Broadway After Dark

Broadway After Dark

A Father and Son Cover 100 Years of Broadway

Ward Morehouse
and
Ward Morehouse III

BearManorMedia.com

Copyright © 2007 by Ward Morehouse III
All rights reserved.

Published by:

Bear Manor Media
PO Box 71426
Albany GA 31707

www.bearmanormedia.com

Book Design by Leila Joiner

Printed in the United States of America on acid-free paper

ISBN 978-1-59393-081-3
ISBN 1-59393-081-X

☐ Preface

BROADWAY AFTER DARK is a compilation of columns, stories, and never-before-published profiles by my father, Ward Morehouse, and myself. The profiles were originally intended for a book called *Stars I Have Known*. The columns of his are representative of those he did for the *New York Sun* from 1926-1950 and after for other newspapers.

My father once said his "reverence" for the theater was "something that has been with me since an afternoon in the long ago when I was taken to a matinee performance of *Mrs. Wiggs of the Cabbage Patch*...." As a child I sat with him and my mother, separately, amazed by the adventures in *Peter Pan* and *Mrs. McThing*, a fantasy-comedy by Mary Chase, the author of *Harvey*. His love of the plays and people we went backstage to see was catching. It later took the form of early efforts to write plays. Audrey Wood, Tennessee Williams' agent, gave Lea Freeman (an older playwright I befriended when I lived at the theatrical retreat The Lambs Club) a $500 option for a play we collaborated on. I have been hooked on the theater, writing plays and columns, ever since. But I must admit my father's theater world has captivated my imagination and heart as much if not more than the theater of the turn of the last—the twentieth—century. This world came to an apex in the late 1920s when nearly 300 shows opened on Broadway in just a single season.

It's my hope that these columns and stories, taken together, will form a portrait of the theater of the last century, and of today. Outstanding stars of the past, such as William Gillette and Laurette Taylor, come alive for today's reader through my father's reporting, and some stars of the past and even into the recent present, such as Katharine Hepburn, span the careers of both my father and myself. Broadway, Off-Broadway, out-of-town previews, tours and showcase productions each have their challenges, their charms, and their idiosyncracies. Here are some behind-the-scenes looks at the actors who entertained, and are still entertaining, the generations of audiences who care about what happens when live performers come out onto a stage, and who come to the theater to be transformed by the magic that takes place on the stage.

The older I get the more I appreciate the influence my father had on me. His two passions have become mine as well—Broadway theatre and New York hotels. Writing about both of these great subjects reminds me not only of the bygone glamour of a dazzling early and mid-twentieth century Manhattan, a land of martini nightclubs and vaulting lobbies everywhere, but of my father. I've paid tribute to my inherited love of hotels in books on the Waldorf-Astoria, the Plaza and, most recently, in *Life at the Top*, a short history of New York hoteldom going back to Mr. Astor. Here, I hope to do justice to the enduring Morehouse affinity for all things Broadway.

You'll find a vast difference between my father's columns and mine. To his immense credit, his are basically the coverage of an insider, someone who sometimes—but not always—was a personal friend of those he was writing about, like the Lunts and Katharine Hepburn. His profiles of some of the greatest stars of the twentieth century are also unique in that they have few if any references to life outside the theater: no mention of movies, radio or T.V. This was the most natural thing, in a sense, because the theater was king for more than half of the last century. My columns are largely an outsider's view of the New York theater, where today Off Broadway has become sometimes even brighter than the Great White Way—but will never shine as brightly as it did when a Broadway show was the pinnacle of American theater.

Ward Morehouse III
Fancy Rock Island
Rockport, Ontario
August, 2006

◻ Laurette Taylor (1884 – 1946)

BORN INTO a poor New York Irish family, Laurette is regarded as one of the leading stage actresses of the twentieth century. Her most notable roles included *Peg O' My Heart*, and an outstanding comeback in 1945 as the first Amanda Wingfield in *The Glass Menagerie*. Tennessee Williams was quoted after her death as saying, "There was a radiance about her art which I can compare only to the greatest lines of poetry." My father's profile is similarly appreciative.

I'VE COME UPON some spectacular and memorable performances in my experiences as a playgoer. Richard B. Harrison's eloquent acting as De Lawd in *The Green Pastures* stays in my memory, as does John Barrymore's stirring Hamlet. Alfred Lunt, in the years before he became a stage immortal, brought gaiety to Booth Tarkington's *Clarence* and he later contributed a captivating performance in the role of Harry Van, hoofer with a soul, in Robert E. Sherwood's *Idiot's Delight*. That same Sherwood's *Abe Lincoln in Illinois* provided a part in which Raymond Massey distinguished himself and Maxwell Anderson's *Elizabeth the Queen* gave Lynn Fontanne the opportunity to establish herself as one of the greatest actresses of her time.

I relished Louis Wolheim's playing as the haggard and heroic Captain Flagg in that unforgettable war play, *What Price Glory*; I was under the spell of Emily Stevens in *Fata Morgana* and again when she brought her extraordinary magnetism to Ibsen's *Hedda Gabler*. I certainly responded to the lyrical beauty of Katharine Cornell's Juliet, to Jane Cowl's loveliness in the same role, and to the savage and relentless characterization that Tallulah Bankhead brought to Lillian Hellman's finest play, *The Little Foxes*. I enjoyed Frank Fay's acting as Elwood P. Dowd in Mary Chase's *Harvey*, but the player who made that comedy-fantasy a special delight for me was Josephine Hull, who was cast as Dowd's harassed and entirely desperate sister.

And there have always been two performances that enthralled just about all of us—the magnificent Jeanne Eagels as the tortured Sadie Thompson in that withering drama called *Rain* and the incomparable—I'm sure that incomparable is the word—Laurette Taylor in the role of the living-in-the-past Amanda in Tennessee Williams' play, *The Glass Menagerie*. If that wasn't the great acting I've never seen it.

LAURETTE TAYLOR had finesse. She had magic. In 40-odd years of acting she appeared in only three or four plays that were actually worth her time, but at the time of her death, following her great performance in *The Glass Menagerie*, she had so impressed those playgoers who had the great privilege of seeing her upon the stage that the vast majority of them, if called upon to name the finest actress they had ever seen, would have made the instantaneous decision in a single word, "Taylor!"

Miss Taylor was a weak, willful, undisciplined and brilliant woman of the theater who dropped to the depths through over-drinking and who went on to achieve, via her performance in *Outward Bound* and *The Glass Menagerie*, one of the greatest comebacks in the history of the American theater. I didn't see Miss Taylor in her early years when she was in the wild, wild, melodramas of Charles A. Taylor, her first husband, the years about which Guthrie McClintic has written fascinatingly in his autobiography, *Me and Kit*. I didn't see her in her first plays for the Broadway stage, such pieces as *The Great John Ganton* and *Alias Jimmy Valentine* and *The Bird of Paradise* but I finally caught up with her when she revived the indestructible *Peg O' My Heart* in the early 1920s, and I got to know her during her years of adversity, following the death of Hartley Manners, her second husband, and after she had scored the greatest hit of her life in *The Glass Menagerie*.

LAURETTE TAYLOR took great pride in that performance and she spoke of it with deep humility.

"I'm sort of kicking the clouds around," she told me in 1945, when she had reestablished herself as the sensation of Broadway. "In playing Amanda, and when I get on the stage, I become Southern. The rest of the time I suppose I'm just American. As for the South, I've never been below Washington except for trips to Florida. I got most of the Southern accent that I use from our author, Tennessee Williams. I really don't know any tricks any more. Acting is really so simple and my advice to young actresses is to try not to become a bedroom thinker but wait until you get to the theater to do your acting. I have never felt that playing Amanda was particularly difficult. It's a part in which you're actually riding on an audience's shoulders. There are actually only two parts in the play—the shrew in the old wrapper and the young girl in the faded blue dress.

"I'd like to go on playing Amanda for as long as they'll let me and I'd enjoy returning to Chicago with the play—it was there that we got off to such a wonderful start—but I don't think I'd want to try any real touring. I haven't enough time left in my life for that…I suppose I'm a Southerner—out of Ireland. I have a peculiar ear for dialect and that might give me an advantage over other actresses. My parents and all my ancestors were born in Ireland and I suppose that's what's the matter with me. I'm Irish all the way through."

Miss Taylor took a gulp of her martini, her third during our dinnertime talk, but she had them under control, and went on:

"The person who had the greatest influence on my life was Hartley Manners, to whom I was married for fifteen years. I'd always imagined our growing old together and when he died it completely threw me. I lost my religion and went in for the longest wake in history. If such a man as Hartley could be taken away from me what did anything matter?...I began drinking harder and harder, and it was only my success in *Outward Bound* that finally pulled me out of it. Then along came this blessed *Glass Menagerie* and I knew I was all right—and that I would be forever.

"Hartley Manners was a graceful man, a gentle man, a wonderful man. He wrote *Peg O' My Heart* for me. I still get royalties from *Peg*—from churches and little theater groups and summer stock and all that sort of thing. My! How old that girl is! She goes right back to 1912 and T. R. and William Jennings Bryan and Woodrow Wilson and the Red Sox beating the New York Giants in the World Series. I loved *Peg* and still do, but it's always made me furious that amateurs haven't wanted to do Hartley's better plays, such as *The National Anthem* and *The Harp of Life*.

"Until this part of Amanda came along I was offered all the old ladies in the world, but I didn't want a part—I wanted a play. I found it, thank God, in *The Glass Menagerie*. And before this I had that great chance in *Outward Bound*. Bill Brady gave me that chance. He was one of the wonderful people to come into my life. He loved the stage; the theater was wrapped around his heart."

◻ Maude Adams (1872 – 1953)

THE DAUGHTER of an actor, Maude left Salt Lake City, performed in touring companies, and made it to Broadway at age 16. She appeared in twenty-five Broadway shows in 28 years, starring in many of them, including the original *Peter Pan* in 1904. She toured extensively and was one of the most popular and enticing actresses of her generation: her demure personality and quiet beauty were magnetic to theatergoers wherever she appeared.

MAUDE ADAMS went on the stage at the age of nine months; she was still on it at sixty, playing Portia, having returned to the theater after a long retirement to make a harrowing, across-America tour in *The Merchant of Venice*. Miss Adams, born in 1872 in Salt Lake City and in an adobe house typical of those of the Mormons, the daughter of Annie Adams and James Kiskadden had a spiritual quality that made her appeal universal. She was quite the most beloved player of her time.

There was something about her that was elusive and ineffable, an indefinable and incommunicable quality that enchanted playgoers and that, upon occasion, bewildered the critics. The rippling laugh, the lilting voice, the quaint tossing of her head—these were attributes that endeared her to audiences. On the practical side, she was the American star with the greatest box-office power from the time of *The Little Minister* in 1897 to *What Every Woman Knows*, which came along in 1911. Her name sold seats. It packed theaters. The evidence was incontestable. People went to see her who never entered a playhouse at any other time. A week's receipts of $20,000 for an Adams play on tour was a normal gross, and that was the day and time of the $2 top ticket.

Miss Adams was known to playgoers, young and old, in cities, towns and villages throughout our land. She never appeared on the other side of the Atlantic—she often spoke of wanting a London engagement—but she was an actress who held her place in the hearts of the theatergoers of the British Isles because of her long and successful association with the plays of James M. Barrie. The imaginative Charles Frohman had to coax the shy Scotsman to write for the theater, but after the success of *The Little Minister* there was no difficulty in getting him to write for Miss Adams. It was Sir James who gave her her greatest success, *Peter Pan*. Its richness has remained undiminished for half a century. Unnumbered thousands of Londoners, during their visits to our shores, were fascinated by Miss Adams as Lady Babbie in *The Little Minister* and by her when she was playing Phoebe of the Ringlets in

Quality Street and they were completely under her spell when she appeared as the irresistible Peter Pan and the managing and indispensable Maggie Wylie in *What Every Woman Knows*.

IT WAS MY good fortune to have had numerous meetings with Miss Adams. Once I got to see her she wasn't at all remote—she was human and warm, wise and gay and humorful. My first luncheon with her was at the Colony Club, which always gave her its careful protection. During an unforgettable two hours in 1932 she laughed pleasantly, her eyes sparkled, her hands fluttered and she frequently clasped them beneath her chin as she spoke of her long tour in *The Merchant of Venice*, of Charles Frohman and James M. Barrie, and she went on to tell me of a dress rehearsal of *The Legend of Leonora*. "Mr. Frohman and Sir James and I sat together and we got to talking about the last act," she said. "I told them I didn't like it. Mr. Frohman protested; he said that it was excellent. Then, all of a sudden, a little voice on my right piped up; it was that of Sir James. 'Miss Adams is right,' he said. 'It is a rotten last act.'"

I called on Miss Adams several times at the Colony Club and stopped over in Columbia, Mo., on U.S. 40, midway between St. Louis and Kansas City, for luncheon with her when she was on the faculty of Stephens College. It was later, in New York, when she summoned me by telegram for a meeting to discuss revisions in the second act of a play I'd written and which had been submitted to her. She undoubtedly had some good ideas for the rewriting of that troublesome second act, but I scarcely heard her words; I spent the afternoon in something of a trance, listening to the music of her voice, which evoked memories of teen-age playgoing in Georgia. She had come to my town as the great star of *What Every Woman Knows* and *A Kiss For Cinderella*.

CHARLES FROHMAN was fully aware of Maude Adams' potentialities when he put her into *The Masked Ball* with John Drew. He was quietly exultant when she again succeeded with Drew in *Rosemary*, and when she brought her girlishness and complete loveliness to the role of James M. Barrie's Lady Babbie in *The Little Minister* the great producer was certain that she could be sure of a devoted following for all the years that she cared to give to the stage. Miss Adams was in *Rosemary* at New York's Empire when Sir James, on his first visit to this country, saw her performance. He was enchanted with her playing, returned to London, and wrote *The Little Minister* for her. It was with that play that Frohman presented her as a star.

Miss Adams had her failures. Juliet, for instance. She was far from impressive in the exacting role of the Duc de Reichstadt, the weakling son of Napoleon, in Rostand's *L'Aiglon*, and she was no more suited to Chanticler of the comb, spurs and tail feathers than she would have been to Lady Macbeth, but these slips were not counted, and certainly not remembered, by her worshipful public. She was triumphant as Lady Babbie and in *Quality Street*. She charmed playgoers with her playing as the Spanish heroine in *The Pretty Sister of Jose*, won them completely when she came forth as Maggie Wylie and it was as Peter Pan that she gave the greatest performance of her career. Barrie had had misgivings about *Peter Pan*. When he sent the manuscript to America he told Frohman that he did not have much hope for it as a commercial property. But Frohman did not share the Scotsman's doubts. He was elated with the play and talked of little else for weeks. He predicted that Miss Adams would be irresistible in her suit of leaves and that Peter of the treetops and the Never-Never Land would become her most popular part. And during the long run at the Empire, as playgoers from six to sixty were swarming into his beautiful playhouse, he had reason to be pleased with his foresight, but he was a man too free of pretensions and of self-importance to go in for self-congratulation. And he was too busy. He was planning to send his great star and the Barrie fantasy to every corner of America.

MAUDE ADAMS, a woman of intelligence and good judgment, with a sense of obligation to her public, made herself a great asset to Stephens College. She became more available than she had been in many years and less mysterious. She even accepted engagements to speak at women's club luncheons. She moved freely about the campus and about the town of Columbia in the years 1937-43, going into town for a vase or a shoe or a Greek ornament or a piece of cheesecloth.

Never sparing herself, she rehearsed her plays until far into the night; she worked on the scenery and the costumes for her productions and she once delayed a curtain for ten minutes while she painted a door. It was the feeling at Stephens that she did a great deal for the drama department, particularly in improving the standards of speech, and it was her contention that this could only be done by dealing with the classics.

Notwithstanding her emergence to some extent during her stay at Columbia, Mo., Miss Adams was enigmatic and self-effacing throughout most of her life. Whenever she sailed for Europe she sought to hide her identity and she was, upon occasion, listed as Miss Kiskadden. Her telegrams were generally signed with the initials "M" or "M. A." During the last decade of her life, in her commuting between the Colony Club and her home in Onteora, N.Y., she always traveled by bus. "It's wonderful not to be known or recognized," she once told me. "I can go where I please and when I please and no one ever bothers me. Also, I enjoy riding on a bus."

It was in 1917, several years following her retirement from the stage, that Miss Adams presented her 300-acre estate at Lake Ronkonkoma, Long Island, to the Roman Catholic Sisterhood of Our Lady of the Cenacle because of her gratitude for the comfort and peace she had found in its convent in 140th Street. It was the same kind of tranquility that she was afforded soon after the turn of the century when she went abroad and sought refuge at a convent in Tours. There she spent a summer in pensive solitude, living as the nuns lived, sleeping in a narrow white iron bed in a room with a wash basin and one small window, which looked out upon a sweep of olive trees.

IN SOME of the towns of America, during Miss Adams' final tour in 1931-32 with *The Merchant of Venice*, the clamor over the return of the beloved Peter Pan approximated hysteria, but there was a word of dissent here and there. Some of the dramatic critics refused to accept her as Portia, and one of the individuals who was unwilling to be impressed was one Mark Anthony, division passenger agent for the Missouri Pacific Railroad.

When the outspoken Mr. Anthony was asked why he wasn't anywhere in sight when Miss Adams's car was in the New Orleans station, en route to Baton Rouge, he said: "Listen. Twenty years ago Miss Adams bawled me out and I haven't forgotten. I've found that Nazimova is the only woman in the world who can bawl out a passenger agent the way that Maude Adams can. I guess she's the loveliest star this country ever had, and I saw her as Peter Pan when I was a kid and loved every minute of it, but I'm staying away from her. She won't forget, she hasn't forgotten, that little run-in I had with her. Frankly, I'm scared as hell of her. She's got a temper."

MAUDE ADAMS crossed prairie and mountain range with her *Merchant of Venice* production and opened at Los Angeles's Biltmore. Richard Pitman, Broadway agent and one of my friends for years, was in constant contact with her. He wired me at the Garden of Allah to call at her dressing room after an evening performance. I did and she was delightful. Would I have lunch with her in New York? She wouldn't forget. Mr. Pitman would call me and perhaps he would join us. Miss Adams played her week in Los Angeles, trouped back East, finished her tour in Newark and went to Ronkonkoma for a rest. And during that summer there came the call from Dick Pitman. We were lunching with Miss Adams on a Tuesday. And so, after fifteen years, my pursuit of her had been rewarded.

There she sat, Maude Adams, lady of the legends, who'd never given an interview in all her life. Time 1:15 p.m. Place: The Colony Club, Manhattan's East Sixties. She laughed gaily, her eyes sparkled, her hands fluttered and she clasped them beneath her chin. She talked of her tour during the melon course. "The tour," she said, "was wonderful. It was thrilling. Twenty-six weeks of it and I was in better health when it was over than when it started. I—I suppose I was a little frightened when I began. It had been twelve years since I had played and the sound of my own voice had a strange, terrifying effect upon me."

Was touring, I wondered, anything like it was when she trouped under the banner of Frohman?

"Just as exciting," she said. "Not a great deal of difference. Just as uncertain. Touring used to be difficult because of lack of railroad facilities. Nowadays an element of uncertainty comes in because theaters are always changing hands. We played in some strange, quaint places. Some tremendous big houses. The biggest, I think, was in Houston. There I had laryngitis, but they told me it would be all right—that in that house they couldn't hear beyond the third row anyhow."

The robot-like waiter had removed the melon. The erstwhile Phoebe of the Ringlets was now jabbing, daintily, at a soft shell crab. I'd asked about the reactions of the theatrical audiences of 1931-32 as compared with those of her Maggie Wylie and her Leonora days.

"They were wonderful to me," she said, and then raced on into quotes: "They often remained in the theater after the performance was over and they waited outside, too. Just like it used to be...We had lots of adventures. In Louisiana we came to a place where the river had just over-flowed and the banks had just failed. In a little place called Missoula, Mont., we had to stay for twelve hours—no train to take us out. The shorter the engagements the better I liked them. The one night stands didn't weary me—they were darlings...Indifferent towns? Maybe Denver and San Francisco. They didn't like us much in either place."

Her hands fluttered and she clasped them. Her eyes danced and she gave her head that quaint, familiar toss.

"They were lovely in Salt Lake. Salt Lake has changed so. It was wonderful when I was there as a child. My parents loved it...The early Mormons, the pioneers, were human, simple, spiritual people." She pried loose a leg of her diminutive crab and took a sip of fruit punch.

Cold cuts had supplanted the soft shell crabs. The animated Miss Adams, speaking swiftly, with varying inflection, was talking of the plays of her past. *Peter Pan*, of course, was her play of plays. For many reasons. But close to her heart and high in her esteem stands *The Legend of Leonora*, which Barrie finished toward the end of his playwriting years.

"Sir James," said Miss Adams, "had written a one-act play with 'Leonora' and when he turned it into a full-length play he found he didn't care for the last two acts. He'd come over for it, however, and at a dress rehearsal Mr.

Frohman, Sir James and I were sitting together in an out of town theater. Mr. Frohman loved Sir James and would rather have put on a bad play than offend him. We were talking about the last act. I said I didn't like it. Mr. Frohman protested. He insisted that it was excellent. Then all of a sudden a little voice on my right piped up—it was Sir James. 'She's right,' he said. 'It is a rotten last act.'"

Her eyes danced as she took a sip of fruit punch. She talked on as the waiter served giant asparagus: "I want a new play—something good and modern. I don't think I want to bring *The Merchant of Venice* to New York...I haven't seen Sir James Barrie in five years...I never made the motion picture of *Kim* because Mr. Kipling refused to have it done unless all of it were filmed in India."...Had she been seeing the plays and movies in recent seasons? She saw *Reunion in Vienna* and she found Mrs. Lunt fascinating. She adored Douglas Fairbanks in *The Three Musketeers*. For her playgoing companions she picks friends of long standing. And she then had in her service her two Marys—one named Reilly and the other Gorman—who'd been her devoted companions for years. I told her I was sure that it was one of the faithful Marys who had blocked my entrance when I called at her Atlanta hotel suite fifteen years before.

She laughed softly as she looked at me over the tea roses and told me of a similar discomfiture suffered by Mrs. Nicholas Longworth, nee Alice Roosevelt. Mrs. Longworth had called to pay her respects but found herself denied entrance. "But I'm the President's daughter!" she exclaimed, indignant. "I don't care," said one of the Marys stiffly, "if you're the President himself. Miss Adams is asleep!"

And then she slammed the door.

◘ William Gillette (1853 – 1937)

MR. GILLETTE made his debut in 1875 in a Mark Twain stage play, with the encouragement of Twain himself, a Hartford neighbor of his family. His acting style, depending on realism rather than the melodramatic declaiming of the nineteenth century, was popular with audiences, if not always with critics. In 1899, he wrote a Sherlock Holmes play, with the blessing of Sir Arthur Conan Doyle, and, for the rest of his life, capitalized on his characterization of the famous detective. His fame paid generously, and for many years he devoted himself to meticulously constructing a modern Norman castle on the banks of the Connecticut River in Hadlyme. It is now operated by the State of Connecticut, and 100,000 tourists visit each year.

WILLIAM GILLETTE was a gallant figure in the American theater, a brilliant worker as an actor, playwright and director for more than four decades. A New Englander of culture, courtesy, and unfailing humor, he had a sure sense of craftsmanship as a dramatist and in his acting he could dominate a scene with an inflection, a glance, a nod, a shrug. He had a way of holding an audience completely as he stood motionless and in complete silence—tall, dignified, impassive, imperturbable. "During my years in the theater," reported the beautiful Marie Doro, of the lovely profile and large bright eyes, "I was hypnotized by two men. One of them was Charles Frohman. The other was William Gillette."

Gillette was a man of many fascinating eccentricities. He had great fondness for using his stage costumes as his regular, off-stage wearing apparel. One of his leading women, invited by him to lunch, was greatly impressed by a bluish-gray coat that he wore, a coat that had a jaunty, military effect and was lacking only in brass buttons. She later learned that he had had the buttons removed and that the coat was one that he had worn in his Civil War melodrama, *Held By the Enemy*. And when he again invited her to lunch she was so startled by his costume she almost lost her appetite. He called for her in his clothes from *Sherlock Holmes*.

He was an actor-playwright-director who disapproved of the women of his companies being seen in public places; he wanted them always to remain aloof, elusive and mysterious. Such was Charles Frohman's policy in guiding Maude Adams to her enduring stardom—and to her life of elusiveness and self-effacement. Gillette liked supper after his performances and he would often consume two dozen raw oysters at a sitting. He had a passion for Chopin, he enjoyed the stories of O. Henry and he liked reading from them aloud. Cats were sacred to him—alley cats or pedigreed. He liked tinkering with things, such as old clocks, and he often rescued a clock that had been pronounced beyond repair, putting it to ticking and to perfect time-keeping. He collected bird cages for years, a hobby that puzzled his associates. Many of them wanted to ask him just why but none of them ever did.

Gillette was a star who never forgot his manners and who seldom lost his temper. He did lose it completely, however, near the close of his Civil War spy melodrama, *Secret Service*, the best play he ever wrote. He was delivering his big, final-act speech when an actor playing a Confederate soldier sneezed. Nearly every player on the crowded stage broke up. They all turned from the audience in an effort to conceal their chuckling, but shaking shoulders were beyond their control. When the curtain fell Gillette was white with rage. He glared at his company and said these words in a low voice: "You people have no right to stand on this side of the curtain. You are only useful out front. That's where you belong. Out there you can giggle your heads off. There are always many idiots in every audience." Then he turned and walked away.

Gillette was witty in conversation, charming in his correspondence, and he wrote many notes, using black ink and red in most of them, and these notes were precise, laconic and frequently profane. For all of his attractive qualities, he had a reputation for being stingy, particularly in little things. His "nearness," as some of his co-players called it, particularly amused Charles Frohman, who was devoted to him. On one occasion, during a trans-Atlantic voyage early in the century, Jessie Busley, an excellent actress who was a member of the company that he was taking to London, had a headache and Gillette gave her two powders. In telling Frohman that her headache was relieved Miss Busley said, "Willie G. gave me two headache powders." And Frohman, his eyes twinkling, said, "Not *two*." But there was also the story of "Matches Mary," who used to peddle her matches outside the New York theaters. During Gillette's revival season at the Empire Theater in 1910—he did five of his famous plays, including *Secret Service* and *Sherlock Holmes*—he invited Mary and her family to occupy a box for the Christmas Eve performance of *Secret Service*. Mary's party had the box bulging with humanity of all ages and sizes and after the performance the great actor entertained his guests with backstage refreshments. When Mary finally decided that it was time to thank him and say goodnight he slipped an envelope into her hands. There were tears in her eyes when she opened it on the sidewalk. It contained her host's check for $100.

Gillette's soundly constructed *Secret Service*, written while he was recovering his health in the mountain air at Tryon, N.C., was a drama that told of the love of a Southern girl for a Northern spy, with its big scene in the War Department telegraph office. At the climax of this scene, the spy, Lewis Dumont, posing as Captain Thorne, a Confederate officer, renounces his duty as he places love above patriotism. Gillette, who had replaced the illustrious Maurice Barrymore, father of Ethel and John and Lionel, in the leading role, gave an electric performance, one that held the playgoers of New York in its spell. He later had great success in the same part in London. But the most memorable performance of his long and distinguished career came with his playing of Sherlock Holmes in the engaging and exciting play that he wrote from the stories of A. Conan Doyle, and a play to which he brought his compelling stage presence and a voice that was dry, crisp, metallic, almost shrill. *Sherlock Holmes* was first presented at New York's Garrick Theater in November of 1899 and it's a tribute to the play's durability, and to the finesse of Gillette, that it seemed to have lost none of its enchantment when it was revived by him thirty years later.

I SAW GILLETTE in that revival of *Sherlock Holmes* and, some years earlier, in *A Successful Calamity* and in Barrie's *Dear Brutus*. I've always felt cheated in having not seen him as the heroic Captain Thorne in *Secret Service*. I first met him prior to the revival of *Three Wise Fools*, his last play for the New York stage, and there then began a friendship that was an infinitely rewarding one (to me, at least) until his death in 1937.

I made my first trip to his fieldstone castle, Seventh Sister, high above the Connecticut River at Hadlyme, Conn., when he was nearly eighty. He was then greatly enjoying his fortress-like retreat and his miniature railroad, which ran over a narrow-gauge track that wound for three or four miles around his vast estate. I shall always cherish the memory of him as he stood beside his undersized locomotive, wearing blue overalls, an engineer's cap and heavy gloves. He was proud of his locomotive and his passenger car and his miles of track—an expression of the mechanical gifts of a man who turned to the stage instead of to engineering. He took me whirling past thickets of birch and hemlock and several minutes later brought me back to our starting point. He then suggested that we go back into his medieval castle and have tea—with rum. Half an hour later, wearing black, with a gold watch looped across his waistcoat, he made an appearance on the balcony above the living room—calm, erect, dignified, commanding. Then he came down the stairs and he spoke—laconic, crackling and shrill. I then had the feeling that the great Mr. Holmes had somehow slipped into the big stone house and was standing before me beside the open fireplace.

He turned to his butler, Takizawa, who shared his love for cats, and said faintly and good-humoredly: "You can make the tea strong with rum, Takizawa. It's a little chilly in here and we want our New York guest to be comfortable."

Takizawa brought the rum-flavored tea and then, for two fascinating hours, William Gillette, reviewed his career from the great days of Charles Frohman to that very moment. "I've had a fine life," he said. "Certainly I've known great people. It's been a satisfying life and I now fear it's near an end."

William Gillette died in 1937 at the age of 81.

◘ Katharine Cornell (1898 – 1974)

Ms. CORNELL made her stage debut at age 18. Three years later, she married Guthrie McClintic, a producer and director. Her first big hit was *A Bill of Divorcement*, followed by *The Green Hat* in 1925, *The Barretts of Wimpole Street*, *Saint Joan* and numerous classics. She made her final stately appearance in 1961 as Mrs. Patrick Campbell in *Dear Liar*. Her husband died the following year and she retired from the stage.

SHE ONCE WORE a green hat and that was during the vogue of Michael Arlen. The stage has seen her as Candida, tender and human and wise; as a vivid and girlish Juliet; as a Saint Joan of transcendent beauty. For a time she was a Malayan princess, brought as a bride of a sea captain into a stern New England community that refused to receive her. She has spoken the verse of Christopher Fry, and she's played drawing-room comedy by Somerset Maugham and in another play by that dramatist she was a jealousy-racked heroine, a pantherine killer who turned a gun upon her faithless lover.

Through these roles and numerous others—and certainly not forgetting that in which she wore the crinolines of Elizabeth Barrett—she has established herself as an actress of range and skill and power and an unearthly beauty of voice. I am, writing, of course, of Katharine Cornell, dark queen of the American stage, daughter of an upstate (New York) theater manager and married to a director-producer, Guthrie McClintic, Miss Cornell has been one of the country's foremost players ever since 1921, when she startled New York with the sheer magnetism of her performance in a drama imported from London, *A Bill of Divorcement*.

Katharine Cornell is by no means a beautiful woman but she often gives the impression of great beauty from the stage. She has a broad face with high cheekbones, a large, expressive and full-lipped mouth, widely separated dark brown eyes, fine chin and neckline, and she is five feet six in her stocking feet. She was born in Berlin February 16, 1898, born there because of father, Peter Cornell, happened to be in Berlin studying surgery. He later gave up medicine, took to theater-managing in Buffalo and it was there that Miss Cornell saw her first plays—Buffalo was a busy port of call for the road attractions—and had her first yearnings for the stage.

She appeared in school plays and wrote them, too, while attending the Merrill School at Mamaroneck and for a time she taught dramatics there. She made her somewhat terrified professional debut in New York with the Washington Square Players (from which the Theater Guild developed), speaking a four-word role. Her single line was "My son, my son" from *Bushido*. Later she learned her trade the hard way, via Jessie Bonstelle's excellent stock company in Detroit. A letter from Miss Bonstelle to William A. Brady got her into the Playhouse offices in 48th Street.

The shrewd and theater-wise Brady, who had by that time produced as many plays as any showman in the history of the American stage, was stirred by the voice of the young actress, as was Mrs. Brady (Grace George). They engaged Miss Cornell for the leading feminine role in a touring company of *The Man Who Came Back*, one of the reigning hits of the time, and Brady later sent her to London to play Jo in *Little Women*. Two seasons or so later she was engaged for the role of the sensitive and outspoken daughter in *A Bill of Divorcement* because of the impression she had made upon Alan Pollock when he saw her in *Little Women*. On the opening night of *A Bill of Divorcement* the majority of the first-string reviewers went to see Helen Hayes in a negligible comedy, *The Wren*, but later the tumult over the Cornell performance, a tumult created largely by Alexander Woollcott and Heywood Broun, had playgoers swarming into the George M. Cohan Theater. Miss Cornell was on her way.

Since her emergence in 1921, Katharine Cornell has grown steadily as an actress. In several instances her plays have not been deserving of her time, but she has generally brought to a role a special kind of excitement. Since *A Bill of Divorcement* her finest performances have been those in *Candida, Will Shakespeare, Romeo and Juliet, Saint Joan* and *The Barretts of Wimpole Street*. And she has demonstrated a mastery of her art in lesser roles—as the fair killer in Somerset Maugham's *The Letter*, as a frustrated pianist in Sidney Howard's *Alien Corn*, as a bitter and ravenous woman in *Tiger Cats*, a pretentious play from the French. A few of her plays, including *Lucrece, The Flowers of the Forest, Herod and Meriamne, That Lady* and *The Prescott Proposals*, can be put down as outright failures.

Miss Cornell has had notable success with revival productions—*Candida, The Doctor's Dilemma*, and Chekhov's *The Three Sisters*, put on with a remarkable cast, and with *The Barretts of Wimpole Street*. The last-named play was in her repertory on her remarkable tour of 1933-34, during which she traveled 16,853 miles, played 74 cities—playgoers in Des Moines paid $7,795.70 to see a single performance—and during which she was greeted in Seattle by an audience that had waited five hours for her flood-delayed train and that was still fresh and eager and expectant when the curtain finally rose at 1:04 a.m.

It was *The Barretts* that Miss Cornell took to Europe for a tour during World War II, going for sixty days and staying six months. To the great majority of those in the GI audiences a stage play was an entirely new experience, for they were kids who had been brought up on the movies. They were gazing upon flesh-and-blood actors for the first time in their lives, and the name of Katharine Cornell was a familiar one to only a scant minority. The GIs were respectful—in their fashion. They frequently yielded audibly to their emotions. They came in upon scenes with cracks that were flip and frequently funny. They expressed themselves in low and sustained whistles. They never failed to yell, "Pass it around!" when Elizabeth was kissed for the first time by the adoring Robert Browning. When a feminine member of the cast came near the dominating father, Edward Moulton-Barrett, without being seen by him, an erstwhile Brooklyn garage mechanic in a down-front seat screamed, "Kick him in the ass, Red."...But the show always went on.

Miss Cornell enjoyed her appearances before the uninhibited GIs, just as she enjoys taking her plays to Atlanta and to New Orleans, to Roanoke and Grand Rapids, to Denver and San Diego and, of course, Seattle. She has been her own manager since 1931 and she likes keeping check on the business details of her productions. She likes to know what things cost—and why. She is a woman who strikes no poses and never assumes an attitude. She has made a great deal of money in the theater, but has continually put her money back into it and it can surely be said that she lives for the theater if ever an actress did. She has never had any desire to appear in films but she enjoys going to the movies. She plays a rather good game of golf (around 105), enjoys long walks and never misses going to the parks of cities throughout America. She has a positive passion for maps.

Miss Cornell has never been over-careful about her clothes, but she likes the feeling of being well-dressed. Her garments are more tailored than fancy; she likes blacks and garnet-reds and good woolens; she wears sweaters at every opportunity. Her figure has never been a source of actual concern; she eats as she pleases and has never found herself alarmingly overweight.

She used to go to the Austrian Tyrol and to Majorca for her vacations, but such trips are now no longer necessary. She has her Martha's Vineyard retreat, Chip Chop, which she loves, and she also has her beautiful west-bank-of-the-Hudson home, twenty miles from New York. The exterior has the look of a royal lodge; the spectacular living room has a ceiling of some sixty feet. She is a familiar figure at her marketing at Martha's Vineyard; she is well liked by the shopkeepers and the islanders and many of the theater's great people have been houseguests at Chip Chop.

Miss Cornell still talks vaguely and wistfully of making a world tour in a repertoire of two or three plays; she is always glad that she got around to playing *Antony and Cleopatra* and she wants to do more Shakespeare. And she's even given thought to Ibsen. I suspect that the day will come when many of the GIs, now scattered to all parts of America, who saw her in 1945, will be sitting back, fairly sedate by this time, and watching her as she plays Lady Macbeth or Ibsen's Hedda. For Katharine Cornell is an actress who still yearns for many roles and who will be active in her profession for as long as she can walk out upon a stage without actually tottering.

◘ Gloria Swanson (1897 or 1899 – 1983)

Ms. SWANSON first appeared in 1914 as a movie extra. A subsequent role was with Charlie Chaplin. Within four years, she was a star, playing in Mack Sennett slapsticks, signed by Cecil B. DeMille, and starring with Rudolph Valentino. Although she made dozens of silent films, her career declined after the advent of the talkies, and she is perhaps best remembered by modern audiences for her audacious portrayal of Norma Desmond in *Sunset Boulevard* (1950). My father wrote about her in 1956.

GLORIA SWANSON, wearing red lounging pajamas and smoking a cigarette, said: "Will you get this straight for me? I'll be 57 in this year of 1956. I was born in 1899 and if I were going to lie about my age I wouldn't reduce it for just a year or two.

"I started in pictures with Essanay at 14. I got to the top, went on the toboggan, and now here I am in the latish fifties, a grandmother and a blessed woman, with more to do than ever before in my life—the theater, radio, television—oh, everything. My apartment's Grand Central station. Everything has become just as exciting as when I was playing *Twentieth Century* on Broadway. I'm in such a rush sometimes I fall into a dead faint. I've even gotten to the point of taking sleeping pills, which is horrible.

"Yes, the age is 57. That's exactly right. Age doesn't matter on the stage but generally, in the movies, any woman in her fifties is an old hag…I'm still looking for an executive-type secretary—somebody over 40. Don't care if it's a man or a woman."

Miss Swanson, very gay and looking very fit, went into the matter of the Rise, the Fall and the eventual comeback of Gloria Swanson as follows and to wit:

"I was 11 years in getting to the top in those wonderful silent films. When I got there I was 26. I knew then that I could only go down, but I clung on. At 32 I started on the toboggan and went down and down and down. Nothing went right for me; everything went wrong. But I got the opportunity to become acquainted with myself. I never expected to make another picture. Then came TV and I had my own show. Two and a half months after I started the show Paramount called me. Would I meet Charlie Brackett? Would I have lunch? Well, I hadn't done a picture in eight years. I didn't know about the importance of Mr. Brackett or Billy Wilder. But I went to lunch.

"Months passed. There were more telephone calls. I went to California and took a test. That was it. I was being asked to take a test after all the starring I'd done for all those years. But I got by with it and they gave me a $50,000 contract to do *Sunset Boulevard*. I could have probably obtained twice that if I'd been tough."

And it was after making *Sunset Boulevard* that Miss Swanson was invited to come to New York to play in the Broadway theater in a revival of the madcap *Twentieth Century*, co-starred with Jose Ferrer. She captivated New York's playgoers for months.

"I loved doing that play and couldn't have done it with anybody except Jose. He was simply wonderful to work with. The reason I took the play in the first place was because he called me. I'd met him only casually in Puerto Rico. The fact that he was born there is to that island's everlasting credit. Jose is good, very good. He has a very fluid quality. He carried that play with me. He set the pace...I'd like New York to remember me for such things as *Sunset Boulevard* and *Twentieth Century* and not for that insane farce, *Nina*, which just shouldn't have been produced at all. I'm told it was funny in Paris. I can't believe it. All I know is that it was dreadful on Broadway and I always felt I was dreadful along with it."

A FRESH CIGARETTE, a sip of tea and Miss Swanson chattered on: "New York's more or less my home, although I've been just about everywhere. I've lived in New York an awful lot and have owned a Fifth Avenue apartment for a long time. I was like a duck in water when I was playing in *Twentieth Century* and I've been dying to find something else just as good. I have to be surrounded by good actors to be any good in a play, but I do know that at the age of 57 I'm bitten with the theater bug. I want to stay in the theater until I'm at least 75 and that still gives me quite a lot of time."

◻ Ruth Gordon (1896 – 1985)

RUTH GORDON started her film career in 1915 and made her Broadway debut the same year in *Peter Pan*. She acted on stage for twenty more years, including a notable run in *The Country Wife* at London's Old Vic. She and husband Garson Kanin then wrote several notable Hollywood screenplays, including *Adam's Rib* and *Pat and Mike*, for George Cukor, Katharine Hepburn and Spencer Tracy. She was back on Broadway in 1956 to portray Dolly Levi in *The Matchmaker*. Her late notable film portrayals in *Rosemary's Baby* (1968) and *Harold and Maude* (1971) made her a perennial cult heroine.

"THE FIRST TIME I ever put my dear little foot on the stage was the night of December 21, 1915," said Ruth Gordon. "That means, as of next December, I will have been in the theater for forty-one years. That's a lot of years. Perhaps I'd better quit counting."

Our Miss Gordon, wearing a beige jersey frock, earrings and cultured pearls, fingered a dozen freshly sharpened pencils as she sat at the bridge table in the living room of her house in East 49th Street, the Turtle Bay section of Manhattan. I was in the presence of the star of *The Matchmaker*, and the author of *Over Twenty-One*, which was a success, and *The Leading Lady*, which wasn't.

"Oh, *The Leading Lady* was great fun because it was all about the theater," she said, "but it just wasn't right. *Over Twenty-One* was the first play I ever did. Nobody seemed to be writing plays in 1943-44 and that's why I did it. A really wonderful experience, playing in your own play and to have it a hit. There was money around our apartment in every drawer. Business was so good that on the night of a big rainstorm two foolish people paid to stand up."

THE NEW YORK stage has known Ruth Gordon for many plays, from the time of her first, Maude Adams' 1915 revival of *Peter Pan* to *The Matchmaker* in this year of 1956. She had an exciting engagement in Booth Tarkington's *Seventeen* and another in *Mrs. Partridge Presents*.

She later played in such pieces as *Saturday's Children* and in *Ethan Frome* and she gave a distinguished performance to the production of *The Three Sisters*. Her co-players included Katharine Cornell and Judith Anderson. It was in 1937 that Miss Gordon took herself all the way to the Rockies to appear as Nora in Ibsen's *A Doll's House*, put on in the old mining town of Central City, Colorado, by the Central City Opera House Association.

"I simply loathed the entire thing," went on Miss Gordon. "Not the play, mind you, but I didn't like that awful town and I hated the Opera House and that dreadful hotel, the Teller House. I didn't even like the people or the mountain air and I despised the altitude, something like 8000 feet. They all knew I hated everything connected with the engagement and I think they were as glad to see me come on back East as I was to be doing it."

And when she got back to New York Miss Gordon, enormously pleased to find that there were no mountains on Manhattan Island, began preparations to play Nora on Broadway. She opened in it and received a fine press, but *A Doll's House* languished. People didn't care about Nora's problems, or Ibsen's, and performances were played to half empty houses. It was then that Alexander Woollcott, in his Town Crier role, told his vast radio audience that it was the duty of every man, woman and child who cared at all about the theater to rush to *A Doll's House* to see Ruth Gordon's beautiful performance. Result: the play began selling out and it got an excellent run.

"That wonderful Aleck," murmured Miss Gordon. "He did so many fine things to help people. That broadcast on *A Doll's House* was quite characteristic of him. I loved him dearly. I've framed his review of *Peter Pan* when I had the part of Nibs. It was an unsigned review and was printed in *The New York Times*. He got his byline later."

RUTH GORDON will write more plays during the next few years. "All that happened to me with *Over Twenty-One* was pretty wonderful," she said. "I was in Washington when I started writing that play. We were at the Hotel Statler. I told the idea to Madeline [Mrs. Robert E.] Sherwood and then told it to my husband [Garson Kanin] for a second time. I really did about twenty complete drafts of *Over Twenty-One*. I got it all finished and came to New York. I first read it to that great man, Ned Sheldon, and then sent it to Max Gordon, who was in the hospital. He called me early the next morning, all excited. He sent the script to George Kaufman and that was all there was to it. A success story from beginning to end."

◻ Alfred Lunt (1892 – 1977) and Lynn Fontanne (1887 – 1983)

ALFRED LUNT, of Wisconsin, and Lynn Fontanne, of Great Britain, married in 1922 and became the outstanding American theater couple for nearly four decades, known especially for their urbane comedic talents. They appeared together in more than 24 plays, including roles written by George S. Kaufman, Marc Connelly, Noël Coward, S. N. Behrman and Robert Sherwood. Although they acted in film, television and on the radio, Lunt and Fontanne are remembered for their compelling stage performances. The pair retired in 1960; a Broadway theater is named in their honor.

ALFRED LUNT AND LYNN FONTANNE represent the most successful man-and-wife acting team in the history of the American theater. Lunt has been, certainly for me, the most fascinating actor on our native stage for the past thirty years. His technique in itself is irresistible—great strides about a living room, sudden changes in inflection and intonation, unsettling, hypnotic stares. Miss Fontanne, incredibly lovely to look upon from a down-front seat, retains her style and sparkle. Her laughter is as contagious as it always was; the zest which has always characterized her performances is undiminished.

Lunt and Fontanne have been delighting audiences of Broadway, London's Shaftesbury Avenue and the American midlands ever since they first appeared together in *The Guardsman*. They had a romp in such plays as *Reunion in Vienna* and *Idiot's Delight*. They supplied vibrant drama in *There Shall Be No Night* and *Elizabeth the Queen*. They brought all of their vast skill and insouciance, their artful and unmethodical and seemingly impromptu style of playing to such negligible comedies as *O Mistress Mine* and Noël Coward's *Quadrille*, which had its finest moments when Alfred was making his speech about the sights and sensations of the American continent, a lyrical description of a great land as seen from the swaying caboose of a freight train.

Their success in the theater has been enormous, but they fret and worry over each play as if it were their very first. They have earned vast sums of money from their acting, but they'll tell you that they have none at all. They look fit and fine, but they'll tell you that they don't feel well and Alfred will ask you, in his jerky offhand fashion, if they look too tired, if they should retire.

Then, when you assure him that he and Lynn will be playing until they're in their eighties, he says: "Time really doesn't mean anything to us. We just go on and on. We do hope that people don't get tired of us. We've now been acting together, God knows, longer than most people have been alive."

The Lunts will also be inclined to tell you, if you talk with them for more than five minutes, that they're a pair of more or less homeless gypsies and notwithstanding the fact that they own a beautiful Swedish manor house in Genesee Depot, Wis. and a charming 16-feet-in-width house in New York's Gracie Square. They will also insist that they're weary of travel but at any minute they're likely to be off for Noël Coward's retreat in Jamaica, for London or for Spain, or for another cross-America tour. They've never regretted turning down *Life With Father*, saying seven years of it would have killed them, and they still talk now and then of trying *Macbeth* and of playing a repertory season in New York. I doubt if they'll ever get around to either. But I shall be expecting to see them in new plays and in revivals of old ones for the next twenty years. These people, this Wisconsin born actor and this British-born actress, they're theater. Our stage has been enriched immeasurably by their presence for three decades.

I'VE HAD EXCITING sessions with Lunt and Fontanne in New York and London, in San Francisco and Chicago, in Lisbon and Atlanta and in Genesee Depot. It's when they're occupying their house of five chimneys in the tiny Wisconsin village, on Route 83, about forty-five minutes out of Milwaukee, it's when they're down on the farm, as they call it, that they actually talk most about the theater, from which they're making a temporary escape.

Alfred, engaged in making his renowned Swedish hamburgers in the spacious and fabulously well-equipped kitchen at Genesee, will suddenly blurt out: "What a fine actor George Arliss was. Oh, I've met some wonderful, wonderful people in the theater. There was Olga Nethersole. One of my earliest memories in the theater was Miss Nethersole being carried up a flight of stairs in Clyde Fitch's play, *Sapho*, around 1901."

And then Lynn breaks in (they're always breaking in on each other but they never miss a word the other says): "Alfred, dear, you couldn't, you just couldn't have been going to the theater in 1901."

"My dear," says Alfred, his voice assuming the proportions of a pleasant roar, "I was very, very young, but I *was* going to the theater…Oh, I was with Margaret Anglin when I was starting. A very fine woman and a very fine actress."

Alfred exhibited a long cigar, prized and preserved since Winston Churchill gave it to him during the time they were playing *Love in Idleness* in London for a wartime engagement.

"We love going to London," spoke up Lynn. "We were there during the buzz bombs and I slept beautiful through all of the racket, but when it ceased I just couldn't sleep at all."

"Those English people," murmured Alfred. "So good, so kind, so courageous...We always enjoyed our mid-afternoon tea in London and we liked those early curtains. And right after the performance we'd come home to dinner."

WE LEFT THE KITCHEN and went into the gay, flower-toned living room, a room with Biblical murals which were painted by Claggett Wilson.

Now Alfred, changing the pace, snapped: "What is the matter with us, really? Here we have this big place and now we go and buy that sweet little house in Gracie Square, the tiniest thing in New York. And what do we do? We go trouping about the country and don't live in either place."

"You know," said Lynn, keeping the conversation on an irrelevant plane, "we do adore Helen Hayes. Alfred says she looks occasionally like Sarah Bernhardt, and if you listen to Alfred he'll probably tell you that he was seeing Bernhardt's plays back in the Nineties and that he was taking her to tea."

"Not Bernhardt, not dear dear Sarah," put in Alfred. "She always had *Camille*...Come on, we'll go back to the kitchen and try those Swedish hamburgers. If you're not hungry we're putting you on the train and sending you back to Chicago."

◻ Robert E. Sherwood (1896 – 1955)

ROBERT SHERWOOD was wounded serving with the Canadian Black Watch in the First World War, and his anti-war topics during the Twenties and Thirties, and then his anti-Nazi dedication in the Forties, were the defining themes of his life. He wrote thirteen plays (including *The Petrified Forest*, *Abe Lincoln in Illinois* and *There Shall Be No Night*), several screenplays, speeches for Franklin Roosevelt and a Bancroft Award-winning biography on Roosevelt and Harry Hopkins, an important F.D.R. aide.

ROBERT E. SHERWOOD, six feet, six and a half and sixty years old, is a Harvard man who discovered that there was a good living to be found in writing for the theater—much more of a living than in editing magazines, such as the old *Life*. So, with the production of *The Road to Rome*, he became a dramatist. Save for time out for book writing (*Roosevelt and Hopkins*) for speechwriting for the late F.D.R. and for a whirl at television, he has stuck to his trade pretty steadily since the late Twenties.

Sherwood is a man of high principles and one of many who regard Franklin D. Roosevelt as a great American. He has a passionate admiration for the British and lived part-time in England for some years. He has always been impressed by Britain's timelessness and steadfastness, by its courage and great spirituality. He will never lose his love for the giant city of London, for the serenity of the surrounding countryside, for the charm of the roadside inns and the geniality and humanity of the pubs.

The plays of Robert E. Sherwood have revealed expert craftsmanship, a mastery of incisive dialogue, a feeling for characterization. His outstanding contributions to the drama have included that touching and nostalgic comedy, *Reunion in Vienna*; that bitter and reflective play on the imbecility of war, *Idiot's Delight*; the serious and extraordinarily effective protest against war that bore the title of *There Shall Be No Night*; the play of irony and comment on our civilization that was called *The Petrified Forest*, and the eloquent drama of Abraham Lincoln's before-Washington years, *Abe Lincoln in Illinois*.

And there is also the fact that Sherwood was one of the founders of the Playwrights' Company, a vital producing organization for New York and the American theater since it was formed in the fall of 1937.

TAKE UP THE STORY of the Playwrights' Company in Sherwood's own words: "We'd been talking it over for some years. Then there came a night that brought on a particularly tempestuous meeting of the council of the Dramatists Guild. It was all about movie money in the theater. After that meeting, Max Anderson and Elmer Rice and I went around to a place called the Whaler Bar for a drink and we knew that the time had come for us to get started. That was our beginning. We knew that Sidney Howard would join with us and we thought of a lot of others. We thought of Sam Berhman. We had to keep in mind the question of reasonableness. Well, we got Sid and we got Sam—and we went ahead.

"We wanted to start with $100,000, which seemed a lot in 1937. The five of us put up $50,000, which was $10,000 to a man. We raised $50,000 on the outside. We started our organization with the idea that it would become so permanent it would outlive not only the usefulness but the actual lives of the original founders...We were very fortunate to get off to a good start with *Abe Lincoln in Illinois*, which was a success. We've had big winners in such plays as *Tea and Sympathy* and *Cat on a Hot Tin Roof*. We've also been extraordinarily lucky to have such men in our employ as Vic Samrock and Bill Fields. Each of them is a positive rock. The idea has worked so far. We're hoping that it will keep on working.

BOB SHERWOOD is unhurried in speech—unhurried and articulate and very thoughtful. He is never one to say, "Now don't quote this." He places dependence in the good judgment of those with whom he's talking. He lit a cigarette, sank into a corner of a divan, crossed his long legs and went along quietly:

"We thought in the beginning that we might fail because our plays were lousy, but not because we didn't have any plays. We knew that some of us would always be writing and we've kept at it pretty well. I think that Max Anderson, far and away, has held the position of being America's most distinguished playwright after Eugene O'Neill. What a marvelous model of patience Max is. You could never imagine anybody more reasonable. Such qualities came out during the production of *The Bad Seed*, which also turned out to be a fine success for the Playwrights' Company. Elmer Rice has done some wonderful things for the theater, and so has Sam Berhman. Everybody knows what a loss the death of Sidney Howard has meant to the stage and to all of us...I think Elmer did a magnificent job in his staging of *Abe Lincoln in Illinois*, and if there's ever been a better performance on any stage than the one Raymond Massey gave in the title part I just haven't seen it.

"I loved Arthur Hopkins, who put on *The Petrified Forest* for me—a fine, sensitive and honest man, Arthur was...I had great success with *Reunion in Vienna* and thanks to those lovely performances of Alfred Lunt and Lynn Fontanne. How lucky can a playwright be when he gets such people to play for him? They were equally wonderful in *There Shall Be No Night* and *Idiot's*

Delight. Alfred's going into his dance in the second act of *Idiot's Delight* provided one of the most delightful interludes I've ever come upon.

"Hollywood? Sure, I liked the dough I got for working out there but my job's the theater. The idea behind this organization was to keep us all out of Hollywood. I'm now in the theater—heart and soul and body and mind. It's something that's to be forever with me. And that's the way I've always wanted it."

◻ Moss Hart (1904 – 1961)

MOSS GREW UP in a New York neighborhood of pushcarts and poverty, and liked to live lavishly after his many stage triumphs, which included six plays co-written with George S. Kaufman (*You Can't Take It With You* won the 1937 Pulitzer Prize for Drama), several of his own, and musical collaborations with George Gershwin, Cole Porter, Irving Berlin and Richard Rodgers and Lorenz Hart. His Broadway hits stretched from *Once in a Lifetime*, a 1930 farce written with Kaufman, to directing Lerner and Loewe's *Camelot* (1960).

◻

MOSS HART, a man of twenty-odd plays, was talking sharply and amiably of matters theatrical. "The day that *Once in a Lifetime* opened I had 95 cents in my pockets and in the world," he said. "The dress rehearsal ran until 5:30 a.m. Sam Harris, who always called me Kid, walked from the Music Box to the Broadway corner with me. He realized I was broke and he put a $100 bill into my hand. I must have felt pretty sure about *Once in a Lifetime*. Instead of taking the subway and going home to Brooklyn I went into the Astor Hotel and got a suite."

And at 11:30 a.m. the time for another rehearsal, it was a glossy young playwright who reported at the Music Box. His clothes had been pressed; he had sent a bellman out for a new shirt and tie. He had had the services of a barber, a manicurist and a masseur and half of that $100 bill, probably more than half, was gone. But he felt good.

Such was Moss Hart's start as a dramatist. The theater had been in his heart and in his head since early boyhood. He had worked as a theatrical office boy. He had read old copies of such exciting journals as the *Dramatic Mirror* and the *Green Book* from cover to cover. He had made his way through the vastly entertaining pages of the old *Theater Magazine* in the bound volumes from 1901 until it expired around 1929. And he never missed an issue of *Variety*, which has outstayed them all, which began in 1905 and which is still flourishing.

Since his debut with *Once in a Lifetime*, written in collaboration with George S. Kaufman, Hart has gone along contributing steadily and brilliantly to the American stage. He and Kaufman supplied an interesting and frequently fascinating play in *Merrily We Roll Along*, a comedy drama that ran backward. Hart and Irving Berlin put together a revue that was remarkably fresh and alive in the one entitled *As Thousands Cheer*. He and Kaufman achieved superb comedies in *You Can't Take It With You*, their story of the mad, happy, daffy, lovable, unmethodical but somehow sense-making family called the Sycamores, and in the engaging and explosive *The Man Who Came to Dinner*, which was based on the tantrums and impromptu rages of Alexander Woollcott. Hart, in calling upon Kaufman in Bucks County, Pa., told him of a terrifying weekend during which he had had Woollcott as a house guest, with A.W. spending most of his time bullying and harassing and torturing other guests and servants.

"Wouldn't it have been terrible," Hart remarked, "if Aleck had broken his leg—and had to stay." They looked at each other. Lightning had struck. They had their play. Eight months later *The Man Who Came to Dinner* was completed.

Moss Hart's solo efforts have included *Lady in the Dark*, which turned out to be an exciting vehicle for Gertrude Lawrence; *Winged Victory*, an Air Force propaganda piece, into which he packed a lot of tumultuous theater; *Christopher Blake*, which contained some of his best writing but which was wrecked by its sheer repetitiousness, and *Light Up the Sky*, an engaging comedy of theater folk.

Have a talk with Moss Hart and you get a lot of chatter that is both entertaining and informative, to wit: "George Kaufman and I had written two plays together before I ever called him George; it was always Mr. Kaufman. He didn't call me Moss or Mr. Hart. He would just say er...er...er...or something like that. I used to smoke cigars and he wouldn't come near me. So I started smoking pipes. George threw me into that.

"George and I will probably write together again. I certainly hope so. Everything I know, whatever I know, I learned from the best teacher in the world—Kaufman. He happens to be the most complicated, as well as the most interesting human being I've ever known and he also has the greatest sense of honor of anyone I've ever met.

"We were having some trouble with *Once in a Lifetime* and Sam Harris came to the rescue. Sam was a real gent, to use a Lindy's kind of expression. He was very smart in a strange sort of way. We just couldn't get a last act with *Once in a Lifetime* and Sam hit it when he said that we needed a quiet scene, that we didn't have one in the play. That led to the writing of the scene on the train."

Moss Hart then revealed that *Once in a Lifetime* had gone to Jed Harris before Sam Harris ever saw it.

"Yes, Jed read it first," he said. "Jed sent for me. He kept me waiting six hours. When he finally called for me to come in he was standing shaving at the bathroom mirror, stark naked. Jed is a man with a real, deep, deep talent. Thank God I didn't do *Once in a Lifetime* with him. I've never done any play with him. I wouldn't want to spend six months in a sanitarium. But I respect him. Jed used to be a very colorful figure. He has become kind of macabre."

Hart put a match to his pipe and went on quietly: "The theater is so ridiculously unsound. Everybody's saying that and I don't think it hurts at all for it to be said again and again. Our basic trouble is mainly that the theater is not now a part of our cultural or national life. Why, I'd like to have a play of mine open in six or seven towns simultaneously and I have the feeling that there could now be a great renaissance, and if this came about the theater could lick Hollywood. Eventually all the guilds and the crafts will have to get together and everybody concerned will have to take the gamble. Everything has gone up and up and up. It cost only $16,000 to open with *You Can't Take It With You*, but *Light Up the Sky* cost $80,000. *Lady in the Dark* opened on Broadway for $119,000 but today that would be around $300,000.

"One of the great mistakes some of us make is railing against the critics. It's the fault of the managers that the critics are so powerful, and all because of our vanity. Give us good notices and we take out those big ads quoting everybody. To start, or to stop, with the critics is complete nonsense. Of course, it's that artillery barrage the day after a play opens that really hurts. It's that concentrated fire. The theater is a floating crap game; you get just one roll of the dice. You're told, on the day after you open, whether you can stay open or not. Perhaps it would help some if the notices could be staggered over the space of a week, but you wouldn't get your line at the box office that way. And I guess that couldn't be done. People who follow the play reviews want the verdict quick. A new play happens to be news.

"It's been my discovery that an audience has a kind of idiot genius; an audience will detect falsity in a play, and reject it, without ever knowing why. I despise anybody who thinks that the theater is easy and I hate the idea of backers who come into the theater just to have fun…I'm going to be writing plays, I hope, for the rest of my life. There's one thing you do learn about playwrighting. Each play is a separate problem, a separate job."

◻ Noël Coward (1899 – 1973)

SIR NOËL started young and never stopped: acting, writing, singing, performing, for audiences large and small. He enjoyed friendships with the high- and low-born, was not ashamed to appear late in life in lucrative Las Vegas revues, and loved his chats with the Queen Mother. He was knighted in 1970.

◻

THERE WAS A PERIOD in World War II during which Noël Coward, the world's jack-of-all-entertainment, gave his friends cause for alarm. He became dangerously near pomposity. He said goodbye to the theater, proclaiming with a most unbecoming solemnity that he was through with it for the duration. He began dabbling in international politics and was forever being whisked away on missions that were mysteriously official. He took his martinis in Government Houses and took himself seriously while sipping them. He became something of a self-appointed High Ambassador to Practically Everything, filling a wartime role not unlike that which had belonged in former years to the Prince of Wales.

Fortunately, however—fortunately indeed for bored, restless and entertainment-hungry Allied troops on ever-alerted but inactive fronts—Noël recovered. With a twitch of his impudent and expressive eyebrows and a Cowardesque grimace or two, he got hold of himself, laughed convulsively at himself, begged the drama's forgiveness for his neglect, and returned forthwith to the only job he knew, the combined job of performing and writing. He visited bases, hospitals and troop concentrations here, there and everywhere giving his one-man show—songs in his fashion, and at whatever piano they had around; stories in his clipped, laconic and amusingly venomous manner, never avoiding impish malice when it could be used to humorous advantage. He gave autographs by the thousands, and always to the accompaniment of his own crisp chatter, his delayed and quivering smile, his cruel-lipped and darting twists of speech.

He gave his concerts, as he called them, throughout the British Isles and the vast Mediterranean area. He appeared in such Near East cities as Teheran and Baghdad, that dusty and over-glamourized metropolis beside the mighty Tigris. He was the theater's, and his country's, royal funmaker in Australia and South Africa. He dropped out of the skies to do his highly specialized act for the maimed and the wounded in scores of hospitals, always finding himself greatly moved by the courage and cheerfulness of the shattered young men of modern war, and never failing to become somewhat apologetic by his own noncombatant status. As a government emissary he had been actually stuffy and was probably the first to become aware of it. As a troops entertainer, paying impromptu calls upon fighting men in remote corners of the world, he was in his own métier, and he contributed vitally to the war effort.

Noël Coward, actor, playwright, composer, lyricist, raconteur and world-traveler, has written farces, comedies, dramas, revues and operettas and he has done the words and music for countless songs. His forty to fifty plays have included such whopping hits as *Private Lives*, *Bitter Sweet*, *Design For Living*, *Blithe Spirit* and *The Vortex*. In *Cavalcade* he gave the theater a stirring panorama of British history and in the wartime film, *In Which We Serve*, which won the New York Film Critics' Award as the best picture of 1942, he was extraordinarily successful in a medium for which he has never had any great interest. He has never been madly keen, as he might express it, to go in for screen acting or writing or producing for any kind of extended period. He is a dramatist who has been booed at first nights—certainly when *Sirocco* had its London premiere—and who has been given thundering ovations. There have been few nights in the history of the New York stage when the tumult within a playhouse has equaled that which came at the final curtain of *The Vortex* on its opening at Henry Miller's in 1925. Since Noël came challengingly to the front as a man of the theater who could do practically anything there have been several epidemics of his plays in both London and New York and at one period in his career he had contracts to supply the clamorous needs of a dozen managements more or less simultaneously.

All of which is difficult to blend with the picture of Noël Coward as a flippant and insecure young man of twenty-one who was a bewildered visitor seeing New York for the first time. Before making that trip to America he had achieved moderate standing as a young actor. He had appeared in such pieces as *Hannele* (in which there was a breathless child actress who called herself Miss Gertie Lawrence), *Charley's Aunt*, *Peter Pan*, *The Knight of the Burning Pestle* and in his own play, *I'll Leave It to You*. His New York stay intensified his desire to succeed as a dramatist and when he returned to London he put in countless hours at his playwrighting. He gave the West End stage *The Young Idea*, *London Calling* and *The Vortex* in which he appeared as Nicky Lancaster, the neurotic son of a neurotic mother. When *The Vortex* opened at the Everyman Theater in November of 1924, Noël was on his way. In another year he had four plays running in London simultaneously.

Noël's earnings in the theater have been enormous. When he was thirty-two, as London's busiest actor-playwright-composer-director, his intake was in excess of $6,000 weekly. He has by no means overworked himself in recent years but his year-to-year income has been a steady one and there are frequent windfalls, such as the $40,000-a-week whirl that he had at Las Vegas in

1955. He will tell you, and very crisply too, that he has never been disgustingly rich. He takes great pride in this property at Jamaica and he owns a house in Kent, behind Dover. He sold the New York apartment that he had bought from Alexander Woollcott and his London flat in Gerald Road, S. W. 1, is taken on lease. During the London blitz he wryly observed, "the Germans are trying to take it from me, piece by piece."

Noël's closest friends include his partners, Alfred Lunt and Lynn Fontanne, and John C. Wilson, who turned from Wall Street to the theater and has never had any regrets. Noël has stayed at many of the world's best hotels and at a few of its worst. He will undoubtedly catch up with any that he has missed, for there are still a few odd spots on this planet that he has not visited, just as there are some luxury liners, tramp steamers and poky river boats on which he has not sailed. Before the war he was traveling light when he moved around the world with twenty or thirty assorted pieces of luggage but his wartime training was such that he's now quite content to be off for Cape Town or Melbourne or Calcutta with only a briefcase, pajamas and a toothbrush.

The affection that Noël has for close friends never prevents his being quietly enraged when their views on a subject—say, on a new Coward play—are not completely in accord with his own. He was certainly more than mildly vexed with the Lunts for turning down *Blithe Spirit*. His pique, however, was of short duration and it is certain that if there's one particular spot in all the world that he prefers to all others it is the Wisconsin village of Genesee Depot, to which he frequently goes as a guest at the Swedish manor house of Alfred and Lynn.

It's one of the legends of the theater that Noël can toss off a play in three days—or even two. He took all of three to write his comedy hit, *Private Lives*, while confined to bed with an attack of flu in Singapore. *Hay Fever*, that gay and giddy comedy that ran for a year in London (but it was received with something less than rapture in New York) was a three-day writing job in London. *Fumed Oak*, a minor masterpiece of a worm that turned, the most popular of the short plays that belonged to the *Tonight at 8:30* grouping, was written in forty-eight hours during one of his freighter trips.

Noël Coward, who first greeted a not-too-responsive world at Teddington-on-the-Thames on December 16, 1899, and who began acting at the age of eleven in *The Goldfish*, a children's play, is a six-footer. He generally weighs around 145. He is very erect, and frequently seems almost military in his bearing. There is definitely an Oriental cast to his pale, lean face, with its small elfin eyes and a friend once remarked that: "Noël could pass any day for a Chinese general if he would dress for the part." He invariably frowns as he smiles. He never gives the appearance of being a dandy, but he wears the best of English clothes. He likes yellow chamois gloves, wears a top hat with authority, and if he were given the choice of a single garment for a thirty-day ordeal on a raft in the open sea, I'm sure that he would ask for an old silk dressing robe—with cigarettes in the pocket.

I've known Noël for a quarter of a century and have found him to be a man of poise, reserve, dignity, humor, generosity and devastating charm. And cynical wit, always. Since his precocious child-actor days he has always had a positive passion for work. He has generally been much more excited over what he was going to write tomorrow than in what he completed yesterday. He has always been fascinated by Charles the Second and wants to play him on the stage. He has never been overwhelmed by a desire to play Hamlet and for this his many friends are thankful. "But it would never surprise us," one of them remarked recently, "to find him turning to the serious plays of Galsworthy or coming forth as Peer Gynt or King Lear."

And then he added: "You see, Noël Coward is a man who likes having a good time. He likes garden parties. He can even take cocktail parties. He likes swimming and yachting and lying on the beach or on a rock in the sun. But he enjoys himself most when he is acting. He has been acting, off stage as well as on, for just about all of his life."

◻ Richard Rodgers (1902 – 1979)

RICHARD RODGERS wrote more than 900 published songs and forty Broadway musicals. He and Lorenz Hart first teamed in the Twenties, with hit shows such as *The Girl Friend* and *A Connecticut Yankee*. They traveled to Hollywood but were back on Broadway in 1935, with an unbroken string of sellouts, including *Pal Joey* and *The Boys from Syracuse*. Hart died in 1943 and Rodgers then teamed up with Oscar Hammerstein II to create *Oklahoma!*, *Carousel*, *South Pacific*, *The King and I*, *The Sound of Music*, and a few failures. In 1990, the 46th Street Theater was posthumously renamed the Richard Rodgers Theater.

DURING THE NEW York theatrical season of 1943-44 a melodrama of men at war called *South Pacific* opened on Broadway and played for a very short run. In early April of 1949 Rodgers & Hammerstein, the foremost showmen of the American theater, presented their magnificent musical play, *South Pacific* without being disturbed at all by the fact that a non-musical piece of the same title had had a metropolitan engagement a few seasons earlier. Such is the impermanence of a title when it is attached to non-success in the theater. Showmen have long contended that there is nothing quite as forgettable as the name of a play which has been a Broadway flop.

The Rodgers & Hammerstein *South Pacific* became, with the passing of two and a half years, a project of global renown. It didn't stay as long in New York as its predecessor, *Oklahoma!*, did, but it won just as much acclaim in its playing across the world. No other management in the theater's history has ever offered a quartet of productions within a ten-year period, to match *Oklahoma!*, *Carousel*, *South Pacific* and *The King and I*. The great Augustin Daly, who produced plays for thirty years, would shake his head in bewilderment.

In writing this piece about Richard Rodgers I want to go further into the extraordinary case of *South Pacific*. Just what did this play with music have that so fascinated tens of thousands of playgoers and that brought it into the consciousness of millions who never saw it? Well, it had these attributes: It made a romantic figure of a man in his late fifties and it brought home to many a man of such age, and even older, that late-in-life romance is by no means unachievable. It delivered, and in romantic terms, a lesson and a message in racial tolerance. And besides making its points on the questions of age and race, *South Pacific* offered an enchanting score, entertainment values in the rowdyism of the Seabees and Marines against an exotic background, and it combined the technical skills of the theater—those of the composer, the lyricist, the scenic designer, the costumer, the choreographer, the stage director—in a collaborative effort that produced extraordinary results.

South Pacific offered something that was incommunicable and indefinable. Playgoers left the theater feeling better than they did when they came in. It was revolutionary in its presentation of a 57-year-old lover and tradition-smashing in the handling of its materials. Consider the lament of the lyrical but agonized Julie of *Show Boat* who listed the shortcomings of her lover while admitting that she couldn't just "help lovin' dat man." And contrast it with the rhapsodic outbursts of Nellie Forbush, who wanted Little Rock and all the world to know that she was in love with a wonderful guy!

RICHARD RODGERS, who comes pretty close to being the top figure in the American theater at the moment, is as direct as he is articulate. He has never told me which of the many scores he has written has given him the greatest satisfaction as a composer and a showman, but I'm sure that the score of *South Pacific* is very close to his heart. A practical man of the theater, Rodgers is interested in every phase of it. He and Oscar Hammerstein 2d. know the exact cost of every yard of costume fabric, they have direct supervision over the settings and the casting and the choreographer. No dancer or singer can get into one of their shows without their complete approval.

"Sure," said Rodgers, several months ago, in a session with me at Dinty Moore's, "the theater is my life's work. If I didn't write for the theater what would I do—sit on my lawn in Connecticut? If there ever comes a time when there are only five legitimate playhouses in New York I'd like to have one of them, and if we ever get down to only one I'd want that to be mine.

"The whole economic situation comes into the story when you get to talking of lowering productions costs. We can't lower seat prices—not much. We can't cut chorus salaries. Things are up, all right. If you did *The Yellow Jacket*, a play with no scenery at all, in today's theater, it would cost $50,000 to put on…Somebody's got to do the theater. Oscar Hammerstein and I are not staying in it for any charitable reasons or because of any sense of duty. It just happens that we're very hot about it.

"We've had the good fortune to be associated with some wonderful people and to have the same kind of people working for us. Now get this straight. Lawrence Langner and Theresa Helburn, who run the Theater Guild, are tremendous people. They've been a force in the theater for 36 years. They dropped *Oklahoma!* right in our laps and it took them months to bully us into doing *Carousel*, and we're mighty glad that we did. We've gone along with the Guild because we like working with them."

SINCE THE MID-TWENTIES, when Richard Rodgers and Lorenz Hart wrote *The Garrick Gaieties* there've been about forty Rodgers shows and hundreds of Rodgers songs. There were several Rodgers & Hart productions that didn't go; that's also been true of Rodgers & Hammerstein operations. *Me and Juliet* paid off, but it was definitely Grade B. And there was *Allegro*, an interesting failure, but a failure nevertheless.

"It all gets back to this," went on Rodgers. "You have to have a smash hit or you have nothing. *Annie Get Your Gun* took eleven months to pay off, but it was a big money-maker. *Allegro* cost us around $250,000 and we never got back a dime of it. Technically it was a departure from anything we'd ever done. We tried to tell a dramatic story with a tremendous amount of music. There was a large dancing chorus, a large singing chorus, a large cast of principals and a 30-piece orchestra. It was all very exciting, but we couldn't get enough of the public interested to make it go...We'll have other flops as we go along. Sure we will. I hope we'll have a few more big hits. But, as I was telling you, I wouldn't know what to do with myself if I didn't do plays. I believe Oscar feels the same way."

◘ Mike Todd (1907 or 1909 – 1958)

MIKE WAS ONE of nine children of a Chicago rabbi. He dropped out of high school, married at 17, and worked as a pharmacist and shoe salesman before starting in construction. He made and lost fortunes and ended up in Hollywood as a studio contractor. After that, he made his own history. His third wife was Elizabeth Taylor, but Todd and three companions died in an air crash in New Mexico the year after their marriage.

THE TIME WAS 4 P.M. Michael Todd, who brought the Todd-AO process into use in motion pictures (perhaps you've seen the screen version of *Oklahoma!*) was wearing a pagoda-red loin cloth and was sprawled out upon the terrace of his Park Avenue duplex, as brown as a Cherokee. He was talking into two telephones.

The summertime sun beat down with the heat of the Pakistan desert. Mike's Japanese secretary, who seemed to come right through the glass, served lemonade. Mike chewed upon a monstrous cigar, snapped orders into both telephones, and began talking to me in his brusque, staccato fashion.

"Hell, I'm in all sorts of show business," he said. "That Todd-AO thing has got me mixed up in pictures. I'll also be doing plenty of TV and I'm not walking out on the Broadway theater, not at all.

"I got plans. We don't get *Peer Gynt* every season, do we? I might try it. Then there are plays by Shakespeare like *Cymbeline* and *King John* that are not around very often. Perhaps I'll try them. And I've been reading up on some of the pieces of the oldtime American theater. There might be a lot of dough in a musical version of that old thriller, *Shenendoah*, and who can say that there wouldn't be audiences for *The Two Orphans* and *The Old Homestead* if they were played straight. I'd even try *The Squaw Man* if Clark Gable would play it and I've got enough sense to know that a show with a sort of a plot and offering all of the George M. Cohan song hits would sell out for a year or two. I'm thinking about it."

SQUARE-JAWED MIKE, the man from Minneapolis, came in upon the New York scene with *The Hot Mikado*. Since that time he has given Broadway such productions as *Star and Garter* and *Something for the Boys* and *Mexican Hayride* and *Up in Central Park*. He enjoyed himself immensely while serving as producer at Jones Beach.

"I'm an artist," he said, "and I don't want anybody to think I'm just a carnival man. When I was running Jones Beach it looked like the biggest thing in America—and it still can be. If that damn thing can actually get going it will draw audiences from everywhere—Venezuela and Rio, Barcelona and the Orange Free State and the Hebrides and the Azores. Also from the Yukon and from Kansas and the Bronx. Jones Beach can be a great asset to New York City. Maybe I'll get another whack at it sometime.

"When I was there we had a slight epidemic of culture, and without hurting anybody. We had *A Night in Venice* and about 330 actors and the moon and fireworks and the ballet and doves flying around."

He reached for one of his telephones and yapped into it: "Remind me to go to Venice in 1957. I don't want to fall in those canals or bother with the pigeons. Just want to see the place. Then maybe I'll come back and produce the play Shakespeare wrote about it. How would Edward G. Robinson do as Shylock? Even if Marilyn Monroe couldn't speak the verse she'd be the best-looking Portia the theater ever had."

MORE TELEPHONE TALK, another cigar. Then:

"You know, there's no magic in the thing called show business. Just a little know-how and a lot of hard work. My average around Broadway was pretty good."

He poured two jiggers of Scotch. "These glasses have false bottoms and they remind me of my Chicago days in the saloon business. I had a good time in that, too...I liked several of my shows, such as *Up in Central Park* and *Mexican Hayride* and *Star and Garter* and I'm one of many who regard Bobby Clark as a great comedian. A man's a fool to ever try a musical show unless Bobby Clark is in it. Bobby doesn't need any songs or any lines; just give him his cigar...*Star and Garter* went along to capacity for quite a time. It got to Chicago and got a terrific panning from the critics. I didn't mind. Sent Napoleon brandy to all of them...Talking about actors, I liked producing *Catherine Was Great* for Mae West. That dame is good box office. Women want to see her. Maybe I'll have Mae and Bobby Clark and Gable and Garbo and Marilyn Monroe all together in a show sometime, and we'll play it in New York at $25 a seat and then tour it all the way to the Saskatchewan. I've never been there, but I hear it's nice...Tell the boys that I'm counting on coming back to Broadway and doing some plays. Honest. Maybe we can try the Todd-AO process in the legitimate theater. Might work."

◩ Jeanne Eagels (1890 – 1929)

ANOTHER GREAT of the American stage of the 1920's was Jeanne Eagels, a former Ziegfeld Follies girl from Kansas City, who appeared in several Broadway productions before her exceptional appearance as Sadie Thompson in the 1922 hit play *Rain*, based on a W. Somerset Maugham story. The intensity of her performance as a fallen woman trying to start a new life on a South Pacific island wowed audiences in New York and on tour for nearly four years. Eagels also appeared in films, starting in 1915, acting with Hollywood legends such as John Gilbert and Leslie Howard. Her final movie, *The Letter* (1929), an early talkie, earned her an Academy Award nomination for Best Actress, but she died before knowing that Mary Pickford had won the Oscar. Here are references from two of my father's books: *Matinee Tomorrow* (1949), and *Forty-Five Minutes Past Eight* (1939).

JEANNE EAGELS (FROM *MATINEE TOMORROW*)

THE FIRST-NIGHT performance of *Rain* was ragged. An after-performance conference became fairly hysterical, with only Harris holding himself in control. Eugene Walter was summoned to do some hasty rewriting, and during the next few days everybody, including the stagehands, had suggestions for changes. Walter wanted to put in a seduction scene, showing the Reverend Mr. Davidson and Sadie together after he had charged into her room, but he was finally overruled. Notwithstanding all the uproar and ruction, there was actually little revision made during the Philadelphia engagement. Most of Walter's time was spent in blasting Colton, whom he called a half-wit, and to whom he applied short, obscene words steadily for twenty-four hours. But Colton wasn't around to hear the vituperation of the author of *The Easiest Way*. The weary and discouraged Colton had stayed alone in his hotel room for most of the Philadelphia engagement.

Rain came into the Maxine Elliott Theater on a November evening in 1922, and the opening brought forth an emotional demonstration never exceeded in the theater of this country and century. First-nighters stood and screamed when the curtain fell upon Sadie's denunciation of Davidson at the close of the second act; they were as wild as spectators at a football game.

I occupied a seat in the rear of the balcony on that opening night and experienced one of the most genuinely stirring moments in all my theatergoing years in the final scene of the third act when Sadie's long-silent phonograph broke into the haunting strains of "Wabash Blues," her gesture of complete disgust with all mankind. She had learned only too bitterly that the Reverend Mr. Davidson, the foe of all evil, who had finally convinced her that she must return to San Francisco and repent her sins, was an idol with feet of clay. Jeanne Eagels had her great night and she was acclaimed, and so was the play, the next day by the enthusiastic critics—Hammond, Broun, Mantle, Woollcott. Miss Eagels achieved a stardom that had been honestly earned and she went on to play the role of Sadie for 174 weeks.

During the long run of the play in New York no one had greater appreciation for the sheer artistry of Eagels than Kathryn Kennedy, her understudy, who fled to New Mexico in the mid-Twenties in a last-chance effort to save herself from dying of tuberculosis. She lived. She decided that the Southwest was to be her home for the rest of her days and started a theater of her own, the Albuquerque Little Theater. And during the year of 1948 Miss Kennedy wrote me thus of the original Sadie Thompson:

'I SINCERELY DOUBT if Jeanne Eagels really knew, in spite of her pretensions, that she was a great actress. She was...Many times backstage I'd be sitting alongside of Rapley Holmes (Joe Horn, the storekeeper of Pago Pago) waiting for my entrance cue and suddenly Jeanne would start to build a scene, and Rap and I would look up from our books at once. Some damn thing—some power, something—would take hold of your heart, your senses, as you listened to her, and you'd thrill to the sound of her...Jeanne was scared and unsure of herself before *Rain* opened. At one of the dress rehearsals she was told John Barrymore was out front with some friends. She stood it for awhile and then she became rattled and couldn't remember her lines, and she walked off the stage and said she wouldn't continue until Barrymore left. They got rid of him, and she went on...Jeanne's surprise at her big hit was actually childlike, but that didn't last long. She began to yell for top billing and a hundred other things. One night about a month after the opening, when she was really the hit of the town, her mother came backstage and said she couldn't get a seat. Jeanne told the stage manager to get her the seat. "I'm the star of this thing, by God!" she yelled, and then she looked quickly at several of us as if she expected us to deny it. Eagels had a fiery temper, and she was a long time fighting loudly for everything that she got, but beneath it all she was a lovable person. We'd all get mad as hell at her, but we had great affection for her.

Jeanne Eagels (from *Forty-Five Minutes Past Eight*)

...I'D NOW KNOWN Jeanne Eagels since *Rain* and had been frequently to her country houses. We met one afternoon at *Le Mirliton*, that charming and delightful little restaurant in Fifty-eighth Street which George Kuhnert had been running for all these years. I told her about my new place upstairs. She wanted to see it immediately. It was exactly what she wanted, she decided. A midtown walk-up, just a tiny place where she could stay when she didn't feel like driving to Westchester. I introduced her to Mrs. Packard, the landlady. Two days later Jeanne Eagels moved into her two-room walk-up above the fruit shop. She wanted to read and sleep and rest. But to her modest quarters she brought cook, maid and chauffeur and I believe there were times when even a butler put in an appearance. Before the coming of the erstwhile Sadie Thompson, life above the fruit shop had never been particularly serene but now, once she had moved in, there was forever bustle on the stairway. Friends began dropping in. The two-room hideaway became something of a salon. There came an afternoon when the crush was so great that she left her callers to their gaieties and fled to her Westchester house for peace, only to find that it, too, was over-run with guests. A great actress, Jeanne Eagels, I thought. And how singular it was (and what a loss for the theater!) that she and Emily Stevens and Holbrook Blinn should all die within a short time of each other. Miss Stevens and Blinn died in 1928. The following year saw the passing of Jeanne Eagels. Her death came with shocking suddenness. She had called at the Park Avenue Hospital in the late afternoon of October 3, 1929, and was waiting a consultation with her personal physician when a convulsion seized her. Death was attributed by the city toxicologist to an overdose of chloral hydrate. The body, in a silver and bronze coffin, was sent for burial to her native Kansas City, which she left in her teens to make her fame in New York.

Jeanne Eagels had moved from Fifty-eighth Street but I continued seeing her frequently. I was not at *The Sun* office when news of her death was received. But when I reached my typewriter the next morning there was a typed memo rolled into the machine. It read: "Please call Jeanne Eagels, 3:10 P.M."

▣ Lost Profiles And Interviews

I'VE INCLUDED THE FOLLOWING section of my father's interviews and profiles not only because they are good but because they have never been published before. Some parts of them have been in his books or columns but they have never appeared together so cohesively.

◻ Helen Hayes (1900 – 1993)

Ms. Hayes first appeared on stage in 1905; her final performance was in a 1971 performance of *Long Day's Journey Into Night*. She preferred the stage to films, but made many memorable movies, including *Airport* (1970), for which she won an Academy Award, and several Disney productions. She is one of the few people to win an Emmy, a Grammy, an Oscar and a Tony.

Helen Hayes is small and slight and is by no means beautiful. Many actresses have had greater vocal range and power, many have had more on-the-surface glamour. But Miss Hayes has magic, a definite star quality once she is on the stage. Such quality has come forth in a great variety of roles throughout a career that has endured since her childhood.

In 1938 I conducted a symposium, "Ten Great Performances," for *The New York Sun*, publishing 150 carefully prepared lists from 150 contributors. Miss Hayes topped the field. Eighty-one of the more or less famous playgoers who listed ten stage performances that had stayed in their memory wrote in the name of Helen Hayes.

The great majority of her supporters were of the opinion that her acting in *Victoria Regina* was deserving of all-time honors. Others recalled her superb work in *Coquette*, in which she played a Southern girl who took her own life at the final curtain. There was also mention of James M. Barrie's *Dear Brutus* and of *Clarence*, the best play Booth Tarkington ever wrote.

I was captivated by Miss Hayes' acting in all those plays and was of the impression that she also distinguished herself in such lesser pieces as *Ladies and Gentlemen*, *Harriet* and *Happy Birthday*. And certainly she brought her very special magic to her characterization as Mrs. Antrobus in the 1955 revival of Thornton Wilder's *The Skin of Our Teeth*.

Helen Hayes' life has been one of a series of stage triumphs and it has also been one that has been touched by tragedy. It struck when her 19-year-old-daughter, Mary Hayes MacArthur, died after a brief illness.

She was desolated by Mary's death, pitifully unprepared to withstand a shock so overwhelming. She needed help, and quickly. It came in the form of wires and letters from all parts of the continent. By such means an entire nation rushed to her aid in a great emergency. Her first impulse had been to give up the theater, at once and forever. To quit the stage, radio and everything else. But…there were all those loving hands reaching out.

"I just had to pick myself up and go on," Miss Hayes told me several weeks after Mary's death. "I've always been so glad that I went back to work. You learn one thing when something terrible happens and that is that every human being has a duty to everybody else...No, 'duty' is not the right word. It's just that everybody owes something to everybody else. It became important to me to show my great friends how I could get through such a crisis.

"Everybody said, 'Just plunge into work.' My doctor said it, that blessed Mayor O'Dwyer said it, everybody said it. Everybody was there trying to help me and I knew that it was up to me to try to do something back for them. Well, I tried...I'll never forget the opening night of *Happy Birthday* in New York. I asked Mary to come down to the theater and sit with me. I knew that her easy calm and humor would help me. I was in my dressing room making up and got to shaking and I said, 'I'm frightened of that dance in the second act.' If Mary had then made a trite remark it would have done no good, but she simply said, 'Suppose you fall down—what do you do? You pick yourself up and go on.' That's what I tried to do after Mary died."

MISS HAYES, speaking quietly and with increasing calmness, fell to talking of many of the plays of her career.

"I've always, always been terrified of first nights," she said. "I've often said to myself, 'This is the last, positively the last,' but then you find yourself going into and going through another one. We just never learn, do we? I'll never forget the opening of *Coquette*. We hadn't been too good out of town and we all felt defeated as we came in. But we opened and a riot greeted us. I got through the first night of *Happy Birthday* because of Mary's simple solution. We had a rather terrible time with *Happy Birthday* in Boston. Opened cold there because of all the tricks and lights and mechanics and our play was sunk on the opening night. We knew that it went badly and they told us so in the papers the next day. But Rodgers and Hammerstein were so full of sweetness and courage and confidence. They kept telling me that everything would be all right, and so it was—by the time we got to New York. Anita Loos, in her writing of *Happy Birthday*, made technical demands of the kind that you'd think only Hollywood could take care of, but Dick and Oscar never turned a hair. They just went right ahead and did all the things that Anita's script called for. They're such wonderful men; we had a love feast all the way.

"Had another rough time in Boston when we went there with Josh Logan's play, *The Wisteria Trees*. On the opening night all hell broke loose; the play just went wild. There was complete apathy from the audience. People sat out there like frozen robins, just sat and stared at us. Then Josh took the play all apart, like a jigsaw puzzle. He had a dictaphone and he walked up and down and after the third week I wanted to smash it to pieces. Whatever and however *The Wisteria Trees* turned out to be in New York it was far, far better than what we had in Boston...I think it was a Virginia accent I used in *The Wisteria Trees*, the same that I tried when I did *The Glass Menagerie* in London. Clement Atlee told me I reminded him of Lady Astor.

"Years ago, when I first came to New York from Washington, I had a trace of a Southern accent, but you can bet I lost it by the time I got to playing *Dear Brutus*. I don't think Mr. Gillette could have taken that Deep-South kind of talk. The first night of *Dear Brutus* still looms out above them all. What a rare and great gentleman William Gillette was...Funny, but you just never know about a play on the road. You never know whether you have a New York play until you open in New York...It's been something dreamy to work with the great people I've known in the theater—Dick and Oscar, Gillette and Tarkington and Alfred Lunt, Anita Loos and Jo Mielziner and Lucinda Ballard, Gilbert Miller and, of course, Jed Harris. What great talent that man really has!"

◻ Forty-Five Minutes Past Eight

LIKE THE EXCERPT of Jeanne Eagels earlier in the book, the following two selections are from my father's first autobiography, *Forty-Five Minutes Past Eight*, published in 1939, his first and perhaps his liveliest book. There's more immediacy in these portraits, more of a breathless "I'm-on-a-deadline-to-finish-this-column-and-finish-this-book" feeling than in his later volumes.

GENTLEMEN OF THE PRESS

I BEGAN THE ACTUAL writing of *Gentlemen of the Press* in 1927. The principal character, Wick Snell, veteran newspaperman, who'd been everywhere and seen everything, was inspired by a man who sat next to me on the rewrite desk at the *Tribune*—Arthur James Pegler, father of Westbrook Pegler. He fumed and he snarled about the injustices of newspaper life; he'd been in the business too long, he'd say, and he'd gotten too little out of it. He was hard and bitter and rasping but, underneath, there was a soft, kindly side, all of which went into the writing of the character of Snell. When I was done with the first act I went to the Lambs Club to see Edward Ellis, now of Hollywood. He was the perfect actor for my leading character. Ellis was polite, somewhat interested, but not particularly encouraging. I later met Leonard Gallagher in Sardi's and outlined the play to him. He was then associated with Guthrie McClintic, who was serving as producer-director for the Actors' Theater and who had brought forth a bright hit in *Saturday's Children*, the comedy by the rising Maxwell Anderson. McClintic and Gallagher took an option on the play and told me to go ahead. But before I was midway in the second act the writing of *Gentlemen of the Press* had become one of the major industries of New York. I had collected four collaborators. When all else concerning the play is forgotten the story of the Five Authors will live on. It was almost fatal showmanship, the whole idea. It was five chins thrust out, not just one. But the legend persists and I shall try accurately to set down the credits. My co-writers were my close friends and they were all co-frequenters of the Chez Florence, Texas Guinan's and the Hotsy Totsy. I hereby present the quartet, alphabetically: Mark Barron of Waco, Texas, John S. Cohen, Jr., of Atlanta, Willard Keefe of Morton, Minn., and Richard Watts, Jr. of Charleston, W. Va. Barron wrote a little dialogue and was a consultant on numerous scenes. Cohen didn't do any writing but delivered himself of some grave and abstract counsel and insisted on putting sex into the second act. Keefe assisted in the writing of several scenes, suggested the curtain of the first act, wrote the best laugh line of the show, and contributed to the general excitement, and to the distress of George Abbott, by falling backstage on the final night at the Apollo, Atlantic City, and suffering a broken leg. Watts didn't do any writing but he was ever-present and was fiercely loyal to the project before and after production.

The title of *Gentlemen of the Press*—an excellent one, I always thought—was contributed by Elbert Severance, who was with the brothers Chanin, architects and theater-builders. The play was finished in December of 1927 and on Christmas Eve the Rialto Typing Service delivered the scripts—original and five carbons. The prettiest script, the one with the red-ribbon trimmings, went to McClintic and Gallagher. Another to Miriam Hopkins and another to Eloise Taylor, now Mrs. Pat O'Brien of Hollywood, who had joined the Five Authors in their nightly rovings and who had heard so much of the dialogue she knew the play line for line. Heard so much that she'd been talking to Tommy Jackson about it, for she had now joined the "Broadway" company as one of the girls of the Paradise Cabaret. Tommy had long had yearnings to produce a play; such inclinations were pretty general in those prosperous pre-Crash years. Now he'd made a hit, he was paid every week, and getting good money. All he wanted was a script. He read *Gentlemen of the Press* behind scenes at the Broadhurst and the next morning he got me on the phone at *The Sun*. Tommy was tough and plain-talking. He said: "I like that goddam show. I'll buy it and produce it. Find out what McClintic is going to do about it." Several days later McClintic, en route to Seattle, sent a wire releasing the manuscript. At 11 A.M. on New Year's Eve, in his office near the Algonquin, Tommy signed the contract for the rights to *Gentlemen of the Press* and paid $500. We began talking about actors. About directors. About try-out towns. It all seemed so swift. And so easy. I went to the New Year's Eve party of the Mayfair Club with the feeling that the play would be in rehearsal within a month.

But it was not quite that easy. Bankroll trouble developed. Tommy Jackson and Hy Kraft, who had become associated with him, peddled the script for backing. Two months passed. I was pretty dejected about the whole business and, after heavy conference with the authorship board—Keefe, Barron, Watts and Cohen—began planning to resell the play after the option expired. Finally, however, Jackson sent the script to George Abbott. Lightning struck. Abbott liked it and said he'd direct it. He suggested a late summer opening instead of a spring production. His name meant then, as it does now, money at the box office, and Jackson & Kraft got a backer within an hour. They could have had a dozen. John Cromwell, who had been playing in *The Racket*, was engaged for the rôle of Snell. Abbott was precise in his casting; he can pass on more players in a given time than any director I've ever known. He had many suggestions for script revision and most of them were good ones. At the beginning of the summer I went to Colorado for a brief stay, wrote an entirely new third act, returned to Broadway and lost it in a taxi! It had to be done over again, and immediately.

We went into rehearsal late in July and hoped to get to town ahead of the competitive newspaper piece, *The Front Page*, written by Ben Hecht and Charles MacArthur and produced by Jed Harris. Jed, however, brought in his play in mid-August. *Gentlemen of the Press* played a week in Atlantic City prior to New York and during that week the Five Authors must have turned George Abbott's hair white. Nobody, certainly none of the five (put up at the Hotel Shelburne at the expense of the management) was ever late for rehearsal, no training rules were broken, but Abbott always feared the worst. Abbott is a man who doesn't drink or smoke and he mildly disapproves of those who do either or both. He has, however, his social side and he is something of a tea-room Don Juan. There never was a man who cared more for dancing, and when he invites a lady out for an evening of dancing she dances! He managed to get in a few waltzes at Atlantic City after putting his authors safely to bed. After a week at the shore—the theater was the famous old Apollo—and with only minor catastrophe, *Gentlemen of the Press* moved on to Broadway and opened at Henry Miller's, on what must have been the hottest night of the year. It was a big opening; a complete sell-out. The orchestra floor could have been sold five times. I stayed away from Forty-third Street, getting the returns at a speakeasy known as the Aquarium. Dorothy Hall and Neal Andrews gave a tremendous after-theater party in Fifty-seventh Street. I got about 400 telegrams. I thought that was tremendous only to learn that Gene Buck once received 2,000!

Some of the reviews were pretty severe, although several critics acknowledged the authenticity of the city-room flavor. The Five Authors build-up had its bearing upon the notices. Gilbert Gabriel, writing in *The Sun*, began his comment with the following sentence: "This is where a critic needs a friend and loses five." Heywood Broun, reviewing for the *Telegram*, paid tribute to the true atmosphere, the characters and the dialogue, but said the story wasn't as strong as that of *The Front Page*. The Five Authors were about ready to head for the East River in a body when things began happening. Paramount called and asked for a price on the film rights. There was inquiry about the London rights (which we sold). A. L. Jones, then of the firm of Jones & Green, and operating the Forty-eighth Street Theater, talked of moving the play into his house. And then *Variety* came out. Jack Lait wrote a beautiful notice, saying that *Gentlemen of the Press* explored the very hearts and souls of newspapermen. And on Saturday evening of the opening week we had a big sale.

Paramount closed a deal within three weeks. Al Jones took over the management and *Gentlemen of the Press* stayed in Forty-eighth Street until nearly Christmas and went on tour in January. During the fall of 1928, several of the critics, Gabriel and Broun included, returned for second glimpses of the play. They both wrote new pieces, glowing pieces. Had we received these notices in August instead of November the play might have taken ranking as an actual hit.

There was a character in the piece called Bellflower, the name of an Atlanta newspaperman and a name that had always fascinated me. The Atlanta Bellflower was a police reporter, the leg-man type who made friends with the cops and the lawyers and the bail bondsmen and who got a lot of news. I didn't put Bellflower as a person into the play; just his name. The actor who created the rôle of Bellflower—one of the skimpiest ever written into the American drama—was that renowned trouper, Russel Crouse. He belonged to New York's writing set, was married to Alison Smith (who did some excellent reviews for the *Morning World*) and he conducted a column on the editorial page of the *Evening Post*. He got a lot of copy out of his stage experience but along about Thanksgiving he decided that he had had enough. Here, at last, was my chance. A chance to act and one that wouldn't lead, necessarily, to a park bench in Roanoke. Saul Abraham, one of the best-known of the Broadway treasurers and a fellow who had great popularity among the Broadway news-getters, was general manager for Jones. William Fields, a Texan come to New York and a leader in his craft, was press agent. The three of us talked Jones into letting me go on as Crouse's replacement. Crouse got $60 weekly. Or could it have been $75? But Al Jones, who had always protested that actors and authors were overpaid, shaved me to $50. Well, I got an Equity card and played Bellflower in Manhattan and Brooklyn. When the show was ready to move on to Baltimore I left the cast. Jones was cutting expenses. So the character was just dropped from the play.

Eugene O'Neill

The pageboy of the Hotel Savoy, all of four feet, bright face and brighter buttons, was at my river-suite door. He extended his tray. "Letter for you, sir…Thank you very much, sir."

I'd been expecting this letter. It was in ink and in writing that was fascinatingly minute:

Le Plessis
Saint-Antoine du Rocher

(Indre-et-Loire)
March 29th, 1930

Dear Ward Morehouse:

Sure thing! I'll be glad to see you. Arrange to come down and stay over night with us. There's a good train from Paris to Tours around two or two-thirty p.m. that gets in Tours around six. Wire me a couple of days ahead so I'll be certain to be here and say what day you're coming and I'll meet you at Tours station. This place is ten kilometers out in the country. You can get back to Paris comfortably by the next evening if you're in a hurry and still have a night and morning here. I warn you I've got nothing much to offer in the way of news since I don't want to declare myself much in advance as to the nature of the work I'm now doing. [It was *Mourning Becomes Electra*.] I'm certain you'll like it here. I can promise you a grand lungful of Touraine country air and a spell of peaceful repose—and you can give me the New York news!

All kindest regards,
Eugene O'Neill

EUGENE O'NEILL, now in California, was then forty-one. He and Mrs. O'Neill (Carlotta Monterey) had presumably happy years in the Touraine. They kept house, thirty-five rooms of house, at Chateau Plessis, removed by a hundred miles and more from the whir of Paris. Their nearest neighbor, a French peasant, wasn't really near. There, in the great gray chateau, isolated and austere, near the river Loire and encircled by a beautiful wood, he found the tranquility which, seemingly, he had sought and had never found in America.

I took the Golden Arrow out of London, my first Channel crossing other than by plane, and was in Tours the next afternoon. That evening, at Chateau Plessis, we sat before an open fire in the large, high-ceilinged living room. Eugene O'Neill talked freely until well past midnight of himself and his writings. His speech was always thorough; it was never hurried.

"If I had any idea," he said, "that I'd have to repeat myself, that I had to stand still, I'd quit writing plays. I'd call it a day. I write primarily for myself, because it is a pleasure, and it would cease to be that if I started repeating. I could have gone on forever with plays like *Anna Christie*, or with the expressionism of *The Hairy Ape*, but I'm interested in trying to do better things.

"Now, this new play of mine is the hardest thing I've ever tried. God knows, it's the most ambitious. I've done the first draft. I'll do a second, then lay that aside and start on something else. Later I'll come back to it, and perhaps I may have something. I don't want to talk of its content. That hurt me with *Dynamo*. I just want to finish it, call a stenographer from Paris, and then mail it to the Guild. I've been at work on it for a year. Carlotta seems to think it's all right." ("Wonderful," was the word Mrs. O'Neill used to me.)

The dramatist-son of a grand old actor sipped his Coca-Cola and sat gazing at the burning wood chunks.

"You see," he said, "I've found out something. I've found out that I ought to take more time. Looking back, to *Dynamo*, I did eighteen long plays in eleven years. That's too much. If I could go back I'd destroy some of these plays, say, four of them—*Gold*, *The First Man*, *The Fountain*, and *Welded*. I've written, I think, forty plays—twenty long and twenty short. In my notebook I have ideas for thirty plays, perhaps thirty-two. That's work for a lifetime."

"Would you," I asked, "destroy *Dynamo*?"

"No, but I'd rewrite it. *Dynamo* had in it the makings of a fine play, but I did it too fast. And it was silly of me to mention a trilogy. And I wasn't surprised that they jumped me about it—that was but natural after *Strange Interlude*."

He paused. "The play of mine," he said, "for which I have the greatest affection is *The Great God Brown*. Next, *The Hairy Ape* and then *Strange Interlude*. My favorite short play is *Moon of the Caribbees*. I think the best writing I've done for the theater was in *Lazarus Laughed*.

"I've been remarkably lucky, I think, in the matter of actors. Certainly the performance of Walter Huston in *Desire Under the Elms* was tremendous. Exactly what I had in mind. And there were splendid performances by Paul Robeson in *The Emperor Jones* and by Lynn Fontanne in *Strange Interlude*.

We rode the next day in his Bugatti racer and got it up to 106 kilometers an hour. We swam in his concrete pool and wandered over his forty acres, with his Gordon setter and Dalmatians coming along. Never one for chatter, Eugene O'Neill, but on this beautiful morning in the Touraine he talked rather constantly.

"I love it here," he said simply. "But I've never had any idea of living here permanently. No nonsense about renouncing America. There's such a thing as being sensibly patriotic. But living away from America has been a good way to get to know America—to see things you couldn't see before."

And so I found Eugene O'Neill when he lived in France. They told me good-bye as the chauffeur whirled through the driveway in Mrs. O'Neill's magnificent French car. He had on a heavy sweater and she was trim in smart Parisian sport clothes. He extended his hand and grinned. "Tell them we're coming back," he said. "We're coming to live in New York or Georgia or California or somewhere."

I was in the big car. The engine roared. The car shot forward and I was off for the Tours train, which was to take me back to the boulevards and the bewilderments of Paris.

THE FOLLOWING SECTION comprises miscellaneous "Broadway After Dark" columns my father wrote from the 1930s to the 1960s for a variety of papers, most notably *The New York Sun*. They reflect his endless curiosity about the people and places, opening nights and closing curtains, of a time when Broadway was always alive and mostly new.

◻ Down by the Jersey Seaside as Winter Comes On — Boardwalk's Quiet, Roller Chairs Empty and It's Nice That Way — Notes on a Curio Called the Elephant House (1935)

ATLANTIC CITY, NOV. 23 — The Boardwalk, that remarkable pine and redwood platform strung out in front of the ocean-front hotels, and which follows the shoreline for a full eight miles from the Inlet to the far-famed Elephant House at Margate, is rather deserted these days. The flow of traffic diminishes with summer's passing. The roller chairs are everywhere, but few are rolling. The ballyhoo of the shopkeepers is stilled. The shops are still there—most of them open—the sun shines, the wind howls and the surf roars, and you have it all to yourself. Or nearly so.

And it's this very fact—the fact that the seaside promenade is uncongested as winter approaches—that brings many of the out-of-season visitors to this strip of Jersey coastline. Peace, quiet, wind, sun (right now)—they get it all and without the mob.

"Yes," said an old gentleman from Ohio, snug in his roller chair blankets and reading "So Red the Rose," "you can't keep me from coming to this place at this time of the year. I don't like crowds. I never did. I like peace. I also like health. Atlantic City, then, is the place for me. I get both. In the summer you couldn't give me the place. But right now—where can you beat it?...Feel that air? Look at the ocean. Why, in July you can't even see it."...He went back to his novel and on with his ride.

How Many Miles Today?

TO MANY ATLANTIC CITY devotees—particularly the health-seekers who come here at this time of the year—the boardwalk presents an eternal challenge. How many miles can they knock off before breakfast or after dinner? Apparently most of these strollers have mastered the knack of boardwalk strolling. They know their capacities, limits, and can judge their distances. It's not as easy, they'll warn you, as you might think. So I found out.

The boardwalk is deceptive. Especially so to one who has never really learned what walking is all about—whose daily stroll generally consists of a hike from Fifty-eighth and Madison, on past the Girl in the Fountain, to the Fifty-ninth street entrance of the B.M.T. And when you set foot on the boardwalk, with the salt air giving you new zest and false courage, you forget that walking isn't one of your accomplishments. The boardwalk looks easy, and you fairly sprint at the beginning. You look ahead and set some sort of mark for yourself. Then another and another. Finally, however, as your legs begin to crumble, you get the impression that the boardwalk has been extended to Cape Hatteras, or somewhere. It was at Ventnor that I desperately asked a fellow stroller about it.

"I wonder," I said, "if this thing ever really ends."

"Hardly ever," he replied. "It's still a good mile and a half to the Elephant Hotel at Margate."

So I put my Fifty-second street legs into reverse and when, after what seemed several years, I finally pulled up at the Hotel Claridge, I realized that I had completed my longest stroll since a little Turkish train broke down in the poppy fields of Turkey, a good six miles out of Broussa.

Conventions and Clams

IF YOU RUN A HOTEL or a remembrance shop or a wheel chair or a skee ball stadium or an auction room at a summer resort you probably expect—and get—dead times in the off season. The boardwalk people are pretty philosophical about that. Those who stay in operation in defiance of winter and slack trade count upon Atlantic City as a convention paradise. Big conventions have a way of happening along at opportune moments and give life to the bars, the cabarets and the gambling spots. Ask any cab driver, or the salt water taffy clerks or the man who sells steamed clams. How the convention delegates do go for the steamed clams! Isn't so easy to get them in Nevada and Tennessee.

Even now with December just ahead, the boardwalk retains many of its summertime attractions. The ponies, the sand artists, the seafood places, the rug and linen auctions—they're still around. In two days of ocean gazing I haven't yet spied a bather. The health baths, however, seem to be more numerous than ever. "Baths for that tired feeling" is the way the billing runs. It's a sort of rule of the resort that all out of season visitors must be complete wrecks upon arrival.

It appears to be a rule, too, that the walkers don't ever ride and that the roller chair occupants disdain walking. The price for a chair is still 75 cents an hour for two persons. The deep sea net haul, apparently a year-round event, is staged twice daily at a pier head. And you can have your photo taken while U wait. The Crane fixtures exhibit, a Boardwalk standby, remains open and you can still buy imported linens, old English gravy boats, hand-painted turtles, rose-scented beans and Persian rugs.

And Where is the Drama?

When Atlantic City is minus a convention, as it is now, the bars reflect the low house-count of the great Boardwalk hotels. Most of the Boardwalk frequenters of the moment are from New York, Philadelphia and northern Jersey. Canada is well represented during the season—also Pittsburgh, Baltimore, Washington, the Midwest and the Far West. Such cocktail spots as the Merry-Go-Round bar at the Ritz, the Mayfair lounge at the Claridge, the Crystal Cafǔ at the Shelburne and the café bar at the Traymore are open right now, but that's all...The theaters? There's a touchy point. In the days of the Boardwalk's theatrical glories the shore got them all—Drew, Gillette, the Barrymores, Lackaye, Cohan, Lillian Russell. Victor Herbert once led an orchestra at the Million Dollar Pier. Diamond Jim Brady was a frequenter of the Shelburne. Managers fought for Boardwalk bookings. But now?

The old Savoy is a Woolworth store. The famous Apollo, the scene of so many premieres, is a film house. The Garden Pier is dark. So is the Globe. The last legitimate attraction to play the Walk, save for a few presentations of an unsuccessful stock troupe, was *The Chocolate Soldier*, with Charles Purcell as the comedy lieutenant that he has been portraying for all these years. This production was given at the Garden Pier in the summer of '34 and exploded after a brief engagement. Can the drama ever make a Boardwalk comeback? No one here believes it. And Broadway has completely lost interest in Atlantic City as a try-out town.

You Missed This, Mr. Rose!

All of which brings us back to the Elephant House, at the far end of the Boardwalk. I finally went there—by motor—because the fellow who runs the deep sea net haul said that he had come upon it all of a sudden on a foggy night, and it had given him the scare of his maritime life. The Elephant House is a creation of tin and timber, twenty times the size of an elephant—it looks like something that might have strayed from *Jumbo* and had become weirdly inflated as it took up its position by the sea. It has stood there by the waves at Margate for years and years, its great trunk lowered in feeding position. In the summertime curious but somewhat jittery vacationists climb the spiral stairway to its belly and pay their money to see a cabaret show. Right now this great tin monster is untenanted, in the care of a glum keeper, who extracts a dime from you before you ascend one of the great hind legs. I worked my way laboriously to the Howdah, gazed out upon the sea and wondered if I wasn't really looking at the Pacific instead of the Atlantic. How did California ever miss this monstrosity? For fair California, as I recall it, leads all the world in the maintenance of lunatic roadside architecture.

November 23, 1935.

🔲 Kit Cornell's Best Play — 'Barretts' Runs a Year — 'Electra' to the Alvin

KATHARINE CORNELL, Buffalo-born, who came to the New York theater via Piccadilly, finishes her New York engagement this evening in the most successful play she's ever had. She closes to absolute capacity. She goes on tour with her prestige increased, her position strengthened, and upon her return to town she'll take up her labors in a new theater—or, rather, an old theater for her. It was at the Belasco that she once played *Tiger Cats*.

The actress, daughter of a Buffalo showman, who is Kit to her East River friends, has tried a dozen and more plays since she gained overnight fame in *A Bill of Divorcement* eleven years ago, and it was not until she ran across *The Barretts of Wimpole Street* that she found that one containing real quality and sufficient popular appeal to keep it on view a full year.

If it were not for some inexplicable booking arrangement that causes the dark-haired daughter of Pete Cornell to pack up and move on to other drama strongholds *The Barretts of Wimpole Street* could stay until Easter and beyond. At the Empire this week they've been putting chairs in the aisles and it's the impression of some of the ticket-selling brethren that Miss Cornell's offering is a far stronger bill right now, as it closes, than it was just after its opening.

PINERO AND 'TIGER CATS'

THE BARRETTS OF WIMPOLE STREET has been at the Empire for a year, minus six weeks in the fall. *The Green Hat*, the next most successful play to come Miss Cornell's way, was good for twenty-nine weeks. Short-run pieces to which she has given her seemingly limitless talents have included the aforementioned *Tiger Cats*, a piece called *The Way Things Happen* and Pinero's *The Enchanted Cottage*.

This actress from upstate, whose title to First Actress of the American theater is perhaps now disputed by Lynn Fontanne and no other, has achieved her year's run under a management that is her own. A salute, I should say here, is due her from showmen for whom she played over the decade—certainly from A. H. Woods, who once sent her trouping in *Cheating Cheaters* and who later reaped no little profit from her glamorous characterization of Mr. Arlen's green-hatted Iris March.

Katharine Cornell's London hit in *Little Women* came two years before the breakfast tables of New York hummed with talk of her sensational playing as Sydney Fairfield in *A Bill of Divorcement*. Taking her career from that moment and that play the findings are about like this:

The Cornell Record

Will Shakespeare. She played Mary Fitton. Fine notices. Short run. Excellent production.

The Enchanted Cottage. A fantasy that didn't come off. Neither performance nor play excited reviewers or playgoers.

Casanova. Done at the Lyceum. A fine performance in an indifferent play.

The Way Things Happen. Something to be forgotten.

The Outsider. William Harris's first-rate production. Moving performance in a good part.

Tiger Cats. Miss Cornell under the Belasco management. Not a success.

The Green Hat. A money-getter. Miss Cornell as Iris. Leslie Howard her leading man.

The Letter. A melodrama. Effective but meretricious, vowed the critics. Started to sell out business, which gradually decreased.

And, also, *The Age of Innocence, Dishonored Lady* and *Candida,* in which she was superb.

So tonight's her farewell in *The Barretts of Wimpole Street,* a good play and good for forty-seven New York weeks. Kit goes a-touring, but she'll be back. The time will be September or October, the place the Belasco, and the play Sidney Howard's *Alien Corn.*

◘ Man of Many Plays (1949)

GLENN ANDERS circled the room, lit a cigarette, fumbled with his eyeglasses, sat down, got up and went to the window, and said: "The greatest actress I ever worked with was Judith Anderson at the time of *Strange Interlude*. Marvelous—simply marvelous! See her now in *Medea* and you'll see what great acting is in our time."

We were in a suite at the New York Athletic Club. Central Park was just below the north windows. Anders, a man of many plays, all the way from *Macbeth* with Sothern & Marlowe to the current *Light Up the Sky*, did some more room circling, sat down again, and rushed into quotes:

"I've been with some great people...Pauline Lord's supreme gift was radiance, and her way of attainment remains a mystery to actors and critics. When you're playing with her on the stage it's just like talking to her in a room...Gertrude Lawrence can be brilliant; there are times when she is undisciplined in her playing.

"Richard Bennet...A fine actor, but I'd rather not discuss him. Often did things for which he should have been shot...Lynn Fontanne has intelligence, taste and beauty, besides being a good actress. When we were doing *Strange Interlude* Julia Marlowe was in the front row one night and at a curtain call Lynn threw her a rose...Tallulah? We were together in *They Knew What They Wanted in London*. Tallulah knew what a hit Pauline Lord had made in the part in New York and she took it all very seriously. Tallulah and I have been great, great friends. She's given me fortitude. She's a girl who'll defy the whole world, even when she's wrong.

NO CRITICS' PET?

GLENN ANDERS, born in Los Angeles, has been in three Pulitzer Prize plays—*Hell Bent for Heaven*, *They Knew What They Wanted* and *Strange Interlude*. He began jotting down his plays one day and decided that he had appeared in sixteen hits. But—

"I haven't a swimming pool like Clark Gable has. I've done a variety of parts, but I've never been a critics' pet. In my case everything depends on the director. If the director is good I'm all right. What I've lacked in the theater has been taste. It's taste that Lunt & Fontanne have. If I'm with a bad director, I'm bad...Moss Hart has been great for me. I want Moss's friendship. I'm an old actor now and I have to have jobs."

Anders took a gulp of ice water, lit a fresh cigarette, took a look at the park, returned to his chair, and went on excitedly:

"Sam Levene, of *Light Up the Sky* is a fine actor. He keeps up his performance and he also dares to tell Audrey Christie and Phyllis Povah off... Jose Ferrer is an actor without inhibitions, without fear. Fine family, fine mind, fine education...Only once in my life have I been in a thoroughly wonderful company and that was when I was playing in *Hell Bent for Heaven*...When *Another Language* came to Broadway on an evening in April some seasons ago we just couldn't give away the tickets, but the next day, after the notices were out, there was a line at the window."

He slapped his hands against his knees, rubbed his eyes, laughed and said: "We're now getting along fairly well backstage at *Light Up the Sky*, but everybody's arguing now...Well, I suppose I've been in thirty plays or so on Broadway. Sounds awful. I guess I've been pretty lucky, too. I'm in something of a rut. I'm not a smarty pants—all I need is a good part and a good director. It's been a nice season and I'm grateful for it."

The New York Sun, May 12, 1949.

▢ Golly, Our Mary's Glad To Be Back!

Traffic spun in Suite 907 at the St. Regis, as it is inclined to do in Trafalgar Square. Room-service waiters were in and out; bellmen came along with roses, yellow and red. The telephone rang and rang; a secretary skipped from room to room, and it was all a very pleasant and continuous commotion. Mary Martin had come home.

"Golly and ye gods," murmured the world-famous redhead from Weatherford, Tex., as she seated herself before a triple-thick lamb chop, "it's wonderful to be back, but it's only for a few days. We went from London to Jamaica by freighter, then flew to New York. We're going to Washington Monday, then here again and sail Wednesday on the United States and then back in May—for good...Summer in Connecticut—we're building a house at Norwalk and it's one-half to two-thirds finished—and into rehearsal, probably in August, for *Kind Sir*.

"Oh, it was four years and five months and one week with *South Pacific* from the time Josh Logan read the first scene—and a year and a week of that time at the Drury Lane in London...When I closed I was drained and dead, terribly in need of refueling—and now I'm going to let my hair grow to my knees, if it will, but I have the feeling it will go straight up. It grows like a weed. Washing it every night for four years didn't hurt it at all."

Sleep, Sun, Rest on a Banana Boat

Miss Martin, so very alive and contagiously gay—her close-cropped hair is now reddish gold and she explains that "the sun has been at it and so have we"—is in New York for the shooting of sequences in the film about the theater, *Main Street to Broadway*, in which she will be playing herself. She and her handsome husband, Richard Halliday, made the two-week London-to-Jamaica trip via the British freighter Corrales, and Mr. Halliday has a Caribbean tan to prove it.

"Oh, that boat," chanted Miss Martin. "We slept and slept—we were horizontal for the first few days. It was a banana boat, going over empty, and I got the best rest I ever had. Dick and I now wish we could go around the world on a freighter—and we will, too...There were only two other passengers, honeymooners, and they were seasick. I learned to play canasta and I read a novel a day—I was simply mad about *Round the Bend*, by Neville Shute—and I reread the manuscript for *Kind Sir*. It's a romantic comedy... I'd often wondered how it would be to be with my husband 24 hours a day. I found out on that freighter. And I loved it. It's such a fine thing in my lucky, lucky life that Dick and I and the children are all together in London...The

London run in *South Pacific* was all very, very stimulating and gratifying, but as for *South Pacific*, I've had it. Had it and loved it. I'd never want to be with a play that long again."

Married 13 Years…'It's Heaven'

Miss Martin will use her time off as she wants to use it—studying French and Italian, taking vocal lessons, making trips to Stratford, taking a motor tour on the Continent and planning, in her own effervescent but well-organized fashion, for the next 10 years of her life, and for about-the-world appearances, no doubt, in Bangkok, Johannesburg, Cairo, Melbourne and Terra del Fuego. Not necessarily in the order named.

Now about that play for next season, Norman Krasna's *Kind Sir*. Miss Martin said:

"My part is that of an actress and Charles Boyer will be playing somebody in the diplomatic service. It will be the first straight play I've ever done. There are only seven in the cast. I think I'm extraordinarily fortunate to have been with Pinza and now Boyer—ye gods!…Oh, that Josh Logan. What's so fabulous about him is his desire to get things right. I want so much to see Josh's *Wish You Were Here* and I want to look in the shop windows…I saw that wonderful Lever building. Oh, honey and my golly, it's all glass!"

Then, reflectively, Miss Martin said that she's loving her life. And, very quietly: "Everything is like Christmas every day—gee whiz! Did you know that Dick and I have been married for 13 years?…It's been heaven."

◘ Busy and Versatile — That's Jule Styne (1954)

THE VERSATILE AND IMAGINATIVE Jule Styne isn't going to produce *Hedda Gabler* or *The Girl of the Golden West* this season. But he seems to be going in for everything else. He will definitely be one of the town's busiest showmen.

He's just completed a brand-new score for Mary Martin's *Peter Pan* to the lyrics of Betty Comden and Adolph Green. He's set to produce *Panama Hattie* for television on Nov. 10 with Ethel Merman in her original role. And his *Rodgers and Hart Songbook: An Entertainment*, with a book by George Axelrod, will enter rehearsal by the first of the new year for a March opening.

Mr. Styne is enthusiastic about the Misses Martin and Merman, as who isn't. "These girls really work," he says. "That's why they're where they are." He is also a firm friend of that strange new medium, television. "The stars of tomorrow are being born on TV at this moment," he said.

It's interesting to note that Fred Coe, one of television's top producers, will be presenting "Tonight at 8:30" (starring Ginger Rogers) and "The State of the Union" on NBC-TV during the next eight weeks. Mr. Coe has replaced Leland Hayward, who has been ill for several weeks.

"I'M TOLD THAT Jean Meegan, that sprightly and witty New York newspaperwoman, has just completed the book for a new revue, *Nice to Visit*, which she and Woody Parker will present off Broadway, "just as soon as all the cash is in hand." Speaking of revues, it's definite, if unexplainable, that this season will see more of them then we have had for many years.

Albert Selden and Morton Gottlieb report from Bucks County that their newest production, *The Facts of Life*, which had its premiere in New Hope Monday night, is a definite Broadway possibility, and that Gaby Rodgers, who played the lead, is "a new find."

More news of theatertown: Joan Fontaine, of *Tea and Sympathy*, will be honored by the officers and directors of The Lotos Club at a cocktail party Sept. 30...Doris Vinton, once of the Follies, has been named public relations director and publicist for Howard Lanin Management, Inc., producers and concert representatives...The entire cast of *Fanny* was moved en masse by plane to Boston, where the Joshua Logan-S. N. Behrman musical opens Sept. 20...*The Moon Is Blue* was done with an all-Negro cast at the Ebony Showcase in Los Angeles recently.

ONE OF THE MORE provocative suggestions of the season comes from The Committee for Postal Commemoration of the Legitimate Theater, founded by Jacques Minkus, head of Gimbel's stamp department. Mr. Minkus wants the U.S. to issue a stamp honoring the theater. How about a series? My suggestions: Edwin Booth, Charles Frohman, Maude Adams and Minnie Maddern Fiske.

World Telegram, September 16, 1954.

◻ Visiting Tokyo Home of 'Teahouse' Mariko (1954)

THE MOTHER OF THE HEROINE of Broadway's great hit, *The Teahouse of the August Moon*, lives in a small, attractive house in the Shibuya-Ku area of Tokyo. I went there for a visit last night and was entertained royally.

My hostess was Mrs. Umeyo Ouchi, whose daughter, Mariko Niki, has contributed such a vivid performance to the play at the Martin Beck. Mrs. Ouchi is a fine-looking woman and she combines humor with dignity, graciousness and zest. She is vastly pleased with the success of Mariko in the New York theater but she isn't very much surprised. During her girlhood in Japan, Mariko showed herself to be a deft and beautiful dancer and it's quite possible that the acclaim that has come to her in New York has been only what was foreseen by her mother, her two physician brothers and her sister, all of whom are now here in Tokyo.

Little English is spoken at the home of Mrs. Ouchi, so it's better to go there with an interpreter. I found a good one in Noriko Inaba, a lively Japanese girl who is working as a secretary in the local offices of the Committee For Free Asia.

We reached the Ouchi house and its garden of roses and willow trees after a 15-minute drive through the drab-looking streets of Tokyo and entered via glass doors that slide back and forth. Greeted by Dr. Kiyoshi Ouchi, we took off our shoes and proceeded to an adjoining room, where we seated ourselves on pillows placed on straw matting which covered the floor. Presently Mrs. Ouchi, widow of a Tokyo doctor, entered, wearing a maroon kimono. She knelt quickly and gracefully and touched her forehead to the matting in a warm welcome. Not knowing exactly how to respond I bowed as low as is possible and took her hand and then, lacking the fluency in Japanese of, say, Louis Biancolli, I turned to my fair interpreter, Miss Inaba, and asked that Mrs. Ouchi be told that I brought words of love from her daughter. There was a joyful response from Mrs. Ouchi, followed by laughter and a few tears. And then a prodigal feast began.

THE FIRST COURSE included helpings of spinach, and green beans, boiled with salted water, and a salad, served as Dr. Ouchi poured Japanese beer and then filled glasses with Japanese rice wine. Then came meatballs and a sweet Chinese sauce, and more beer and more rice wine. Next there were pork cutlets and strawberries and tea from a great kettle. And, finally, Sukiyaki, consisting of meat, bamboo shoots, Japanese onions, beans and dried fish, was cooked right before us. By this time I well knew that I was going to have a tough time getting up off the floor.

When the Sukiyaki was finished the glass doors slid back and two little girls, Sachiko Ouchi, aged 10, and Yoko Ouchi, aged seven, both wearing flaming red kimonos, entered and went into the pretty routine of a Japanese dance. They were so good at it Mrs. Ouchi, who has been taking dancing on her own account, got up and charmed us all with a dance known as "Under the Willows in the Rain."

IT WAS ALL delightfully staged. Later, after I had managed to get to my feet and into my shoes, Mrs. Ouchi said that she was very happy to know that her daughter was married to a fine man (Bernard Dekle, native of Statesboro, Ga.), that she hoped Mariko would be returning to Tokyo as soon as she has finished her run in her play, and that if she ever sees *The Teahouse of the August Moon* she will have to see it in Japan. "It would be wonderful," she said, "to be with my daughter in New York, but it is just too far. Bring the play over here—and bring Mariko with it."

World Telegram, June 8, 1954.

◻ 'Look Homeward' May Set Record For Drama Profit (1958)

IT SEEMS ENTIRELY LIKELY that *Look Homeward, Angel* will eventually take its place as the top money-getter in the non-comedy, non-musical play field in the history of the American theater. Traditionally, a drama is harder to sell to playgoers than a comedy, such as *Life With Father*, which stayed around for 3,224 performances. Its total intake through the years ran well into millions.

But *Look Homeward, Angel* is now playing to more than $40,000 on the week at the Barrymore and showmen generally are predicting a run of three years for this magnificent play. Its weekly profits, above the costs of presentation, are more than $10,000 a week.

Its $40,000 plus weekly gross is greater than that ever achieved by such powerful plays as *A Streetcar Named Desire* and *Death of a Salesman*. Going along at a $6.90 top for orchestra-floor seats, *Look Homeward, Angel* is piling up more money in a week than some of the legendary hits of Broadway's yesterday's totaled in three.

I HAVE IN MIND such super successes as *Rain* and *Within the Law* and *The Lion and the Mouse*, all of which belonged to the category of dramas.

And there was an early-century hit entitled *Paid in Full*, the story of a thieving cashier of a steamship line who was saved from prison by his wife's intervention. *Paid in Full* had a Broadway run of six months, quite remarkable for 1908, and was accepted as a terrific money-maker. But one of its producers, the late Lincoln A. Wagenhals, told me the truth about it several years ago.

"We didn't make a dime on *Paid in Full* in New York," said Mr. Wagenhals. "In fact, we kept it going at a loss. But we were using Broadway as a show window, as an advertisement for things to come. During the next two seasons we had seven or eight companies playing it in all parts of America and we cleaned up."

Anyway, back to the matter of *Look Homeward, Angel*—

Everybody associated with this project will get rich, more or less. They will include the producer and the author and the leading players and Actress Mildred Dunnock, who took the Kitti Frings manuscript to Kermit Bloomgarden. For such service she will receive 2 percent of Mr. Bloomgarden's share of the profits. It will run to more than pocket money.

Long Island Daily Press, January 27, 1958.

◻ The Shuberts

THE STORY OF THE SHUBERTS is one of America's success stories of the 20th century. It began around the turn of the century with a haberdashery in Syracuse and moved on to Broadway.

Since the year of 1901 and a flimsy comedy called *The Brixton Burglary*, the Shuberts have been operating theaters, hiring actors, producing plays. They are not building playhouses any more (nobody is) but notwithstanding the terrifying costs of 1960-61, the sharp decline in play production and the shrinkage of the Road, there are still 18 Shubert theaters in New York and a total of 25 available for legitimate attractions in America.

There were three brothers Shubert—Sam S., Lee and J.J. A train wreck near Harrisburg in 1905 cost Sam his life; Lee died several years ago. J.J. is still at his desk daily in the Sardi Building.

And now his son, John, who is actually running the empire, is vice-president of the Select Theater Corporation, which operates the chain of houses.

I've heard the Shuberts called hard names by members of the profession; I've also heard of them being spoken of as benefactors to fellow-managers, to authors, to actors. I know that the firm has been one of a great deal of unpublicized generosity. Two of Broadway's great managers received weekly checks from them in final, impoverished years.

MEET JOHN SHUBERT. He is 52, slightly gray and soft-spoken. He is a graduate of the University of Pennsylvania, had a great deal of out-of-town theatrical experience, and joined the family firm in 1934. He will soon make his debut as a Broadway producer, solo. He will present *Julia, Jake and Uncle Joe* in late January. This is a comedy by Howard M. Teichmann.

I talked with John for an hour or so the other afternoon in the Playbill bar of the Hotel Manhattan.

"I believe that the Shuberts are the only management that actually built houses," he said. "Our oldest is the Lyceum, which was opened in 1903. We always did well with the Shubert Theater and the Booth and the location has had something to do with it. Playgoers will go into these theaters if they'll go anywhere.

"The Shuberts had 72 theaters in the chain in 1928—half of them owned, half leased. We love the Winter Garden and shall always have it. It was a breadwinner during the Depression—had eight successes in a row.

"Lee became business manager of the New Theater after it opened in 1909 at 63rd Street and Central Park West. Otto Kahn wanted to move the Met to the New but the Met never moved. Now there's the Lincoln Square project. I hope it can pay. I don't feel that it will affect the Broadway situation in the Forties and the Fifties. It really might augment everything. You just can't lick the transportation facilities around Times Square."

John feels that 42nd Street has, however, become dangerous. "The Bowery used to get the old bums. Now 42nd has become skid row and its getting the young people."

JOHN POURED TEA with milk and told me about *Julia, Jake and Uncle Joe*, which will bring the legend "John Shubert Presents—" to the houseboards.

"Howard Teichmann and I were working together on some material about the Shuberts for the University of Wisconsin and I got interested in his play. The principal characters are supposed to be Brooks and Oriana Atkinson. I think Brooks is recognizable. In the play the character wears a bow tie, a tweed suit, gold-rimmed glasses and is a bird-watcher. Myles Eason, an Englishman, plays Brooks, and Claudette Colbert plays Oriana. Claudette is the most energetic and disciplined woman I've ever seen. Oriana has been attending our rehearsals but I haven't seen Brooks yet. We open around January 25.

"I'm doing a book myself on the Shuberts, and as they appeared to me. Sam S. came to New York in 1897, Lee in 1899 and my father in 1901."

JOHN, OVER HIS SECOND cup of tea, told me that he knew that his father and Lee Shubert weren't on the 1905 train with Sam S., but that William Klein, the attorney, was. He said that he never saw Lee relax except when he was in Florida, that his father's health is good, and that the Shuberts own the Sardi Building but have no interest in the restaurant.

"I hang out at Sardi's," he said. "I used to go Toots Shor's. I belong to the Lambs but don't get there often. I seldom get to the off-Broadway theaters and I'd hate to tell you how many on-Broadway shows I haven't seen. I live in 54th Street and am married to Helen Ecklund, formerly a ballet dancer at the Winter Garden. I married her to get her out of the Winter Garden.

"There are no Shubert plans for building a new theater. The costs are too much and a small theater just can't make it...I think sudden death for a play is to be preferred to a lingering death...Our operation is now primarily real estate, but I hope to devote time to producing a play or two every year...And I think the theater in New York is a pretty healthy business, all things considered. There's nothing else like it anywhere in the world."

The New York Sun, 1930s.

THE THREE SELECTIONS THAT FOLLOW are an Associated Press story about my father from the 1940s, a review of my father's biography of George M. Cohan by playwright George S. Kaufman, and a piece in *The New York Times* magazine section in which my father focused a spotlight on many of the greatest plays and performances of the 20th century.

◻ Ward Morehouse Twits the Laggard Scribe

REPORTER, TRAVELER, AUTHOR OF 'U.S. 90' SEEKS MORE
DAUNTLESS CHARACTERS (1940S)

ACCORDING TO THE LEGEND—apparently important to the perpetuation of newspaper lore—reporters usually have a book or a play they hope one fine day to write. Either that or they have tucked away amid the pile of junk in their desks a manuscript they hope to finish. Anyhow, that's the legend.

The fact of the matter is, however, that most scribes have no intention of troubling themselves with words after the whistle blows. And those who do generally sever their connection with the Fourth Estate long before their books are in the drugstores or their plays have begun to bring the angel a return on his investment.

Ward Morehouse has defied all these procedures. He has written books, magazine articles, plays and films. And he has remained in the newspaper business as a working newspaperman.

Mr. Morehouse, in case you are in doubt, is the man who conducts a column, "Broadway After Dark," in *The New York Sun*. He is also author of *U.S. 90*, a play which will have its first performance tomorrow night in the Paper Mill Playhouse, Millburn.

THE WILY NEWSMEN

MR. MOREHOUSE is shortish, bespectacled, has a kindly outlook on things and conducts himself during his waking hours in a manner which suggests he has only a few minutes left before catching a train. His friends will tell you that a day with him rivals anything Olsen and Johnson ever dreamed of.

In the matter of extra-curricular writing among newspapermen, Mr. Morehouse, when consulted between rehearsals for *U.S. 90* last week, was of the opinion that his brethren were "frightened about being creative." By this he did not infer that they shrank from going long-haired or artistic. Rather, they deplored the loss of security in breaking away from the Saturday pay check.

"But," inquired Mr. Morehouse, "if people who work for newspapers don't write, who will?"

And then, as if to awaken the dormouse valor of laggard scribes and put brimstone in their livers, he came forward with the consoling information: "I have never written an unproduced or unsold word."

This statement was followed by an interval of heckling at the hands of his between-rehearsal dinner companions. But Mr. Morehouse was not to be budged.

"Anyhow," he said in summing up the qualifications for a newsman who would desert the city room for the muse, "it takes a dauntless character."

Dauntless Mr. M.

THE DAUNTLESSNESS of Mr. Morehouse's own character is, of course, under something of a strain since he must sandwich it between his work at the *Sun*. Under the circumstances, however, he does very well.

It is the feeling of some of Mr. Morehouse's friends that his creative writing is a newspaperman's way of escaping the barrage of facts to which he is subjected daily. In any case he seems to draw from his wanderings a wealth of impressions which, to assure his peace of mind, he must get on paper either as a book, article or play.

This is demonstrated, for example, by Mr. Morehouse's play, *Gentlemen of the Press*, which sprang from his association during the speakeasy era with a group of newspapermen, among whom were Mark Barron, Richard Watts, John S. Cohen and Willard Keefe. After the group had spent a summer living in an apartment lent them by Frances Goodrich, the playwright, Mr. Morehouse had the yen for a play about newspapermen. He had much authentic material upon which to draw, in addition to that which was contributed, wholecloth, by his roommates.

Other impressions have gone into Mr. Morehouse's films, among which were *Big City Blues*, *Central Park*, *It Happened in New York* and the Hollywood version of *Gentlemen of the Press*. What gleanings did not find their way into these efforts, or the many articles he has turned out for magazines, went into his book *Forty-Five Minutes Past Eight*, a recounting of his life in the newspaper business and theater.

Reverence for Stage

UNLIKE MANY THEATRICAL writers, Mr. Morehouse's palate, even after years of pounding the Broadway beat, can hardly be called jaded. He has a deep reverence for ability in the theater and his loyalty to such stars as Mrs. Fiske, Maude Adams and Ethel Barrymore is inexhaustible. His loyalty to the theater as a whole is best shown by the fact that he is considered by those who know him to be one of the outstanding historians of the stage in America.

Mr. Morehouse's current theatrical offering is the result of twelve transcontinental auto trips, using Route 90—the Old Spanish Trail—which picks its way along the Gulf of Mexico, past New Orleans and Houston and then goes on to El Paso. The play, which is in eleven scenes, is described as a cross-country romance.

This, then, would be the latest of Mr. Morehouse's impressions seeking an outlet. He is a much traveled man. He has seen 68 countries and has the handsome distinction of owing a bar check at the King David Hotel in Jerusalem. But of all places on earth, it is the highways of America in which he takes most delight—beyond Broadway.

"There is," he allows, "more copy and wide wonder in America than all the ruins from here to Patagonia."

The neon signs, the sheepherders, the barbecues and the great immensity of the land are some of the things which have caught his eye and mean America to him. And as Jim Stone, the chief character of his play expresses it, he "likes to look and wander and talk to the people."

Jim is a young man who is trying to find something in the world that has meaning for him.

And does he find it?

"Well," said Mr. Morehouse "He thinks he does—he hopes he does."

Associated Press, 1940s

◻ The Yankee Prince (1943)

George M. Cohan, Prince of the American Theatre. A biography by Ward Morehouse. 240 pp. Philadelphia: J. B. Lippincott Company. $3.

THE THEATRE, OF COURSE, is one of the most ephemeral of the arts—only the radio has a briefer span. The elder statesman and even the retired business man may reasonably expect to give benevolent advice for years and years, but even the greatest figures of the theatre have a way of vanishing from the scene long before their days are over.

The moving picture *Yankee Doodle Dandy* undoubtedly did a lot to keep the name and achievements of George M. Cohan in the public mind, and now Ward Morehouse has made a further contribution with a fond and generally readable biography. It is subtitled, somewhat awkwardly, "Prince of the American Theatre," and it goes a long way toward avoiding the chief pitfall of the average theatrical biography.

That pitfall is, of course, the danger that such a book will become merely a record—a succession of dates and plays and places. "In such and such a year he wrote…" Mr. Morehouse, delving beyond the scenes, has contrived to make his book something more than that. He has made an honest effort to catch the character that was George M. Cohan. It is no idolatrous treatment of its hero, this book. Mr. Morehouse is keenly alive to Mr. Cohan's weaknesses—a little inclined to take his talents for granted. Near the end of the book, in the words of a woman friend of Cohan's comes the nearest thing to a real analysis of his character—not quite a satisfactory analysis, but almost. It is the portrait of a man who stood alone most of the way, whose friendships were fewer than the legends of Broadway would have you believe.

His name was not Cohan but Keohane, and he was not born on the Fourth of July. These are just two of the book's minor surprises. But in the main it is a reminder that here is a man who was the greatest of them all in his day. The succession of Cohan popular hits during the first twenty years of the century was astonishing. His personal popularity with the playgoers was enormous. Let a Cohan play falter and Mr. Cohan would jump into the leading role overnight—and simultaneously the crowds would storm the theatre.

That was the story of *A Prince There Was*, from which the handsome Robert Hilliard was ejected to make room for Mr. Cohan. Mr. Morehouse describes the ensuing court action, but mysteriously omits Mr. Cohan's discerning remark about Hilliard. The latter was then a man in his sixties, white of hair and majestic in appearance. He had been an actor for perhaps forty years. Cohan, despite the lawsuit, was gentle with him. "A nice fellow," was the way he described Hilliard, "but stage-struck."

Little Johnny Jones, Forty-Five Minutes From Broadway, Seven Keys to Baldpate, Get-Rich-Quick Wallingford, Hit-the-Trail Holliday, Broadway Jones—all the Cohan triumphs cannot be listed, because many of them never bore his name. Then came the great climax of "Over There"—a war song that increases in stature as no comparable one emerges from the present war.

His effect on the American popular theatre, of course, was gigantic. In a way, it may be said that he founded it. For years and years most of the popular American plays showed the Cohan influence—he gave way, finally, to what might be broadly called the O'Neill period. Today it's every man for himself, and not a bad idea.

There is one more Cohan anecdote that Mr. Morehouse omits, and it's one of the best. It goes back to the early days of the radio. Listening to it for the first time, a friend of Cohan's remarked to him: "Well, there goes the American theatre." But George M. Cohan was wiser. "Listen, kid," he said, "the only thing that will keep an American in a room is a dame."

SOURCE: George S. Kaufman, *The New York Times Book Review*, December 5, 1943, page 5.

◻ Moments of Magic On Broadway

AS A NEW SEASON STARTS, A REVIEWER RECALLS SOME PAST
PERFORMANCES THAT MOVED HIM DEEPLY. (1961)

JUST AFTER THE CLOSE of the French and Indian war—that was the war, I believe—I struck New York for the first time and my courtship of the metropolitan drama began forthwith. From time to time, I've been disappointed in it, confused and heartened by it, and occasionally overwhelmed, but my devotion has remained changeless and unchanging.

Now, within a very short time, Broadway will be in the whirl of a new season, and many fresh excitements are promised. For the moment I'm leaving the matter of prophecies and predictions to others and am concerning myself with thrilling moments in the theatre of other years.

Since 1920 I've been privileged to see some performances of greatness...

Jeanne Eagels in *Rain* is the first that comes to mind. If I were told that there was but one play for me to see, my choice would be that one, with Miss Eagels again playing the tormented Sadie Thompson on the rain-soaked island of Pago-Pago. To me it remains the most substantial play within all of my playgoing experience.

Its opening, on a November night in 1922, brought forth an emotional demonstration never exceeded in the theater of this country. First-nighters stood and screamed when the curtain fell upon Sadie's denunciation of the fanatical Reverend Davidson at the close of the second act; they were as wild as spectators at a football game.

As the gaudy harlot from San Francisco, the strikingly attractive Miss Eagels moved about the stage with pantherine grace, part woman, part animal. Frightened and angered by the hot-eyed missionary, then penitent and subdued, and finally rebelliously free again, she gave a magnificent performance that made her a star. For five punishing years she played this role, and there are those who believe it drove her to desperation and to an early, tragic death.

To this day, whenever I find myself in the vicinity of Thirty-ninth Street, where the old Maxine Elliott Theatre stood, I imagine that I can hear the melancholy strains of "Wabash Blues" as they came from the gramophone in Sadie's room in Joe Horn's run-down hotel.

IN 1924, THE THEATRE got a fresh, resounding smack in the face from *What Price Glory?*, the best modern war play in the English-speaking theater, and the first to be presented with something approaching realism. The heroes of this Laurence Stallings-Maxwell Anderson chronicle were foul-mouthed, lice-ridden brawlers, portrayed by Louis Wolheim as Captain Flagg and William Boyd as Sergeant Quirt. The American theatre had never seen anything like those two, nor heard speech as rough and frank as theirs.

It brought greater freedom to dramatic dialogue and introduced into the language Sergeant Quirt's plaintive exhortation, "Hey, Flagg, wait for baby!"

An extraordinary token of the appreciation of the crowd at the premiere was the sight of Alexander Woollcott who, beside himself with joy, had managed somehow to propel his bulky figure to the top of his aisle seat and stood in it, waving and cheering.

FOR YEARS LYNN FONTANNE and Alfred Lunt have been as inseparable as Dun and Bradstreet, refusing to act apart. But I do not forget the remarkable facility for characterization revealed by Miss Fontanne by herself in Eugene O'Neill's five-hour drama, *Strange Interlude*, which opened Jan. 30, 1928, and became the most talked-about entry of the season.

This bold and ambitious work, an attempt to present the essence of a woman's life from girlhood to middle age, was hailed as a classic in some quarters, and in others, less enchanted, as "the Abie's Irish Rose of the pseudo-intelligentsia." It was, nevertheless, a fascinating attempt to present the whole life of a character.

In the complex role of Nina Leeds, who rushed into a series of love affairs after her fiancé was killed in the war, Miss Fontanne was on stage most of the time in each of nine long acts. But if the part was exhausting, her art was inexhaustible. She brought to it not only a warm and lovely presence, but also subtlety, unflagging energy and wide-ranging emotional command. (The part was first offered to Alice Brady, who turned it down.)

O'Neill used in this play a variation of the old aside, allowing his characters to give voice to their secret thoughts, a device now called "stream of consciousness." Miss Fontanne mastered this difficult technique to an astonishing degree, giving her asides a dimension that eclipsed those of her fellow players. "How we poor monkeys hide from ourselves behind the sound of words," said Nina Leeds, summarizing the substance of the play.

FOR THE LUNTS as a team, I choose Robert Sherwood's *Reunion in Vienna* of 1931, a fair comedy made memorable by the adroitness of their playing. In it they exhibited the daring playfulness, the graceful high-jinks which have made them the privileged wantons of the theater. Wherever they choose to lead, we willingly follow.

Who is likely to forget in this play the meeting, after a lapse of ten years, between Lunt and Miss Fontanne, his mistress of the past, now respectably married? He glimpses her first in a mirror. He turns around ever so slowly, gazes at her with heated eyes, circles her like a hunter, approaches her, runs his hand over her bosom and derrière, lightly slaps her cheek, and plants on her lips a long unnerving kiss. She does not speak, nor betray a tremor of emotion, but when the kiss is over one can see she has crumbled.

THRILLING MOMENTS were supplied by Laurette Taylor, the incomparable Laurette. Few actresses have attained the perfection she displayed in Tennessee Williams' first play for the New York stage, The Glass Menagerie, in 1945.

As a faded Southern belle, living in fretful discontent with a son and daughter in a St. Louis tenement, she scaled the heights of acting and made it look as easy as a stroll down a country lane. She captured a Southern accent magically and with her mumblings and pauses, her detached, half-completed sentences, she brought to life a woman both pathetic and monstrous, the character named Amanda Wingfield, unable to forget her white-columned girlhood.

How can anyone forget this frowsy, run-down slipper of a woman sitting at the telephone patiently and cunningly corralling magazine subscriptions from indifferent friends in the D.A.R.? Or the sly, relentless way she prodded her son to bring home a Gentleman Caller, somebody, anybody, who might marry his crippled sister? Or the moment when she turned on her son to ask "Why? Why? Why?" in a desperate outburst of pain and bewilderment?

It was a portrait made up of many small strokes—subtle shifts of emphasis, sudden bursts of energy, vague little movements, and tired little pauses. It was unforgettable.

I DID NOT, to my regret, see John Barrymore's Hamlet. But I had the good fortune to see him give a great performance in Sem Benelli's The Jest, adapted for the American stage by Edward Sheldon. It was played in 1919 and 1920 and co-starred Lionel Barrymore.

A lurid medieval melodrama set in Florence, The Jest presented John as the weakling painter Giannetto (a role played in France by Sarah Bernhardt) and Lionel as his brutish tormentor, Neri. The violence of the play, the appearance of the famous Barrymore brothers in sharply contrasting roles, and the beauty of John's performance captured the imagination of the public. Dorothy Parker said the articles written about The Jest would have filled the Public Library.

John's physical appearance flashes to my mind—a slim, handsome figure in leaf-green tights, enveloped by a white cloak, his face ghostly white, his hair flaming red. He was eloquent in voice and intonation, and inspired in his use of pose and gesture.

ANOTHER GIFTED PLAYER to come out of the Twenties was Katharine Cornell, dark and lithe, with high cheekbones, a full expressive mouth and widely separated dark brown eyes. Others may prefer her in *The Barretts of Wimpole Street* or *Saint Joan*. But she gave her best performance for me as the womanly heroine of Shaw's *Candida*, playing the part first in 1924 and returning to it in other seasons.

Miss Cornell brought compassion and understanding to this perfectly constructed stage piece and, as well, a voice that is one of the most expressive instruments of the theatre. She plumbed the depths of Candida's character or, as H. T. Parker, the Boston critic, put it, she "achieved the part by mental and spiritual sensibility." Her quick intelligence and her Duse quality were impressively evidenced.

Candida is Shaw's testimonial to love and to the lasting ties of marriage, but it is also high comedy. Miss Cornell encompassed all facets. The long scene at the end, in which Candida chooses between her husband Morrell and her youthful suitor Marchbanks, was made by her playing one of the most poignant scenes of the modern theatre.

RICHARD B. HARRISON was a 65-year-old beginner on the Broadway stage when I saw him act De Lawd in Marc Connelly's *The Green Pastures*, the Pulitzer Prize play of 1930. Novice though he was, he gave a performance that was a triumphant amalgam of majestic humility and all-wise naïveté.

Harrison, a one-time Pullman porter, dining car waiter, elocutionist and dramatics teacher, was discovered by Connelly in a Harlem casting office. Both in physical aspect—he was tall, gray-haired and noble in bearing—and in the gentle goodness of his character, he was ideally suited to play the benign overseer of an all-Negro Heaven.

In all the annals of the New York theatre, no actor has had an entrance line to equal his, nor one as potentially dangerous. "Gangway," shouted a dark-skinned Angel Gabriel, interrupting a celestial fish-fry. "Gangway for de Lawd God Jehovah!" And onto the stage strode Harrison, immensely dignified, radiating warmth and loving kindness. From that moment, the success of the play was assured.

Whether commanding the sun to be "a mite cooler," then remarking gratefully, "That's nice," or complaining mildly, "Being God is no bed of roses," Harrison was faultless.

It was a triumph also for Marc Connelly, whose play, suggested by some stories of Roark Bradford's, had been refused by the foremost producers of the day. At the final curtain, somewhat like a goal-kicking quarterback, he was borne on stage on the shoulders of his broadly beaming actors.

I REMEMBER, TOO, the exquisite delicacy of Frances Starr in the 1921 revival of *The Easiest Way*, Eugene Walter's harsh, convention-shattering story of Laura Murdock, a Wall Street man's luxury-loving mistress who made a futile struggle for reform and honest love. Miss Starr, now living in Manhattan's Mitchell Place, brought a new type of courtesan to the American stage. She did not swing her hips, or roll her eyes flirtatiously, or caper about the stage. She was admirably natural and unaffected.

I still recall some of the things she did as Laura—brushing off the milk bottle, sewing a glove, and , above all, her cry at the end of the play, "I'm going to Rector's to make a hit and to hell with the rest."

NOR DO I FORGET the powerful performance of Florence Reed in *The Shanghai Gesture* in 1926, the John Colton rococo tale of Mother Goddam, a Manchu princess betrayed by her English lover and sold to junkmen. Despite critical derision, it became a super-hit for producer Al H. Woods.

Miss Reed's recitation of the "I survived" speech, in which she recounted the tortures she endured at the hands of the junkmen, remains one of the most volcanic tirades in the history of melodrama.

ANOTHER OCCASION that is vivid in memory involved but one performer—Judy Garland, in her celebrated comeback at the Palace a few years ago. The opening night produced unabashed sentiment on both sides of the footlights, with a tearful Judy whispering "I love you" to the wildly applauding audience that would not let her go. Then, at the climax, sitting like a weary child at the edge of the stage as she sang "Over the Rainbow."

AND THERE WAS THE RHAPSODIC interlude in *My Fair Lady* when Julie Andrews as the Cockney flower girl Eliza Doolittle learning proper English speech, finally said with slow, painstaking correctness, "The rain in Spain stays mainly in the plain."

"I think she's got it," Rex Harrison, as her mentor Henry Higgins, exclaimed cautiously. Then, as she repeated the sentence successfully, the note of exultation rose in his voice. "By George, she's got it! By George, she's got it!"

And the exultation of the audience rose, too, as Miss Andrews, Harrison and fellow actor Robert Coote broke into a playful, happy tango, the perfect expression of their relief and joy at Eliza's conquest of ladylike speech.

I HAVE NAMED in the preceding paragraphs those players and, to some extent, those plays, which have had an especial appeal for me and provided me with unforgettable moments. But I cannot end this piece without recording my deep appreciation for the theatrical pleasures supplied by such performers and players as these:

Helen Hayes in several works, but particularly in *Coquette*...Pauline Lord as Anna Christie...Emily Stevens in *Fata Morgana*...Jane Cowl as Juliet...George M. Cohan in anything...Tallulah Bankhead as the voracious Regina Hubbard in *The Little Foxes*...Jessica Tandy, the pathetic Blanche Du Bois of *A Streetcar Named Desire*.

Alec Guinness and Cathleen Nesbitt in *The Cocktail Party*...Lee J. Cobb in *Death of a Salesman*...Paul Lukas and Lucile Watson in *Watch on the Rhine*...Dudley Digges in *The Iceman Cometh*...Laurence Olivier as Oedipus and Ralph Richardson as Falstaff...Mary Martin in *South Pacific*...Martha Scott in *Our Town*...Gertrude Lawrence in *Lady in the Dark*...and Josephine Hull in *Arsenic and Old Lace*.

Those are my unforgettables.

The New York Times Magazine, September 17, 1961.

Katharine Hepburn (1907 – 2003)

HARTFORD NATIVE and Bryn Mawr graduate, the great Kate quickly moved from student productions to a bit part on Broadway in 1928. Four years later, her work in *The Warrior's Husband* as an Amazon princess made her a Broadway name and she headed for Hollywood. Hepburn worked on and off the stage for decades, but perhaps is best remembered for her many films, including *The Philadelphia Story*, which was written for her, first as a stage comeback, and then as her return to Hollywood box office gold. One of her last stage appearances was in the 1971 musical *Coco* for which she earned a Tony nomination. Her final Broadway role, ten years later, won another Tony nomination for her work in *The West Side Waltz*. She died at her family home in Fenwick at age 96, and Broadway's shining lights were dimmed for an hour to honor her more than 60 years on the stage.

KATHARINE HEPBURN is quick and gay, slim and freckled, profane and vital and she is, I suppose, singularly intelligent. She could have made a career for herself as headmistress of a fine girls' school had she ever felt she could have been content with so humdrum a life. Instead, she turned to the theater and to the theater's ever-lasting good fortune.

"I'm generally taken to be an intellectual," she said to me as she sat cross-legged in the rear garden of her home in New York's Turtle Bay section, "but I do nothing but go on hunches. When I'm appearing in a play all I do is to do the play—and rest and eat. I'm always so terrified on opening nights I wish I could be dead drunk through the first performance. I still think it would be a good idea to open plays with a matinee performance and then the poor bloody actor would have less time in which to do a complete freeze. But that matinee idea is Ruth Gordon's—not mine.

"I've had seven or eight plays in New York. Those first nights, brother! They do get steadily worse. They're terrifying, they're horrifying, honestly. I'd like to own a theater in Brooklyn and just never open on Broadway…I'll never forget the first night of *The Philadelphia Story*. Dear Phil Barry protected me in that play—with the writing, I mean. And on the opening night the Lord came down and helped me get through. During the first performance of *As You Like It* I felt much easier. In that play I could change things around—not the words, but the movement."

Miss Hepburn, now wearing an old white sweater, brown gabardine pants and old, thick-soled shoes, accepted the challenge offered by *As You Like It*, which gave her her first Shakespearean role, and she was triumphant.

"I always wanted to play Rosalind and I always knew I was going to do it," she said. "I had a good time playing the part and I learned a lot. Somehow, before trying that play, I'd often thought that the audiences were just sitting out there, waiting to lynch me, but Rosalind got me to believing that people had come to the theater to have a good time and that there was great friendliness out front."

The lithe and bonny Kate, "sometimes Kate the curst but the prettiest Kate in Christendom," had a good time during the shooting of the film, *The African Queen* in the African wilds but she had an even better time in playing *As You Like It* in New York and on tour throughout America.

"When I was trying to learn to play Rosalind," she said, "I got to wondering to myself what the hell acting really is. I like to act but I also like to do many things—to clean a room, to walk, to ride my bike, to play tennis, to fiddle around in this garden. I don't like to do anything unless I really like to do it. I wouldn't have done *As You Like It* without help from the wonderful Constance Collier (Miss Collier died in 1955). She worked with me for about six months, every afternoon. Miss Collier was wise; she had a real zing and a zest for all that was good in life. She had a passionate belief in life and in people—and so have I."

The afternoon sun slanted into Miss Hepburn's pretty garden. Caught in its rays her lean and freckled face took on a curious beauty. The Hartford-born daughter of a distinguished surgeon lit her second cigarette and chattered on:

"Hell, I like seeing plays. *Death of a Salesman* has been my favorite for some time. I think Elia Kazan is the best damn director there is. George Cukor is wonderful—I've been with him a thousand times. I loved working with John Huston on *The African Queen* and it's always been fun doing pictures with Spencer Tracy. Spence is a great, great actor. He has such simplicity. I respect him and I love him...I love walking, as I've said. I walk around the reservoir in Central Park very often and you're always meeting the same people. Something funny happened the other day. I was wearing old pants like these—I always wear the same things all the time—and a man who had been walking behind me came alongside. Without even a glance at me, without a pause, he just muttered, 'If your gams are so damn beautiful why don't you show them?' And then he walked on."

She took a turn around the garden, glanced up at her four-story house, and said:

"I own this place, and without a mortgage. Rented it first, then bought it. I've always rented in Hollywood, never owned anything. I'd be afraid to be buried in Hollywood. It's so dry. I prefer Hartford, in the state of Connecticut. It's nice and damp...I've often thought I'd like to go to England and live for a long time. The truck drivers in London whistle at me when I walk around in slacks and I get strange looks from the desk clerks at Claridge's, but I do love those British. They're the toughest race in the world. They can go through anything and they have a passionate belief in themselves...My next play? I never know. I don't like to talk about any plans that I might have; it's a phobia with me. But I do know that there's an enormous field of absolutely fascinating stuff to do in the theater—so many fine things just lying around."

I STARTED WRITING sporadically about show business for *The Christian Science Monitor* in the 1970s and continued as a reporter and theater columnist for the *New York Post*, Reuters, *New York Sun*, *amNewYork*, and the *Epoch Times*. It's my hope that these columns and stories, taken together, will be a portrait, however sketchy, of some of theater for the last and current century through some of their biggest stars, including Katharine Hepburn.

I had done my first interview with Hepburn for Reuters after they hired me to write a column called "The Business of Broadway." In early 1994, I joined the *New York Post* where I had started as a copy boy in 1969, as its Broadway columnist. The column, called "On- and Off-Broadway," immediately began making waves writing about Faye Dunaway suing Andrew Lloyd Webber, and Disney planning that a stage version of the blockbuster film, *The Lion King*, was coming to Broadway. Disney and its minions were so incensed with the story that they forced *The Post* to print a retraction. But two years later, when Disney broke the story in the *New York Times*, that a stage version was indeed heading to the Great White Way, *The Post*, in a banner headline, proclaimed "The Lyin' Kings," referring to Disney and its denial that the famed movie would be made into a musical. In late 1998, after Matt Diehel, my editor in *The Post*, left the paper, I knew my days were numbered. And only a matter of days later, I was given a generous severance payment and the next month started freelancing frequently for *People* magazine and the following Fall, for People.com. Being a national publication, *People* picks stories to do based on their appeal to readers across the country: the appeal of the Broadway theatre is limited to personalities who already have a national name. I was fortunate to keep ties to the City Editor of the *New York Post*, Stuart Marguer and I freelanced for *The Post* occasionally after leaving People.com where I wrote long profiles of stars like Liza Minnelli, Nathan Lane and Jack Lemmon. In May 2000, I got what may have been the last "interview" with screen legend Katharine Hepburn. I stayed all of ten minutes, stammering just a few questions, fairly dumbounded by how much she had aged since I last saw her in person five years earlier in New York. (She had moved to the family home on Long Island Sound in Fenwick, Connecticut.)

Meeting *New York Sun* "Knickerbocker" columnist Gary Shapiro by chance at the New York Book Expo in May 2002 set in motion my joining the "new" *New York Sun* the following month. At first, I had freedom to write not only about theatre in a kinder, gentler way than I did in *The Post*, but to cover news of books, music and the social scene. It wasn't uncommon for me to fill half a broadsheet. Moving from The New York page to the arts page in December 2003 curtailed my writing about things other than theatre. I also found myself no longer reporting to Stewart Marques who had joined the *Sun*, and whom I had worked for occasionally in the *Post* since 1994. By the time of the 2004 Tony Awards, I had been hired by *amNewYork* as its "Broadway After Dark" columnist. Besides the paper's much larger circulation, there was a feeling of camaraderie and support I no longer felt at the *Sun*. Some have called *amNewYork* a New York *USA Today*. In any case, it seems to be the wave of future journalism: short and highly readable articles with the emphasis on local news.

After two years with *amNewYork* I moved to *The Epoch Times* and TimesSquare.com. I was a copy boy in the *New York Post* in the early 70's, graduating to an assistant make-up editor and, briefly, a police and general assignment reporter. Covering Jackie Robinson's funeral, I found myself sitting in the midst of his immediate family and got my first real scoop at a time when every reporter in town was seeking to talk to them. After joining *The Christian Science Monitor* in 1972, I got my first by-lines reporting on stories about the New England fishing industry and the first efforts to improve the quality of old opera recordings. *The Monitor* taught me the importance of direct, clear writing. Leon Lindsay, its New England editor, advised me, "Your first job is to tell the story clearly. If the reader doesn't understand it, it doesn't matter how well it's written." Aside from stories on consumer issues, electricity and car insurance rates, I did a number of series which took me out of the office throughout New England for as long as two weeks at a time. One was about New England railroads; another rural poverty; still another was about New England's freight and passenger trains which took me to the northern fringes of Vermont and Maine. I wrote about the proposed Dickey Lincoln hydroelectric dam, talking to those who felt it would bring jobs, as well as wrote about those who never wanted the natural beauty of Northern Maine to be compromised. I later traveled to the Amazon jungle with a fellow *Monitor* correspondent, Clayton Jones, now that paper's chief editorial writer, to do a series about living with a tribe of Indians on an Amazon tributary on the Columbia-Brazil border. Soon after I was sent to New York for a month "try-out" where I tried to get New York on the front page of the paper, doing stories on the Brooklyn Bridge to the Statue of Liberty. After I was assigned to New York I did more writing about the theater, eventually becoming chief theater columnist for the *New York Post* for five years.

I've included three of my own Katharine Hepburn stories, including two interviews, in this section. They appeared decades after my father wrote his profiles. Mine don't quote her as much but offer, I hope, an interesting contrast.

◻ She's A-O-Kate

Exclusive: Rare interview with Oscar's winningest star, Katharine Hepburn

Clad in white slacks, tennis shoes and a red sweater, four-time Academy Award winner Katharine Hepburn fretted over what her guest wanted to drink with lunch.

"There's juice, or soda—or you can have what I'm having," she said. "What do you want?"

"What are you having?" I asked.

"An ice-tea sort-of-thing," said Hepburn, her long gray hair twirled loosely in her trademark bun. She matter-of-factly pointed to a goblet filled with a brown-sugar-colored drink, chock-full of ice cubes.

"Help yourself."

The one and only "Kate," as some friends call her, was in the spacious second-floor living room of her Manhattan townhouse yesterday as we chatted about the present, past, her favorite leading men and two-time Academy Award winner Tom Hanks, who, with *Apollo 13* a solid hit, seems to have a good chance of three Oscars in a row (and, eventually, of challenging Hepburn's Oscar record).

The great actress—already 88 this year—was in good form, suffering little from the "shaking" disorder that has dogged her in recent years.

But she couldn't conceal the grief she still feels over losing her longtime secretary, Phyllis Wilbourn, who worked for her for 39 years and died this past April. "I miss her terribly," she said. "Everyone loved Phyllis."

Wilbourn went everywhere Hepburn did, including her visits to her family home in Fenwick, Connecticut, near the mouth of the Connecticut River.

She still divides her time between her country home and her New York townhouse.

"I was lucky to be able to buy this house," she went on, referring to her home in the Turtle Bay section of Manhattan, which she bought in 1932. "I was walking down the street and I saw it was for sale and I bought it—because I had the money."

Her neighbor is Stephen Sondheim. "I keep his mail for him," she said. "But I don't think he's ever been in this house."

"I love movies," she continued, as Nora, her cook for 24 years, handed Hepburn vanilla ice cream with chocolate chips and her guest started in on a heaping plate of fresh chicken salad with grapes. "But I don't see as many as I should. Is he (Hanks) good?...I want to see that movie."

"But doing well in a part is not so much a matter of talent," she continued in the clear, crackling tones that are unmistakable to almost anyone over the age of 12. "It's really luck—choosing the right material. I was lucky enough to get material that the critics liked."

Each of her Academy Award-winning performances, beginning with *Morning Glory* in 1933 and ending with *On Golden Pond* 50 years later in 1982, was dependent on "having a good script," she said.

But, today, she added, while "people are always sending me things, I rarely see any thing that is really very good."

Hepburn misses the glamour that used to pervade show business in the old days, but finds that today's crop of actors can often be just as exciting as the studio icons of yesteryear.

"The important thing is having personality," she said. "If you're an actor and don't have personality, you're in trouble. It really doesn't matter how you look."

For her part, she denied that she herself was particularly attractive, but did admit to having "spirit."

Her last role was *Love Affair*, released late last year and starring Warren Beatty and Annette Bening. She said she enjoyed doing the film—a remake of *An Affair to Remember*, starring Cary Grant and Deborah Kerr (which itself was a remake of the original 1939 *Love Affair* with Irene Dunne and Charles Boyer)—and called Beatty "a fine actor."

Hepburn first came to the attention of the American public on Broadway in the late 1920s in a play called *These Days*. After being in several more plays, she made her motion-picture debut in 1932 in a supporting role in *A Bill of Divorcement* starring John Barrymore. The following year she won her first Academy Award for Best Actress in *Morning Glory*.

She went on to receive three more Academy Awards for Best Actress in *Guess Who's Coming to Dinner* in 1967, which co-starred Spencer Tracy in his last movie, *The Lion in Winter* (1968), and *On Golden Pond* (1981).

In her best-selling autobiography, *Me*, published in 1991, Hepburn for the first time talked about her own love affair with the late actor Spencer Tracy.

Yesterday at lunch, she simply said, "Spencer was a great actor."

She was more eager to talk more about the theater.

"I don't think the theater is as interesting as it used to be when I was a kid," she said, "because there was more that you could do."

Does she miss acting?

"Not really," she laughed.

"You don't love it?" I asked.

"I love life," she said.

SOURCE: *The New York Post*, Thursday, July 20, 1995

◻ Hepburn to shun spotlight on her 90ᵗʰ b'day

OLD SAYBROOK, CONN.—One of Hollywood's last remaining living legends celebrates her 90ᵗʰ birthday tomorrow.

But there will be no fireworks, champagne toasts or star-studded parties for Katharine Hepburn.

Instead, one of cinema's greatest divas will spend a quiet day—virtually alone—in her isolated mansion on a peninsula that curls into windswept Long Island Sound at the mouth of the Connecticut River.

If it's warm, neighbors in her exclusive seaside community may see the four-time Oscar winner walk haltingly on the arm of John Elmore, her driver of many years.

But Hepburn, who's in failing health, is more apt to be sitting before a roaring fire, gazing out at the lighthouse offshore and remembering brighter days.

That was when her seaside home in the tony Fenwick section was a veritable Hollywood East and her beloved "Spence" would stay here. In fact, Spencer Tracy's bathrobe still hangs in her bedroom closet.

"There's no celebration planned," Ellsworth Grant, Hepburn's brother-in-law, told *The Post*. "She's too out of it. There's no reason to do it."

Although a medical scare last year led her to move to Fenwick permanently—giving up the townhouse on East 49ᵗʰ Street in Manhattan that she bought in 1932—she has no serious health problems.

"She has the disease of old age," Grant said. "She walks a little, talks a little, but her memory is pretty much gone."

But her fans aren't willing to forget.

Old Saybrook will mark the occasion quietly tomorrow when First Selectman Laurence Reney visits Hepburn with a bouquet of flowers from the town.

Also tomorrow, city Parks Commissioner Henry Stern will rename a half-acre garden in Dag Hammarskjuld Plaza the "Katharine Hepburn Gardens."

And Sen. Joseph Lieberman of Connecticut has asked President Clinton to bestow the Presidential Medal of Freedom, the nation's highest civilian honor, on the great film star.

Lieberman's request is expected to be fulfilled.

Writer Henry Josten, a Hepburn pal, says that even if she were more up to it, "Kate" wouldn't want any fanfare.

Josten says 15 years ago, the actress objected to renaming the causeway that runs from Old Saybrook past her home the "Katharine Hepburn Causeway."

"If they do that, I'll never use it again and take the long way around to get home," Josten says Hepburn warned at the time.

Hepburn didn't turn away all local honors.

She once shelled out $10,000 for a fire engine the town needed—a deed repaid when the firemen named the vehicle "Old Kate."

Some said everything she did hinged on her mood.

"It all depended on what side of the bed she got up on," said Josten. "She could be the most charming person alive or bite your head off."

In luncheon interviews with her in 1994 and 1995, she told this reporter she had finally come to the point where she no longer minded being called a "living legend."

"I think it's all right to be called one now. I've been around a hell of a long time. I think I'm entitled to be called a legend, don't you? And I am living!"

SOURCE: *The New York Post*, Sunday, May 11, 1997

▣ My Dinner With Kate Hepburn

HOLLYWOOD LEGEND Katharine Hepburn, who turned 91 in May, "has never been better."

That's how a longtime friend and Connecticut neighbor, actor-artist Max Showalter, says the four-time Oscar winner was when he had dinner with her several nights ago at her home in Old Saybrook, Conn.

Showalter, who played Marilyn Monroe's husband in the film *Niagara* (using his acting pseudonym Casey Adams), told *The Post*: "Kate is in wonderful condition. She's a New England survivor. We had a good time and a lot of laughs."

There are no signs, Showalter said, of the acute stomach flu that landed the star of *The Philadelphia Story* and *Bringing Up Baby* in the hospital early last year, giving family, friends and her millions of fans a big scare.

"Kate has a marvelous appetite," Showalter said. "She has breakfast at 10:30 a.m., lunch at 1, snacks at 4 and dinner at 6. She doesn't talk much at all about the old days. She's enjoying life now."

Showalter said he told the outspoken, once-raven-haired beauty—her hair is totally white now—that "people are interested in publishing a book of my photographs of celebrities that I've taken since I was a young actor.

"And Kate said, 'I hope there are a lot of me.' I said, 'But you've never let me take any of you!" And she said, 'And I won't let you start now!' "

Hepburn has moved permanently from her landmark Manhattan townhouse on East 49th Street to the windswept Old Saybrook mansion, overlooking Long Island Sound, that her late father, a Connecticut doctor, built in the early part of the century.

Henry Josten, a longtime friend of Hepburn's and a columnist for the *Pictorial Gazette*, a local newspaper, remembers when Hepburn had the house rebuilt almost from the ground up following the 1938 hurricane that damaged many homes along the Connecticut shoreline.

"We had a story in the paper at the time that when it was finished, it would be 'one of the grandest homes on Long Island Sound and would cost the astounding sum of $15,000.' Now you can't buy a doghouse around here for that!"

"She walks a little, talks a little, but her memory is pretty much gone," said Ellsworth Grant, who has a home nearby and was married to Hepburn's late sister, Marianne. "She could die tomorrow or live for another five or 10 years."

New York Post, October 29, 1998.

◻ Kate Hepburn:
'Tell everybody I'm doing fine'

KATHARINE HEPBURN wants to set the record straight—she may be 92 and living in seclusion, but she's still in good spirits.

In a rare interview, the feisty Hollywood legend shot down rumors that she is bedridden.

"Tell everybody I am doing fine!" Hepburn told *The Post* as she sat in the comfortable living room of her rustic seaside home in Old Saybrook, Conn.

"I am OK."

Dressed in a purple jumpsuit, the four-time Oscar winner rested on a large settee in front of a roaring fire and a picture window with a sweeping view of Long Island Sound.

The legendary star has spent all her time in this quaint home since moving out of her posh Midtown townhouse in the mid-1990s.

And while she occasionally invites an old friend or a neighbor over for afternoon tea, Hepburn's reclusive lifestyle has fueled speculation she's seriously ill.

But, although Parkinson's disease has limited her mobility and her speech, Hepburn insists that all the chatter could not be further from the truth.

The actress confessed that she's still a big eater—enjoying homemade meals prepared by her cook.

Her best friend, actor Max Showalter, recently told *The Post* his famed friend sits down to four square meals a day and "eats like a horse"—a fact Hepburn confirmed with a broad grin.

"Oh, yes, that's true," she admitted, as her cook, Maureen, stood by and nodded in agreement.

Hepburn's mood turned dark as she asked about Showalter, who has been gravely ill with cancer at Essex Meadows Hospital in nearby Essex, Conn.

The actor, who played Marilyn Monroe's lover in 1953's *Niagara*, has been Hepburn's closest confidant since the death of her longtime love, Spencer Tracy.

She nodded with approval when told that Showalter is hanging in there.

Neighbors say Hepburn—who delighted audiences in classics such as *The Philadelphia Story*, *Adams Rib* and *The African Queen*—still ventures outside when the weather permits.

"Miss Hepburn has good days and bad days, like most of us," said friend and neighbor Henry Josten, first selectman of Old Saybrook.

SOURCE: *The New York Post*, Friday, March 10, 2000, by Ward Morehouse III and Bill Hoffman

☐ Can the Old Shelburne survive amid casinos?

The grand hotel of Atlantic City's gilded age is still open to wayfarers—for the present

Perched atop the grand old Hotel Shelburne here, the 11-room "George M. Cohan Suite" is one of the last remnants of America's gilded age of hotels.

For less than $50 a night, you can stay in one of the suite's seven bedrooms—where the Duke and Duchess of Windsor once slept. And for $750 you can have the entire floor all to yourself.

But you'd better hurry: Both the suite and the hotel face an uncertain future as casino gambling prepares to make its debut.

The push for new and less costly ways to operate hotels could mean an end to the rose-colored marble floors, velvet (but faded) draperies, and chandeliered ballroom of yesteryear.

The Malumat family—the grand old Shelburne's owners—hope the hotel can be renovated along with what Lewis Malumat calls "the resurgence of Atlantic City." But that is in the future. The Shelburne is elegantly chiseled Americana—the roomiest suite at New York's Waldorf-Astoria, after all, boasts only four bedrooms.

Present-day visitors to the Shelburne's penthouse suite often can't believe their eyes. "When I got off the elevator and saw the dining room, I thought 'Where are they leading me?'" said a guest recently. "When people say 'a penthouse' this is what I always thought one would look like."

From the suite's 11-story vantage point, guests can look through six-foot-wide windows at the crashing waves of the Atlantic Ocean, framed by a somewhat rickety Boardwalk.

While planners hope that eventually up to 25 casinos will mean a new lease on life for this seaside city, the days when George M. Cohan, wearing his familiar straw hat and carrying a cane strolled along the Boardwalk are gone forever.

Drama critic Ward Morehouse once wrote: "George M. Cohan was a familiar figure on the Atlantic City's Boardwalk when this resort held its place as the most desirable tryout town in America, when Broadway's famous figures—producers, playwrights, actors—were forever swarming to the shore for their weekends. Atlantic City finally died as a show town; the venerable old Apollo surrendered to the films, and the Broadway crowd gradually discontinued trips to the old Shelburne."

But today some of the great and near-great in the entertainment world continue to visit the Shelburne. Comedian Danny Thomas recently stopped there, and Julius Schoenholtz, a retired Broadway costume designer, still frequents the Shelburne. "I like the service and the food," he says.

A still popular story about the Shelburne's penthouse is that George M. Cohan once dropped everything he was doing in New York and stormed down to Atlantic City when he found out that his suite had been rented to another guest. The man with the kangaroo walk and the out-one-corner-of-the-mouth talk wasted no time in telling the intruder to leave. And, the story goes, the party wasted no time in leaving.

The Christian Science Monitor, September 21, 1977.

Alberta Hunter's Songs— Just Like It Used to Be

"*I spend my days rejoicing because of the love I have for you.*"

This lyric epitomizes what New Yorkers think of one of the world's great jazz and gospel singers, Alberta Hunter, who, at 82, is making a big comeback here.

"The hottest thing in town," wrote *Cue* magazine of Miss Hunter, whose glamorous jazz, gospel, and Broadway career recently resumed here at the Cookery restaurant after a 20-year lapse. During those years, Miss Hunter worked as a nurse at Goldwater Memorial Hospital on Roosevelt Island.

"You would take a chance on me, a woman 82 years old?" Miss Hunter asked Cookery owner Barney Josephson when he offered her a job singing "Pennies From Heaven," "Downhearted Blues" (which she also wrote), the gospel number "By and By," and others three times a night.

She answers her own question: "That's the hand of God behind me and the hand of God in him (Mr. Josephson)."

The black singer began her career just as the 20th century was dawning. At 8 she ran away from her Knoxville, Tennessee, home to peel potatoes, and eventually to sing, in windy Chicago.

Dedication pays off

She was a small, gawky child when she sang in Chicago's honky-tonk bars. In that seamy atmosphere she practiced the old-fashioned virtue of self-improvement.

Her dedication paid off as her name hopped from marquee to marquee—from the George M. Cohan Theater on Broadway to the Drury Lane Theater in London, where she played the part of "Queenie" in the immortal musical *Showboat*.

She also managed to find time to write songs for a contemporary named Bessie Smith, regarded as the greatest blues singer of all times. She is still writing music and recently did the entire score for the soon-to-be-released Geraldine Chaplin movie *Remember My Name*.

In 1954, Alberta Hunter's mother passed on, and "I decided I was through with show business," she says. "I went to the Harlem YWCA and applied for a nursing job." It was not as easy as just applying and getting the job, so she went to school to get training for the nursing post.

"I was never late once," she says of her days at Goldwater hospital, her clear, brown eyes warm and unblinking. But mandatory retirement came knocking at her door last year, and she had to give up career No. 2.

Career No. 3 starts

CAREER NO. 3 BEGAN when she attended a party with her old friend Mabel Mercer. She sang at the party, and word got to Mr. Josephson, a longtime New York impresario, that Alberta Hunter was still around.

"Don't' tell me she's still around!" Mr. Josephson exclaimed when he was told about her soon after the party.

The rest is—as they say—history. He heard her sing and offered her a six-week engagement at his restaurant. That was in the fall. Now, Miss Hunter says, "I'll stay right here until it [the Cookery] closes up."

Mr. Josephson doesn't want her to do anything else.

"I hope all your troubles are small ones," is Miss Hunter's closing line to her packed audiences. Indeed, listening to her sing, even small troubles seem to disappear.

The Christian Science Monitor, March 3, 1978.

◻ CENTER STAGE

"Goodbye to All That" Len Cariou
The star talks about life before and after Teddy and Alice

"The body blows were terrible. He ran away for two years. I think he felt he was going to lose it all. But he was able to deal with it, and came back and became one of the great citizens of this country."

Len Cariou, one of Broadway's finest actors, is talking about Teddy Roosevelt's pain in losing his wife and mother the same week. Cariou portrayed the bombastic 26th President in the short-lived Broadway musical *Teddy and Alice*. His words could also describe his own anger about the fate of the lavish show. It closed January 10th, after 88 performances in New York.

In an interview at the Friars Club a few days before *Teddy and Alice* closed, Cariou lashed out at Frank Rich, chief drama critic of *The New York Times*. He called Rich's review "irresponsible journalism" and partly blamed it for the musical's demise. But unlike Roosevelt, Cariou, 48, is not about to run away. If anything, he will lose himself in doing what he loves best: acting—somewhere, anywhere, in his native Canada, in regional theater in the United States, or even off-off Broadway, where he did a play with his wife last year.

Cariou is perhaps best known for his Tony award-winning performance in the title role in *Sweeney Todd, the Demon Barber of Fleet Street*. At the Friars, he was so angry he hardly touched his stew. Graying somewhat, with the weather-beaten good looks of a Kirk Douglas, Cariou stared across the wood-paneled dining room into space.

"A monster has been created," Cariou fumed about Rich. "I think it's irresponsible journalism. If somebody wanted to make a case for it, they could easily go after his ass! The producers in this town have allowed that thing to get way out of proportion and I think they have to fight it. The way to fight it is to go to the paper and say, 'Look carefully at what this guy is doing.' Rich has gotten worse. He doesn't seem to be able to deal with reality. It's entirely possible he doesn't like theater."

Rich's review of *Teddy and Alice* said it "combines the educational mission of 'My Weekly Reader,' with the entertainment agenda of a half-time show at a high school football game." Rich conceded that Cariou, "fitter of voice and looks than in recent outings, brings dignity and honesty to a role that, as written, amounts to little more than a sketch for Harold Hill in *The Music Man*."

Cariou continued, his anger building, "Rich learned at John Simon's breast. [Simon is drama critic of *New York* magazine.] "Now, there's one of the most vitriolic people who ever put pen to paper. For some of the things that man has written, he should be strung up, by his balls! He's said absolutely unconscionable things about people, personally attacking them."

Cariou first stepped on stage professionally at the Winnipeg Rainbow Stage Theatre in Canada. He next went to the Manitoba Theatre Center, where he appeared in *The Taming of the Shrew*, *Mother Courage and Her Children*, *Mr. Roberts*, and *Who's Afraid of Virginia Woolf?*

Always in command, Cariou says exactly what he wants and never a syllable he doesn't. The clarity he has brought to his vastly varied roles on stage is also a hallmark off stage.

"Classical theater is what really turns me on," he said, as some of his anger subsided. "I spent most of the first twelve years of my career as a classical actor. I came to New York in 1969 and did *Applause*, but went back to classical theater because I love it. It's wonderful. It's wonderfully challenging. I will always go back to it."

A glance at his credits will tell you a lot about his acting in the last 30 years. They range from the spectacular peaks of Shakespeare to the flatlands of television. He has never sunk to the artistic depths of a TV sitcom. At the Stratford Shakespeare Festival in Ontario, he played Brutus in *Julius Caesar*, Prospero in *The Tempest*, the title character in Coriolanus, and Petruchio in *The Taming of The Shrew*. He has also played leads in *Le Bourgeois Gentilhomme*, *Mahagonny*, and *Timon of Athens*. At the Guthrie Theater, he was in *As You Like It*, *The Skin of Our Teeth*, and played Orestes in Tyrone Guthrie's production of *The Oresteia*, which also came to New York.

On Broadway, he starred in the American Shakespeare Festival's production of *Henry V* and received Tony nominations for his roles in *A Little Night Music*, and *Applause*. Other Broadway credits include *Dance a Little Closer* and *Cold Storage*, a role he recreated for television. But it comes as no surprise that this classical actor's most acclaimed TV role was on PBS. In *There Were Times, Dear*, Cariou portrayed a man suffering from Alzheimer's Disease. Critics applauded the rare compassion and clarity he brought to the role.

Cariou's biggest commercial film success was in *The Four Seasons*. Roles in other major movies have eluded him, despite at least one concerted effort to establish a film career.

"There was a time when I said I'm going to make a shot at the film industry," he related. "I came very close to doing three films and lost them all for whatever reasons. I felt really bad about it and I was bemoaning the fact that this had gone on for six months."

Doing another play snapped the self-pity. And Cariou will co-star in a movie to be released this spring called *The Lady in White*, about a young novelist growing up in upstate New York. This movie's director didn't need advice about Cariou's qualifications: He had seen him in *Sweeney Todd* seven times.

Unlike many actors, Cariou doesn't let his agent pick properties for him. "He called me the other day and said, 'Somebody has just sent you a script for a television pilot.' He said, 'I wouldn't send it to you on a dare. It was written by a child of 12.'" Cariou will look at it himself.

Several months before *Teddy and Alice* opened out-of-town, Cariou appeared with his wife, Canadian-born actress Heather Summerhays, in an Actors Equity showcase at the Baldwin School in Manhattan. Many lesser known actors, let alone their agents, won't even consider showcases. Not Cariou, and there's a major reason for it.

"That's a mistake some actors make," he said. "I really think you have to exercise your acting muscles, you know. I really do. If you don't exercise, they atrophy. And I've seen that." Moreover, he added, "You gotta give something back to the theater. But, also, it's not unselfish. I really believe it. I've seen too many actors who haven't worked for a year. Then they've been given a job and all they've done is wait on tables. All of a sudden, you go into auditions and somebody says you happen to be the right type. 'You're it!' And you've got a week to show up ready to go. And when you get into rehearsal you're just so rusty it's apparent immediately. 'Did you make this resume up, for Christ's sake? I thought you were a pro.' Then you say you haven't worked on stage in a year. It's something that happens a lot. Actors go into television. They want to do theater and they have been in television and they haven't done anything on stage in three or four years. At least some of them have enough sense to say, 'Boy, I can't do that because I need about six months to get into shape.' Theater is just a totally different way of working."

For the foreseeable future, Cariou plans to live in New York, on Manhattan's West Side. But his more permanent home is acting before a live audience, no matter how small the stage. He loves acting so much that only in the last few years has he felt the need to take a vacation. No, he doesn't want to be a producer or theater manager. Nor a director, if it takes too much time away from acting. However, he has directed regionally and on and off Broadway, and remains Artistic Director of the Manitoba Theatre Center.

What about doing more films?

"If a film career is going to happen, it's going to happen," he said. "If it doesn't, it doesn't. There's nothing I can do about it."

But act. Somewhere. Anywhere. And brilliantly.

Theater Week, February 8-14, 1988.

LIKE MY FATHER I've been fortunate enough to have had some good press about my books and plays.

Story of Waldorf Astoria Links Hotel With History

—Jennifer Braun

"WELL, I WAS ALMOST born at the Waldorf, you know," says author Ward Morehouse III, whose latest work, *The Waldorf Astoria: America's Gilded Dream*, hit bookshelves this month.

"Of course, I didn't find that out until recently. But my parents lived there until *very* shortly before I arrived, I've been told."

Morehouse offers this jesting explanation as to why he chose to write, in effect, the biography of a hotel—or rather, as he terms it, *the* hotel: New York's Waldorf Astoria.

"There really is something about the Waldorf in particular. It's a piece of history. Everyone knows about it. A first-generation immigrant would know about it because it's famous throughout the world," Morehouse notes.

Heads of state throughout the world, at any rate, know about the Waldorf. Stories about the visits of Queen Elizabeth II, Emperor Hirohito, the Duke and Duchess of Windsor, General Douglas MacArthur, PLO chairman Yassar Arafat and a whole slew of American presidents can be found in the pages of *Gilded Dream*.

It took five years of research on the great Park Avenue hotel for Morehouse to complete *Gilded Dream*. Interviews with the Waldorf's staff from managers to busboys, all of whom have brushed elbows with the elite during the course of their work at the hotel, comprised a great deal of his work.

As the finishing touch to his research, Morehouse himself spent a weekend at the hotel. That same weekend, he reports, the Waldorf was visited by Secretary of State James Baker and actress Elizabeth Taylor.

Morehouse, son of a former drama critic for *The Star-Ledger*, Ward Morehouse II and Joan Marlowe Rahe, also a journalist, worked for the *New York Post* and *The Christian Science Monitor* before becoming a freelance author and playwright.

Morehouse has had six of his plays produced in New York; the latest, *Mr. Doom Gets a Letter*, will open at the Kauffant Theatre off-Broadway in September.

As for his plans for the future, Morehouse jokes, "It has been suggested that I make a living out of this hotel writing. Maybe if I was offered a royal suite somewhere for about six months? But right now I'm not planning on it."

Morehouse says he has been approached by several other large New York hotels who want similar treatment, but he notes, "I love the Waldorf for its people and its history, both serious history like the Big Four conference of 1946 and fun history like the 'April in Paris' Balls. People like a good story, and the Waldorf has lots of stories to tell."

No other hotel has quite as much history to write about, Morehouse feels, aside from the Kitty-Kelley-esque "dirt" that Morehouse avoided in his book.

"As a general policy I tried not to tell stories that would hurt anybody," he notes.

The Waldorf Astoria: America's Gilded Dream, published by M. Evans and Company, is available in hardcover in New Jersey bookstores for $22.95.

By Jennifer Braun, *Newark Star-Ledger*, July 23, 1991.

◘ The Life and Times of the Fabulous Waldorf

—Caroline Drewes of The Examiner *Staff*

WHEN HE DIED back in the '60s, an irreverent friend suggested his tombstone be inscribed "Room Service, Please."

And it is true that Broadway theater critic/columnist/playwright/world traveler Ward Morehouse, pal of Walter Winchell and flamboyant man of his time, did have a penchant for living in hotels.

All told, Morehouse lived in 29 Manhattan hostelries.

His son, Ward III, says his father once kept a bear while residing at the Plaza.

More to the point, Ward III narrowly escaped being born at the Waldorf, in a suite on the 15th floor, "where my parents were permanent residents... They moved as they wished from one hotel to another."

His parents were divorced when he was two years old and he says he grew up in hotels with his mother, grew up to follow in his father's footsteps both in the fields of theater and journalism. Given all that, it seems well-nigh inevitable that Morehouse should tackle the past and write a book about the fabled Waldorf.

The Waldorf-Astoria: America's Gilded Dream (Evans; $22.95) is a gently gossipy history of an institution that has occupied its present position—an entire block on Park Avenue at 50th Street—for 60 years. Built in 1893 by William Waldorf Astor on the site where the Empire State Building now stands, it was moved from downtown Fifth Avenue in 1930.

COLE PORTER AND THE DUCHESS

MOREHOUSE'S ACCOUNT is laced with anecdotes about the glittering characters who have passed through its portals, some of them, (like Gen. Douglas MacArthur, who retired there, Cole Porter, and the Windsors) to make their home in the Waldorf-Towers.

The rich and super-rich, and the noted, kings, presidents, diplomats, scientists, screen stars, politicians, make up his cast of characters, from Lillian Russell to Elizabeth Taylor, from J.P. Morgan to Imelda Marcos.

There was Elsa Maxwell, the world's most famous party giver, also a resident and good friend of Porter who dedicated "Mis Otis Regrets" to her. "Though many people considered her as homely as a billy goat," Morehouse says, "Sir Cecil Beaton, who possessed a rare eye for beauty, signed one of his photos of her as a mature woman, 'She was beautiful.'"

Maxwell's party-giving had a racy side to it. "She ran one of the most exclusive bordellos in New York from her Towers apartment. 'She was the

"Madam of the Waldorf,'" says a former hotel executive who knew her well. 'She would get anything you wanted, women for men, men for men, women for women...'

"This little 'business on the side' evolved from her talents as a matchmaker for her friends...Her clients did not indulge their pleasures in her suite, but she would run the operation from there, as well as serving tuna fish salad to her pimps every Sunday. Each of them would throw an unmarked envelope containing the week's take into an empty punch bowl."

A FIVE-YEAR TASK

THE AUTHOR, in town the other day touting his book, says the task took five years off-and-on of interviews with employees, and guests. (The Waldorf has 1,832 rooms, and some 1,800 employees.)

He considers it an effort to make a great hotel come alive through its personalities, as he reconstructs a time when "people worshipped their heroes."

After 35 years, MacArthur's widow, Jean, still lives in a suite with a 40-foot living room. She is friendly but declines to talk about her late husband.

Richard M. Nixon accepted the Republican presidential nomination in the Grand Ballroom. George M. Cohan gave his last public performance on the stage there. He was dying but he sang a little and danced a little to a packed house that gave him a standing ovation.

Nikita Khrushchev was stuck in the elevator between floors at the Waldorf, to the consternation of his KGB guards who immediately whipped out their guns. When Frank Sinatra rides the elevators, Morehouse says, no stops are permitted. The singer pays a million dollars a year for a suite where Porter lived for a quarter of a century.

Xavier Cugat was once caught bowling in the hall in his birthday suit with two young girls. The Duke of Windsor was far friendlier than the Duchess. "Old-time waiters and waitresses were used to the Duchess's outbursts. 'You serve her something wrong, even alone in her room, and she would go through the roof,' said one of them. Cruel!"

A good-looking man with pale gray eyes and a friendly, easy, unassuming manner, Morehouse was a cultural correspondent for *The Christian Science Monitor* for 10 years.

HEART IN THE THEATER

"But my heart was always in the theater—my mother, by the way, was an actress in the '40s. I wrote a play that was produced off-Broadway, it got a good review in the *Times*, and I was hooked. It's a high you don't get in journalism. I used to hate being 'on' all the time, I thought, enough of this, I'd just like to be me. Actually, the theater and journalism are tied together. What is a newspaper article but a small play, a scene in somebody's life?"

(The idea for the Waldorf book came after years of covering events at the hotel for the *Monitor*. "I sort of fell in love with it." One conclusion after his research: There's something sad about living in a hotel. People are very alone.")

Morehouse says he has had six plays produced in New York, "including *The Actors*, which lasted—barely—a year off-Broadway in 1986." The last play, *Mr. Doom*, is based on an original story by his father.

During his brief stay in San Francisco—his first time here—he was billeted at the Campton Place Hotel, dined at Trader Vic's, took the cable car to Fisherman's Wharf, poked his nose in the Sheraton-Palace, the Hyatt Union Square and the Ritz Carlton. Approved of them all.

By Caroline Drewes of *The (San Francisco) Examiner* Staff, August, 1991.

◻ The New York Times Book Review

—Richard F. Shepard

MR. ASTOR'S LITTLE INN

THE GRAND CITIES of the world have their grand hotels, the bed-and-breakfasts for the mighty and the moneyed. Ward Morehouse 3d explores one of New York City's grandest in THE WALDORF-ASTORIA: *America's Gilded Dream* (Evans, $22.95). Mr. Morehouse, a former reporter for *The Christian Science Monitor*, is more of a guide than a historian, embellishing his meanderings about the Waldorf with entertaining anecdotes and portraits of those who have been the lifeblood of its fame, such as Elsa Maxwell and Cole Porter. The Waldorf is 60 years old this year, and the author reminds us that it opened during the Great Depression, the descendant of the original Waldorf-Astoria that occupied the site, until 1929, where the Empire State Building now stands. It is a hotel big enough to handle Golda Meir and Yasir Arafat at the same time, without embarrassment to anyone, and vast enough to need computers to sort out the task of housekeeping, with a staff of nearly 400 for the 1,850 rooms to be cleaned. Mr. Morehouse writes of pleasures and scandals, of the hard facts of running a hotel and of its romance. This is not the last word on the Waldorf-Astoria, and the publisher is to be chided for neglecting to provide readers an index. Even so, the hotel comes off well in the hands of its appreciative Boswell and one will find *The Waldorf-Astoria* to be a pleasant buffet.

Richard F. Shepard, *The New York Times Book Review*, September 29, 1991.

🞏 Broadway-Come-To-Town

—Tom Coffey

AT WARD MOREHOUSE'S funeral that soft December day in 1966, the proper ladies of Statesboro who surrounded the grave site registered complete shock when, following the minister's words of committal, a fellow stood and, after a few opening bars by an accordionist, started singing George M. Cohan's "Give My Regards to Broadway."

It was the Great White Way-come-to-town, that touching episode marking *finis* to a brilliant career of the Savannah-born journalist who wrote his "Broadway After Dark" column for New York papers from 1926 almost until the day he died. His burial was in Statesboro on the Franklin lot, his widow being Becky Franklin, a journalist herself and a native of nearby Register.

That tender *coup de grace* at the cemetery, which brought tears to a lot of eyes as the shock ebbed quickly, followed the funeral service two days earlier in a New York church, into which Ward's casket was rolled while the organ played Rodgers and Hart's "Manhattan." Such deviations from the staid and the customary are done frequently for people in show-biz.

But there's more, not an encore in music but in drama. A play Ward Morehouse began writing in 1910, when he was a Savannah High School student, is coming to our town on Saturday. Ward never finished it, but son Ward Morehouse Jr. did, and just recently.

The younger Ward, second-generation writer who has penned plays and books himself, will be here Saturday afternoon at 2 o'clock while City Lights Theatre people, under the talented Leslie Gordon's direction, give a dramatic reading of the play whose ending came over 80 years after its beginning. The play's title is *Mr. Doom Gets a Letter*.

Tomorrow, the 16th, Ward Jr. will lecture at Georgia Southern College, and on Sunday at 5 p.m. he will be at Georgia Historical Society (Gaston Street door) to lecture and autograph his new book, *The Waldorf-Astoria: America's Gilded Dream*.

Likely you've already read the details of young Ward's anticipated visit, but allow me to share briefly the warm feeling that comes from the knowledge of a son's demonstrated reverence for his father and mentor so many years later, especially a son who has inherited some of the old man's talent.

I met the elder Ward only once, and just briefly one day when he visited the *Evening Press* newsroom and found still on the job three staffers with whom he had worked here under the late editor William G. Sutlive. Mister W.G., he recalled then, made his reporters walk on opposite sides of the street lest, bunched up, they might miss a news story. (The elder Sutlive's son

John, who succeeded him as editor, imposed that same requirement when I was a young reporter.)

Brief as the meeting was, Ward's fame as a theater critic, reporter and world traveler preceded and followed him out of our newsroom. He wrote several plays, among them *Gentlemen of the Press*, which ran 128 performances in New York and was made into a motion picture.

He also wrote five books including a biography of George M. Cohan, whose song we heard at the Statesboro cemetery.

And Ward Sr. was like another Savannahian who struck it big in showbiz. Neither he nor the late songwriter Johnny Mercer ever really left home. They always kept in touch with the old hometown, and came back often. (Savannahian H.L. "Lukie" Bowyer is Ward's nephew, and his late brother Morehouse Bowyer bore the family's name from the maternal side.)

The elder Ward's journey to Broadway was from the *Evening Press* by way of the *Atlanta Journal*, and his widow Rebecca was a reporter for the Atlanta paper.

Ward Jr. is a son by an earlier marriage, and it was by about 15 minutes that he missed being born in New York's Waldorf, where his parents live. Hence, his choice as the subject of the new book. Young Ward has a fine heritage, and let's wish him continued success.

Tom Coffey, *Savannah Morning News*, July 15, 1992.

☐ 'Dark' Sheds Light on a Legend—Morehouse Portrayal at Norwalk

—Gloria Cole

WHEN BROADWAY THEATER critic, columnist, bon vivant, raconteur and boulevardier Ward Morehouse died in 1966, they played "Give My Regards to Broadway" at his funeral and some wag suggested his tombstone should say, "Room Service, Please."

It would not have been inappropriate. The much-married and well-traveled Morehouse had lived in 29 different hotels and his home-cooked meals were always in restaurants.

"One time when he was in Hollywood with his second wife, actress/producer Jean Dalrymple, Gary Cooper brought them a game bird he had shot," said his son, Ward Morehouse III, whose play about his father, *Broadway After Dark*, runs September 11-26 at Norwalk's Rainbow Theatre. "As his wife was preparing it for dinner, my father started crying. 'Here we are in the most glamorous city in the world, among the most glamorous people in the world and we're sitting here like a couple in the Bronx,' he said."

Flamboyant as his lifestyle was, it was also eccentric, according to the younger Morehouse, a journalist, author and playwright who has had ten plays produced. "My father loved wild animals and I once had a lion cub as a pet while I was growing up in New York City," he said, "My father owned monkeys and kept a raccoon at the Algonquin."

When he lived at the Plaza, he had a bear cub who used to get into the hotel kitchen and tear it apart looking for food. He finally had to give it to the Ringling Brothers when it got to be a thousand pounds.

The play, named after the elder Morehouse's column which ran in New York newspapers for 40 years, highlights a life of highlights and features Morehouse's relationships with George Bernard Shaw, Talullah Bankhead, Alexander Woollcott and others, as well as his lifelong love affair with the theater.

"My father always wanted to be a playwright." Morehouse said. "He had two plays produced on Broadway. Unfortunately his play *Gentlemen of the Press* opened the same night as *The Front Page*. As a critic, he always went out of his way to let the actors or playwright retain their dignity, even with a bad review.

Even so, he lost one of his best friends, a playwright who was my godfather, because he gave him a negative review. He loved theater people and he never saw any conflict between his role as a critic and socializing with theater friends. His love for the theater gave him compassion; he knew how tough it was."

"What's Doing" column by Gloria Cole, *Fairpress*, September 10, 1992.

◻ Liz Taylor and Mike Todd

MIKE TODD, the famed film producer of the 1956 film version of Jules Verne's "Around the World in 80 Days," which starred David Niven and Shirley MacLaine, in a happy moment with a young Liz Taylor before Todd died in a plane crash. Many people don't know it now but, before his film career, Todd produced many Broadway shows including an acclaimed revival of "Hamlet." Born Avrom Hirsch Goldbogen, Todd also produced "The Hot Mikado" at the 1939 World's Fair.

photo credit: Corbis

John Barrymore and "The Fortune Hunter"

THIS IS A FAIRLY rare photograph of John Barrymore in the comedy "The Fortune Hunter." Produced by Cohan & Harris, song-and-dance man George M. Cohan who was also a prolific Broadway producer, theater manager and owner, and his partner Sam Harris. The "great profile," as Barrymore came to be known as in silent films and talkies, played Nat Duncan, a young man who seeks his fortune by marrying the richest girl in town. The play's author, Winchell Smith, had to read the play aloud to George M. Cohan before Cohan would produce it. Barrymore became a star with his appearance in the show, thereafter doing a series of light comedies before such heavyweight material as "The Jest" and, of course, "Hamlet" before becoming a silent screen star.

◻ Robert Morley

BORN IN 1908, one of Robert Morley's best known film roles was that of Katharine Hepburn's missionary brother in "The African Queen." Known and loved for his wit and crisp English diction, he co-wrote and acted in the play "Edward, My Son," which my father, Ward Morehouse told Ben Bodne, the late owner of The Algonquin Hotel, that he was seeing in London. "I thought he was seeing his son, his real son, Edward, in London, but he was seeing the play," Bodne told me. Sheridan Morley, the highly-able and prolific theater journalist and biographer, is his son.

🞑 William Gillette

BORN IN HARTFORD, Connecticut in 1853, Gillette was best know for writing, producing and performing in "Sherlock Holmes," a play he adapted from the fiction of St. Arthur Conan Doyle. He earned so much money in this and other plays that he built a fieldstone castle on the banks of the Connecticut River that is now open to the public in the spring, summer, and fall, and is replete with genuine secret passages and four-foot thick walls. He died in 1937 but not before spending some time at New York's Plaza Hotel where he wrote to the hotel in red ink that he would like one of their larger rooms because the time was fast-approaching when he'd soon move to much narrower quarters.

photo credit: Corbis

◻ Gloria Swanson

GLORIA SWANSON, perhaps best known to modern day audiences for her riveting portrayal of a faded silent screen goddess in "Sunset Boulevard" opposite William Holden, a goddess who like the real life Swanson had made it big in silent films in an era when "They had faces!!" Swanson declared in the film. But Swanson also brought her highly comedic gifts to the 1950's Broadway revival of "Twientieth Century," about a producer, played in the 1930's film version by John Barrymore. She adored being on Broadway and, according to an interview she had with my father, couldn't wait to return in another play.

photo credit: Glyn Lewis

◻ Jean Dalrymple

Legendary producer Jean Dalrymple, who ran the New York City Center for 25 years, is seen here flanked by Robert Wagner, the late New York City mayor and Bert Lahr, who was in numerous plays but became a movie legend beloved throughout the world as the "Cowardly Lion" in "The Wizard of Oz," starring Judy Garland. Dalrymple is getting an "Outer (Critics) Circle Award in this photo.

photo credit: Glyn Lewis

🞑 Liza Minnelli and Donald Billings

EXTRAORDINARY SINGER/ACTRESS Liza Minnelli, who starred in "Minnelli on Minnelli" and other shows on Broadway has a tender moment with Donald Billings, the husband of photographer Rose Billings.

photo credit: Rose Billings

◻ Richard Gere and Anne Jackson

RICHARD GERE started on Broadway before his good looks and terrifc acting ability took Hollywood and the movie-going public by storm. Anne Jackson starred in numerous shows on and Off-Broadway and is married to Eli Wallach, one of the most prolific character actors of the 20th and now the 21st Century. Jackson was nominated for Tony Awards, Broadway's highest honor, for her performances in Tennessee Williams "Summer and Smoke" in 1948 and she and Wallach were in "The Tiger and The Typists" off-Broadway for which she won a Village Voice Obie Award. Gere amazed critics and audience alike for his adroitness in the hit film version of the Broadway blockbuster "Chicago" but he had started out in the chorus.

photo credit: Rose Billings

◻ John Lindsay and Lillian Gish

THE LATE JOHN LINDSAY and the late film and stage actress Lillian Gish share amused looks sitting together at a Broadway Tony Award ceremony. Gish was in a number of Broadway plays. Lindsay should have been an actor, his critics complained. I interviewed him in the late 1970's after her had returned to "civilian life" as an attorney with a major law firm. Gish made her stage debut in "The Little Red School House" and died in 1993. A US Congressman before he was Mayor of New York City, Lindsay was Mayor from 1966-1973.

photo credit: Glyn Lewis

◫ Carol Channing, Jerry Herman and Pearl Bailey

CAROL CHANNING, who won the 1964 Tony Award for Best Actress in a Musical for playing the title role in "Hello, Dolly," with music and lyrics by Jerry Herman, "didn't play Dolly—she was Dolly!" some veteran Broadwayites said. Herman went on to write the music and lyrics for "Mame" and other shows and Pearl Bailey played "Dolly."

photo credit: Glyn Lewis

◻ Sandy Dennis

SANDY DENNIS won the 1964 Tony Award for best (dramatic) actress in a play for her role in "Any Wednesday." Her movie roles included "The Out-of-Towners" and then in 1982, "Come Back to the Five and Dime, Jimmy Dean, Jimmy Dean." Once referred to as a "critic's darling," Dennis won an Oscar for her performance in Edward Albee's "Who's Afraid of Virginia Woolf?"

photo credit: Glyn Lewis

◻ Ward Morehouse

WARD MOREHOUSE, critic, columnist and bon vivant shares a lighter moment with my mother, then Joan Marlowe Morehouse, now Joan Marlowe Rahe, his assistant at The New York Sun (in uniform), Willy Priory, and a woman with the big hat who I believe to be the late actress Jane Wyman.

◻ Zero Mostel, Betty Blake and Joan Marlowe Rahe

ZERO MOSTEL, with the mustache, is flanked by Betty Blake on his right, and Joan Marlowe Rahe, so were co-editors and co-publishers of the Theatre Information Bulletin for nearly a half century. I met Mostel at New York's Sardi's Restaurant when I was a young man studying to be an actor. "It (the theater, show business) is a horrible business," he told me. But the Brooklyn-born actor would himself win the hearts of theater lovers around the globe with his Broadway roles, including Pseudolus in "A Funny Thing Happened on the Way to the Forum" and Tevye in "Fiddler on the Roof."

photo credit: Glyn Lewis

◻ Christopher Plummer and wife Elaine Taylor

DESPITE HAVING STARRED or been featured in more than 100 movies, and dozens and dozens of stage roles Christopher Plummer remains best known for playing Captain Von Trapp in "The Sound of Music" opposite Julie Andrews. He won his seventh Tony Award nomination for his portrayal of the title role in Shakespeare's "King Lear" at New York's Lincoln Center and been a member of the company of Britain's National Theatre and the Royal Shakespeare Company.

photo credit: Rose Billings

Edward Albee and Marian Seldes

EDWARD ALBEE, widely considered the greatest American playwright since Tennessee Williams, had almost instant success with his 1959 play, "The Zoo Story," about a drifter who plans his own murder. He would go on to win Pulitzer Prizes and Tony Awards but in the early 1990's his career seemed to wane. Overlooked by some critics, Albee went on doing what he did best: write plays. He would go on to write some of his finest work, notably "Three Tall Women," which co-starred Marian Seldes, a longtime friend and colleague, with the drama winning the 1994 Pulitzer Prize. A great champion of Albee's and a number of gifted playwrights, Seldes is the daughter of the late Gilbert Seldes, the literary critic who was an early supporter of F. Scott Fitzgerald at a time when many critics dismissed his some of his work as mediocre.

photo credit: Rose Billings

◻ Carol Burnett and Sheldon Harnick

CALL THIS PHOTO "Once Upon a Mattress" meets "Fiddler on the Roof." Burnett, the star of CBS-TV "The Carol Burnett Show," made her Broadway debut in 1959 in the musical "Once Upon a Mattress." Harnick, who wrote the lyrics for the Broadway blockbusters "Fiddler on the Roof," a true masterpiece, "The Apple Tree" and "She Loves Me," began his musical career playing the violin but found he had a gift for writing comedy and an even greater gift writing lyrics. Burnett, who grew up in a troubled family living in a Hollywood boarding house, and would later co-author with her daughter a poignant Broadway play about her childhood, found her greatest gift was making people laugh.

photo credit: Rose Billings

◻ Alec Baldwin

BEST KNOWN AS a film and TV star, the good-looking Long Island, New York native is an avid and talented stage actor with a special flare for comedy. He played the egomaniacal Broadway producer in a revival of "Twentieth Century" with a keen sense of the colorful style the play was originally written in and adroit comic timing. Planning to attend law school he reportedly enrolled in acting classes on a dare and, in 1980, was cast in TV's "The Doctors." I saw him play the title role in an Off-Broadway production of Shakespeare's "MacBeth" and although the reviews of the play were mixed he never seems to stop expanding his acting horizons and in this way is more like the great English actors than Hollywood stars.

photo credit: Rose Billings

🎦 Ethel Barrymore and Rebecca Morehouse

ETHEL BARRYMORE made her Broadway debut in 1903 at Broadway's beautiful Hudson Theatre in a comedy called "Cousin Kate." In a subsequent play at the Hudson she uttered this final line in a play, "That's all there is—there isn't any more." But, personally, the actress would go on to be one of the 20th Century's greatest stage and screen stars. In this photo, she's seated with Rebecca Morehouse, my father widow, and a great journalist in her own right, having been on the staff of The Atlanta Journal, Time Magazine and Playbill. Barrymore's brothers, John and Lionel, also became great film actors after years on Broadway. Her great niece is film star Drew Barrymore, the granddaughter of John Barrymore.

◻ Kitty Carlisle Hart

PERHAPS BEST KNOWN for her star-turn in the Marx Brothers classic 1935 film "A Night at the Opera," Hart absolutely sells out whenever she sings at Feinstein's at the Regency, New York City's premier cabaret room, which is really more of a throwback to the glory days (and nights) of elegant New York nightclubs. The widow of playwright Moss Hart, who co-authored "The Man Who Came to Dinner," "George Washington Slept Here" and other plays with George S. Kaufman, Hart once told me that she used to go out with Broadway and classical American composer George Gershwin before she dated Hart. "If I had married George I'd be rich!" she laughed. In the 1960's, Hart was a regular panelist on the TV show "What's My Line."

photo credit: Rose Billings

🔲 Eli Wallach and Anne Jackson

ELI WALLACH and his wife, Anne Jackson, have to be called something like "America's first husband-and-wife acting team." Their individual careers are staggering. Together, their credits alone would fill up a small book. The odd thing about them both is they have remained very, very nice people—and funny. At a 2006 fund-raising dinner at New York's Tavern on the Green for Primary Stages, a highly-respected Off-Broadway theater, Wallach told of picking up the phone, saying hello, with the party on the other end of the line asking, "Anne?!"

photo credit: Rose Billings

Joel Grey

I call him just Mr. Musical Comedy because there's not a more talented actor alive today with his credits in "Cabaret" and "George M" on Broadway. He's not a bad film actor, either, having won an Oscar for Best Supporting Actor for his performance in the film version of "Cabaret" over Al Pacino in "The Godfather." Pacino was widely-expected to win.

photo credit: Rose Billings

🔲 Donald Smith and Donna McKechnie

DONALD SMITH, one of New York City's all-time great entertainment publicists and singer managers, is seen here with Donna McKechnie, one of Broadway's all-time greatest musical comedy stars having been in "Chorus Line," "Company," "Promises Promises" and many others.

photo credit: Rose Billings

◻ Christine Ebersol

MANY BROADWAY INSIDERS think Christine Ebersol, star of the 2006-2007 Broadway musical "Grey Gardens," will win the 2007 Tony Award for Best Actress in a Musical for her performance. In reviewing "Grey Gardens," The New York Times chief drama critic Ben Brantley said "Christine Ebersol and Mary Louise Wilson command the stage like nothing I've seen before."

photo credit: Rose Billings

A NUMBER OF MY OWN stories and columns follow.

"*Broadway After Dark*" *is celebrating its 80th birthday this year. It was the title of a column written by my father, the late drama critic and theater historian, Ward Morehouse. He began writing it in 1926 when he was with the old* New York Sun, *and I have continued on with the column since his passing. After being the Chief Theater Columnist for the* New York Post *for five years, as well as authoring a number of books, I have regularly contributed the column to* The Epoch Times *since January 2006. While the name "Broadway" is synonymous with Broadway Theater, here, I use it as my father used it, in the sense of entertainment and celebrities in general.*

◻ Producing Ain't So Simple, Simon

NEIL SIMON'S VETERAN PRODUCER has picked one of Broadway's hottest male leads, Nathan Lane, to star in the playwright's next show—while at the same time he struggles to keep Simon's latest play alive.

Emanuel Azenberg, who has produced 16 Simon shows, has chosen Lane, a Tony nominee for *Guys and Dolls*, for *Laughter on the 23rd Floor*, a play based on Simon's experiences as a TV comedy writer for Sid Caesar.

While he gets *Laughter* ready for November, Azenberg is fighting to keep the musical version of Simon's *The Goodbye Girl* alive after it opened to mixed reviews in March. He says the musical is slowly gaining momentum. And he feels Simon has written one of his best plays in *Laughter*.

But since Azenberg produced the critically acclaimed *The Lion in Winter* 26 years ago, with the late Robert Preston and Rosemary Harris, he's seen great changes on Broadway, few for the good.

"For one thing, the quality is disappearing because we cannot really compete economically with film and television," he said. "It's risky for stars to come here because agents can add. They see their clients coming back to Broadway at say, $20,000 a week [when they can get] $2 million for three-month movie commitment."

Azenberg's partial panacea for the ailing theater is to give several top directors, including George C. Wolfe, Mike Nichols and Jerry Zaks, a theater and "their directorial talents will attract actors and writers."

"We have to do something like this to ensure that quality theater will survive," he said. "I'm 59 years old. And my perception is that the quality of the writing and the quality of the acting and the quality of the directing has diminished since I started in the business."

New York Daily News, June 5, 1993.

▣ B'way Comes Their Way

THE BROADWAY THEATER may be having troubles on the street where it lives, but it is doing great in San Francisco, Atlanta, Washington and Schenectady, N.Y.

Therein lies a tale of how the cities where producers used to try plays out before taking them to the "Great White Way" are now the places where they make their profits.

In short, Broadway is now America.

"Broadway is no longer a physical location," said Harvey Sabinson, executive director of the League of American Theaters and Producers.

"It's a very long street. Wherever you go these days, there's Broadway. The most fabulous trend in the theater right now is that the money is made on the road," he said in an interview, adding:

"Markets have opened up that never existed before. You may have a blockbuster that makes money in New York on Broadway, but by and large you make your money on the road. All of which points out one thing—these days it's a national business, it's not just a New York business."

"The road" is booming these days for several reasons.

Dozens of cities have huge new theaters that are often better equipped and more comfortable than some of the older Broadway houses. In addition, many producers are profiting by learning from mistakes of the past.

They have always tried to recoup some of their investment with pre-Broadway tours of shows before the generally tougher New York drama critics review them. But now road shows are much better than they were, theater sources say.

"Producers have finally learned that they can't send anything on the road that isn't any good like they used to," said Jean Dalrymple, a Broadway producer and publicist.

"They ruined the road for a while by sending out second-rate stuff. And even if it wasn't second-rate, it wasn't up to Broadway standards. Audiences have always wanted the best. When they didn't get it, they stayed away. Now they're getting it and they're flocking in."

The League of New York Theaters and Producers was founded in 1930 to help suppress ticket speculation. In 1985, its name was changed to the League of American Theaters and Producers. Currently, it has more than 300 members, about three times the number it had 20 years ago.

Major Broadway touring shows substantially outnumber those along the Great White Way. As of this week, there are 28 major touring shows compared with only 18 shows on Broadway. And the theater boom beyond Broadway is of much greater magnitude than just the touring companies, although that is where the money is. The number of nonprofit professional theaters has leaped from 195 in 1980 to more than 320 today.

During the 1992-93 season that ended May 30, Broadway touring productions took in a record-breaking $621 million in ticket sales, a 23 percent jump from the previous season's record of $503 million, according to the latest figures compiled by the League. That is almost triple the 1987-88 season's sales of $223 million for touring productions.

On Broadway itself, sales also climbed to a new high of $327.7 million, an increase of 11.9 percent from the $293 million in the 1991-92 season.

While Sabinson and others are pleased about more money being made on Broadway, he stresses that "the phenomenon is what happened on Broadway throughout North America."

The stable of long-running Broadway tours includes *Cats*, *Phantom of the Opera*, *The Secret Garden* and *Les Miserables*. There were also new tours of *Crazy for You*, *Miss Saigon*, *The Will Rogers Follies*, *Guys and Dolls* and *Six Degrees of Separation*.

While many musicals and straight plays are being performed in huge new theater complexes from Savannah to Dallas to Los Angeles, others are being booked in renovated theaters such as Proctor's in Schenectady.

New York Post, July, 1993.

🔲 City Center Is Bringing Back Revivals

RETURNING TO ITS ROOTS, City Center will begin producing revivals of classic American musicals early next year for the first time in 26 years.

And borrowing a page from what millions of people throughout America remember most about the early glory days of City Center, seats for these new revivals will be much cheaper than the nearby shows on Broadway—perhaps an average ticket price of $20, with a top of $45.

The first effort: *Allegro*, a 1947 Rodgers and Hammerstein musical about a young doctor corrupted by success.

Also tentatively planned are *I'd Rather Be Right*, the Franklin Delano Roosevelt takeoff by George S. Kaufman and Moss Hart, with score by Rodgers and Hart, and *Lady in the Dark*, with score by Kurt Weill and lyrics by Ira Gershwin.

"Our heritage is rich with these tremendous shows and these tremendous composer-lyricist teams," said Judith E. Daykin, City Center's executive director. "So it seems to me that the niche for City Center is to mount concert versions of these old shows."

While a full orchestra will be used for each show, actors won't be required to memorize their lines or songs but be permitted to "hold their books," making them "concert versions" of the originals, Daykin said.

While it has helped subsidize some of its resident dance companies, City Center has not produced musicals or plays since 1968 when Broadway producer Jean Dalrymple left City Center after running it for 25 years.

Daykin, whom many in New York's theatrical community credit with breathing new life into City Center, was managing director of the Brooklyn Academy of Music (BAM) for 15 years before assuming the reins of City Center in January of 1992.

Daykin said she now has had enough time to think about whether City Center should go back to producing shows itself, and she now believes it should on a limited basis.

"The way I and my advisory committee see things, we probably won't be presenting those shows that might realize fully produced productions (at other theaters) but rather those where the books are a little creaky and they might not make it today," Daykin said.

"But, generally, the scores for many of these shows were wonderful and deserve to be seen again, which is why we're calling the shows, 'Encores! Great American Musicals in Concert.'"

Daily News, August 30, 1993.

◻ Playgoers Putting the Nix

ON THE EVE of the Theater Development Fund's 25th anniversary, its half-price TKTS booth in Times Square is in trouble.

While the fund tries to reverse a decline in sales of half-price tickets, it is turning to television to promote its other programs and is more actively soliciting contributions from corporations and foundations.

"Ticket sales at the half-price booth are off by 10 percent in the last year," Thomas F. Leahy, president of the fund, the largest public service organization for the theater in the United States, said in an interview.

"We want to do something about it before it becomes a major problem that could force us to make substantial cutbacks in the services we offer to producers and the theater-going public," Leahy added. "We don't know whether the drop in sales is related to the shows available or to the quality of life in Times Square—there are so many variables."

Leahy said he hopes one thing that will boost sales a bit is a new electronic billboard the fund is installing the better to display the shows for which its half-price tickets are available.

Anyone can buy a TKTS ticket—if they want to wait in line for a couple of hours.

The TKTS booth at Broadway and 47th Street opens for business at 3 p.m. every day except Wednesday, Saturday and Sunday, when it opens at noon.

Sometime before noon and 3 p.m. the box office managers of both Broadway and Off-Broadway shows send unsold tickets for that afternoon's or evening's performance to the TKTS booth.

New York Post, September, 1993.

☐ B'way Producers Want Estefan to Be: Miz Gloria

RICHARD JAY-ALEXANDER wants Gloria Estefan for *Les Miserables*—and he thinks he'll get her.

Jay-Alexander, the head of superstar producer Cameron Mackintosh's North American operations, has asked the singer to join the Broadway cast of *Les Miz* while he struggles to prop up the slightly faltering seven-year-old hit and open up a brand new market for it in the Far East.

Jay-Alexander, who is also directing the new road company of *Les Miz* that will play Singapore for 11 weeks beginning in January, wants Estefan to replace Andrea McArdle, who was the original star of *Annie* on Broadway and in London.

McArdle joined the cast of *Les Miz* earlier this year in the emotionally charged role of Fantine.

Jay-Alexander hasn't gotten a definite "yes" from the pop superstar, but in an interview before he left for Singapore he was confident he would.

Several other major cast changes for the musical based on the Victor Hugo novel set just before the French Revolution are definite, however, he said.

Craig Schulman, who has played the lead role of Jean Valjean well over a thousand times, more than any other actor, will star in the 11-week Singapore tour.

He will be replaced on Broadway by David Fisher, who has played Valjean in a production of *Les Miz* in Jerusalem and who also happens to be a Jewish cantor.

Les Miz played to less than 85 percent capacity during the week Aug. 30-Sept. 5, down from 93 percent the previous week, according to *Variety*'s weekly Broadway box office figures.

By contrast, Mackintosh's production of *Phantom of the Opera* continues to play to standing-room-only crowds and his *Miss Saigon* is selling close to capacity, *Variety* reports.

It is no major surprise that after seven years ticket sales for *Les Miz* are sputtering a bit.

But Jay-Alexander sees the slump as part of the larger picture of Broadway's "seasonal dives." He expects sales will pick up as the fall season goes into full swing and more creative group sales marketing efforts are launched.

"People accused *Les Miz* of being 'the McDonald's of musicals.' I say to them, 'You carefully watch the show and tell me this is a copy.' The show set a new standard for musicals on the road."

New York Post, September 22, 1993.

◫ Now and Forever, 'Cats' Has 11 Lives

CATS IS STILL the cat's meow as it celebrates its 11th anniversary on Broadway.

The Andrew Lloyd Webber musical based on T.S. Elliot's *Old Possum's Book of Practical Cats* opened October 7, 1982 with the dubious distinction of being America's first mega-musical, in which sets and costume were as important as music and staging.

Despite mixed reviews *Cats* quickly became a popular favorite and paved the way for a decade of British imports in the same mold, including such hits as *Miss Saigon* and Lloyd Webber's *Phantom of the Opera*.

And, at a time when some producers scramble to sign film and pop stars to sell tickets, *Cats* has thrived without any major names, even in its original cast.

"The allure of *Cats* is cats," said Gerald Schoenfeld, chairman of the Shubert Organization, one of the show's producers. "It's truly an ensemble show."

After more than 4,500 performances *Cats* is the third longest-running musical on Broadway, trailing only *A Chorus Line* and *Oh! Calcutta* and well on its way to living up to its famous tag line: "Cats—Now and Forever."

Worldwide, *Cats* companies have grossed "in excess of $1.2 billion," Schoenfeld said. Lloyd Webber's British-based Really Useful Co., another of the producers, estimates that total gross receipts are closer to $1.5 billion.

Schoenfeld said *Phantom* may eventually rank as the highest grossing show of all time, in terms of dollars.

"But as a percentage of return on investment I don't think there's any other show that will touch *Cats*," he said.

"If you add up the total number of companies and the return on the investment in those companies I would say that it would be close to 20 times. In New York, it's 10 times."

Only one company of *Cats* is currently touring the United States. It has bookings in cities through mid-1995 and is already the longest continuously running road show.

But the musical has blazed a trail, Schoenfeld said.

"*Cats* has opened up territory that has not been exploited before in such places as Eugene, Ore., and Boise, Idaho, and Fayetteville, North Carolina—hardly places where Broadway shows had gone before," he said.

"Now *Evita* is playing in a large number of smaller places, but *Cats* really opened up territories," Schoenfeld said. "In a sense, it's a return to what the theater was 70 to 80 years ago when the dramatic shows were playing everywhere."

Still propelled by a high-powered TV ad campaign, box-office receipts for *Cats* are running at a healthy pace, but Schoenfeld wouldn't predict if it would run another 11 years.

But even if it doesn't, there is a consolation that is music to an investor's ear.

"We're making a profit," Schoenfeld Said.

New York Post, October 7, 1993.

🔲 "HELLO, JERRY!"

NEW YORK—BY THE SAME TIME next year, there may well be four major revivals of Jerry Herman shows in or on their way to New York, London, Tokyo and other cities around the world.

The biggest news is Carol Channing has now definitely said "yes" to doing a world tour of *Hello, Dolly!* according to Herman, who wrote the book and lyrics for the show with which she has become virtually synonymous.

In an interview with Reuters here before he left for his home in Beverly Hills, Herman said this brand new revival starring the most famous Dolly of them all will include stops in Japan, some European cities and a six-week limited engagement on Broadway.

Hello, Dolly! was the biggest hit of Broadway's 1963-1964 season and has become one of the most popular musicals of all time.

Besides *Hello, Dolly!*, major revivals are slated for *La Cage aux Folles*, *Mame*, and even *Mack & Mabel*, Herman's least known Broadway musical, which is about the movies' silent era.

"There's a possibility that I'll have my four children back on the boards," Herman said.

First up is this year's 10th anniversary revival of *La Cage aux Folles* beginning in December, which Herman said will star LeRoy Rheims and Walter Charles.

"We have 37 major American cities booked already," he said.

The rehearsals for *Hello, Dolly!* will "begin in July and we're starting on the West Coast and probably in San Francisco and stay there for four weeks."

Herman added that he thinks the production will open in New York sometime next winter, possibly as early as December.

Why does he think *Hello, Dolly!* is being revived again aside from Carol Channing's own great popularity?

"The story is timeless in the sense it's not for letting the parade pass you by," Herman said. "Taking that last chance in life. I think so many people can identify with that theme and there's no generation that won't understand and relate to it."

Mack & Mabel, which was first produced in the 1974-1975 season, was Herman's least commercially successful Broadway show. While he admitted that some may not have liked the book's unhappy ending, he said the musical remains a personal favorite of his.

And at least according to Herman, the London producing team of David Cole (Cole) and Guy Kitchen (Kitchen) are hoping to do a revival of *Mack & Mabel* in London next year.

At the same time, two producers in this country, Jon Wilner (Jon Wilner) and Peter LeDonne (LeDonne), l have also expressed strong interest in doing the show. Herman's hunch is that they will team up with Cole and Kitchen to produce a London production.

"I really think we're going to be seeing a London production of *Mack & Mabel* before we see it here," Herman said.

Lastly, "a very big producer who I cannot name" is talking about reviving *Mame*, Herman related.

With Angela Lansbury in the title role?

Probably no such great fortune, Herman replied.

"I don't think she wants to come back to Broadway. If she did, we'd welcome her with open arms. She is Mame!"

Besides working with producers of planned revivals of these shows, Herman has been busy writing some new individual songs and is looking for "the right material" to write a new musical about.

During the past year, he spent six weeks recording a new CD of his songs and Elektra (Elektra) Entertainment, a division of Warner Communications, Inc., has just released the CD entitled "Michael Feinstein Sings the Jerry Herman Songbook," which features Herman at the piano.

Herman has high standards for new musical material.

"It's got to be wholesome in its own way. I don't want to do a musical with people getting shot. I really don't. I want the audience to be able to escape for two hours. There's enough horror in the world. You turn on the late news and it's overwhelming."

Reuters, October 27, 1993.

◻ Little Orphan "Annie Warbucks" is Going to the White House

NEW YORK—KATHRYN ZAREMBA, who plays "Annie Warbucks," and the entire cast of the sleeper hit Off-Broadway musical comedy—even including Annie's not-so-little dog "Sandy," played by part Airedale Cindy Lou—have been invited to perform at the White House Christmas party on December 17th.

"Even Cindy Lou's understudy, Cosmo, is going to Washington in case Cindy Lou gets sick," Dennis Grimaldi, one of the producers of *Annie Warbucks*, said in breaking the news to Reuters.

"We just got word of the invitation and we're delighted to be going," Grimaldi said in an interview with Reuters December 2.

Grimaldi went on to say that the cast, which includes Harve Presnell, who plays Daddy Warbucks, will sing some selections from the show during the Clintons' Christmas party on the morning of December 17. Then they will fly back to New York that afternoon for a regularly scheduled performance that evening.

There are several ironies to the story, not the least of which is that one of the scenes in *Annie Warbucks* actually takes place in the White House during the administration of President Franklin D. Roosevelt. In fact, FDR is a character in the musical.

Might President Bill Clinton be asked to be in the show?

"I don't think so," Grimaldi said with a big smile, adding with an even bigger smile, "But he might play his saxophone."

While President Clinton may be more than happy just to enjoy watching others perform, producer Grimaldi has a lot to smile about in connection with *Annie Warbucks* these days.

"The chances of *Annie Warbucks* moving to Broadway are better than 50 percent," Grimaldi said, addressing the rumors that have been flying around the New York theater community for the last several weeks.

"It's doing very well downtown at the Variety Arts but having the possibility of going to Broadway is something that Martin Charnin and Charles Strouse and Tom Meehan have always wanted," Grimaldi said. "And it's very heady when somebody—a money source—wants you to come to Broadway. But we haven't signed anything yet...A decision will come in the next few months because if we want to move it to Broadway it would be a move in the Spring."

Until *Annie Warbucks* opened at the Variety Arts this past August there was very little to smile about for either the musical's producers or Charnin, who wrote the lyrics and directed it.

With music by Charles Strouse and book by Thomas Meehan, *Annie Warbucks*, the sequel to the mega-hit *Annie*, which closed in 1983 after six years, grossing somewhere around $25 million, almost never opened in New York at all.

The sequel had problem after problem on the road and actually a version of it closed just prior to opening on Broadway. Finally, after many rewrites, it opened Off-Broadway at the 499-seat Variety Arts Theatre and has settled into a highly successful run.

In fact, the box office has been so healthy that Grimaldi and the show's two other producers are confident of recouping their $1.2 million investment much earlier than they originally expected.

Reuters, December 2, 1993.

☐ Plaid

NEW YORK—DURING THESE SOBERING days on and Off-Broadway the grass is very much greener for at least one Off-Broadway show.

While five new Broadway plays have closed in the last six weeks, and three long-running Off-Broadway shows have announced they are closing early next year, *Forever Plaid* shows every sign of running—well, forever—in cities around the globe.

Worldwide ticket sales of *Forever Plaid* will top the $31 million mark this weekend, according to Eugene Wolsk, the show's producer.

Companies of the funny, four-character gentle spoof of 1950's groups like the Four Lads are currently playing in New York, Boston, Minneapolis, Philadelphia, Tampa, Toronto and London.

And within the next year alone, Wolsk said eight more companies will open in Honolulu, Chicago, Dallas, San Diego, Seattle, Vancouver, Sydney—and hold onto your plaid jacket—even in this country's country music capitol of Branson, Missouri.

Moreover, the $31 million that the show will have racked up in ticket sales by this weekend doesn't include a lucrative sideline of peddling everything from *Forever Plaid* sweatshirts and cummerbunds to CD's and music videos.

"It's been a very, very profitable show," veteran producer Wolsk said. "The return to the original investors is in the neighborhood of 800 to 900 percent on their investment."

Not bad for something that *Forever Plaid* creator Stuart Ross started in Teaneck, New Jersey, with a $600 cash advance on his Visa Card in 1989.

In May of the following year, Wolsk produced the show Off-Broadway for a little over $140,000 in a converted Manhattan restaurant called Steve McGraw's. The New York production has remained there ever since, with profits buoyed by group sales to teenagers and senior citizens alike.

To date, there have been 24 *Forever Plaid* companies, not counting the eight slated to open in the next year.

"We may not be dealing in Broadway numbers but $31 million Off-Broadway is a very big number," the producer said.

And as veteran of many years of producing on and Off-Broadway, Wolsk said the success of *Forever Plaid* Off-Broadway has taught him a big lesson.

"It's taught me to stay away from Broadway. This is the most profitable show, in percentage terms, I've ever produced."

The Brooklyn-born Wolsk also produced the hit Off-Broadway play *Driving Miss Daisy* as well as the critically-acclaimed play *The Lion in Winter* on Broadway.

But the business of producing, co-producing, licensing and marketing the various *Forever Plaid* companies has kept Wolsk and his partner Laura Stein, who is also his wife, so busy he said there's no time to even think seriously about producing another play.

In *Forever Plaid*, the "Four Plaids," as the singing group calls themselves, sing nostalgic standards like "Matilda" and "Three Coins in the Fountain."

Last year, enthusiastic *Forever Plaid* fan President George Bush invited a Washington, D.C. company of the show to play the White House. That same year, a Denver *Forever Plaid* company did the show as a fundraiser for President Clinton when he was campaigning in Colorado.

But the bottom line of this show really has nothing to do with politics. Rather, *Forever Plaid* seems to have a permanent silver lining—but color it green.

Reuters, December 14, 1993.

◻ Disney to Ink Broadway Deal

THE WALT DISNEY CO. and the New York State Urban Development Corporation have hammered out an agreement for the entertainment giant to take over the dilapidated New Amsterdam Theatre on West 42nd Street.

Disney would build an entertainment complex in the landmarked Art Nouveau Theater, which was home to the famed Ziegfeld "Follies" between 1913 and 1927.

Under the agreement the UDC would provide Disney a 3 percent loan of $20 million to help renovate the badly deteriorated theater, said Stewart F. Lane, a Broadway theater owner whose holdings include a 50 percent interest in the Palace Theatre.

Disney's production of the musical *Beauty and the Beast*, adapted from its animated film of the same name, starts previews March 9 at the Palace Theatre.

Lane said Disney would also put up $8 million in cash in the deal for the New Amsterdam.

New York Post, February 3, 1994.

◻ Prince

NEW YORK—NINETEEN-TIME Tony Award winner Harold Prince says he'll fight financial and artistic pressure to bring his hit Toronto revival of *Show Boat* to Broadway before next Fall—when he also said the first road company of his mega-hit, *Kiss of the Spider Woman*, will be launched.

Prince's remarks about *Show Boat*, and *Kiss*, both of which he directed, came in an exclusive interview with Reuters December 20.

Prince said it would be a mistake to put *Show Boat* into the Gershwin Theatre earlier than the Fall even though the theater, where *Show Boat* has been slated to go for some time, has just become available after *The Red Shoes* closed Sunday.

The director's revamped revival of the 1927 Jerome Kern classic musical opened in Toronto to ecstatic notices in October.

Prince also directed *The Phantom of the Opera* and *Kiss of the Spider Woman*, the two hottest musicals currently entrenched on Broadway. They are playing to more than 100 percent (including standing room) and 99.7 percent capacity, respectively, according to *Variety*'s Broadway latest box office figures published this week.

At the same time, Prince said there are now seven companies of *Phantom of the Opera* playing throughout the United States and Canada, including the Broadway company. A total of 14 companies of this Andrew Lloyd Webber extravaganza are playing worldwide.

"I don't want *Show Boat* put into the soup of revivals," Prince explained. "There seem to be a lot of revivals coming in. But this is, strictly speaking, not a revival. Not in the same sense.

"There are six numbers that were never in the show that were written at the time [1927]. And I would like to separate *Show Boat* off from the revivals."

A Broadway revival of *My Fair Lady* opened two weeks ago and revivals of *Damn Yankees* and *Carousel* are slated to open in the next several months.

"I think I have some pressure I can apply (on the producer and Gershwin Theatre owner)," Prince continued. "I want to bring it in with the same Toronto cast. So I think that will be October."

In the interview, Prince also squelched rumors that Chita Rivera, Tony Award-winning star of *Kiss of the Spider Woman*, may bow out of that show soon after it celebrates its first anniversary in May.

"Chita's very happy [in the musical] as she deserves to be," Prince said.

But he went on to say that Carol Lawrence will again substitute for Rivera when she takes another week's vacation from the highly demanding title role later this winter.

As to Andrew Lloyd Webber's recently announced plans to produce movie versions of *The Phantom of the Opera* and other of his shows himself, Prince said he was firmly opposed to a movie of *Phantom* anytime in the foreseeable future.

"I don't want a movie of *Phantom*," he said. "I just hope they forget it. It's going to be a long way off, anyway. And, you know, the best musicals do not necessarily make the best musical movies. *Cabaret* made a successful one, as did *The Sound of Music*. But, by and large, movie musicals are not as good as the originals—by miles...This doesn't mean they don't make money. They're just not as good."

Never one to rest on his laurels even though they include 19 Tony Awards both as a director and a producer, beginning with *The Pajama Game* in 1954, as a producer, Prince said his latest directing project is called *The Petrified Prince*.

He said it's based on a script Ingmar Bergman once intended to do as a movie.

"It's a small, dangerous musical," Prince said. "It's really a black comedy. It's difficult. I've been working on it with the composer and lyricist for three years. I think we're getting there. But at this point in my life there's no point of doing anything I would perceive as easy.

"Essentially, it's about a young boy, a prince, whose father dies. The boy is paralyzed and cannot rule—and we see the effort that gets him out of the wheelchair and assert himself. The thought behind it is that people tend to be paralyzed for one reason or another psychologically and the musical examines what it is that makes them move."

Will he first do the new musical in Toronto, as he did *Kiss of the Spider Woman* and *Show Boat*?

"I don't know," he said. "It's still a long way off. It certainly won't be Broadway. You can't afford to open here and fail."

Reuters, February 15, 1994.

◻ Sting and James Taylor Join Forces for Brazil Show

RIO DE JANEIRO—ROCK SUPERSTARS Sting and James Taylor are teaming up for the first time to jointly perform in the Brazilian city of Sao Paulo March 19 and 20.

Neither his two music history-making gigs with Taylor in Sao Paulo, nor any of his concerts in three other Latin American countries this month will go to help the endangered Amazon rainforest, one of the superstar's favorite causes.

Instead, Sting is due to hold a $1,000-a-ticket benefit concert at Carnegie Hall in New York April 9 to raise funds for the Amazon and its Indian inhabitants.

"We never try and mix rock 'n' roll with rainforest benefits," Sting's manager, Ken Turner told Reuters March 18 on a short holiday stop here before flying down to Sao Paulo for the concerts with Taylor.

But Sting, who has already performed in Costa Rica and Venezuela during this current tour, says he remains as committed as ever to his favorite cause for which he set up his own foundation, The Rainforest Foundation.

Sting believes widespread development has decimated millions of acres of rainforest in the vast Amazon River basin, a major source of the world's fresh air and water.

In a news conference with reporters here, Sting said his concerts with James Taylor in Sao Paulo came about quite by accident.

"We are very good friends and we found out that we were both going to be in South America at the same time so I thought that rather than compete for the same audiences we should sing together and have the same audiences," Sting said. "Taylor's been one of my idols."

Following the concerts in Sao Paulo, Sting and Taylor will perform in Buenos Aires March 25 and 26.

Asked as to his plans following the tour, Sting replied: "I'm going to go home and sleep for a couple of days."

Reuters, March 18, 1994.

◻ It's Not 'Fair'!

(Today, *Post* Weekend Plus begins "On and Off Broadway," a new column that brings you the inside track on what's happening on the Great White Way. It's written by Ward Morehouse III, who was a staff correspondent for *The Christian-Science Monitor* for 10 years. The author of *The Waldorf-Astoria: America's Gilded Dream*, Morehouse later was a drama critic for the *Monitor* and is a theater reporter for Reuters. His father, the late Ward Morehouse, was a drama critic and columnist whose column, "Broadway After Dark," ran in *The New York Sun* and Newhouse newspapers. Look for "On and Off Broadway" every Friday.)

THINGS AREN'T TOO "luverly" at *My Fair Lady*.

Michael Moriarty, the surprise choice to replace Richard Chamberlain in the hit revival, "has been behaving like a willful little boy" and "riding roughshod" over cast members at rehearsals, according to one of the show's supporting actors.

Chamberlain makes his final exit from the musical this Sunday after a year-long triumph as Professor Henry Higgins, first on the road, and beginning in December, on Broadway. Moriarty, a brilliant actor, has been rehearsing with the cast for the past two weeks. Paxton Whitehead takes over the Higgins role next week and Moriarty is scheduled to start April 8.

Director Howard Davies is having to do a delicate balancing act between encouraging Moriarty and placating discouraged cast members. One person is even threatening to resign.

"Maybe it will all straighten out and he'll turn out to be a genius, but I've never seen anyone who came into a show and took over like he did," one actor complained.

Moriarty was not available for comment, but Richard Kornberg, the press agent for *My Fair Lady*, denied that Moriarty was causing any waves whatsoever. "Everybody's in seventh heaven with him," Kornberg told me.

Moriarty is no stranger to controversy. While starring in the TV series "Law and Order," he locked horns with U.S. Attorney General Janet Reno over the issue of TV violence.

HAVING FIRST FALLEN in love with Broadway nearly 70 years ago, Katharine Hepburn says she'd like to return to the Great White Way for one last valentine.

Over lunch at her New York townhouse, the star told me she'd go back to the Broadway stage, "If I found something I liked. But," she quickly added, "then I don't know what the hell I'm going to be doing."

The once-avid theater-goer says these days she's "not mad about sitting in a theater, especially if I don't like the play!"

And in a rare comment about the late Spencer Tracy's drinking, the four-time Academy Award winner told me: "I know a great many people who had a great drinking problem, including Spencer. So I was not inclined to the bottle."

Hepburn, 87, just starred with Anthony Quinn in her 50th film, *This Can't Be Love*, on CBS-TV.

NOT CONTENT WITH ACTING onstage from time to time, movie star Steve Martin has written a one-act play which will be performed in the Ensemble Studio Theater's 17th annual festival of new one-act plays, May 5 through June 12.

Martin's play is called *WASP* and it begins performances June 1. But the fledging playwright has some heavyweight competition, including John Guare, Christopher Durang and Marsha Norman. Tickets are $25. E.S.T. is at 549 W. 52nd St. Reservations: (212) 247-3045.

THE BOX OFFICE hasn't opened for Tommy Tune's new production of *Grease*, but the revival has already racked up more than $3 million in advance ticket sales.

With soap star Ricky Paul Goldin (who played Dean Frame in "Another World") in the John Travolta role, Tune's new take on the 1972 musical opens for previews April 23. And the box office opens tomorrow, with Goldin leading a block party in front of the Eugene O'Neill Theater on West 49th Street...Odds are Jeff Calhoun will make Tony Award history this year with twin nominations for best choreographer for both *Grease*, which he's also directing, and *The Best Little Whorehouse Goes Public*, which he co choreographed with Tommy Tune.

Is Mayor Rudolph Giuliani become a Broadway booster? On a recent edition of "The Broadway Hour" on WPAT-AM 93, Giuliani said, "the arts are as important to New York in the 1990s as steel was to Pittsburgh in the 1950s." And George Wachtel, director of research and government relations for the League of American Theaters and Producers, says Giuliani, who relishes Broadway openings, "will be more proactive for the theater than any mayor since John Lindsay."

WHEN JAZZ LEGEND Annie Ross finishes her stint at Rainbow & Stars April 23, she's off to London to be in the musical *Sweet Lorraine*. Ross has received a career shot in the arm from her role in Robert Altman's movie *Short Cuts*.

"You just keep on doing what you do and do as much of it as you want to do," she said. "I refuse to be put into one of those little pigeon-holes."

"Tony 'n' Tina's Wedding" celebrates its 2,000th performance off-Broadway on April 6, just as producer Joe Corcoran flies to Boston to complete negotiations for a Boston company of *Wedding*, the third longest-running off-Broadway show...*Forever Plaid* starts the beginning of its fifth year at Steve McGraw's in May...

Fred Papert, president of the 42nd Street Development Corporation, on Disney taking over the New Amsterdam Theater on 42nd Street: "My concern is that we come up with a 1990s version of 42nd Street instead of a 1990s version of a Kansas City mall."

Papert's own baby is the proposed 42nd Street Trolley project, which would consist of 13 electrically powered trolley cars replacing buses. And Papert says we can expect to hear those trolleys ding-a-linging next year.

New York Post, April 1, 1994.

☐ Miller Spins Gold for Amy

BROADWAY IS CERTAINLY having a love affair with Hollywood—and stars' professional and personal lives are crisscrossing like the streets in Times Square. Here's how:

Amy Irving, starring in Arthur Miller's new play, *Broken Glass*, which opens Sunday, says she's at "the high point of my professional life. Creating a role on Broadway for Arthur Miller is as good as it gets."

The star also told me she was thrilled that ex-husband Steven Spielberg was "seeing the show this week." But Irving never thinks she'll work professionally for the man who is also Hollywood's most successful director.

"I think it would be awkward for his own personal life," Irving said.

"But we're great friends and we spend a lot of time together."

A who's who of Hollywood is piling through the doors of the Booth Theater to see *Broken Glass*. Actor Dennis Hopper saw it Tuesday, and told me, "I was very moved by Amy's performance."

Hopper said he could be coaxed to come to Broadway "if the right thing comes along." But what he'd really like to do is a play about the late heiress Mabel Dodge, who befriended D.H. Lawrence and Georgia O'Keeffe at her adobe house in Taos, N.M. Hopper once owned Dodge's house.

Incidentally, Hopper got mugged in Central Park this week—as part of the storyline for a segment of "Effie Abroad," the hit Australian TV series starring Mary Coustas that is filming in the Big Apple.

Simon Curtis, director of *The Rise and Fall of Little Voice*, tells me has been "getting notes" from his beautiful movie star wife, Elizabeth McGovern. The play opens May 1.

"I just want unqualified praise," Curtis said. "She's more realistic."

Little Voice is about an emotionally tormented young woman with a remarkable voice able to mimic the styles of Judy Garland, Barbra Streisand and others.

Curtis first met McGovern 10 years ago when a mutual friend invited them to a performance of Marsha Norman's *'night, Mother*. But Curtis says that their romance didn't bud until McGovern did a play for the BBC called *Tales of Hollywood*, which Curtis was producing. The couple has a 9-month old daughter, Matilda.

Actor Eli Wallach's on a religious role "roll." Sunday's his last performance playing Noah in Clifford Odets' *The Flowering Peach* at Lyceum Theater. Next, he will play an Italian priest in a new film called *Honey Sweet Love* starring Ben Cross.

But Wallach's quick to say it's not typecasting.

"I usually play Mexican bandits!" Wallach told me.

Susan Egan, who plays Belle, the Beauty of Disney's *Beauty and the Beast*, says the musical has had an adverse effect of sorts on one aspect of her personal life.

"I'm going to have to elope when I get married," Egan joked. "I've been spoiled by all the beautiful gowns I wear in the show."

And no, Egan said she had no immediate plans to elope. Hey the show just opened!

Off-Broadway's also going to Tinsel Town for talent. Leslie Jordan, starring in *Hysterical Blindness* at the Theater on Vandam Street, is best known for appearing as Murphy's secretary in "Murphy Brown" as well as recurring roles in "Reasonable Doubts," "Hearts Afire" and other sitcoms.

Leslie told me his New York theater debut is causing him some major problems—all spelled MOM.

In *Hysterical Blindness*, which Jordan wrote and is a comedy about his growing up in Tennessee, he describes a psychosomatic disorder his mother once had.

"If she got angry her eyes would snap shut," Leslie said, adding that his mom now claims Leslie's "just like Patti Davis, who wrote about her parents, the Reagans."

And no, Mrs. Jordan won't be at the opening May 19. But friends John Ritter and Walter Matthau are expected to attend.

Practically all Hollywood has wanted to know whatever happened to reclusive writer-director Terrence Malick after he made *Days of Heaven* in 1978. Well. Malick's alive and well and heading for Broadway, of all things, via a slight detour in Hollywood.

But he's not making a movie. Rather, he's currently sequestered in a warehouse there for a few weeks directing workshop productions of his recently written first play.

Sansho the Bailiff is set in the Dark Ages and deals with a Japanese family's fight to retain its basic humanity against overwhelming odds. Robert Geisler, who along with John Roberdeau is producing *Sansho the Bailiff* on Broadway next season, told me he "revels that Malick's working again and Broadway's got him." Geisler and Roberdeau produced the critically acclaimed Broadway revival of Eugene O'Neill's *Strange Interlude* a decade ago.

New York Post, April 22, 1994.

◻ After Dismal Fall, Revivals Bring Upbeat Note to Season

NEW YORK—BROADWAY IS ON THE REBOUND. After a dismal start, with only two shows that opened last fall surviving thus far, Broadway has had two solid hits in the past month.

And even some of the most conservative theatrical veterans are forecasting that the 1993-94 season will end on an upbeat note as it increasingly relies on big names of the past.

A revival of *Carousel*, which was first a hit in London last year, opened at Lincoln Center's Vivian Beaumont Theatre March 24 and received 20 positive reviews.

And British TV and film star Diana Rigg just scored a major triumph in the title role of *Medea*, which was also first done in London last year.

"I'm always optimistic at this time of year, as I was early last fall," said Gerald Schoenfeld, chairman of the Shubert Organization, New York's largest owner of Broadway theaters. "My optimism last fall was short-lived, but now I think there's really room for optimism."

More than a dozen new Broadway shows are opening in the next month.

These include a major revival of *Grease*, which was first produced on Broadway in 1972, a brand new Arthur Miller play, *Broken Glass*, and Disney's *Beauty and the Beast*, which opened Monday after doing standing-room-only sellout business in previews at the Palace Theater.

"There are a large number of impressive credentials in the shows that will open," Schoenfeld also said in an interview in his office atop the Shubert Theater, where the Gershwin musical *Crazy for You* is enjoying a long run.

"Stephen Sondheim and James Lapine have a new musical, *Passion*; *The Inspector Calls* is opening here soon after being such a big hit in London. Anna Devere Smith, in a one-woman show called *Twilight: Los Angeles* (about the 1992 Los Angeles riots), is a major talent. And there's Diana Rigg in *Medea*, another production from London.

"The theaters on the south side of 45th Street were dark for the last four months and now they're lit and there's excitement in the air," Schoenfeld added.

And while Jackie Mason's new one-man show, *Jackie Mason: Politically Incorrect*, recently opened to very mixed reviews at the Royale, one of those theaters on 45th Street, it already has a huge advance sale for a one-man show.

"We already have a half-million dollars advance and expect to run at least a year," said Jill Rosenthal, Mason's manager.

Reuters in the *Chicago Tribune*, April 28, 1994.

◻ Joan's Tribute

JOAN RIVERS MAY or may not strike gold on Broadway in *Sally Marr...and Her Escorts*. But when the show opened last night she had already done the thing uppermost in her heart: fulfill a dream of her late husband, Edgar Rosenberg.

"The play was Edgar's idea," Joan told me this week. "And he was the one who kept on saying, 'You've got to go back, you've got to go back to Broadway!'"

In fact, she is dedicating the show entirely to Edgar. (Rosenberg committed suicide in 1987. On May 15, NBC will air "Laughter and Tears," the story of his death and aftermath. It stars Joan and their daughter, Melissa.)

"Now I'm finally taking my journey and I hope audiences come with me," said Joan.

As for life after Broadway, Rivers would like nothing more than to be a full-fledged movie star.

"If Shirley MacLaine dies, I'll do all her roles," she joked.

She and producer Marty Richards have laundry lists of stars to replace Joan on Broadway if the play is successful. Her first choice is Bernadette Peters.

"Bette Midler also would be insanely good in it," she added.

WITH A REWORKED FINALE and new lyrics to three songs, *Passion*, the new Stephen Sondheim/James Lapine musical, is heading confidently either for the Tony Award record books or the chopping block when it opens on Monday.

Sources say even some of the musical's producers are divided about how it will be received by critics. But after countless revisions, the number of unintentional laughs that some lines got in early previews have trickled down to nearly none. And, every night, at least during the past week, *Passion* received standing ovations.

After nearly six weeks of previews, *Passion* was finally "frozen" Tuesday night.

"We had a lot of things go in yesterday," said Jere Shea, the musical's male heartthrob, who plays Giorgio. "Of course, during the performance we had our share of train wrecks!"

Another potential pitfall for the handsome actor: his wife Elaine's reaction to his romantic interludes on stage. In one scene, for example, Shea and actress Marin Mazzle are naked and in the throes of, well, the title of the show.

"Elaine and I have a lot of trust and respect for each other and we have a very solid marriage," Shea told me. "She's a rock."

Perhaps not surprising, but the cast member quote here last week that "Richard (Chamberlain) is a superstar and Michael Moriarty is a stupid star" went over like a backstage mention of *Macbeth* with the publicity people at the now-defunct *My Fair Lady*.

Publicist Richard Kornberg even tacked up a note in the theater which said, in effect, that the person I quoted was disloyal and should get out of the theater.

In fact, this individual had the show's best interests at heart and fervently wanted the brilliant "Law and Order" star to succeed. But he didn't, showing that dramatic genius isn't necessarily all it takes to cut it in a Broadway musical. It closed on Sunday, by the way.

"Michael had the guts and the drive and the commitment but, unfortunately, it didn't work for him or for us," producer Fran Weissler told me. "There are not too many fine, high-visibility actors who really sell seats. They are great actors but they simply don't sell tickets.

"It was very hard to replace Richard Chamberlain. And it was very hard for Richard Chamberlain to replace Rex Harrison. A lot of stars didn't want to replace Rex and some terrific actors didn't want to replace Rex and Richard."

Despite its losing last weeks on Broadway, Weissler told me that she and her husband, Barry, are going full steam ahead with plans for a road tour of the show.

But it's unlikely, said Weissler, that Chamberlain would be on the tour.

"I would have liked Richard to extend but he made certain demands which we felt were excessive and we couldn't honor those," Fran Weissler said.

Meanwhile, the Weisslers have something right around the corner to keep them plenty busy. Their production of *Grease*, starring Rosie O'Donnell, opens next Wednesday, and has a hefty $3 million "advance"—the dollar amount for tickets sold for future performances.

With preview audience comments ranging from wildly enthusiastic to "The Best Little Snorehouse on Broadway," Tommy Tune's production of *The Best Little Whorehouse Goes Public* gets a gala opening night on Tuesday.

One unusual aspect of the show, though, seems to be getting universal raves—the small Las Vegas-style "lounge act" performed by Susannah Blinkoff and Ryan Perry in the lobby before the actual show. (Blinkoff also happens to be the daughter of Carol Hall, who wrote the music and lyrics for the show.)

After their lounge act, Blinkoff and Perry scurry to the orchestra pit where they join Nancy LaMott as the musical's three "pit singers"—augmenting what's being sung onstage.

"It's such an unusual experience to have a mother in the same business," Blinkoff told me. "I can't even describe what a blessing it is to sing her songs."

It appears that *The Rise and Fall of Little Voice*, which got creamed by several critics this week, won't turn out to be the Little Broadway Show That Could—as some of its producers had hoped even with the negative notices. It's expected to close tomorrow.

Peggy Hill Rosenkrantz, one of the show's producers, said the $1.4 million show had an advance of $55,000 going into its opening week, not that bad for a straight play. But with the negative reviews, the show sold just $700 worth of tickets this past Monday, Rosenkrantz said, adding it needs to make $170,000 a week to break even.

But as of late yesterday, Roseroots told me that there "had been such an outcry" from *Little Voice* supporters that she and her fellow producers were having a meeting today to see if they could keep it open at least another week.

Too bad the producers didn't do it off-Broadway where the zany show about an introvert who can sing up a storm might have found a home—and an audience—for some months.

ON MONDAY, "Girls Night Out," Larry O'Daly's long-running stand-up comedy TV series, will begin shooting in its new uptown home at the Blue Angel, 327 West 44th Street.

Each segment of "Girls Night Out," which airs on Lifetime Television, features a different celebrity host, and, like Letterman, is shot before a live audience. O'Daly said he is trying to get *Grease*'s Rosie O'Donnell to do the honors for a segment later this month.

Broadway investors often crop up in strange places. For example, Dick Button, the former Olympic figure skating champion-turned-broadcaster, was an investor in *The Rise and Fall of Little Voice*.

And while it looks like this play will fall faster than Tonya Harding, there seems to be no stopping Button's backing for the theater. *The Rise and Fall of Little Voice* is actually the 43rd play in which he has invested.

"I've done well in the theater—better than the S&P index!" he told me. Sorry, I don't have Button's home number. Try CBS.

New York Post, May 6, 1994.

◻ Redgrave Isn't Crying Woolf on Play

VANESSA REDGRAVE is definitely not afraid of Virginia Woolf—or Broadway.

Producer Lewis Allen says Redgrave—considered by many to be the finest actress alive—and Eileen Atkins will co-star on Broadway in *Vita and Virginia*, the two-character play Atkins assembled from the letters between Virginia Woolf and Vita Sackville-West.

"Vanessa hasn't signed yet, but she's all set to do it," Allen told me yesterday. Allen and producer Robert Fox originally staged the play in London but without Redgrave. Among other things, the play deals with Woolf and Sackville-West's lesbian affair.

The lean and lanky Redgrave will play Vita Sackville-West. And Atkins, currently in Washington, D.C., in her one-person play about Virginia Woolf called *A Room of Her Own*, will play Woolf. Allen said *Vita and Virginia* is now scheduled to start rehearsals Oct. 3.

If the opinion of the most revered and most senior member of the board of the American Theater Wing counts for anything, Disney's *Beauty and the Beast* will win the Tony for the best new musical over Stephen Sondheim's *Passion*.

But legendary producer, director and press agent Jean Dalrymple told me she voted to give *Beauty and the Beast* the Tony only after seeing it a second time.

"Nothing can beat *Beauty and the Beast*," Dalrymple, now 92, told me. "It's got absolutely everything. But when I first saw it, I thought it was something for kids. And I didn't know why so many people [including other Tony voters] liked it. I went back and I liked it myself. It was wonderful."

What does she think of *Passion*, which is the only other real contender?

"I loved that, too," Dalrymple said. "It's a beautiful show. And Donna Murphy is extraordinary. She will win for best actress in a musical."

But Dalrymple, a former Tony nominating committee member, agreed with other Tony voters who feel *Passion* is not truly exhilarating theater. And, in all honesty, a number of voters, who asked not to be quoted, told me they found *Passion* just plain boring.

And despite the musical's overall critical acclaim, "the boring factor," as it has been called, is a major cause of concern for a great many Tony voters. They say that, if *Passion* gets the Tony, it may send out the wrong signal to prospective theatergoers: that if they aren't too thrilled with *Passion*, they may give up on wanting to see other new Broadway musicals.

IS JACKIE MASON'S threat to sue the American Theater Wing over not letting him be a presenter or performer at the Tony Awards a genuine beef or a publicity ploy for his one-person show, *Jackie Mason: Politically Incorrect*?

Some of each, undoubtedly.

But this week's splashy press conference, in which he accused Isabelle Stevenson, powerful president of the American Theater Wing, of treating him unfairly, seems to have brought him no results. Stevenson has merely dug in her heels.

Sources say the real reason Stevenson and others don't want to have Mason as a presenter is simply because they are afraid "he's a wild card" who might embarrass either specific Tony officials or the Broadway theater in general.

PROFESSIONALLY AND PERSONALLY, Mia Farrow seems to be adjusting to life after Woody Allen just fine.

She's had one of the high points of her career with her role in the movie *Widow's Peak*. And just this week, Farrow was on Broadway briefly but very brightly for a benefit performance for the Irish Repertory Theater at the Booth Theater.

None other than Katharine Hepburn introduced the show, which was billed as "Yeats: A Celebration!" Backstage, as everyone prepared to go on stage, the dauntless Hepburn couldn't believe how beautiful Mia looked.

"Is that Mia with all that hair?" Hepburn said playfully, ruffling Farrow's shoulder-length curly blond hair.

Farrow later told me she will star in a new movie, *Reckless*, which will begin shooting in the next several months, and even said she hopes to be in a Broadway play in the not-too-distant future.

On the home front, Mia has recently been spending a lot of time with her mother, actress Maureen O'Sullivan, who just left town on Monday. "I gave her one of my poems," she said, another sign that her creative juices seem to be flowing just as freely as ever.

A close friend of the actress told me "it won't be long before she's dating again—if she isn't already."

WITH RAVE REVIEWS for her recent cabaret engagements, Mary Cleere Haran may be the best known of the performers helping celebrate the 75th anniversary of the famous Algonquin Round Table. The series begins Monday.

But it's singer Sidney Symington, grandson of Eve Symington, a popular singer of the 1920s, who has the strongest connection to the Round Table itself.

Humorist Robert Benchley used to meet regularly with Dorothy Parker, Alexander Woollcott, George S. Kaufman and other critics and playwrights around an actual round table to trade jibes and gossip. And it was Benchley who once wrote Eve Symington, "I'm so upset I missed your show. I could shoot myself and probably have!"

Actor Steve Martin has been riding his bike to and from rehearsals and performances of *WASP*, the one-act play he's written currently being performed at the Ensemble Studio Theater (EST) on West 52nd Street.

And now Martin can count on doing a little more cycling: *WASP* and the other one-acts in the production have been so successful that EST is extending their run for a few weeks beyond the original June 12 closing date.

New York Post, June 10, 1994.

☐ Faye Won't Fade Into Sunset; Webber Sued

LIKE A REAL-LIFE Norma Desmond, actress Faye Dunaway, jilted by the world's most powerful theater man, will be gunning for Andrew Lloyd Webber—in court.

"Faye's going to sue the pants off Lloyd Webber," a close friend of Dunaway's told me.

"She will be going forward with a suit against Andrew Lloyd Webber and the Really Useful Group," Bob Palmer, Dunaway's manager, told me late yesterday. "We'll have an announcement of the details either Friday [today] or Monday."

Two weeks ago, Lloyd Webber fired Dunaway, whom he had previously picked to replace Glenn Close as Norma Desmond in the Los Angeles cast of *Sunset Boulevard*, the latest Lloyd Webber mega-musical. Dunaway's singing voice wasn't right for the role, Lloyd Webber said thorough a spokesman.

While Plamer wouldn't comment on the amount Dunaway is suing Lloyd Webber for, insiders estimate that it could well be many millions of dollars.

Added to the fact that Dunaway stood to make hundreds of thousands of dollars in the role of the faded movie queen—immortalized by Gloria Swanson in the classic 1950 movie *Sunset Boulevard*—is the deep emotional pain that friends say Dunaway has suffered since she was summarily dismissed by the creator of *Cats* and *The Phantom of the Opera*.

Dunaway reportedly had not actually signed a contract before Lloyd Webber let her go and announced he would terminate the Los Angeles production of *Sunset Boulevard*. But there's little denying she had an "implied contract,"—and such word-of-mouth contracts have increasingly been upheld in the courts in recent years.

And Dunaway won't be the only Broadway performer heading to court soon. Tony Award-winning comedian Jackie Mason and his producer Jill Rosenberg told me this week they are definitely filing suit against the American Theater Wing and Isabelle Stevenson, the Wing's president.

Mel Sachs, the new attorney Mason has hired for the case, told me that "a lawsuit is in the process of being commenced on behalf of Jackie Mason in regard to his unfair treatment and exclusion from the Tony Awards."

On the eve of the Tony Awards telecast June 12, Mason held a press conference outside the theater where his current one-man show, *Jackie Mason: Politically Incorrect*, is playing. Among other things, he accused Stevenson of treating him unfairly by not even allowing him to be a presenter at this year's Tony ceremony.

And in talking to him this week, Mason again vehemently denied his planned lawsuit was "a publicity stunt" to sell more tickets.

Rosenberg told me last week that a suit had not been filed up to that time because of concern a judge might throw it out of court for being "frivolous." But this week she said sufficient legal grounds had been found to sue and "we're definitely going forward with the suit."

Next Wednesday at 11 a.m., Broadway will be rolling out the red carpet for itself and the world.

According to its organizers, the third annual free outdoor "Broadway on Broadway" concert promises to be bigger and better than last year's event, which attracted nearly 45,000 people.

Held on a 40-foot stage stretching along Broadway from 43rd to 44th Streets, this year's extravaganza celebrates current productions as well as Broadway shows playing around the world.

"It's Broadway's own musical salute to New York and all those who love the theater," says Harvey Sabinson, executive director of the League of American Theaters and Producers. "It's also a travelogue for out-of-towners to see Broadway's great numbers in one visit."

The League sponsors "Broadway on Broadway" along with the Times Square Business Improvement District.

"Broadway on Broadway" will feature numbers from *Beauty and the Beast*, *Blood Brothers*, *Carousel*, *The Who's Tommy*, as well as one from Hal Prince's new production of *Showboat*, which opens here in September. These and other numbers will be introduced by Jamie Farr (*Guys and Dolls*), Nathan Lane (*Laughter on the 23rd Floor*), Rosemary Harris (*An Inspector Calls*), and many others.

Incidentally, with all its woes, Broadway has at least this good news: Even after Wendy Wasserstein's *The Sisters Rosensweig* closes July 16, the Great White Way will still boast 22 shows. This compares to 19 last year at this time.

NO MATTER WHAT roles she plays, Loretta Swit says she's still having trouble shedding her image as Major Margaret "Hot Lips" Houlihan in the hit TV series "M*A*S*H."

"I want to be who I am but people put me in a pigeonhole," the blond bombshell told me. Swit is currently starring in a revival of the musical, *The Song of Singapore*, at the Wesport Country Playhouse.

"'M*A*S*H' was the highlight of the lives of all of us who were in it," Swit told me. "But I'm Loretta Swit, not Margaret Houlihan."

Showing just how far she'll go to get away from her Hot Lips image, Swit's set to star again in a national tour of the one-woman show, *Shirley*

Valentine. Valentine is a plain, matronly housewife. For glamorous Loretta Swit, that's got to be real acting.

WILLIAM A. HENRY 3RD, the drama critic for *Time* magazine who died last week, took more sheer enjoyment in living than anyone I ever knew. He loved theater, books, food and people with an all-consuming passion.

"I think I was born saying 'more.'" Henry once told me. We had known each other since we were young reporters in Boston.

Bill's Herculean writing feats were well known. He seemed to write *Time* cover stories with the same ease and relish as his drama reviews. But he also spent endless hours doing pro bono work for organizations such as the Theater Critics Association, New York Drama Critics Association and New Dramatists.

He was also so secure in his own journalistic genius that he took great pleasure in helping many colleagues, including myself, try and climb up rungs he had long since risen above.

If it ever comes time to name another theater after a drama critic, Bill Henry should be at the top of the list.

New York Post, July 8, 1994.

◻ New Diamond in Giant's Cap

ARTHUR MILLER and Edward Albee, two sleeping giants of the American theater, are suddenly alive and taking Broadway and off-Broadway by storm.

After a 14-year absence from the commercial Broadway theater, Miller's latest play, *Broken Glass*, starring Ron Rifkin, Amy Irving and David Dukes, opens at the Booth Theater April 24. This coming Wednesday, just before the matinee performance, Robert Whitehead, one of the play's producers, will host a celebration for the 50th anniversary of the playwright's Broadway debut.

And in an exclusive interview this week in New York, Miller revealed for the first time that Ron Silver was replaced with Dukes in *Broken Glass* because Silver "just wasn't right for the part." Silver had told *Variety* he was unhappy with the role. Miller added that Silver's departure was "sort of mutual in that we all agreed."

Set in Brooklyn in 1938, *Broken Glass* is the story of a woman (played by Irving) battling a crippling ailment, while her husband (played by Rifkin) is forced to confront his own long-hidden shame.

The husband talks of revering his wife almost like a goddess, and there are bound to be comparisons to Marilyn Monroe, who was once married to Miller. But the playwright, now 78, told me the character of the wife "has nothing to do with Marilyn. It's set 20 years before we knew each other." He added, however, that "the characters are composites of people I know," at least opening the door slightly for some speculation.

America's foremost playwright also told me that his movie *The Misfits*, which starred Monroe and the late Clark Gable, remains his favorite of the relatively few movies he has written. Miller also revealed that a deal has been struck for Kenneth Branagh to both direct and star in a movie version of Miller's play *The Crucible*, with 20th Century Fox producing it.

The box-office advance for Albee's *Three Tall Women* continues to climb through the roof of the 400-seat Promenade Theater following the announcement it won this year's Pulitzer Prize for drama and, as of mid-week, had topped $300,000, according to producer Daryl Roth.

Albee, absent from Broadway even longer than Miller, flew in from Texas Wednesday to celebrate with cast members Marian Seldes, Myra Carter and Jordan Baker. Another reason for rejoicing was Roth's formal presentation to investors of checks representing 10 percent of their investment—amazing since the play has been at the Promenade barely a week.

WHEN *FALLEN ANGEL*, the new rock 'n' roll musical starring Living Colour's Corey Glover opened at the Circle in the Square Downtown last night, there was a fallen angel of sorts in the audience.

Ivan Boesky, the notorious Wall Street financier, was there to applaud his playwright-songwriter son, Billy Boesky. No financial support, however, has been forthcoming from the former felon, production sources said.

Fallen Angel features 10 rock and roll songs, seven of which the younger Boesky wrote.

Broadway's cash registers are jingling these days. For example, Diana Rigg's *Medea* at the Plymouth smashed box office records for a straight play at a Shubert-owned theater, ringing up ticket sales of $130,000 on a single day this week. *Medea* opened April 7 and as of tomorrow the limited engagement will have 75 performances left…

FOR SIX DECADES, "Broadway Ballyhoo," Radie Harris's twice-weekly column in the *Hollywood Reporter*, was must reading for just about everyone in the entertainment industry on both coasts.

Harris doesn't write her column anymore. But, now, several book publishers are vying to publish many of her old columns along with new material about stars who were her personal friends over the years.

One story that may not be in her new book is about the late Harvard-educated Broadway producer Vinton Freedley. Harris and Freedley were lovers for 20 years and Harris tells me that one day she met Freedley's wife, who thanked her profusely for "taking such good care of Vinton. You made him so happy he didn't leave me."

New York Post, July 15, 1994.

▢ 'The Lion King' to Hit Broadway

THE LION KING may roar into Broadway.

With one eye on the phenomenal Broadway success of *Beauty and the Beast* and the other on the more than $157 million *The Lion King* has grossed in movie houses, top Disney officials are seriously considering moving Simba and friends to the Great White Way.

"We'd love to do a stage version, since it's been so well received as a movie," said Robert McTyre, vice president of Walt Disney Productions.

"It's so successful as a movie we can't ignore it. It's all animals—which makes it difficult to do. But we thought that about *Beauty and the Beast* and we didn't think we could do that, either."

Some veteran Broadway observers had reservations about whether the Disney movie's all-animal cast would translate well onstage.

But others point out Broadway is certainly no stranger to humans playing animals.

"Technically it's very possible—look at *Cats*," said George Wachtel of the League of American Theatres and Producers.

Walt Disney Attractions already has done a 20-minute live version of *The Lion King* for Disney World's Magic Kingdom.

And Disneyland in Californian stages a *Lion King* parade that has a big production number in it.

For his part, McTyre stressed that turning *The Lion King* into a full-fledged musical "isn't the highest idea on our list at the moment.

"Right now we're working on licensing the stage version of *Beauty and the Beast* internationally and rolling out companies in the United States and Canada.

Beauty and the Beast has continued to break box office records.

It continues to be the highest grossing musical on Broadway and ticket sales have soared over $700,000 in recent weeks.

In May, McTyre said that if ticket sales continued at their rate the show would recoup its entire $12 million investment by April 1995.

But ticket sales got even stronger.

'Beauty & Beast' Showtime to Be a Half-Hour Earlier

THE BROADWAY SHOW most popular with the under-5 set is getting a new curtain time.

Starting after the Labor Day weekend, evening performances of "*Beauty and the Beast*" will begin at 7:30 p.m. instead of the traditional 8 p.m. Broadway starting time.

Disney officials said the company wants to make it easier for parents to bring school-age kids to weeknight performances—and still get them up in time for school the next day.

New York Post, July 21, 1994.

(Note: Disney demanded a retraction for this story, denying it was bringing *The Lion King* to Broadway. The show opened several years later.)

🔲 Minskoff Theater Sails Into 'Sunset'

A MULTIMILLION-DOLLAR private mansion is going up on Broadway and 44th Street.

It's part of the set for Andrew Lloyd Webber's *Sunset Boulevard*, starring Glenn Close. With rehearsals starting next month, here's the first-ever sneak peek of the mammoth *Sunset* transformation now taking place inside the Minskoff Theater.

First of all, all the theater's seats have been entirely ripped out. The so-called "continental" (no aisle) seats, popular in the 1960s when the Minskoff was built, are being replaced by new plush seats with aisles.

Walking through the dust-laden lobby, you immediately see a huge plastic tube hanging from the ceiling as if it were part of a surrealistic sculpture at the Whitney Museum. Dust-strewn air is pumped out of the theater through the tube as the noise of circular saws unceasingly screams in a race against time to build suitable platforms for new seats.

On stage, 30-foot-plus thick steel girders, similar to ones used in Manhattan's skyscrapers, are piled in neat rows waiting to be fitted in place prior to the *Sunset* mansion literally "being hung" from the girders.

"The house itself weighs about 30,000 pounds," Olan Cottrill, the head carpenter for the mega-musical, told me this week.

"There's a metal superstructure under it," he said, explaining that "the outer part of it is wood but the structure underneath is metal. It's more complicated than building a house. You don't have to fly a house on- and offstage!"

The house itself—with its gargantuan winding staircase which some audience members who saw the London and Los Angeles productions of *Sunset* applauded more than the show's music—is being constructed in Washington, D.C. It will then be disassembled and shipped to New York on flatbed trucks.

All parts of the mansion and other scenery in the show have to be in place here when the "dry technicals" (the rehearsals just for the computerized scenery) begin next month. Once the bugs are worked out of all the mechanical operations, Close and company will join the set for rehearsals.

Lloyd Webber's Really Useful Co., which is producing *Sunset*, isn't saying exactly how much the set costs. But the New York production as a whole is budgeted at $13 million. So it's a pretty safe bet you might be able to buy the real thing in Beverly Hills for a price far below that of bringing Beverly Hills to Broadway.

SPEAKING OF SETS, *Show Boat* producer Garth Drabinsky told me this week that the set of *Show Boat*, which begins previews Sept. 22 will cost "eight million U.S. dollars." The set has been constructed in Canada, where labor costs are cheaper.

Friends and acquaintances of Glenn Close in the affluent New York suburb of Bedford are bursting with anticipation and curiosity about the star's Broadway showing in *Sunset*.

At the same time, this same excitement seems to be mixed with a certain degree of fear. Some of the actress's friends say they are under strict orders not to say where she lives or reveal anything about her movements.

The Bedford area is also home to Jill Clayburgh and her playwright husband, David Rabe, Christopher Reeve, and Susan Sarandon and her lover, Tim Robbins, among many other major stars. Average-sized houses here would be considered mansions elsewhere, leading some people to call Bedford "Beverly Hills East."

It was Close herself who announced to the world that she lived near Bedford when she introduced some of her local friends and neighbors in a segment of "Saturday Night Live" last year.

One of them was Asoka Galpotthawela, manager of the Shell gasoline station in Bedford. "Nobody knows where she lives," Galpotthawela told me this week.

On the other hand, residents say that Close is far from being a hermit and is often seen in and around town with her 6-year-old daughter, Annie Maude.

"You look so much like Glenn Close," an area resident told me recently about an encounter Close had with a stranger at a shop in the vicinity.

"Don't tell anybody, but I am Glenn Close!" the actress is said to have replied with a smile.

Jim Crookston, who works at Stewart's market in Bedford, and who was also on "Saturday Night Live" with Close, said he expected to go to *Sunset Boulevard* but certainly didn't expect the renowned actress to give him tickets for the new musical.

"I don't give her free groceries," Crookston told me.

BRIAN DENNEHY MAY STAR in a new Broadway production of Brian Friel's play, *Translations*, later this season. According to producer Joseph Harris, the brilliant TV and film star is only a matter of days away from signing for the lead role in the new production, which, if it's produced as planned, will be Dennehy's Broadway debut.

Translations, which was first done off-Broadway at the Manhattan Theater Club in 1981, is set in Ireland in 1833, and deals with an Irishman's attempt to save Gaelic, his native tongue, from extinction. Dennehy got raves in the play when he did it at the Abbey Theater in Dublin last year.

EVEN AFTER NINE YEARS—and with business slipping a bit—*Nunsense* is proving to be a hard "habit" to beat.

You can be certain you will begin seeing "last weeks" ads for the long-running off-Broadway musical currently starring Dody Goodman. But don't expect the Little Sisters of Hoboken, as the nuns are called in the musical, to vacate the Douglas Fairbanks Theater altogether.

Dan Goggin, the show's creator, has decided to close *Nunsense* because "business has naturally slipped a little after nine years." But when it closes Dan plans immediately to open the sequel to the show, *Nunsense II*, at the same theater. *Nunsense II* actually started performances on the road two years ago and has already racked up an incredible $12 million in ticket sales.

Meanwhile, the original *Nunsense*, which opened in December 1986, has spawned over 400 companies and become the longest-running off-Broadway show next to *The Fantasticks*.

PERFECT CRIME, the mystery thriller which is currently off-Broadway's fourth-longest running show, celebrates its 3,000th performance a week from tomorrow. Earlier this year, *Perfect Crime* moved to the Duffy Theater, a former burlesque house across from the TKTS booth in Duffy Square, where it has been doing brisk business.

But some people are still coming to the theater expecting quite a different kettle of fish from the understated acting in the mystery thriller. Are they ever surprised when they find out this cast keeps its clothes on.

Tony Kushner's *Angels in America* may not close Labor Day weekend as its producers announced last month. A sharp increase in box-office receipts—caused in part by people who have wanted to finally see the two-part Tony Award-winning epic before it closes—has prompted *Angels* producers to consider keeping the show open through fall, if not longer.

New York Post, August 15, 1994.

◻ Tune's Fair Lady

MELISSA ERRICO, who as flower girl Eliza Doolittle was Broadway's latest *My Fair Lady*, is starring with Tommy Tune in Barry and Fran Weissler's $6 million production of the new musical *Busker Alley*.

Without knowing Errico had landed the job, I went to a rehearsal of a workshop production of *Busker Alley* this week and couldn't believe my ears.

As I stood in back of the crimson-and-gilt Nederlander Theater and heard one of the characters sing the line, "It takes a bit of getting' used to you," it sounded like Errico. Getting a better look at the young woman with long dark hair and dressed in a low-plunging leotard, I knew it was one and the same.

The six-week workshop at the Nederlander continues to the middle of next month, after which the musical will go on the road prior to coming to Broadway. And harmony seemed to be the order of the workshop—at least when I saw it.

"A more loving company would be hard to imagine," actor Drew Eliot, one of the *Busker* cast members, told me. "We're one family."

And producer Fran Weissler told me "some things are looking too good and you say to yourself, 'Oh, my God. So it really is looking wonderful.' But we've only had 12 days of rehearsing a brand-new show and it's too soon to tell."

Jeff Calhoun, who directed *Grease*, is directing *Busker*, the story of London's street singers before World War II. And as for Tune, "starring in it—that's his [only] role," Fran Weissler said. "We really have a great relationship with Tommy that Barry and I treasure. This is our fourth show together."

Jazz Show Boat, now in its third week at Michael's Pub, has a new addition. Joining singer Gail Wynters in jazz renditions of some of the hits from the Kern-Hammerstein *Show Boat* score is the brilliant pianist Frank Owens. Owens co-produced Lena Horne's new hit CD, "We'll Be Together Again"—a sure bet for the Grammys this year. (Then, again, Horne herself had once been a sure bet to star in the last movie version of *Show Boat*. Ava Gardner got the role instead.)

Owens is well known to Broadway audiences for his work in *Ain't Misbehavin'* and *Sophisticated Ladies* and as the accompanist for Petula Clark (soon going on a national tour of *Blood Brothers*), Johnny Mathis, as well as the incomparable Horne.

THE LEGAL "HONEYMOON" between actress Faye Dunaway and impresario Andrew Lloyd Webber may soon be over.

The behind-the-scenes legal maneuvering between the lawyers for Dunaway and Lloyd Webber appears headed for trial in open court.

And if it does, the opening of Lloyd Webber's scandal-splotched musical *Sunset Boulevard* could pale by comparison.

Who'll Emerge 'Victor'-ious?

Broadway is buzzing about Julie Andrews returning to the Great White Way in a Blake Edwards stage version of her hit movie *Victor/Victoria*. But the biggest question is who Andrews' love interest will be. James Garner played it in the movie.

There's even wild speculation that producers are trying to lure Robert Redford back to Broadway. But there's no official word from anyone connected with the show.

"It's only August!" Peter Cromarty, the show's publicist, said.

With music by the late Henry Mancini, *Victor/Victoria* is scheduled to go into rehearsals around November and open first in Boston in February. It's due here in March.

New York Post, August 19, 1994.

🞎 B'way Gets in Shipshape

Lavish revival might just be
the theater hit of the decade

Show Boat fever is steaming onto Broadway.

Having racked up the biggest advance ticket sale for any revival in Broadway history—and with celebrities ranging from Israeli Prime Minister Shimon Peres to Monaco's Prince Albert showing up at the Gershwin Theater—the blockbuster revival of *Show Boat*, which opens Sunday, promises to be the biggest theatrical event of the decade.

At least until Andrew Lloyd Webber's *Sunset Boulevard* opens the very next month—on November 17.

One thing's for sure, though: Hal Prince's blockbuster revival of the 1927 Jerome Kern-Oscar Hammerstein III musical will set new standards for grandeur that could well earn it the title of Broadway's *Gone With the Wind* for many years to come.

With more actors than any previous Broadway musical, 73, wearing more costumes than ever, 500; and with more than 50 scene changes over a span of five generations, no Broadway musical has ever matched the size and scope of *Show Boat*. Even the musical's orchestra has 31 musicians, 25 percent more than most big Broadway musicals. And with more than 800 lights—Broadway lighting high water mark—the production will try and create the illusion that the steamboat *Cotton Blossom* is floating down the mighty Mississippi.

Even its ticket prices are bigger—$75 for a top orchestra seat (*Miss Saigon* actually started out with a higher $100 top seat but subsequently scaled it back to $65. The top *Sunset Boulevard* ticket is $70.) The musical's advance ticket sale, meanwhile, is over $12 million, a bigger advance for any revival in Broadway history.

However, the show's budget of approximately $8.5 million, is well under the roughly $12 million that *Beauty and the Beast* and *Sunset Boulevard* each cost to mount.

Now, rewritten and restaged and recast, the new *Show Boat* is drawing heavily upon the genius of Hal Prince, widely considered America's greatest theater director. As such, this production of *Show Boat* has also done something no other revival has ever done on such a grand scale. Aside from its basic plot and score, Prince's revival, or as he prefers to call it, "re-creation," is a veritable collage of what he considers the best of the musical's earlier Broadway productions and three film versions.

For example, the brooding spiritual, "Mis'ry's Comin' Around," was deleted from the original 1927 version during out-of-town tryouts. But the reintroduction of "Mis'ry," coupled with many other attempts to bolster the musical's innate realism, have added a completely new dimension to *Show Boat* that breaks the bonds of mere bigness.

Show Boat producer Garth Drabinsky and Prince both decided from the very start of their collaboration in 1988 that "gritty realism" would be at the very heart and soul of the show.

"We didn't want to do just another revival," Prince told me. "We wanted the characters to be real people.

New York Post, September 29, 1994.

◻ It's in the 'Wind'

ONCE AGAIN, Tony Randall's National Actors Theater is turning to both classics and established stars for its new Broadway season at the Lyceum Theater.

And while NAT's fourth season isn't set in stone, Randall has his heart set on doing a revival of *Inherit the Wind*, the blistering 1955 drama based on the 1925 Scopes "monkey" trial.

The National Actors Theater is also seriously wooing Helen Mirren, star of the hit PBS series, *Prime Suspect*, to re-create her London triumph in Ivan Turgenev's *A Month in the Country*.

In an exclusive interview, Randall, NAT's artistic director as well as its president, said that "I want to do *Inherit the Wind* very, very much. I've put a deal together twice now to do it. Twice it sort of fell through. It's such a big production as far as actors (around 40) that I want to do a co-production.

"So I tried to put it together with other theaters and we were almost there and I thought we were going to announce it and each time it fell through," he continued. "But I'm going to do it yet!

"The first play is going to be in December. I'm still juggling things."

The strong possibility that the theater will produce *Inherit the Wind* this season seems even stronger since recent fund-raising efforts are paying off handsomely. For example, ticket sales for the theater's annual benefit at the Pierre Hotel Oct. 4 are already approaching the half-million dollar mark.

"The benefit has been very successful," said Fred Walker, the theater's managing director. "We've had a great response to it, which we're thrilled about."

Among other celebrities, David Letterman is scheduled to attend the gala and do a special "top 10 list." Randall has been a frequent surprise guest on Letterman's "Late Show."

Paul Muni, Ed Begley and Tony Randall starred in the original production of *Inherit the Wind*, which was based on the real-life courtroom drama between William Jennings Bryan and Clarence Darrow and their battle about the origins of man. Randall played an obnoxious young reporter loosely based on journalist H.L. Mencken, who covered the case as a young man. Stanley Kramer directed the 1960 movie version starring Spencer Tracy and Fredric March. Gene Kelly, playing against type, got Randall's role.

Judy Kaye, who won a Tony for Best Supporting Actress in Andrew Lloyd Webber's *Phantom of the Opera*, has become yet another possible Glenn Close replacement in Lloyd Webber's *Sunset Boulevard*.

And like Chita Rivera, Kaye told me she's also discussing the possibility of starring in the Toronto premiere of *Sunset*, set for October 1995, and being co-produced by Garth Drabinsky, the producer of *Show Boat*.

Close's contract calls for her to be in the Broadway production of *Sunset* for nine months.

Kaye herself will be honored as one of "The Leading Ladies of Broadway" at a gala for Musical Theater Works Oct. 3. In the past decade, MTW has produced 36 world premieres of new musicals.

Cy Feuer, veteran producer and the president of the American League of Theaters and Producers, says what Broadway needs most is more new material—not just more revivals.

"We can't keep on looking forward to what we used to do," he said. "Young people have to take it forward."

On Monday, Oct. 3, the United Jewish Appeal will honor Feuer and his longtime producing partner Ernie Martin with its Lifetime Achievement Award at a celebrity gala at the Pierre Hotel.

Feuer and Martin produced the original productions of *Guys and Dolls*, *Can-Can* and *How to Succeed in Business Without Really Trying*. Matthew Broderick will star in *How to Succeed* this spring—one revival Feuer admitted he's excited about.

'Passion' Days Are Cooling?

DESPITE AN AGGRESSIVE new TV advertising campaign, a growing number of Broadway insiders say the days are growing short for Stephen Sondheim's *Passion*. Some don't expect it to last much past the holidays.

But Gerald Schoenfeld, chairman of the Shubert Organization, one of the producers of Passion, said that he expects it to last "Much longer" and well into the new year. And other Shubert executives say that the new TV ad campaign is beginning to have a positive impact on the box office.

If that happens, it'll be none too soon. Receipts have recently hovered just over 50 percent capacity, according to *Variety* figures. And at that level, *Passion*, which swept 10 Tony Awards last June, is doing worse than any other musical on Broadway.

The show's major problem seems to be a lack of good word-of-mouth, necessary for any show's long-term success. And, apparently, theater party business, an increasingly important part of Broadway ticket sales, could be better if it wasn't for what some consider the musical's gratuitous nudity.

New York Post, September 30, 1994.

◻ Throwing in Towel

AN AGE-OLD Broadway tradition, matronly attendants in ladies' rest rooms has now become a thing of the past in many theaters.

Actually, only the mammoth Shubert Organization, Broadway's biggest theater owner-operator, has let all the matrons go at its nine occupied theaters, including the Winter Garden, where the immensely profitable *Cats* is now in its 12th year.

Under a new contract with Local 54, the League of American Theaters and Producers, the bargaining agent for all the theater owners, won theater owners the right to terminate all their rest room matrons. The Nederlander Organization, the second largest theater owner, has opted to keep its matrons while the Jujamcyn Theaters (the third largest Broadway theater group) has kept two of six matron jobs.

"It's got to hurt Broadway," said Howard Chaiken, president of Local 54 of the Service Employees International Union (SEIU), AFL-CIO.

"My hope is that they are going to get so many complaints in the ladies' rooms from those who pay good money to see a show that the theater owners will have to hire them back," Chaiken added.

Harriet Slaughter, a labor negotiator for the League, said a primary reason for letting the matrons go is cost.

"You don't want the ticket price to go up, do you?" she asked.

But ticket prices are headed up anyway. One need look no farther than *Show Boat* and *Sunset Boulevard* with top prices of $75 and $70, respectively. And some insiders say the matrons' salaries represent only a small part of the multimillion-dollar costs of owning and operating legitimate theaters these days.

"They claim it's too costly and a luxury they can't afford," Chaiken explained.

But "sheer greed" is how another insider described the situation.

"It's disgraceful," said an usher in one of the Shubert theaters. "They've picked on people least able to fight back."

Four of the eight matrons who used to work in Shubert houses have found other types of jobs in the Broadway theater community. All of them were given severance pay—$300 for each year worked. Some had been matrons for decades.

IN A BID TO BRING attention to *First Night*, the struggling new romantic comedy at the Westside Theater, producers Scottie Held and Anne Baker are sponsoring a contest to find the most romantic couple in New York.

Contestants are being asked to write a 200-words-or-less explanation of why they are the most romantic couple. They are also being asked to check off three names on a special "made for each other" list. This list includes Warren Beatty and Annette Bening and The Donald and Marla.

First prize is a New York hotel and theater weekend, and a "Love Scope" forecast by Arlene Dahl, one of the contest judges. Winners will be announced Nov. 11.

Pacino Comes Full Circle

CIRCLE IN THE SQUARE producer Ted Mann is going after even bigger fish than Mercedes Ruehl and Academy Award winner Estelle Parsons (who will star in his theater's coming revival of Michael Christopher's 1977 Pulitzer Price-winning play, *The Shadowbox*, opening Nov. 20).

"We have been speaking to Al Pacino about a project, but that won't be ready for at least a year," Mann said.

Circle, a Broadway house, will reopen when previews for *The Shadowbox* begin Nov. 4. Budget and other problems have kept the famed theater dark for the last several years.

Pacino had first starred in two one-act plays, *Salome* and *Chinese Coffee*, at the Circle in the Square before taking the plays elsewhere.

Woody or Would He Not?

SOME ACTORS' AGENTS have been scratching their heads over a casting notice for a new one-act play by Woody Allen which will be produced off-Broadway in February at the Variety Arts Theater.

Julian Schlossberg is producing Allen's *Central Park West* along with new one-acts by David Mamet and Elaine May.

The casting notice says that the lead woman in *Central Park West* should be 40 to 50, "a bit dizzy" and "very sexual."

Some say this might well apply to characters that Mia Farrow, Allen's ex-gal pal, played in his movies.

But the notice goes on to describe the character as being "Jap-ish" (for the not-very-politically correct Jewish American princess) and like "Marlo Thomas."

Tickets Scarce for Really Big 'Show'

SHOW BOAT, which opened Sunday to resounding rave reviews, is sending shock waves along the Rialto.

Opening with a $12 million advance—the biggest ever for a Broadway revival—he advance has grown steadily every day this week with longer and longer lines at the box office of the Gershwin Theater, according to a spokesman for producer Garth Drabinsky. In short, *Show Boat* has become the hottest ticket in town. Just try to get seats for the next several months.

And like heaving a boulder into a small pond, *Show Boat* seems to have blasted the Broadway theater out of its post-Labor Day doldrums. But over the long haul, *Show Boat*'s ripple effect might also have a detrimental impact on older, struggling musicals such as *Passion*.

"When you have a great new show like *Show Boat*, the total number of people going to Broadway shows skyrockets," said George Wachtel, director of research for the League of American Theaters and Producers. "Theatergoers who have waited to see a new musical come to Broadway again. But a few shows which have been around for some time might be hurt in the long run."

New York Post, October 7, 1994.

◻ Broadway

FOLLOWING A RECENT exclusive Post revelation that Disney's *Lion King* may be Broadway-bound, here's a show that's coming in like a lamb.

Shari Lewis and Lamb Chop are headed to the Great White Way.

"Broadway needs a holiday show for children and Lamb Chop fits the bill and appeals to kids and adults alike," producer Jimmy Nederlander Jr. told me. "I'm planning to make this the first of special holiday children's shows on Broadway every year."

Shari Lewis and Lamb Chop on Broadway will open Dec. 8 for an initial one-week run at one of the Nederlander-operated theaters on Broadway.

Lamb Chop is joining an evermore crowded field: Nickelodeon and Dodger Productions announced earlier this week that they would present a new stage musical adaptation of Charles Dickens' *A Christmas Carol* at the Paramount Theater in December. This will compete for the kids' market against Radio City Music Hall's "Christmas Spectacular" and Disney's *Beauty and the Beast*.

Rock 'n' roll appears here to stay on Broadway. Beginning in February, a new rock 'n' roll show recently renamed *Smokey Joe's Cafů*, will join *Grease* and *Tommy* on the Great White Way. With words and music by rock 'n' roll legends Jerry Lieber and Mike Stoller, *Smokey Joe's* opens at the Doolittle in Los Angeles Nov. 17 and begins previews on Broadway Feb. 10. Among many others, Lieber and Stoller wrote "Love Potion No. 9" and Elvis Presley's "Hound Dog."

The New York producers of the show, formerly called *Baby, That's Rock 'n' Roll*, include Tom Viertel and Steve Baruch and Richard Frankel Productions.

CATS JUST KEEPS ON purring along. The longest-running show currently on Broadway celebrated its 5,000[th] performance Sept. 28. The musical is also the third longest-running production in Broadway history.

To celebrate, the Shubert Organization and the other producers of *Cats*, invited children who normally wouldn't get to see the show. Up to 1,000 kids from Big Brothers/Big Sisters of New York City, The New York State Mentoring Program and The Boys Club of New York were treated to the Sept. 28 Wednesday matinee.

Cats celebrated 12 years on Broadway Oct. 7, when it began its 13th year. And original cast members Marlene Danielle and Susan Powers are still here.

The rivalry between the $12 million production of *Sunset Boulevard* and the more than $8 million revival of *Show Boat* spilled over into a battle of the blockbuster first-night parties.

Show Boat producer Garth Drabinsky virtually booked the entire first floor "Banquet Level" of the Plaza Hotel for 1,800 guests for the musical's opening night party Oct. 2. This includes the Plaza's ornate gilded ballroom and huge adjoining suites. Broadway first-nighters and other VIPs were sent special gold-embossed invitations.

Not to be outdone, Andrew Lloyd Webber is casting about for equally opulent space for his opening night party for *Sunset Boulevard* on Nov. 17.

But the Plaza is definitely out of the running, because according to Harvey, Lloyd Webber's party planners "wanted a sit-down dinner for 1,200, which we were unable to do. The ballroom will only accommodate a sit-down for 500."

Asked why the guest list for *Sunset* seemed to be far smaller than that for *Show Boat*, one Broadway insider quipped: "Lloyd Webber's not inviting the press!"

"And the ex-Norma Desmonds whom he's fired," said another.

One Broadway insider said Lloyd Webber had personally nixed the idea of having his party in the grand ballroom of Broadway's Marriott Marquis (in the next block from the Minksoff Theater, where *Sunset* will be performing) because he thought it was "too shabby." But Adrian Bryan-Brown, the New York press representative for *Sunset*, said he very seriously doubted this was true and that, in fact, the grand ballroom of the Marriott Marquis, where the annual Tony Awards ball has been held in recent years, was already booked on Nov. 17.

Thousand Islands Sun, October 12, 1994.

◻ Will Jerry Raise Devil?

THE PRODUCERS of *Damn Yankees* are in negotiations with a major star to replace Tony Award nominee Victor Garber as the devil. Garber is leaving the cast of the Broadway show after the holidays.

Sources say that comedian Jerry Lewis is one of the top contenders to play the flamboyant role in what would be his Broadway debut. *Damn Yankees* producers would neither confirm nor deny the report.

Insiders say the choice of a star like Lewis, coupled with the growing popularity of Tony nominee Charlotte D'Amboise (for *Jerome Robbins' Broadway*) as Lola, the devil's sexy foil, could add to the momentum which has been building for the show. The revival, which opened last March, already has its biggest advance since last May, about $2 million.

Over the past two decades, Lewis, who broke into show business on the Borscht Belt circuit in the 1940s, has been much more closely associated with his popular Muscular Dystrophy Association telethons than with movie or TV features. But insiders say his international name recognition and his often dizzyingly impish humor could be just the right combination for a winning *Damn Yankees* team.

"Our business is very, very strong throughout the end of the year," Mitchell Maxwell, the lead producer for *Damn Yankees* said. "But, as you know, *Carousel* is closing in January and everyone is concerned about making it through the traditionally leaner months of January and February. So with Victor leaving after the holidays we will be seriously talking to a major star for the devil."

D'Amboise, who took over the role of Lola from Bebe Neuwirth in September, has been getting standing ovations at almost every show. But it's no secret some potential ticket buyers are less familiar with her than they were with Neuwirth, who was a fixture on "Cheers." And for the past two months, several other *Damn Yankees* producers have been pressing Maxwell to team a major star with D'Amboise.

"Broadway used to be about making stars," Maxwell said. "And I think we have a star in the making with Charlotte. But, now, we're also going for a recognizable name."

Lewis teamed up with Dean Martin in 1946 and they became one of the hottest entertainment acts in the country. A decade later, Lewis went his own way and starred in a string of hit movies such as *The Nutty Professor* and *The Geisha Boy*. While his movie popularity has waned here at home, Lewis is still widely regarded as a major star in Europe, and especially France, where he was awarded the Legion of Merit.

Caruso Rumored to Inherit 'Heiress'

The Lincoln Center Theater will produce a gritty new revival of the classic play, The Heiress, (originally suggested by Henry James' novel, Washington Square) at the Cort Theater in March, The Post has learned.

The play's first Broadway production in 1947 starred Basil Rathbone and Wendy Hiller. In the subsequent movie, Olivia de Havilland played the title role and the late Montgomery Clift was catapulted to superstar status as her darkly flamboyant, engaging and ne'er-do-well suitor.

Sources say the play hasn't been cast. But one report along the Rialto has linked former "NYPD Blue" star David Caruso, who wants to do Broadway anyway, with the Clift role.

Still Standing "Tall'

Now in its ninth hit month off-Broadway, Edward Albee's Pulitzer Prize-winning play *Three Tall Women* remains one of the most-sought-after tickets in New York, has a huge (for off-Broadway) $300,000 advance, and continues to draw major celebrities like bees to a honeycomb.

But despite recurring interest in bringing it to Broadway, producers Elizabeth McCann, Daryl Roth and Jeffrey Ash plan to keep *Women* right where it is.

"We're delighted being where we are," Ash said. "I produced *Other People's Money* and had a lot of offers to take it to Broadway. Even Donald Trump wanted to move it. But we sold out almost every night off-Broadway for 990 performances."

In recent weeks, Tom Cruise and his wife, Nicole Kidman, Meryl Streep, Faye Dunaway, Stephen Sondheim, Christopher Walken and "NYDP Blue" star Sharon Lawrence have trekked to the Promenade Theater.

Barely a month after it opened, there seems little doubt that Hal Prince's revival of *Show Boat* will be one of Broadway's top critical and box office smash-hits of the decade.

Not to be outdone, Andrew Lloyd Webber's *Sunset Boulevard*, starring Glenn Close, had its first public performance at the Minskoff Theater Tuesday. And the latest musical in town is already winning raves and varying degrees of respect from the theater-goers who've seen it.

"It's fantastic," said fashion designer Adolpho, who was in the star-studded audience Wednesday evening. "I'm coming again—once is not enough...Glenn Close is more than sensational!"

But well-known New York socialite Patsy Patterson said Close "Tried too hard, somehow overacting—but she's fascinating. Gloria Swanson [who starred in the original Billy Wilder movie] was sort of cool about it. She played the perfect movie star."

Joan Rivers said, "I like it. I'm happy to be seeing it, but I'm a cheap date." Broadway ticket broker Al Spitainy said it's not "a classic" like *Show Boat*, but "in some ways the music is better" than music in other Lloyd Webber shows.

SINGER/SONGWRITER Amanda McBroom, best known for writing the song "The Rose," will be the first singer ever to record a live album at Rainbow and Stars. McBroom, who's currently headlining at the nightspot, will record the album live on Nov. 9 and the DRG Records CD will simply be called "Amanda McBroom: Live From Rainbow and Stars."

COHEN'S 'COMEDY' IS COMING

ALEXANDER H. COHEN, the legendary producer who has been recurrent in the New York theater ever since 1941, may well begin to turn back the pages of Broadway history in more ways than one when he and Max Cooper present their new musical revue, *Comedy Tonight*, starring Dorothy Loudon, Mort Sahl and Michael Davis. Preview performances begin Dec. 14.

Cohen says that *Comedy Tonight* will just be the first of a whole new series of reviews he plans to produce that have their genesis in his old "Nine O'Clock Theater" series. This became 10 successive Broadway revues, including *An Evening With Mike Nichols and Elaine May* and Victor Borge's *Comedy in Music*.

"When *Comedy Tonight* eventually closes—and I hope it will be a long, long time from now—I'll present another revue at the same theater [the Lunt-Fontanne] with other stars just as I did in the 'Nine O'Clock Theater,'" Cohen said.

New York Post, November 4, 1994.

▣ Jerry Pitches for 'Yankees'

IN A MOVE THAT even took many theater insiders by surprise, *Damn Yankees* will take a two-month break starting Dec. 31 to avoid the traditional winter box-office blues and rehearse Jerry Lewis, who will make his Broadway debut as "the devil."

It's too early to tell whether other Broadway shows might follow suit.

But industry sources say this much seems certain now: The hiatus and addition of Jerry Lewis are almost certain to help turn "*Damn Yankees*," which opened last March, into a solid financial success. And in the larger picture, the concessions the producers obtained from the theatrical unions could signal a whole new spirit of cooperation between producers and the unions.

Post Plus was first to report on Nov. 4 that there was a very good chance that legendary comedian and film star Lewis would replace Victor Garber as "the devil" after Garber left the cast of the musical in January. The part would be Lewis's first on the Great White Way.

"We feel this opportunity will enable our show, as well as many shows in the future, to circumvent the seasonal downward box-office trend and survive what can be an irreversible financial hardship for any Broadway producer," said principal *Damn Yankees* producer Mitchell Maxwell.

"The hiatus has become reality through the enormous cooperation generously given by all the union and professional associates involved with our production," he added.

Harvey Sabinson, executive director of the League of American Theaters and Producers, said that the *Damn Yankees* agreement "shows some flexibility" on unions' part.

"But I don't think it's a trend," he added, explaining that in the past unions have agreed, under isolated circumstances, to make concessions and permit a show to suspend performances for a limited period of time. This happened, he said, when Dustin Hoffman was doing *Death of a Salesman* in the mid-1980s.

Maxwell and his partners reached the agreement to shut down *Damn Yankees* for the two worst months for Broadway attendance with Local One (Stagehands) of the International Alliance of Stage Employees (LATSE), Local 802 of the American Federation of Musicians and other theatrical unions.

Traditionally, there has been a great deal of friction between a number of Broadway producers and the unions over the issues of work rules as well as salaries.

In fact, many producers have felt that Broadway would face a major strike when Local One's contract is up next July.

Manny Azenberg, Neil Simon's producer, said as painful as it might be, a major shutdown of the industry may well be necessary to adequately address problems that have been compounded over many years.

Azenberg plans to produce Simon's latest play, *London Suite*, Off-Broadway this spring for far less money than it would take to do it on Broadway. He said *London Suite* can be produced for $600,000 off-Broadway compared to $1.6 million or $1.8 million on Broadway.

Everyone's focused on the stagehands, and that's an issue, but it's the totality of the number that's the problem," Azenberg said.

Alan Myers, one of the business agents of Local One, refused to speculate whether work rules or salary differences might precipitate a strike.

"When we get to the bargaining table we'll talk about what's on the table," he said.

Myers also stressed that his local is as concerned about not having enough plays on Broadway as the producers or anyone else in the ailing industry. "We want as much theater as possible," he said.

New York Post, December 8, 1994.

◻ The New Norma

"OF COURSE, I'M NERVOUS. I always have butterflies before an opening. But I'm nervous for a different sort of reason than you might think. I want people to love the show—it's that kind of nervousness.

"And I'm also under a great deal of more pressure in this situation than I usually am when I perform because people's expectations are so huge about this show and their feelings about Norma Desmond."

So said a dog-tired but suddenly radiant-looking Betty Buckley, her huge eyes sparkling and her finely chiseled cheekbones glistening in the afternoon sunlight streaking into the lounge of a Times Square hotel.

After all, Buckley, 48—who first fell in love with the Broadway theater back in her native Fort Worth, Texas, when she saw a production of *Pajama Game* when she was just 11 years old—has been waiting a professional lifetime for her own close-up in what she calls "the most spectacular role of all."

Fresh from her year-long triumph in London where she replaced Patti Lupone as the faded silent-screen giant in Andrew Lloyd Webber's musical stage version of Billy Wilder's classic 1950 movie, *Sunset Boulevard*, the last few days have been a whirlwind of recordings, costume fittings, interviews—and more recordings.

Even *Sunset Boulevard*'s musical director David Caddick told me Buckley's done the equivalent of six shows in the past two days recording a new album of the show which will be sold at the theater.

Buckley, who has her first dress rehearsal today, said "I've had to make my peace with a role which everyone has their own expectations about. I want to provide them with a silhouette. But I believe I have a responsibility to share my feelings [with the audience] about Norma Desmond. "At the heart of it all, it's a love story," Buckley said. "And the audience has to feel that."

A number of London reviewers certainly did and, to be sure, Buckley got unanimous raves for every aspect of her West End performance as an actress as well as a singer.

Nor is she scared of comparisons to superstar Close. "It's been demonstrated there's room in the world for many interpretations of Norma Desmond," Buckley said. "So I'm not so intimidated by my predecessors. I admire them all very much. Patti and Glenn and Elaine Paige, who took over for me. And the understudies whom I've seen as well. Everyone has been just wonderful. The only Norma Desmond I haven't seen is mine. But it feels right."

Buckley made her Broadway debut in the musical *1776* 26 years ago in 1969. She won the 1982 Tony Award as Best Featured Actress in a musical for the role of "Grizabella" in *Cats*. She also starred in Lloyd Webber's 1985 musical *Song & Dance*.

She followed Bernadette Peters into *Song and Dance* and that musical, which had been a hit with Peters in it, closed relatively soon after Buckley took over. But, then again, *Song and Dance* was not nearly the hit that *Sunset Boulevard* has become.

"Glenn Close gives a performance that one can greatly admire but Betty Buckley really makes you care about Norma Desmond," says producer Timothy Childs.

Meanwhile, other veteran Broadway observers say they believe Buckley may be so well received that the musical, which opened with the largest ticket sale advance in Broadway history (estimated at more than $40 million), may well continue to soar to new box office heights.

"I don't want to denigrate Glenn Close in any way but having seen Buckley in London she is the ultimate person to play that role," said a well-known Lloyd Webber associate. "She is spectacular."

Patti LuPone reportedly received a settlement of close to $1 million after Lloyd Webber picked Close instead of her to be in the Broadway production. LuPone's contract stipulated that she would open Broadway.

Faye Dunaway was hired to replace Close in the Los Angeles production of the musical but was subsequently fired because Lloyd Webber said she couldn't sing well enough. Dunaway filed a $6 million lawsuit against Lloyd Webber and his Really Useful Company alleging that she was used as a scapegoat for closing a financially ailing show. She and Lloyd Webber subsequently reached an out-of-court settlement in January and a source close to the litigation said Dunaway pocketed more than $1 million.

New York Post, June 29, 1995.

◻ Second Siege Underway in Battle of B'way

Merrick Claims Tony's Are Un-'Fair'

The Battle of Broadway opened a second front yesterday, as the producers of *State Fair* prepared to launch a blue-ribbon blitzkrieg at the shell-shocked Tony Awards.

Legendary producer David Merrick threatened a suit that—along with Julie Andrews' decision last week to decline her nomination—promises to turn next month's televised awards ceremonies into a grand night for bickering.

In an angry letter to the Tony Administration Committee, Merrick complained that 11 Rodgers and Hammerstein songs in *State Fair*—most of the show's score—were disqualified because they were lifted from the movie or other stage productions.

Only four songs from the show were allowed consideration for Best Original Score, he noted.

Merrick argued that the entire score from *Beauty and the Beast* qualified when it was up for nominations a couple of years ago—though some of its hit songs also were in the movie version.

"Partial scores obviously cannot compete with entire scores," Merrick wrote. "This is not fair competition! The Tony committee has a duty to see that justice is done."

Merrick said he might be "forced to take legal action if we cannot resolve this quickly and amicably."

Sources said Merrick could ultimately try to get an injunction to stop the June 2 Tony telecast. But a spokeswoman for *State Fair*, Susan Schulman, said there's been no decision on what action to take.

A spokesman for the Tonys, Keith Sherman, noted that the rules have been "amended" since *Beauty and the Beast*.

Now, he explained, songs in Broadway plays cannot be considered for Tonys if they were taken directly from movies.

"We believe they've been fairly treated and we think this is a closed issue," Sherman said.

But Schulman angrily asserted: "The issue is not the nomination but the rules that were changed in midstream!"

The flap is the latest scandal to beset the Tonys.

Last week, *Victor/Victoria* star Julie Andrews withdrew her nomination because she was disgusted that her commercially successful show received so few other nominations.

The other commercial hit on Broadway, *Big*, also failed to win the fancy of the nominations committee.

Instead, the committee weighed in favor of two closed shows and two newcomers with decidedly more urban themes, *Rent*, and *Bring in da Noise, Bring in da Funk*.

"The outrage of the general public and the upheaval within the theatrical industry caused by this year's Tony nominations has definitely undermined the dignity and prestige of this year's Tony Awards," Merrick said in his angry letter.

Victor/Victoria producer Tony Adams said he was not informed of the rules change that could have disqualified some songs from the show—though *Victor/Victoria* did not receive a Tony nomination for its score.

Some Broadway insiders say the latest flap smacks of a publicity stunt.

State Fair hasn't been doing well at the box office in the past two weeks. According to *Variety*, tickets were down last week to $189,609. The previous week's sales grossed $202,879, and for the week before that, $269,846.

Break-even is considered $310,000, sources said.

New York Post, May 15, 1996.

◻ New Queen of 'Victoria'

THE BROADWAY THEATER, often shockingly inept since the fall, took on new vitality last night when Raquel Welch gave her first public performance as Julie Andrews' replacement in the gender-bending smash-hit musical *Victor/Victoria*.

Welch's *Victor/Victoria* was as enormously engaging as unexpectedly polished, according to a cross-section of audience members at the Marquis Theater last night.

"Raquel was surprisingly good," said Judi McMahon, a New York skin-care specialist.

"And as for looks—forget about it! Who wouldn't want to look like that," McMahon added.

And from the moment the curtain went up on Paris by night in the 1930s, when the statuesque actress, sporting a curly red wig and purple coat, stepped on stage as a down-on-her-luck cabaret entertainer, Welch had the audience eating out of her hand.

Welch first captured public attention 31 years ago as the half-naked cave girl fighting prehistoric beasts in the sci-fi thriller *One Million Years B.C.*

She made her Broadway debut in 1983, replacing Lauren Bacall in *Woman of the Year*, where she broke attendance records at the Palace Theater.

And if last night's overwhelmingly enthusiastic final-curtain standing ovation was any indication of how she was going to do this time around on the Great White Way, *Victor/Victoria* is victorious still.

Welch was particularly enchanting to last night's theatergoers in the show's big production numbers like "Le Jazz Hot," which turned West 45th Street into Las Vegas East. And as to whether she's convincing as a woman playing a man playing a woman, nobody seemed to care.

"She's too beautiful to be a man," commented one audience member, "But you don't hear me complaining."

"All the hard work she did at rehearsals seems to have paid off," said co-producer Tony Adams, who was nervously standing at the rear of the Marquis Theater eyeing her every movement.

"The audience loves her," Adams added.

But the biggest compliment of the night may have come from director Blake Edwards, who wrote the story, or "book," for the stage show, which is based on his hit 1982 movie of the same name. Insiders say Edwards and Welch had often "had words" about his direction of her in the show.

"But Blake rushed to try and be the first to greet Raquel backstage," said one production insider.

"He was bedazzled."

New York Post, June 11, 1997.

▢ 'Freak' Streak to B'way

JOHN LEGUIZAMO'S HIT off-off-Broadway one-man show *Freak* is coming to Broadway as early as Christmas, *Post* Plus has learned.

Subtitled "A Semi-Demi-Quasi-Autobiographical Comedy," and co-authored by David Bar Katz, *Freak* is about what it was like for Leguizamo to grow up as a Latino in Queens. In the show, he plays everyone from his first girlfriend to a WASAP do-gooder.

Freak will be the TV and movie actor's Broadway debut.

The show, which recently wound up a sold-out engagement at PS 122, begins performances off-Broadway on Tuesday at the Atlantic Theater on West 20th Street. It's slated to run there through Oct. 18.

"After this, the plan is to open at a small Broadway theater around Christmas," a production insider told *Post* Plus yesterday.

"We think it will be the most electric solo show since Whoopi Goldberg took Broadway by storm at the Lyceum Theater in 1984," said a major backer of the show.

Leguizamo is no stranger to off-Broadway. Six years ago, his *Mambo Mouth* was a big hit and he followed it with the equally successful *Spic-O-Rama*.

On TV, he co-starred in Fox's "House of Buggin'" and played a whole host of film roles, including Chi Chi Rodriguez in *To Wong Foo, Thanks for Everything, Julie Newmar*.

Broadway theaters being considered for *Freak* include the Booth and Longacre.

IN A BROADWAY FIRST, $125 "VIP suite seats" went on sale Wednesday for *Ragtime*, the musical extravaganza which begins previews at the new 1,850-seat Ford Center for the Performing Arts on Dec. 26.

But Canadian impresario Garth Drabinsky, chairman of Livent, which is producing the $10 million musical, says he's not actually hiking basic ticket prices.

"The additional cost [above the basic $75 orchestra seat price] is for the service," Drabinsky told *Post* Plus. "There are hundreds of other seats in the same area that don't have the service."

However, a spokeswoman for the show, Mary Bryant, admitted that the $125 seats would be in better locations than for regularly priced tickets. "They're the prime of the prime," she said.

Apart from the better location, this extra cost buys access to a VIP lounge where free sandwiches and drinks are served, as well as a souvenir program. All the usual telephone service charges are included in the $125 price tag.

"If someone wants another drink, no one is going to stop them," Drabinsky said. "It's a special service that we have been very successful with, beginning at the Pantages Theater in Toronto. We have sold thousands of these seats over the years."

Fifty $125 VIP tickets will be sold for every performance. The price is $115 for Wednesday matinees.

Roundabout Return of 'Cabaret'

The Roundabout Theater, which had to abandon its plans to produce a so-called "site-specific" revival of *Cabaret* at the Supper Club last spring, is edging closer to finding space to produce the Kander and Ebb musical this spring.

And, once again, the production is set to star movie actress Natasha Richardson.

"We're negotiating with Club Expo about doing *Cabaret* at the Henry Miller Theater in the spring, and I'm hopeful it will work out," Todd Haimes, the Roundabout's producing director, told *Post* Plus.

"Things look good, but as I learned from the Supper Club experience, nothing's set until it's signed," Haimes added. "We're keeping our fingers crossed." Club Expo uses the Henry Miller for private parties.

Like the Supper Club in the Edison Hotel, the Henry Miller now has no permanent seats. Tables and chairs would be added to make it look like a cabaret.

'Funny' Feeling About Whoopi

Superstar Whoopi Goldberg is mulling a return to *A Funny Thing Happened on the Way to the Forum*, production sources say.

Goldberg, who replaced Nathan Lane in the revival, left the show July 13 to make a movie.

Her possible return, Broadway insiders told *Post* Plus, might coincide with companion Frank Langella's stint in the title role of *Cyrano* at Broadway's Roundabout Theater. *Cyrano* will begin performances Oct. 29.

"Whoopi wants to be with Frank when he's in New York and it would be wonderful for *Forum*," said one knowledgeable Broadway insider. "She'd only need a few days of brush-up rehearsals."

TV actor David Alan Grier, who took over the part of Pseudolus from Goldberg, is expected to exit *Forum* at least by mid-November.

"He's staying until Nov. 15—unless he has to leave earlier to make the production schedule of his new TV series," Jackie Green, a publicist for "*Forum*" said yesterday.

Green said she couldn't confirm or deny whether Goldberg might come back to the show.

An assistant to Jeffrey Hunter, Goldberg's agent, also said he couldn't confirm or deny Goldberg's interest.

Diana's Life Worth a Play: Playwright

Playwright Arthur Miller, some of whose work is being produced this season by off-Broadway's acclaimed Signature Theater Company, says the late Princess Diana would undoubtedly make a great subject for a play.

And the 81-year-old Miller should have a better idea about this than almost anyone alive today—wholly apart from his being one of the country's greatest dramatists.

After all, Miller was married to Marilyn Monroe, who, like Diana, died at age 36, and his grief over her death is obvious in *After the Fall*, his play about her. (Of course, "Candle in the Wind," Elton John's tribute to Princess Diana, was originally written about Monroe.)

"It's got all the ingredients of a great play," Miller told *Post* Plus exclusively. "Diana was beautiful; she looked great, and she tried to buck the establishment."

New York Post, September 12, 1997.

☐ 'Capeman' Slip Slides Away — B'way's Biggest Flop — Curtain Closes on Paul Simon's $11 Million Musical Bust

December 11, 1997

'How I fell in love with the Capeman'

RELATIVES OF THE TWO teenagers murdered by Salvador "The Capeman" Agron who are protesting Paul Simon's soon-to-open Broadway spectacular about the killer teen have a surprising ally: his former girlfriend.

But for a very different reason.

While the loved ones of the teens who were stabbed to death in late 1959 on a Hell's Kitchen playground are seething at what they see as the "glamorization" of the caped killer, the outraged gal pal of Agron says Simon's show does not reveal the tender side of the man she loved.

"The character that was on stage was not the Salvador Agron that I knew," Gail Peck fumed. "I knew Sal for 10 years. It was not him."

"After his release [from prison], he worked day and night for other people in the community—the people who, like him, had been so poor as a child.

"That was not in the production at all," Peck said—although she said Simon talked to her "for hours" in the late 1980s about what the real Agron was like.

The 50-year-old management consultant saw the first preview of the $11 million show at the Marquis Theater last week. Marc Anthony portrays Agron as a young gang leader and Ruben Blades appears as Agron after his release from prison. The musical will open officially on Jan. 8.

Peck was a corporate sales manager in Manhattan and doing community work with Agron's therapist in 1976 when she met Agron, who was in a maximum-security prison after having had a death sentence commuted to life without parole.

"He asked if we could help [get him out], and we started to contact all the people he knew from all walks of life," she said. "Sal was the kind of person who built relationships with all kinds of people.

"He was a very, very charismatic person...and I started to work on the campaign to get him out and we got very, very close and we fell in love."

Peck, who lived with Agron for a year after his release from prison in 1979, said the former West Side gang member changed his life dramatically after his death sentence was commuted for slaying Robert Young and Anthony Krzesinki.

"He was in love with the love of changing, in love with freedom, in love with helping others—none of this was in the show!" she said.

"Simon didn't convey the agony he went through to become the man he became, the man I loved. He transformed his life—and that was completely erased."

Peck said that when Agron was freed, he worked relentlessly for the poor—but the character played by Blades does not.

"That was not in the production at all," she said. "The only part that was Sal was when they had videos of Sal. Those were the only moments of the man I knew."

Peck said that she lived with Agron on West 115th Street near Columbia University after his release. He then moved to The Bronx and lived with his mother until he died in 1986 at age 43.

She said their relationship ended because Agron could not adjust to life outside prison.

"It was hard. It was over—not our friendship and our passion and compassion for each other—but it was over, our life together."

Why did he kill the two teenagers?

"We didn't talk about that," said Peck, who is single. "He talked a lot about his life in the poorhouse and with the nuns. He said he got into a bad situation."

She added: "He tried to love, the best he could, the families of the victims. The more they turned their backs on him, the more he tried to love."

Ironically, Peck said she's certain Agron would be applauding the relatives.

"His voice would have been with them," she said. Their right to protest. To do what they feel deeply."

Is Nichols Tailor-Made for 'Capeman' Alterations?

POP SUPERSTAR Paul Simon, whose controversial first Broadway musical, *The Capeman*, is in previews, has asked mega-director Mike Nichols to help shore up the troubled show, sources in and outside of the production have told *Post* Plus.

The move comes as tensions have risen at the Marquis Theater, where the $11-million show opens officially Jan. 8.

"At times it's almost intolerable, working in the show," said one production team member.

Capeman producers are downplaying any role Nichols may play. The director, who is married to ABC-TV personality Diane Sawyer, saw a performance of *The Capeman* on Tuesday. Nichols was brought in to "doctor" *My One and Only*, the hit 1983 show starring Twiggy and Tommy Tune.

"He's one of Paul's oldest friends," co-producer Dan Klores told *The Post* yesterday, adding that Nichols will not be helping the production.

However, Klores didn't rule out that Nichols might make suggestions to help tighten *The Capeman*, which tells the story of notorious New York killer Salvador "The Capeman" Agron, who stabbed two 16-year-olds to death in 1959.

Regardless of what role Nichols plays, insiders say the partnership between Simon and famed director-choreographer Mark Morris, the show's third and current director, is under severe strain. At press time, none of the three could be reached for comment.

Morris joined the production earlier this year after two other directors, Argentine director Susana Tubert and Eric Simonson, had parted ways with Simon.

And now comes word that Morris, who's making his Broadway directing debut with *The Capeman*, will leave New York today for the better part of a week to work on a show in California.

"It's an odd time to leave a show," said a Broadwayite not connected to *The Capeman*. "It's like leaving your wife when she's going to have a baby."

Klores said Morris "will be in California for four days working on a dance project, but that was all part of the deal."

"Mark's done a wonderful job," he added.

New York Post, December 11, 1997.

▣ 42nd St.'s New Pleasure Palaces

THE BATTLE OF 42ND STREET's theater leviathans has begun.

Canadian mega-impresario Garth Drabinsky's new 1,821-seat Ford Center for the Performing Arts—where the $8 million musical *Ragtime* opens officially on Sunday—is now in direct competition with Disney's 1,747-seat New Amsterdam Theatre, where *The Lion King* opened to rave reviews just two months ago.

And a *Post* Plus comparison of the two performance palaces—which face each other across the revitalized thoroughfare—shows the Ford Center topping the New Amsterdam in setting new standards of comfort on the Great White Way.

FORD, NEW AMSTERDAM RAISE LEVEL OF LUXURY FOR PLAYGOERS

THE FORD CENTER's seats are roomier, its sightlines are significantly better in its third-level balcony and its restrooms are on a par with some in the city's finest hotels.

But in key staffing areas and convenience, the Ford Center, where *Ragtime* opened for previews on Dec. 26, seems to lag behind the New Amsterdam.

"The Ford Center is the most lavish and comfortable theater on Broadway," said New York theater producer Jamie Cesa.

And Clifford Lane, brother of Broadway theater owner and veteran producer Stewart Lane, calls the Ford Center "the Ritz Carlton of Broadway theaters."

In fact, the Ford Center itself is getting such raves that in some cases they seem to be overshadowing people's enthusiasm for the show it houses, which is based on the E.L. Doctorow novel of the same name.

Frank Gruzinski, a bartender at Sardi's, the landmark Times Square eatery, said that "most people, when they come in here, talk about the show they've seen. With *Ragtime* at the Ford Center, they seem to be raving mostly about the theater.

Stewart Lane, co-owner of Broadway's Palace Theater, where Disney's *Beauty and the Beast* is playing, said, "Livent clearly had the advantage of starting from scratch and incorporating every comfort and convenience that are all but impossible to have in the older theaters."

On the other hand, many theatergoers attending performances of *Ragtime* are complaining loudly about the Ford Center's service, with some of their harshest comments reserved for its box-office policies.

"It was a nightmare," fumed one theatergoer, who requested anonymity. "We first went to the theater's 42nd Street entrance and were told we couldn't get in that way, and when we walked around the block [to the 43rd Street entrance], there was a big line snaking out to the sidewalk, and it was driving rain."

"It was like being on a maiden voyage of a new passenger liner. Nobody knew quite what to do," said another irate patron.

Livent sources say the company will open the 42nd Street box office after the show opens officially on Sunday.

Overall, say Broadwayites, Disney and Livent have raised the bar for theater standards along the Great White Way.

"Both the New Amsterdam and the Ford Center are truly palaces, and people are going to gawk and feel a real sense of stature when they go to shows in both of them," said George Wachtel, president of Audience Research and Development, an industry organization.

And producer Dennis Grimaldi said that both theaters are going to "set new standards of comfort for Broadway. And whether they like it or not, the other theater owners are going to be forced to make changes."

New York Post, January 14, 1998.

▣ It's Curtains for Top Flop 'Capeman'

March 6, 1998

BATTERED BY ANGRY protests and savage reviews, Paul Simon is pulling the plug on his crippled musical, *The Capeman*—making it the biggest flop in Broadway history.

The curtain will go down on the $11 million show for the last time on March 28—after just 59 previews, 69 regular performances and a never-ending stream of snafus.

Cast members wept when they got the bad news yesterday, even though many insiders believed the end was near.

"This is a wonderful show, and I'm so sorry it has to close so soon," star Marc Anthony said, still crying an hour before the 8 p.m. curtain.

Simon, who made his Broadway debut with *The Capeman*, was out of the country and issued only a brief statement.

"What I enjoyed the most apart from the creative process was the intensity with which the audience, in particular the Latino audience, responded to the play," he said.

A friend from the production said the pop icon "is very upset and says he will never do another Broadway show."

The Capeman chronicled the fall and redemption of Salvador Agron, a cape-wearing gang member who stabbed to death two teenagers in Hell's Kitchen in 1959.

The subject matter infuriated victims' rights groups, who were thrilled by the show's early death.

"Happy days are here again," said Cornelius Fanelli, the 71-year-old uncle of one of Agron's victims, Robert Young.

"That musical was a disgrace," he said. "Now I hope he isn't going to write a musical about O.J. Simpson. I hope he's learned not to make any more musicals about people who've had heartache like this."

The Capeman was plagued by problems even before it opened.

The show went through three directors before Tony winner Jerry Zaks was called in to revamp it, the opening was delayed by three weeks, and several preview performances were canceled at the last minute.

When the show finally opened, the reviews were scathing—although critics did like Simon's soundtrack.

One reviewer said that seeing the musical was "like watching a mortally wounded animal."

Buoyed by $6.5 million in advance ticket sales, Simon and the other producers decided to keep the show open.

However, the advance quickly evaporated, and the show has been playing to half-empty audiences at the Marquis—while blockbusters like *Lion King* and *Ragtime* siphoned off ticket-buyers.

Broadway veterans reacted to the closing with told-you-so shrugs.

"Simon let his ego get in the way of his judgment," long-time publicist Michael Alpert said. "He thought he was better than Broadway, and he wasn't."

Pointing to the involvement of Simon, Nobel winner Derek Wolcott and choreographer Mark Morris, he added: "The pedigree of the production was impeccable, but the execution didn't live up to it."

Veteran producer Arthur Cantor borrowed a line from *Annie Get Your Gun* to describe the *Capeman* dilemma.

"In a variation of the Irving Berlin lyric, 'There's no business like show business'—there was no business for *Capeman*," Cantor said.

The Capeman eclipses 1996's $10 million loser *Big* as the Great White Way's greatest failure. Other top turkeys have included the $8 million *Red Shoes* and the $7 million *Sideshow*.

But there may be a little life left in the murder-themed musical.

There are plans under way to develop national and international touring productions, and a concert tour featuring the show's music may be in the works.

New York Post, March 6, 1998.

☐ Play on Broadway

Hot new parts for the young at art

The canyons of Broadway are alive with the sounds of talented children these days.

The revival of *The Sound of Music*, which opened last night, features seven youngsters as the von Trapp kids joining the pantheon of pint-sized players on the Great White Way.

In spite of the grueling routine of live theater—and the slim prospects of a long career—the tiny thespians told *The Post* they're thrilled about their big break.

"This is fantastic!" gushed Ryan Hopkins, a 12-year-old from Florida who is getting the chance to play Friedrich von Trapp after years of voice and dance lessons.

"This is a dream come true."

Tracy Walsh, a 10-year-old from upstate Armonk who plays Brigitta von Trapp, is already thinking about her memoirs.

"I want to definitely be an actress," the precocious grade-schooler said. "In my spare time, I would like to write about the whole experience."

Other current Broadway shows that have juicy parts for the small-fry set include *Titanic, Capeman, Les Miserables* and *Ragtime*.

At the New Amsterdam Theatre, 11-year-old Scott Irby-Ranniar won raves as the young Simba in Disney's *The Lion King*.

"It's really cool working on Broadway—but I don't get out of homework, not at all!" the East Harlem prodigy said.

There may be close to 100 children, including understudies, working on Broadway right now, experts said.

"There are more kids on Broadway than there have been in a long time, and you have to point the finger at Disney," said Robert Fresco, a theater director.

In addition to *The Lion King*, the Magic Kingdom also produced *Beauty and the Beast* and is planning to bring *The Hunchback of Notre Dame* to the stage.

Many Broadway kids have stars in their eyes—dreams of seeing their names on movie-theater marquees and talent agents beating down their doors.

But theater vets warn that making the transition to adult stardom is difficult if not impossible.

For instance, the original star of the original *Annie*, Andrea McArdle, was practically a household name after she burst onto the scene in 1977.

She's since carved out a career for herself as a working actress, appearing in *State Fair* several seasons ago, but her star has certainly waned.

Unlike McArdle, a later *Annie*, Sarah Jessica Parker, parlayed her experience into a big-time career. She's now a sought-after movie actress and stage star.

Then there's the case of the Hines brothers, Maurice and Gregory, who co-starred in the 1954 production of *The Girl in Pink Tights*.

Gregory Hines' career took off, and he went on to bigger theater parts, movies and TV as an adult. Maurice, on the other hand, works behind the scenes as a Broadway director and choreographer.

Despite the pitfalls, talented kids all over the country are dying to be Broadway babes.

Joanna Pacitti, 13, who was bounced from the Broadway revival of *Annie* last year, is still waiting for her next shot at New York's great stages.

"Despite what happened to me, I learned there are many rewards and enriching experiences that are possible for young people who work in the theater," she said.

'Rent' Hike Tix Off Honchos

Broadway producers were tight-lipped yesterday on whether they'll stick with current ticket prices or go along with the *Rent* hike.

But they blasted *Rent* for raising top ticket prices to $80 amid sensitive labor negotiations between Broadway musicians and producers.

"It couldn't be worse timing," said one producer, requesting anonymity.

Rent producers have been besieged by calls from angry colleagues along the Great White Way, the source said.

Officials with the trendy hit musical sent memos out to ticket-sales offices this week advising them of the price hike, which kicks in June 30.

The increase—the first since 1994—is initially only for the four most popular weekend performances.

Richard Kornberg, spokesman for *Rent*, said that although orchestra seats will cost more, 130 mezzanine seats will drop from $75 to $35 four days a week.

New York Post, March 13, 1998.

🔲 Frank Sinatra: 1915 – 1998

Ol' Blue Eyes —
Wife with him as he succumbs to coronary

Frank Sinatra, a larger-than-life icon of American pop culture for more than half a century, died last night of a heart attack.

He was 82.

The legendary entertainer's wife Barbara, was by his side when he was pronounced dead at 10:50 p.m. in the emergency room of Cedars-Sinai Medical Center in Los Angeles.

Other grief-stricken family members arrived at the hospital a short time later to bid a final farewell to the "Chairman of the Board."

"Frank Sinatra is a stranger to no one," his teary-eyed spokeswoman, Susan Reynolds, said.

"He [was] a comfort during sad times and a co-celebrant at happy occasions." Sinatra had been ailing and had not been seen in public since January 1997, when he was rushed to the hospital after suffering a heart attack.

He was in and out of the hospital several times since then, most recently just two weeks ago.

He was rushed to the hospital by ambulance last night after complaining of chest pains.

"Frank was in worse shape than his family let on," a close pal said.

The family was planning a private funeral.

Son Frank Sinatra Jr., accompanied by a crying woman, and daughter Tina Sinatra left the Sinatra mansion in Bel-Air early this morning without speaking to reporters.

"Barbara is doing fine. She's very strong. All the family are with her," one woman at the Sinatra home said.

"It's very sad," said close family friend Jerry Weintraub, also leaving the Sinatra estate several hours after the singer's death.

As word of Ol' Blue Eyes' death spread across the country, tributes began pouring in.

"Frank Sinatra was a true original," entertainer Mel Torme said. "He held the patent, the original blueprint on singing the popular song, a man who would have thousands of imitators but who, himself, would never be influenced by a single, solitary person."

"He just had a natural grace," said actress Betty Garrett, who appeared with Sinatra in *On the Town* and *Take Me Out to the Ballgame*.

Perhaps more than anyone, Sinatra represented the World War II-generation success story, the swaggering survivor of rocky marriages and career setbacks who achieved spectacular success in more than one field.

His songs were often intensely personal, reflecting his sharp swings in fortune, from pauper to piper, Democrat to Republican, pawn to king.

During the early 1950s when his signing career stalled, his movie career crashed and his second marriage collapsed, Sinatra sang torch songs in the "Wee Small Hours" of how he was "Glad to be Unhappy."

In his comeback, Sinatra's "Ring-a-Ding-Ding" songs were upbeat, urging listeners to "Come Fly With Me" because "I've Got the World on a String."

Then in the post-Rat Pack 1960s as he considered retirement, an introspective Sinatra sang of being in the "September of My Years" and mournfully recalling "The World We Knew."

Sinatra also had the unique ability to tackle a song originated by someone else—such as Liza Minnelli's "New York, New York"—and make it "a Sinatra song."

Few of his intensely loyal listeners seemed to mind that, for example, Rodgers and Hart's "The Lady Is a Tramp," is about a woman reflecting on her own life.

Once Sinatra recorded it, it was a Sinatra song and no one else's.

Before he became "the Chairman of the Board" or "Ol' Blue Eyes" he was simply "The Voice," a baritone band singer from Hoboken, where he was born the only child to Italian immigrant parents on December 12, 1915.

He chose his career at age 18 after seeing Bing Crosby croon on stage while dating his future wife, Nancy Barbato, a plasterer's daughter from Jersey City.

After minor successes, such as winning a Major Bowes amateur talent contest, the scrawny (5-11, 135-pound) singer earned his big break at the Rustic Cabin, a Route 9W roadhouse where he sang—and served as head waiter—for $25 a week.

Bandleader Harry James heard Sinatra on a WNEW radio broadcast from the cabin and signed him with a $50-a-week raise.

After breaking into the music charts with "All or Nothing at All," Sinatra left James for Tommy Dorsey's band, where he developed a following of teenagers with modest hits such as "I'll Never Smile Again."

But it was after buying out his contract with Dorsey that Sinatra became a sensation. When he opened at Broadway's Paramount Theater in December 1942 thousands of bobby-soxed high school girls besieged him, causing a near riot.

When he returned to the Paramount on Columbus Day two years later 30,000 girls, ignoring Mayor Fiorello LaGuardia's curfew order, flooded 43rd Street.

Sinatra's sudden success inevitably led to a movie career, which began with well-received films, such as *Anchors Aweigh* and *On The Town*, but also some bombs like *The Kissing Bandit*.

Movies changed his life. By 1951, his 12-year-old marriage to Barbato was over, and he had moved to California. After a tortured romance—expressed in his "I'm a Fool to Want You"—he married Ava Gardner.

Sinatra was also romantically linked during his Hollywood days to Judy Garland, Marilyn Monroe, Lana Turner, Kim Novak and Juliet Prowse, among many, many others.

SOURCE: *New York Post*, May 15, 1998.

Broadway's Biggest Night is THE MANE EVENT

WOMEN SCORE FIRSTS WITH DIRECT APPROACH

BROADWAY MADE HISTORY twice in the same night when Garry Hynes and Julie Taymor became the first—and second—women ever to win the Best Director Tony Awards.

"This is just spectacular, spectacular," said Taymor, who was honored by both the award and a standing ovation from the audience for directing the Disney musical *The Lion King*.

Hynes won Best Director of a Play for *The Beauty Queen of Leenane*, a dark melodrama set in Ireland that received six nominations.

It was the first time in 51 years of Tony Awards that any woman has picked up a Best Director award. Speaking of the dual win after the show, Hynes said, "I hope it will help other women. It's another barrier broken."

Taymor said the *Lion King* winning the Best Musical award is "spectacular to the 10,000th power." As for her history-making award, she said, "I don't think too much about being a woman—but I'm incredibly pleased."

Earlier, presenting the prize to Taymor, Sandy Duncan said, "It's history in the making, and it's great."

Stockard Channing, who presented Hynes' award, said being part of the historical moment was "a real honor."

Emcee Rosie O'Donnell drew huge applause from the Radio City Music Hall crowd when she noted, "This is a history-making year."

Other than Taymor and Hynes, the nominees in the Best Director categories were all men.

The two women won the awards within five minutes of each other—and both faced formidable competition. Taymor was up against heavyweights Sam Mendes and Rob Marshall, who helped the popular *Cabaret* revival. And Hynes won out against Michael Mayer, who directed *A View From the Bridge*, which won the award for Best Revival.

Theater insiders had predicted the female pair would sweep the Best Director awards—but the historical odds were against them.

Women directors have been few and far between on the Great White Way.

There were three women directors of Broadway productions this year—the third was Susan H. Schulman, who wasn't nominated for the revival of *The Sound of Music*.

New York Post, June 8, 1998.

◻ TV Audience Missed Out on Off-Color Commentary

SOME OF THE MOST COLORFUL MOMENTS IN LAST NIGHT'S CELEBRATION OF LIVE THEATER TOOK PLACE OFF CAMERA:

AFTER THE SHOW ended, celebs fanned out to post-awards bashes. Leading the pack was Best Actor in a Musical winner Alan Cumming of *Cabaret*, who donned a leather jacket and tall platform shoes.

"It's in homage to the departure of Ginger Spice," he joked.

DURING AN OFF-CAMERA commercial break, Rosie O'Donnell got in a dig at Barry and Fran Weissler, producers of the mega-hit revival *Chicago*. It seems they had wanted more than $100 each for costumes from their show, which were used in one of the Tonys' musical numbers.

"Where are the Weisslers?" Rosie called out. Spotting them, she announced: "Oh, there they are. They're the cheapest people in this theater."

EARLIER IN THE EVENING, O'Donnell got a lesson in New York's tough pedestrian laws.

Before the show started, she tried to cross Sixth Avenue to talk to cheering fans on the west side of the street—but she was stopped by cops, who said it would have been a safety hazard.

Rosie wasn't amused—she walked away, cursing and muttering under her breath. She still seemed to be simmering as the evening progressed. Before the live telecast began, she shocked the audience with an expletive-laden pre-show speech.

She instructed people in the audience to keep quiet during the opening musical number—a salute to Broadway divas.

Otherwise, she explained, "You'll f--- it up!"

ROSIE WASN'T the only star who was swearing.

When Irishman Tom Murphy stepped onstage to accept his Featured Actor in a Play award, he informed the crowd that *The Beauty Queen of Leenane* is "a great f---ing play"—before TV censors could bleep it out.

SEAN CONNERY, one of the producers of Best Play *Art*, said he had a personal reason to be happy about another winner—*The Lion King*.

"Thank God I have shares in Disney," he quipped.

New York Post, June 8, 1998.

◻ 'THE LION KING' —
Six Tonys Are Claws to Rejoice

THE LION KING became the pride of Broadway last night, mauling the competition and devouring six Tony awards, including Best New Musical.

Ragtime, Cabaret and *The Beauty Queen of Leenane* were the other big winners at Radio City Music Hall, taking home four awards each.

Julie Taymor and Garry Hynes became the first women to win Best Director Tonys in the 51-year history of the awards. Taymor won for Best Director of a Musical, *The Lion King*, and Hynes for the play *Beauty Queen of Leenane*.

"This is just spectacular, spectacular," a triumphant Taymor exulted as she received her award to a standing ovation.

The King's closest competitor, *Ragtime*, took home awards for Best Book in a Musical, Best Original Score, Orchestrations and Best Featured Actress, Audra McDonald.

"I want to thank my parents in Pittsburgh for the piano lessons," said composer Stephen Flaherty, who wrote the score for *Ragtime* along with lyricist Lynn Ahrens.

Terrence McNally, who won for his adaptation of the E.L. Doctorow novel *Ragtime* for the stage, declared, "This is for freedom!"

McNally was referring to his controversial new play about a gay Jesus called *Corpus Christi*. The upcoming production was briefly shelved because of bomb threats, and the writer thanked "the theater community who came together when I was in trouble."

Beauty Queen took a trio of top acting awards in addition to Best Director, but it was upset for Best New Play by the comedy *Art*.

Best Featured Actor Tom Murphy made CBS censors blush when he proclaimed, with an Irish twang, that *Beauty Queen* is "a great f---ing play."

Anna Manahan, who plays the cold and controlling mother in *Beauty Queen*, was visibly touched—and used better language—when she snagged Best Featured Actress honors.

"My heart is very full," she said, thanking "the generosity of all my friends for lighting candles for me."

Best Actress went to Marie Mullen, who plays Manahan's spinster daughter.

Cabaret also captured a quartet of awards, including Best Revival and Best Actress for Natasha Richardson, who plays the sexy Sally Bowles.

"This has been the most terrifying and most thrilling journey of my life," said Richardson, who thanked husband Liam Neeson—passed over for a Best Actor nomination—for being her "constant inspiration."

And she dedicated the win to her father, director Tony Richardson.

"It is a Tony, after all," she quipped.

Best Actor in a Musical went to the show's star Alan Cumming, who joked, "I want to thank everyone Natasha Richardson thanked—except Liam Neeson."

Ron Rifkin, who plays a Jewish shopkeeper in the show, won Best Featured Actor in a Musical. He said he gave up acting in 1984 and "went into the coat business" before returning to the boards.

"I'm so completely shocked I can't tell you," Rifkin cried.

Oscar-winning actress Helen Hunt presented the award for Best Actor in a Play to Anthony LaPaglia, for his portrayal of Eddie Carbone in the Arthur Miller classic *A View From the Bridge*, which won the Best Revival of a Play honors.

"This is absolutely mind-blowing. I blanketly thank everyone in the world right away," LaPaglia said.

He told his fellow nominees, Richard Briers, John Leguizamo and Alfred Milina, "I share this with you, but it's coming back to my house."

Despite lavish production numbers, the night wasn't flawless.

John Leguizamo's microphone didn't work when he performed a bit from his one-man show, *Freak*, and superstar-actor-turned Broadway producer Sean Connery was ignominiously cut off when he tried to say a few words as he accepted the Best New Play award for *Art*.

The awards show was hosted for the second year in a row by TV talker Rosie O'Donnell, who helped turn poor ratings around last year and kept this year's show light and quick.

New York Post, June 8, 1998.

◻ Footlights of Broadway May Beckon

THE DEATH OF ENTERTAINER Kay Thompson—who penned the internationally beloved *Eloise* books—has raised the prospect that *Eloise* may now be exploited as a movie or stage musical for the rising tide of pre-teen-girl audiences.

Longtime friends say that Thompson patterned the precocious 6-year-old Plaza resident on Liza Minnelli when Minnelli, who was the author's goddaughter, stayed at the posh hotel with her mother, the late Judy Garland, in the early 1950s.

The original *Eloise* book was published in 1955. It and three *Eloise* sequels—*Eloise in Paris* (1957), *Eloise at Christmastime* (1958) and *Eloise in Moscow* (1959)—were all illustrated by noted artist Hilary Knight.

But after a made-for-TV version of *Eloise* failed to live up to expectations, Thompson subsequently turned down numerous requests to turn the books into feature films or Broadway shows. However, with Thompson's passing, one Broadway producer—who requested anonymity—told *The Post* yesterday that he has approached Harvey Schmidt and Tom Jones—creators of the world's longest-running musical, off-Broadway's *The Fantasticks*—about coming up with a show based on the original *Eloise* book.

Broadwayite Kevin McCollum, a co-producer of the mega-hit musical *Rent*, also sees great potential in *Eloise*.

"*Eloise* is a wonderful subject," McCollum said. "And she has the advantage of being 'pre-sold' to audiences."

However, Thompson is said to have been so emphatic about protecting the legacy of the spoiled but lovable little girl that she may have put severe limits on her heirs from marketing *Eloise*.

"We won't know for a long time because we don't know what her will says," Knight said yesterday. "Kay was very protective of *Eloise* when she was alive and I'm sure she'll continue that," he said.

Nevertheless, Knight—who for years has felt that *Eloise* might make a wonderful musical—added that "there might be something that can be done" now.

Publishing experts believe that's a possibility even in a case where an author's will says, in effect, "I never want my book to be done as a movie or for television."

Said New York literary agent Howard Sandum: "At times, in various court cases, this has been broken or revised if it was shown that it was the wish of the author to have the material exploited in better ways than he or she could see based on present options."

New York Post, July 8, 1998.

◻ 'Footloose' Shaky in D.C. Run —

NYC-BOUND MUSICAL IS GETTING A FINE-TUNING

WASHINGTON, D.C.—*Footloose*, the most highly anticipated musical set to open on Broadway this fall, is getting mixed reviews from the audiences seeing it in out-of-town performances here this week at the Kennedy Center.

Despite standing ovations at the final curtain, many audience members felt that the show's dance numbers needed to be more exciting and its storyline streamlined.

Based on the hit 1984 movie—starring Kevin Bacon as a big-city boy who dances his way into the heart of a small town—the $6.5 million stage adaptation of *Footloose* started previews here Tuesday. It opens officially on Saturday night.

Production insiders say the show's creators—including *Chicago* director Walter Bobbie, who also co-adapted *Footloose* for the stage with lyricist Dean Pitchford—are feverishly trying to smooth the transitions between musical numbers and hone the book.

Almost every audience member interviewed by *The Post* said the cast—led by Jeremy Kushnier, who plays young high school student Ren McCormack, the Kevin Bacon role—could not be better.

"Everyone was just terrific—they threw themselves into their parts!" raved Mary Toman, theatergoer from Los Angeles who attended the first preview with her 7-year-old daughter, Mary.

Overall audience reactions, though, were more muted.

"I must say I expected a lot more," said Ben Phillips, a Washington-area resident who saw *Footloose* at its first preview with his 6-year-old son, Mark.

"The movie made me want to see it, but I was a bit disappointed," Phillips added.

Some parents were dismayed about the show's occasional use of expletives.

"It's not appropriate for young children like my daughter," Toman said. "We had to leave the show and go to the lobby when that language was used."

Several theater professionals, however, said they think the show stands a good chance of success on the Great White Way.

"The show is going to be judged not on the book but on how good the music and dances are," said veteran Broadway producer Michael Frazier, who is not associated with the musical.

"Unquestionably, it's going to be one of the big hits of the fall if not the entire season," said Carol Levine, a theater marketing executive. She also is not connected with the show.

"So what if it doesn't have a book," she added. "It doesn't have to. The young people will love the dancing and the music."

New York Post, August 27, 1998.

🔲 'Rent' Finally Pays Off for Play Doctor

A WOMAN WHO helped co-author the monster hit musical *Rent* with the late Jonathan Larson won't have to worry about paying her own rent anymore.

Under a court settlement with Larson's multi-million-dollar estate, Lynn Thomson—a "dramaturge," or play doctor, who helped ready *Rent* for production—will receive several hundred thousand dollars, a percentage of its continuing worldwide royalties, and so-called "title page credit" for her contribution, sources familiar with the settlement told *The Post*.

Thomson will receive credit on all future playbills for *Rent*, said a press rep for the show.

Initially, Thomson, a drama teacher at Brooklyn College, was paid $2,000 to help mold the show for production—a process common in the theater. After she threatened legal action, saying she had written nearly half the storyline and 9 percent of the lyrics, the producers offered to pay her another $10,000.

Under terms of the settlement, both sides have been forbidden to talk about it.

But Russell Smith, Thomson's attorney, told *The Post* that "the issues that Lynn raised regarding royalties, credit and the right to publish her own book about developing the show have all been settled."

"I'm very, very happy!" said Thomson yesterday.

"But after fighting for over two years, the [results of] the settlement [are] just beginning to sink in," she added.

Larson, 35, died in January 1996 three months before the show was transferred from off-Broadway's New York Theater Workshop to Broadway's Nederlander Theater. Since that time, *Rent* is estimated to have raked in more than $250 million before expenses.

Last summer, a U.S. Federal District Court judge in Manhattan dismissed Thomson's claim that she was a joint author of *Rent*, specifically citing the U.S. Copyright Act law that describes such a work as "Prepared by two or more authors with the intention that their contributions be merged into inseparable or interdependent parts."

Larson's lawyers had successfully argued that the late playwright had never intended Thomson to share any kind of credit. However, they freely acknowledged that Thomson had made a considerable contribution to the finished work.

Smith appealed the case to the U.S. Court of Appeals, and early last month the higher court upheld the decision of the lower court.

At the same time, the appeals court left the door open for further legal action when it stated that Thomson may have had some copyright claims on specific material she contributed.

And as Smith was in the process of filing a new suit claiming copyright infringement—and asking the court to delete all her material from *Rent* productions around the world—Larson's estate agreed to settle the case.

Along the way, Thomson received heavyweight theatrical support from playwrights Tony Kushner (*Angels in America*) and Craig Lucas (*Prelude to a Kiss*). Both contended Thomson was being cheated out of her fair share of the profits.

Lucas, for example, testified Thomson, "transformed the play."

Thomson testified that Larson "talked about acknowledgement and how it was very important to him and he would never claim something that was never his."

New York Post, September 9, 1998.

◻ New Tunnel Vision

CONTROVERSIAL NIGHTCLUB czar Peter Gatien, owner of the Tunnel and the soon-to-reopen Limelight, will co-produce *Largo Desollato*, a play by former Czech President Vaclav Havel, at the Tunnel.

Previews start September 18. The play, about a family trying to survive a totalitarian regime, will run through Oct. 17.

"This is only the first of a series of off-Broadway shows I'm hoping to do at the Tunnel and the Limelight," said Gatien, who is co-producing with the Chelsea Theater Company.

'CABARET' TO BOOGIE AT STUDIO 54

LIFE WILL BE a *Cabaret* at the infamous Studio 54, *The Post* has learned.

Pace Theatrical Group, co-producers of the long-running musical *Jekyll & Hyde*, is set to transfer the nonprofit Roundabout Theater's monster-hit revival of *Cabaret* from the Kit Kat Klub on West 43rd Street to the Studio 54 space, at 254 W. 54th St., as early as November, according to Pace, Studio 54 and Roundabout sources.

"We're going to be sorry to see them move," said Douglas Durst, a Roundabout board member and president of the powerful Durst Organization, which owns the Henry Miller Theater (as well as the Condé Nast office tower under construction next door).

"But *Cabaret*'s lease…is up later this year, so it's good economic sense for them to move to a larger venue at that time."

The much larger Studio 54 space—which was originally built in 1923 as the Gallo Opera House and in the late 1970s became the renowned disco—is expected to have a seating capacity of more than 1,000. The orchestra section of the Kit Kat is set with cabaret-type tables and chairs, a pattern expected to be repeated.

The Roundabout revival of *Cabaret*, currently co-starring Jennifer Jason Leigh as pre-World War II Berlin nightclub singer Sally Bowles, has been playing to sold-out houses since it opened at the 500-seat Kit Kat Klub in March.

And while Roundabout sources say the show produces a steady stream of revenue—*Cabaret* charges a Broadway-high $80 for orchestra seats—it's simply not the moneymaker that Pace executives think it can be when moved to Studio 54.

This is despite the fact that Pace may have to renegotiate contracts with actors in the show and pay Broadway-scale salaries, according to Actors Equity sources.

Daltrey's Musical: You Better, You Bet

Rock superstar Roger Daltrey—who will play Scrooge at Madison Square Garden's fifth annual production of *A Christmas Carol*, starting Nov. 27—says he is hard at work writing a new Broadway musical.

"I've been working on it a couple of years now, and it's coming together quite well," the former Who lead singer told *The Post* in an interview yesterday.

"It's a love story, based on a classic tale. I don't want to tell you which one because a lot of people are looking for ideas, but I'm going to try and raise money to do it next year."

What convinced him to do *A Christmas Carol* was "because it's different than a normal Broadway show," he said.

"Not a lot of theater really interests me. But what I like about his show is it's the closest thing to what we British call 'pantomime,' which is how most kids see their first theater in England. It's big spectacle kind of stuff that doesn't take itself too seriously."

Cast Changes Next Month for 'Pimpernel'

Rachel York—who co-starred in *Victor/Victoria* last year—and TV star Rex Smith will replace Christine Andreas and Terrence Mann, respectively, in the Broadway musical *The Scarlet Pimpernel*, starting Oct. 10.

Douglas Sills will continue to lay the title role in the Frank Wildhorn musical, which is based on the novels by Baroness Orczy and set during the French Revolution.

Smith, who had a long-running role on the TV soap "As the World Turns," previously starred on Broadway in *The Pirates of Penzance*.

Pimpernel, which opened to mixed reviews last fall and has been playing to barely half-filled houses in recent weeks, got a new lease on life this summer when Cablevision, which owns Madison Square Garden and Radio City Music Hall, became a co-producer.

And, to listen to executive producer Tim Hawkins, things look a lot rosier for *The Scarlet Pimpernel* this fall.

New York Post, September 11, 1998.

◻ 'Millie' Made Thoroughly Modern

IN YET ANOTHER example of a movie musical being rewritten for the theater, *Thoroughly Modern Millie*, the 1967 film starring Julie Andrews and Carol Channing, is heading for Broadway next year.

New music will be provided by Jeanine Tesori, who wrote the music used in the recent Lincoln Center Theater production of *Twelfth Night*. The movie *Millie* included then-new songs written by Sammy Cahn and Jimmy Van Heusen and also incorporated oldies from the flapper era. The film is set in 1922.

Millie will open on Broadway next season, its producers say.

Produced jointly by Fox Theatricals—which is not associated with 20th Century Fox studios—and superstar actress Whoopi Goldberg, the new production will have a new book by Dick Scanlan, who collaborated with the late Richard Morris. Morris wrote the 1967 screenplay.

"We just finished our second workshop production of the show and everyone, including Whoopi, was delighted with the way the musical is shaping up," Tesori said yesterday.

"We've tweaked the book to make it more politically correct than it was in 1967," Scanlan said. "But we've taken a lot of pains not to lose the show's sense of fun."

The 1967 movie tells the story of an ambitious Jazz Age flapper who falls in love with a stock boy who turns out to be a multimillionaire. It includes an unflattering picture of Asian men involved in the "white slave trade."

"That is being changed," Scanlan said.

As THE POST FIRST reported, *Cabaret* will move to the former Studio 54, 254 W. 54th St., as of Nov. 12. The show announced yesterday that Nov. 8 will be the final performance at its current home, the Kit Kat Klub—the former Henry Miller's Theater—on 43rd St.

'ELECTRA' MAY MOVE TO B'WAY

For the first time since 1994, when Diana Rigg starred in an acclaimed revival of *Medea*, Greek tragedy is returning to the Great White Way.

Princeton University's McCarter Theater is in talks with the Shubert Organization, which owns 16 Broadway theaters, about moving the McCarter's highly praised production of *Electra*, Sophocles' ancient tale of incest. It stars Zoe Wanamaker as the half-mad Electra and Claire Bloom as her murderous mother, Clytemnestra.

Electra, which officially opened in Princeton to a number of rave reviews last week, is set to close there Oct. 4.

Shubert and McCarter insiders say that if all goes according to play, the show, which has a cast of nine, may move to either the 1,096-seat Longacre Theater or the 1,084-seat Cort Theater as early as November.

New York Post, September 25, 1998.

◻ Ticket-Fraud Probe Widens

As ATTORNEY GENERAL Dennis Vacco continues to broaden the scope of his investigation into Broadway ticket fraud, new details are emerging about possible improper, though not necessarily illegal, activity at Broadway's half-price TKTS ticket center in Times Square.

Knowledgeable sources have told *The Post* that, all too often, tickets in the best seating locations are sold for half-price at the TKTS booth to theater-industry insiders.

And unlike the average theatergoer, who must queue up in the long lines that stretch out from the TKTS booth at Broadway and 47th Street, these individuals "usually go right to the head of the line and pick up their tickets," one source said.

The TKTS booth was established a quarter-century ago to sell the tickets that producers don't expect to sell for full price at the box office or over the phone.

"I don't think anyone is making money on this," one source said of the alleged scheme, "although, theoretically, they could be turning around and selling them for full price.

"But at the very least it's really unfair to the show's producers and theatergoers alike to take good seats out of circulation and sell them at half price," the same insider continued. "It's just not right."

David Corvette, a spokesman for Vacco, declined to comment on whether the attorney general's probe was targeting the TKTS booth along with other Broadway box-office operations.

"We cannot confirm or deny specific aspects of our ongoing investigation," Corvette said. "But we are interested in the practice of 'ice' (alleged bribes paid to box-office employees in return for choice seats) wherever it occurs.

Veronica Clapool, managing director of the Theater Development Fund, which operates the TKTS booth, strongly denied that any employees of the TKTS booth were involved in anything improper or illegal.

GLADYS GUNG-HO FOR GOSPEL

GRAMMY AWARD-WINNING superstar Gladys Knight is taking the midnight train to Broadway.

Knight, who first broke into show business when she won the first prize of $2,000 on Ted Mack's "Original Amateur Hour" back in 1952, will star in the gospel musical *Abyssinia*, set to open on Broadway in or around February.

Abyssinia, which was first done by Musical Theater Works as a workshop production in 1986, was adapted by composer Ted Kociolek and Lyricist James Racheff from a novel for young adults by Joyce Carol Thomas.

While it's successfully been done in a number of places outside New York, including the highly regarded Goodspeed Opera House in Connecticut, the so-called "feel good" gospel musical has never been produced on or off-Broadway.

Described by its director, Josephine Abady, formerly of the now-shuttered Circle in the Square Theater, as "a small musical with a big heart," *Abyssinia* is being co-produced by MJM Productions.

"Gladys has this wonderful window of opportunity to do *Abyssinia*, and we're taking full advantage of her desire to do it," said Abady yesterday.

The story of *Abyssinia* revolves around a young singer who, molested by a neighbor, becomes mute until the regains her faith in God and in her fellow man.

Knight, 54, will play one of those close to the girl who helps her regain both her faith and then her voice.

The singer's first major professional singing success came as a member of the group Gladys Knight and the Pips. One of the group's biggest gold singles was "Midnight Train to Georgia," which became No. 1 in 1973.

'Tiny Alice' Gets a Big Revival

A revival of Edward Albee's '64 play *Tiny Alice* will open on Broadway before the end of the 1998-99 season.

Co-produced by Daryl Roth and Elizabeth McCann, who also co-produced Albee's Pulitzer Prize-winning *Three Tall Women* several seasons ago off-Broadway. *Tiny Alice* "will basically be the same Mark Lamos production that was done this past year at the Hartford Stage Company," Roth said.

"We're hoping to get Richard Thomas, who headed the cast in Hartford, but he's not signed yet," Roth added.

Tiny Alice originally starred the great English actor Sir John Gielgud. "It's a beautiful play—one of Albee's best—and we will open in either March or April," Roth said.

Filled with metaphysical symbolism, the play proved to be so confusing to some theater critics that playwright Albee held a press conference in the lobby of Broadway's Billy Rose Theater (now the Nederlander Theater) to explain it. He said critics—and the public—were reading too much into it.

New York Post, October 9, 1998.

◻ Valerie's Pearls

AS A CHILLY WIND whipped across Union Square, Valerie Harper was running to get back to rehearsal.

So the very last thing she needed was the stranger who stopped her and asked, "Aren't you Valerie Harper—Rhoda?"

"You bet I am!" the actress beamed, running off.

"I love being known as Rhoda," Harper said, her long hair curling obediently about her neck and shoulders. "But I want people to give me a chance to act someone else."

And now she's getting that chance, starring as Nobel Prize-winning novelist Pearl S. Buck in *All Under Heaven*, by Dyke Garrison.

The one-woman play began previews last night at off-Broadway's 299-seat Century Theater on East 15th Street, right off Union Square. The official opening night is Nov. 16.

The four-time Emmy Award-winning actress seems an unlikely aspirant to portray Buck, the now obscure literary giant, who wrote *The Good Earth*, a novel about life in China, and later helped provide foster care for hundreds of Asian-American children fathered by American servicemen.

"The idea for a play about Buck, who died at 80 in 1973, came quite by accident.

Three years ago, Harper and her husband, producer Tony Cacciotti, received a Christmas card from comedian Dom DeLuise, who wrote that he had given a donation to the Pearl S. Buck foundation in their names.

"I told Tony what a great woman she was and we should do her story," Harper said.

Harper herself had learned a little about Buck's life and work as a child.

"My mother loved books and especially Pearl Buck—although she read a lot more than I did at the time," the actress said with a disarming grin.

Born in Suffern, N.Y., Harper was just out of high school when she began her professional career as a member of the now defunct corps de ballet at Radio City Music Hall. She then landed successive chorus jobs in the Broadway musicals *Li'l Abner*, *Take Me Along* (starring Jackie Gleason) and *Wildcat* (starring Lucille Ball).

But it was playing the exasperating yet often lovable Rhoda Morgenstern on TV's "The Mary Tyler Moore Show," which lasted seven seasons, that made Harper a household name.

Her own "Rhoda" series ran for five seasons. But a later sitcom called "Valerie," which initially fared well in the ratings, was short-lived.

"Valerie" was canceled after contract talks with NBC hit a snag. Harper later claimed that she had been fired because the network didn't want to pay her enough.

New York Post, November 4, 1998.

◻ B'way Giant Cantor Dies at 81

LEGENDARY BROADWAY producer Arthur Cantor—whose long-running hits included *A Thousand Clowns* and *All the Way Home*—died yesterday afternoon at age 81.

Cantor, a resident of the Dakota apartment house on Central Park West, died of a heart attack at Mount Sinai Hospital, following a bout with pneumonia.

"His heart just gave out," his son, David, told *The Post*.

Cantor—who brought more than 50 plays to stages along the Great White Way, Off-Broadway and London's West End—was a consummate showman until the end, his son said.

"Just hours before he died, he was reading the theater section of *The New York Times*, saying, 'Look at all these shows. Can you believe the prices they're getting? They'll be getting $100 soon,'" David said.

Cantor was one of the first proponents of discounted tickets for families and groups, his son said.

A native of Boston and graduate of Harvard University, Cantor first produced Paddy Chayefsky's drama *The Tenth Man*.

Other credits included the Pulitzer Prize-winning *All the Way Home*, *Gideon* and *On Golden Pond*.

Well-known stars in his shows included Rex Harrison and Julie Harris in *In Praise of Love*; Claire Bloom, in *Vivat! Vivat Regina!*; Maggie Smith, in *Private Lives*; and Ingrid Bergman, in *The Constant Wife*.

He also produced *Dylan Thomas Growing Up*, *A Party with Bette Comden and Adolph Green*, *The Biko Inquest*, *St. Mark's Gospel* and *The Hothouse*.

Most recently, he presented the long-running hit *Beau Jest*, and Eileen Atkins as Virginia Woolf in *A Room of One's Own*, both at the Lamb's Theatre.

Cantor is also survived by a daughter, Jacqueline. His wife, Deborah, died in 1970, and another son, Michael, who appeared in the movie *Dirty Dancing*, died in 1991.

New York Post, April 9, 2001.

◻ Broadway's Flair for the Dramatic

THE GREAT WHITE WAY IS STILL DOMINATED BY MUSICALS, BUT SERIOUS WORKS ARE PULLING THEIR OWN WEIGHT

WHILE MEL BROOK'S new musical comedy *The Producers* is grabbing headlines over stories by delirious critics and setting records for ticket sales, serious Broadway dramas are back on the Great White Way, too, attracting impressive audiences.

Six dramas and one comedy-drama—nearly double the number in recent seasons—are currently on Broadway stages. And make that eight dramas, if you count Neil Simon's *The Dinner Party*, which is advertised as a comedy but is more serious than a typical Simon play.

Broadway theater continues to be dominated by some two-dozen splashy musicals, ranging from *The Producers* and *The Full Monty*, both new this season, to long-running revivals such as *Kiss Me Kate* and *The Music Man*. Many have earned record or near-record box-office receipts: *The Producers* is the first musical in history to charge a top price of $100 on regular Friday and Saturday evenings.

Musicals have dominated Broadway for several decades as producers cater to out-of-town tourists, many from foreign countries, for whom musicals more easily cut through language barriers.

Two plays, the revival of *One Flew Over the Cuckoo's Nest*, starring Gary Sinise, and the Irish import *Stones in His Pockets* have enjoyed big upticks in sales recently.

For the first time in eight years, a drama playing on Broadway, David Auburn's *Proof*, has won the Pulitzer Prize for Drama. The last Broadway drama to win the coveted award was Tony Kushner's *Angels in America* in 1993.

In the intervening years, Off-Broadway and regional plays won Pulitzers for drama, including Off-Broadway productions of Margaret Edson's *Wit* in 1999 and Donald Margulies' *Dinner With Friends* last year.

August Wilson's *King Hedley II* and Arje Shaw's *The Gathering* have also made it to Broadway this year. Both used successful runs Off-Broadway as a showcase before transferring theaters.

The new Broadway dramas include:

THE GATHERING. Largely a vehicle for its star, Hal Linden, this Holocaust drama derives much of its power from Linden's stellar performance.

Perhaps best known for his starring role in the "Barney Miller" TV series, Linden does the most chillingly brilliant acting of his lengthy stage career. He is hamstrung to some extent by playwright Shaw's overly ambitious attempt to make Linden's character, Jake, funny as well as poignant and haunting. Yet one can only applaud Linden's wrenching combination of rage and forgiveness, which has a Tony Award written all over it.

ONE FLEW OVER THE CUCKOO'S NEST. This generally powerful revival of Dale Wasserman's acclaimed antiestablishment play based on a Ken Kesey novel (and made into a 1975 film that earned Jack Nicholson an Academy Award) is diluted by Gary Sinise's energetic and engaging, but relatively unmoving, star turn.

Sinise plays Randle P. McMurphy, a quixotic nonconformist who rallies other patients in a mental ward against the stern and authoritarian rule of Nurse Ratched. But compared with Nicholson's edgy, unnerving, and complex characterization in the same role, there's too much of a cheerleader sameness to Sinise's handling of the part. The play's second act is more melodrama than dramatic tragedy.

STONES IN HIS POCKETS. Conleth Hill and Sean Campion give remarkable performances as two film extras on location in Ireland who in turn play 15 different characters ranging from an American film diva to her highly belligerent bodyguard. The play, by Marie Jones, takes on a magical life, thanks to these two extraordinary actors.

First produced in Belfast in 1999, *Stones in His Pockets* received rapturous reviews on London's West End and several top prizes before moving to Broadway this spring. Its major flaw, however, is that it tries too hard to be serious even though it is essentially a comedy.

JUDGMENT AT NUREMBERG. Abby Mann's forceful and faithful adaptation of his 1950s "Playhouse 90" teleplay and his 1961 film of the same name starring Spencer Tracy is one of the best "courtroom" dramas Broadway has seen in years. (It is, however, not for the squeamish, as there are unnecessary filmed sequences of the Nazi death-camp horrors.)

Maximilian Schell won an Oscar in the movie (in which Spencer Tracy played an American judge) as a young German defense lawyer. He now plays Ernst Janning, a once highly moral Nazi judge corrupted and co-opted by the Third Reich.

Schell, as the once decent and honorable Janning, is most moving when, after being sentenced to life in prison for crimes against humanity, he still questions whether he did anything wrong.

George Grizzard as a U.S. judge and Joseph Wiseman as a doctor testifying against Janning are equally wonderful.

The Christian Science Monitor, April 27, 2001.

Producer Recounts a Golden Age in Hollywood

MARTIN JUROW, the producer of such classics as *Breakfast at Tiffany's*, *The Pink Panther*, and *Terms of Endearment*, may have never become a major Hollywood producer, but his new book offers rare personal insights into the world of Hollywood and some of its greatest stars.

Written without the rancor or bitterness that seem to characterize other Tinseltown autobiographies, *Martin Jurow Seein' Stars: A Show Biz Odyssey*, published by Southern Methodist University (SMU) Press, features clear and colorful writing from Philip Wuntch, the long-time chief film critic for *The Dallas Morning News*.

In a joint interview with Jurow and Wuntch at Jurow's comfortable Dallas home, where he lives with Erin-Jo, his wife of more than 50 years, Wuntch is emphatic about his regard for the producer.

"What the movie industry desperately needs now is Martin Jurow," Wuntch says. "We've just come off a terrible summer filled with totally mediocre quality, and all the films Martin produced and all of the films he worked on in any capacity were above average. They were character-driven and quality-driven. Today, the plots and characters are there really to service special effects."

Working as an agent and studio executive before becoming a full-fledged producer, Jurow represented and worked with such stars as Katharine Hepburn and Frank Sinatra, as well as legendary producers Jack L. Warner and Hal Wallis.

Jurow's book also contains a lot of humor, even though some of his encounters with rich and famous authors and actors seemed anything but funny to him at the time.

Discussing his plans to produce the film version of Truman Capote's best-selling novella *Breakfast at Tiffany's*, Mr. Jurow says in his book that his vision for the production "seemed to ignite his [Capote's] enthusiasm, but my loyalty to his ideas was about to be sorely tested."

It seems that Capote, the author, wanted to be Capote, the actor, and play the film's leading man, a part that went to suave star George Peppard. But Jurow's years of clutch thinking and smooth talking were about to pay off in a masterstroke of cajoling.

"Truman, the role just isn't good enough for you," Jurow says he found himself suddenly explaining, "All eyes will be on Holly Golightly through every frame of the picture. The male lead is just a pair of shoulders for Holly to lean on. You deserve something more dynamic, more colorful."

"You're right, I deserve something more dynamic," Jurow recounts the egotistical author replying.

Like many film, screen and stage luminaries, Jurow had first wanted to be an actor, but soon realized his greatest talents were on the business and production side of theater and film.

As a child growing up in Brooklyn, Jurow first became enthralled with show business while attending live vaudeville performances on Sunday afternoon family outings. He attended William & Mary College in Williamsburg, Va., playing many leading roles, before going to and graduating from Harvard Law School, which prepared him for the business side of Broadway and Hollywood productions.

Early in his career as a producer, Jurow hired the now-famous director Blake Edwards, after having seen his work on the comedy *Operation Petticoat*, starring Cary Grant. It marked the beginning of a close professional association and friendship. Edwards would go on to direct Jurow's production of *The Pink Panther*, as well as its many sequels.

Jurow also recalls in his book how Frank Sinatra, in a major slump as a singer and actor in the 1950s, landed the plumb role of Maggio in the early 1950s movie *From Here to Eternity*.

While Jurow was head of William Morris's East Coast film department, he asked Sinatra if he could act as his representative for his next movie role. Having little faith in his own slim prospects, Sinatra agreed, and Jurow approached Hollywood producer Harry Cohn about casting him as Maggio.

Cohn couldn't see Sinatra playing a bitter loser, but Jurow persisted. And one night, Jurow says he went over to the home of his friend George Woods, a nightclub impresario, to "recount my woes."

Mr. Woods was having dinner, Jurow says in his book with an associate of reputed mobster Meyer Lansky named Vincent Ado, aka "Jimmy Blue Eyes." Sensing Jurow's melancholy, Jimmy Blue Eyes asked him what was bothering him. After telling him he had gotten nowhere with Cohn, Jurow says Jimmy Blue Eyes said, in a scene which seemed to come right out of an Edward G. Robinson movie, "Cohn. He owes us."

"Mr. Sinatra never knew the full story of what had transpired, but he was always courteous to me," Jurow relates in his book.

As an agent, Jurow had his share of more experienced mentors, too, but few as glamorous as four-time Oscar winner Ms. Hepburn, who was one of the "stable" of stars in the talent agency Jurow was working for at the time. "She, a professional actress, became a mentor to me, hotshot Harvard Law School grad," Jurow writes. "She pointed out aspects to each contract, explaining their ramifications in diction as precise as her cheekbones."

Jurow, who moved to Dallas with his wife and daughter in the late 1970s, where he continued to produce films as well as teach college film courses, has had more time in recent years to reflect on his experiences when he was in the Hollywood and New York centers of the entertainment world. But his overall feeling for the industry hasn't changed that much over the past 60 years.

Looking at a gallery of signed star photographs, ranging from Hepburn to Kirk Douglas to Peter Sellers, lining the front hallway of his modest but comfortable Dallas home, Jurow paraphrases the title of a famous Jimmy Stewart movie, one he had nothing to do with making or casting: "It's been a wonderful life!"

The Christian Science Monitor, October 19, 2001.

WHEN I STARTED working for *The New York Sun* in June 2002, I started using the same name of the column my father used. He began his "Broadway After Dark" column in *The New York Sun* in 1926 and it seemed appropriate that I, working for the new *New York Sun*, would use it now, and my editor, Seth Lipsky, enthusiastically endorsed the idea.

☐ Salvador Dali's Favorite Sports Artist

EARLY HAPPY BIRTHDAY wishes to artist Al Hirschfeld, who will be 99 on June 21. He still brings his sketchbook to shows. He has sketched every star from Groucho Marx to Jerry Seinfeld.

It's OK to call LeRoy Neiman, one of America's greatest living painters, a sports artist—now. After all, he's painted the likes of Babe Ruth, Michael Jordan, Kentucky Derby winner Secretariat, and his close friend Muhammad Ali.

Time was, however, some 40 years ago when he first moved to New York, the still striking artist told me over lunch at Tavern on the Green, that he took offense at the sport's artist title. "I was offended because I had only been doing sports conspicuously for a few years," he said. "I was a painter and go way back in painting long before that."

Messrs. Neiman and Ali were in Las Vegas Saturday for the sale of copies of a serigraph of Mr. Neiman's painting of Mr. Ali called *Athlete of the Century*.

Next up for Mr. Neiman is a book of prints of paintings of New York City restaurants, including Rao's, Le Cirque, Café Des Artistes, and Tavern on the Green. A portrait of the late Frank Sinatra is in Mr. Neiman's painting of Rao's even though Mr. Neiman said late Chairman of the Board may have never set foot in the uptown celebrity haunt. "I did it because Sinatra is a symbol of the place," he said.

Over lunch, Mr. Neiman also talked about friend Salvador Dali. "We were having our picture taken at the Hammer Galleries and I had a cigar and Victor Hammer, who was alive then, comes charging over, saying 'Get rid of that cigar.' And Dali says, 'No, good prop!' That was a real Dali-ism."

THE PRINCE AND THE PAUPER, a promising new musical based on the Mark Twain novel of the same name, began preview performances on Friday in the Lambs Theater, located in the historic Standford White-designed Lambs Club building at 130 West 44th Street. The show seems especially suited for the clubhouse, where late song-and-dance man George M. Cohan regaled members with stories of his years in Vaudeville, and Mark Twain himself smoked his pipe in front of a roaring fire. Not that Twain's ghost inhabits the club, but with its turn-of-the-century ambiance it can seem pretty spooky at times.

"I was working in the theater by myself at 2:30 a.m. the other night and I was a nervous wreck!" Carolyn Rossi Copeland, who is producing the show, told me.

WITH ALL THE BUZZ about Martin Scorsese's long-awaited Miramax epic *Gangs of New York*, starring Leonardo DiCaprio and Cameron Diaz—now set to be released December 25, 2002—little if anything is mentioned about its once famed author Herbert Asbury, who wrote the book *The Gangs of New York* in 1928. But that may soon change after historian Craig Rosenthal publishes his book that he has spent 10 years researching and is now shopping to publishers.

Asbury, who died in 1963, was a journalist with a long association with New York City-area newspapers and dedicated one of his books to his former boss, George "Keats" Speed, the last editor of the old New York *Sun*. He was an editor at *Collier's Magazine* in the 1940s and wrote books ranging in subject matter from a small town prostitute named "Hatrack," in his hometown of Farmington, Mo., in his book *Up From Methodism*, to the oil industry in *The Great Flood*.

UP CLOSE: Martha Stewart's daughter Alexis stretching her sweater over her Mom Martha's shoulder's Friday night in the slightly chilly Westport Country Playhouse in the early minutes of the theater's production of *Our Town*, starring Paul Newman, Jayne Atkinson, Jane Curtain and Mia Dillon... Joanne Woodward, artistic director of the Playhouse, told the *Sun* during the intermission that theater's next show will be John Van Druten's *Voice of the Turtle*, which first opened on Broadway in 1943. "I love that play. I saw it when I was a teenager during the war," she said...If you think ticket prices to *The Producers* are high, try paying $2,000 for two seats to see *Our Town* in Westport. New York advertising exec Bruce Burton did exactly that—but the cost also included dinner with *Our Town* director James Naughton and his wife. The $2,000 went to Shakespeare on the Sound, which is run by Mr. Burton's wife, Sheri.

Over the weekend, the Lester Lanin Orchestra, which has played for every American President since Dwight Eisenhower (with the exception of George W.), played for the 75th anniversary of the Brooks School in North Andover, Mass. It played for Brooke Astor's 100th birthday party this past March and the Adrian gowns exhibit opening at the Costume Institute of the Metropolitan Museum of Art on May 13. The seemingly ageless Mr. Lanin is no longer on the bandstand but the orchestra still gives out his signature "beanies." Mr. Lanin found the original prototype beanie in a novelty store on upper Broadway...

The New York Sun, June 11, 2002.

◻ Baryshnikov Plans Move to Off-Broadway Theater

IN A MOVE EXPECTED to be a cultural coup for New York City, Mikhail Baryshnikov may be moving off-Broadway—literally—the *Sun* has learned.

The world's most famous living dancer is in negotiations to move his world renowned White Oak Dance Project into several upper floors of a new seven-story off-Broadway theater complex under construction at 450 West 37th St., near 10th Ave., east of the New York City Convention Center, according to well-placed sources at White Oak and the West 37th Group, LLC, which is developing the site.

White Oak, one of the world's most celebrated dance companies, would move into space slated to be completed by spring 2003 above three state-of-the-art off-Broadway theaters (with 499, 399, and 299 seats) on the first three floors of the new building. Averitt Associates is designing the structure. White Oak currently has administrative offices in Philadelphia and at the Howard Gilman Foundation here in New York, and has rehearsal space at the 7,000-acre White Oak Plantation in Yulee, Florida, owned by the Gilman Foundation.

"Having Baryshnikov will help make the complex a destination point not just for theater but for the arts in general," a source close to building project told the *Sun*. White Oak is expected to have administrative and rehearsal space there.

"We have the space," said one White Oak source, who requested not to be identified.

Alan Schuster, one of five managing partners of the complex, told the *Sun* that constructions was scheduled to be completed by next spring, but would not discuss prospective tenants. Christina Steiner, with Baryshnikov Productions in Philadelphia, could not be reached for comment.

White Oak was formed in 1989 with choreographer Mark Morris to perform modern dance works. By December 2001, it had given some 600 performances in 30 countries. It presented works at Princeton University's McCarter Theatre earlier this month and will be performing Wednesday through Sunday at the Jacob's Pillow concert arena in Becket, Mass.

CALL HIM ONE NICE GUY. Woody Allen, who apologized to jurors and shook hands with Judge Ira Gammerman after the actor's lawsuit against his former producer, Jean Doumanian, was settled last week, went out of his way to sign an autograph for an eight-year-old fan when he was shooting his "Spring Project" movie starring Jason Biggs in Manhattan's John Jay Park on the East River.

"As we left the park, we saw Woody in the passenger side of the front seat of a black car with three other people. Sydney pointed to him," said the girl's mother, who declined to give her last name. He saw her and waved. "They all got out of the car and headed into the park. Sydney ran after them with me tailing behind and said, 'Excuse me, Mr. Allen!' He stopped first and then the others stopped. Sydney handed him a piece of paper and pen and he said 'sure' and signed an autograph. Sydney and I both thanked him and he said 'Sure, no problem!'"

"I JUST WANT PEOPLE to know that life goes on after the Carlyle!"

So said Barbara Carrol, one of the world's greatest jazz pianists, who after 24 years at Bemelman's Bar in the Carlyle Hotel is "happy to be getting back to my classical jazz roots." In her first extensive interview since a contract dispute with the hotel earlier this year, Ms. Carroll said she has only fond memories of working at the hotel and she's eagerly looking forward to three appearances at the JVC Jazz Festival, June 24, 25, and 26 and to performing at Birdland with her trio on July 17.

Looking radiant at lunch at Nirvana on Central Park South, she told me, "I came to the Carlyle for two weeks and that stretched out to 24 years. You create a following of people who keep coming back and they bring people who keep coming back and that's how one becomes established in a place like Bemelman's."

Over the years, Ms. Carroll has played not only bebop and jazz but also every conceivable kind of pop—from entertaining at top cabaret rooms like Bemelman's to appearing on Broadway in the Rodgers and Hammerstein classic *Me and Juliet*. One of her happiest memories of Bemelman's is the late Jack Lemmon staying late one night and playing on her piano.

"When I first came to the hotel it was owned by [the late] Peter Sharp who was such a marvelously interestingly, knowledgeable man who attempted to make his hotel the best in every possible way," she said.

THE 18-YEAR-OLD Castillo Theatre at 500 Greenwich Street will be opening its 2002-03 season this October with Heiner Müller's rarely produced masterwork *Hamletmachine*, under the artistic direction of Fred Newman, who will be writing original songs for the production. Müller, considered by many to be the most important European playwright since Bertolt Brecht, wrote plays steeped in history. Mr. Newman's unorthodox productions of Mr. Müller's works are typically infused with American popular culture, music and comedy.

Hamletmachine, which deconstructs Shakespeare's *Hamlet*—the script is just seven pages long—is the German writer's most-produced play in America. Noted avant-gardist theater and opera director Robert Wilson directed the American premiere of the play at New York University in mid-1980s. This production will be Castillo's second *Hamletmachine* (the first was an all-female version in 1996).

Hamletmachine will be cast from within Castillo's resident performing ensemble and will likely include Jeremy Black, who played the clone of Hitler in the film classic *The Boys of Brazil*, and David Nackman, who appeared on Broadway in Neil Simon's *Broadway Bound*.

YOU CAN NOW CALL him top banana. Actor and songwriter Daniel Linden Cohen, who won last year's John Lennon Songwriting Contest, has hit the national music scene with a CD aimed at the kids-market called "Danna Banana," which includes songs like "Teeny Houdini" and "Eleventy-Four." Mr. Cohen is pleased and surprised by its success. "As a writer and performer, it's having my dreams come true. With three kids myself, I guess you could say I've been duly inspired," he told the *Sun*. He's now is working on a kids-only opera, which he expects to finish this summer, and, on a "Danna Banana" CD sequel.

UP CLOSE: Amber, with such hit singles as "If You Should Read My Mind," belting out a new song, "The Need to be Naked" at the second annual "Tulips & Pansies: The Headdress Affair" benefit for Village Care of New York at the Super Club…Arthur Webb, president of Village Care, which services some 1,200 AIDS patients every day, says the fundraiser brought in $250,000, about $95,000 more than last year's event…Former *Rent* and *A Beautiful Mind* star Anthony Rapp, judging the wild and crazy headdresses by DKNY Jeans, Liz Claiborne and other designers, told the *Sun* he's headed to Boston to appear in the title role of *Henry V* for the seventh season of Free Shakespeare in the Park on the Boston Common…Another judge, two-time Oscar nominee Sylvia Miles, said she has a role in the first episode of the new season of HBO's "Sex in the City."…At a reading of a new play he's written, Tony Noto, the co-producer of the musical *The Fantasticks*, told the *Sun*, "If no one else does it, I definitely plan to produce *The Fantasticks* for its 50th anniversary in 2010." The show closed in January after a record 42 years. Mr. Noto's own play is about a black conservative radio talk show host and a white liberal city councilman from the Times Square district…Tony-Nominee Kate Burton and Oscar-winning stage veteran Estelle Parsons joined 200 people at the Players Club—once the Victorian home of actor Edwin Booth (the brother of John Wilkes Booth, who killed President Lincoln)—to celebrate the 4th annual Otto Rene Castillo Awards for Political Theatre, which honor performance artists and cultural organizations doing cutting-edge theater. Among this years honorees were performance artist Laurie Anderson, Ishmael Reed, and the MISSING TEXT

The New York Sun, June 18, 2002.

◻ New Producers in Town

MOVE OVER LINDA Bloodworth-Thomason and Harry Thomason, the pals of President Clinton who produced "Designing Women." Reality TV gurus Bertram van Munster and his wife Elise Doganieri are back in the U.S. following whirlwind trips from Kansas City to the Middle East preparing for the upcoming seasons of their TV shows, the new ABC reality series "Profiles From the Front Line" and "The Amazing Race," which received an Emmy nomination this year and will start its second season on CBS this fall. They produce the shows with Jerry Bruckheimer ("Bad Company," "CSI: Crime Scene Investigation.")

"Profiles from the Front Line" will pay homage to the brave men and women in the U.S. armed forces who are fighting terrorism overseas. "This is going to be a very visual reality show with a strong patriotic message," Mr. van Munster told the *Sun*. The Pentagon and the Department of Defense are lending their full support to the production.

While things couldn't get much better for one of TV's hottest producing couples, Ms. Doganieri, a native New Yorker who now lives in Los Angeles, misses New York. "I will always love New York," she told the *Sun*. "In L.A., everyone drives, so you can't walk if you want to go out for dinner. And when it comes to pizza and gourmet Italian food, New York's is the best. It would be great if Balducci's and Ben's Pizza opened L.A. locations…I miss them both. They don't know how to make a Sicilian pizza out here!"

LIVE, NO-ONE-UNDER-18 admitted-without-a-parent-or-guardian adult entertainment will open off-Broadway or possibly on Broadway in the upcoming New York theater season.

But it's not what you may think. *Adult Entertainment* is the name of a new six-character comedy by playwright/comedienne Elaine May, director Mike Nichols' former comedy partner, and the show's age caveat is for language, not nudity. The play will open off-Broadway "unless I can find a star," the producer and president of Castle Hill Productions, Julian Schlossberg, told the *Sun* in an interview in his office high above Central Park. Stanley Donen, who directed such classic films as *On the Town* and *Seven Brides for Seven Brothers*, will direct *Adult Entertainment*. The play is about a group of people in the pornography industry who band together to form their own company.

"At this point I'm not sure if it's going to be on Broadway or off-Broadway," Mr. Schlossberg continued. "What will make it go to Broadway is if some major star came aboard. You never know if a major star might be interested. When you're dealing with Elaine May and Stanley Donen you can't get too much better for some stars."

Meanwhile, Mr. Schlossberg, who produced the movies *Widow's Peak* and *In the Spirit* as well as *Fortune's Fool* currently on Broadway, said he wants "to get Vanessa Redgrave to do another play in New York. We've talked about it." He produced *Vita and Virginia* with Ms. Redgrave and Eileen Atkins.

"When I was growing up there were five performers that all I wanted to do was meet," he said. "I just wanted to shake their hands, and tell them what they meant to me. They are Sid Caesar, Alan Arkin, Elaine May, Mike Nichols, and Woody Allen. All five I've now worked with."

IN A SURPRISE announcement made from the stage of Carnegie Hall last night, entertainer Michael Feinstein told the audience that he and the entire 100-piece Israeli Philharmonic Orchestra will go on an eight-city American tour in August. Mr. Feinstein also introduced a special performance by the Arab-Israeli Music Ensemble, which consist of members of the Israeli Philharmonic and the Arab Music Group. The upcoming Michael Feinstein-IPO tour comes on the heels of the CD from Concord Records, "Michael Feinstein With the Israeli Philharmonic Orchestra," recorded in Tel Aviv and released May 7.

UP CLOSE: Self-effacing Academy Award-winning star Kevin Kline, who this week became the first American actor to win the Shakespeare Guild's Gielgud Award (named after the late English acting giant John Gielgud) telling family, friends and fans at Lincoln Center's Alice Tully Hall Tuesday, "I leaned over to Phoebe (Phoebe Cates, Mr. Kline's wife) and said this is my kind of night! Not because I'm an egomaniac, which I am, but I am so insecure!"… Raymond Benson signing his new James Bond novel *The Man with the Red Tattoo*, (Putnam) at the Jack Spade shop selling gadgets and menswear in Soho…Down the block, Kate Hudson and Matthew McConaughey shooting a scene from their new Paramount film *How to Lose a Guy in 10 Days*…*TV Guide* staff writer Mary Murphy writing a book on actor Robert Blake, awaiting trial for allegedly murdering his wife.

New York Sun, June 21-23, 2002.

◻ Jazz Star Lionel Hampton Still Makes Music at 94

THE DAWN OF A NEW era for the Apollo Theater finds 94-year old Lionel Hampton, America's greatest living jazz legend, jubilant and introspective about his days and nights at the historic 88-year-old Harlem playhouse.

"If you got a standing ovation from the people in the second balcony you knew you had made it!" a loquacious and upbeat Mr. Hampton told the *Sun*. *Harlem Song*, which opened July 7 and pays homage to great urban composers like Duke Ellington and Sam Cooke, is the first open-ended Broadway-style musical to play at the Apollo.

"When I first played there I felt the presence of greatness and ghosts," Mr. Hampton said as he played a few notes on his "vibes" (Vibraphone). "I didn't see any ghosts—but I felt the ghosts were there."

Born in Louisville, Ky., Mr. Hampton began studying music with the strict Dominican Sisters at Holy Rosary Academy in Kenosha, Wisc. His idols were Louis Armstrong and a drummer named Jimmy Bertrand, who used to toss his sticks high into the air. He met Armstrong in 1930 and the first tune they recorded was "Memories of You" by Eubie Blake. But Mr. Hampton's greatest fame would come when he joined the Benny Goodman Quartet several years later. "Benny and I were close friends," Mr. Hampton said. "The first time blacks and whites played together was with Benny…I had such respect for his musicianship. I liked him, too, as a person. Some people thought he was hard, gruff, but he had a good heart. When I was younger and coming up, I idolized him. He let my wife, Gladys, travel with the band and he used to say, "I'm going to put you in the hands of your wife so you won't get into trouble!" We played the Pennsylvania Hotel in the famous Mad Hatter room."

Mr. Hampton is looking forward to seeing *Harlem Song* at the Apollo, where he still holds the record for the number of performances in a single day—ten—which he set in 1946.

RCA/Bluebird is repackaging as CDs most of the original 78-rpm single records Mr. Hampton recorded in the 1940s with Harry James, Nat King Cole, Johnny Hodges, among others. Along with the Benny Goodman quartet sides, they are today considered the birth of classic jazz. In those performances, Mr. Hampton plays vibes, drums, piano, and sings ("Sunny Side of the Street" was his first big vocal hit).

HAVING JUST PRODUCED Thornton Wilder's Pulitzer Prize-winning classic play *Our Town*, starring Paul Newman, which broke box office records, the Westport Country Playhouse seems headed for one of its most successful seasons in its 72-year existence. The show's producer said he has secured space to bring the show to New York for an eight-week run with Mr. Newman in the starring role.

Mr. Newman's wife, legendary Oscar-winning actress Joanne Woodward, is the artistic director at the Playhouse and she's planning to take the famous summer theater year-round. "Eventually, hopefully, we will work year-round," Ms. Woodward said. "But not necessarily all theater. Some of it, hopefully, will be concerts and maybe opera or mini-opera."

And despite escalating costs and other problems, Ms. Woodward, says she's bullish on live theater "because we've gone past the whole television thing in a way. We used to have terrible feelings about the fact that television was taking away all the good writers when we did live television. But what it did was find a lot of writers. It was a place for them to work. Some of the greatest writers have started in television. And, now, I think there's so much going on in television; it's so fast, that we need to come back to theater. To me, it's really the place where an actor has to learn and where a writer has to learn. You have to pay your dues."

About how her marriage to Mr. Newman has lasted so long, Ms. Woodman smiled. "I think a lot of it is luck. It's important if people are willing to give and take a little. And forgive and take! Splitting up household chores helps, too. He cooks. I clean."

SHORT TAKES: Who says radio is dead? It's the 32nd anniversary of the nationally syndicated radio show, "One Minute Please," hosted by Dr. Tom Haggai, chairman/CEO of IGA (the worlds' largest voluntary supermarket network). An ordained minister, Dr. Haggai gives a short inspirational message on each show and says he first got used to short messages as a quarterback on his college football team. "Each huddle was a matter of seconds," he said. More a matter of minutes than seconds, Dr. Haggai, who has flown more than 5 million miles to IGA stores around the globe, said he never suffers from jet lag because he takes catnaps on planes.

The New York Sun, July 17, 2002.

◻ Newman Means Broadway

PAUL NEWMAN hasn't been on Broadway in more than 40 years. But he is poised to play the Stage Manager in *Our Town*, the classic American play about small town life, in October, sources close to Mr. Newman told the *Sun*.

"Paul only wants to do it for four weeks but we think we can persuade him to do it for eight weeks beginning in October," James Naughton, who directed the production of *Our Town* with Mr. Newman at the Westport Country Playhouse in Connecticut last month. "We got the rights to the play after the Roundabout Theatre, which was going to do it on Broadway, dropped them."

TWIGGY WAS THE WORLD'S first supermodel. She took Broadway by storm in the musical *My One and Only*, and now hopes that the Bay Street Theatre's current production of Noël Coward's classic comedy *Blithe Spirit* will come to Broadway.

Wearing fashionably faded blue jeans and sunglasses, Twiggy talked about plans to be in a new 1920s period musical with Tommy Tune, about meeting Noël Coward in Jamaica, and about her friendship with (and love for) ex-Beatle Paul McCartney.

"You'd make a great Elvira [the attractive ghost in *Blithe Spirit*]," Coward told her at their first meeting. A photographer took their picture, but she lost it. Then "about six years ago when I was preparing to do *Blithe Spirit* in London I was cleaning my bookshelves and a little thing fluttered down. It was the snapshot of Noël Coward and myself!"

"Paul [McCartney] is one of my best friends and Paul's [late] wife Linda was one of my dear, dear friends," Twiggy told the *Sun*. "I still miss her all the time. She was an extraordinary woman." Twiggy attended Mr. McCartney's marriage to Heather Mills and told me, "I love him dearly and I'm very happy he's happy."

ACTRESS JENNIFER ROBERTS is making her New York City debut in *Veronique*, a play by the late John O'Hara which is having its world premiere at off-Broadway's Bank Street Theater. The script calls for someone to try to kill her in Act II. Life seemed to be imitating art when Ms. Roberts was rushed to the hospital with a gash in her forehead.

Ms. Roberts was coming off stage during a blackout and ran into a brick pillar. A minute or two passed, then the director came out and announced she needed medical attention and the curtain came down on that night's performance. Five stitches and a good night's rest later, Ms. Roberts returned to the show. But this time any reference to blood was strictly in the script.

"Making Books Sing," a unique in-school performing arts program from off-Broadway's nonprofit Vineyard Theatre, has become an independent organization. Created in 1996 by Barbara Krieger, the founder and former executive director of the Vineyard, the program grew from serving 180 students in to serving more than 5,000 in some 30 schools today. Being spun off is "a natural next step in its development," Ms. Krieger told the *Sun*.

"Our first project was *The Merry Muldoons*, a fun vaudevillian-style opera based on a book by theater historian Brooks McNamara," Ms. Krieger told the *Sun*.

"Our programming interests have shifted in recent years to theater woks inspired by books that celebrate the multicultural origins of the children we serve and expose them to art forms from around the world.

"Last year, we produced a cross-cultural opera called *Beautiful Warrior* that was an enchanting journey through 17th-century China incorporating Peking and Western opera, Chinese instruments, shadow puppets, and martial arts choreography. Our upcoming production, *Bird Woman: The Story of Sacajawea* tells the story of a Shoshone girl's travels as a guide on the Lewis and Clark Expedition."

The New York Sun, July 19-21, 2002.

◻ Bogdanovich On His Wife, a Call Girl, a Detective, and a Judge

PETER BOGDANOVICH, who found relaxation and profit directing the *The Cat's Meow* partly aboard a sumptuous 1920s yacht in the Mediterranean, is planning to shoot his next movie, a screwball comedy called *Squirrels to the Nuts*, much closer to home in Manhattan and Brooklyn, the *Sun* has learned.

"*Squirrels* is about a guy who is directing a play on Broadway and his wife and a call girl he gets involved with and a detective and a judge," Mr. Bogdanovich said. "It's a wild ride. We're just starting to talk to actors about it."

His highly praised film *The Cat's Meow*, starring Edward Herrmann as the late newspaper czar William Randolph Hearst, and Kirsten Dunst, as his longtime paramour Marion Davies, comes out on DVD in August. Mr. Bogdanovich takes some credit for Ms. Dunst's co-starring role in *Spiderman*, which he didn't direct. "She auditioned for it while we were shooting *The Cat's Meow*. They were coming to Athens with Toby McGuire [who played the title role in *Spiderman*] and I told her, 'Make them wait and you'll get the part!'

"In *The Cat's Meow* all the stuff aboard the yacht was shot in a small fishing village off the Mediterranean coast of Greece," he said. "Why? Because it was the only place we could find a yacht that was big enough and get the 'period' right. Also, San Diego and Los Angeles are much too 'grown up,' much too modern-looking. The movie is set in 1924. I had done *Paper Moon* set in the 1930s. But I had never done one in the 20s. It was great fun. I love that period. We used 58 songs from the period."

JULIE ANDREWS, whose Broadway singing career ended after the 1996 stage version of the film *Victor/Victoria*, may soon perform a non-singing stage role.

"She's done two sort of 'conversations with shows' for us and we would love her to act here," Emma Walton, co-artistic director of the Bay Street Theatre in Sag Harbor, and Miss Andrews' daughter, told the *Sun*. "And we're actually talking to her about the possibility of directing a play." After *Victor/Victoria*, Ms. Andrews had an operation to remove nodes on her vocal cords but has not sung in musicals since.

"Julie's a wonderful director," Ms. Walton's co-artistic director Sybil Christopher, the late Richard Burton's first wife, told the *Sun*. "If she sees something that needs to be done she's very lucid. She's very, very clear about what she wants."

New York's venerable Folksbiene Yiddish Theatre, America's oldest professional Yiddish theatre, has finally obtained the rights from Barbra Streisand's production company to adapt into Yiddish and produce Off-Broadway Isaac Bashevis Singer's acclaimed play *Yentl*. The world premiere of *Yentl* in Yiddish will open Folksbiene's 87th consecutive season in the fall and will star director and actress Eleanor Reissa (nominated for a Tony for the musical *Those Were the Days* in 1991) and will be directed by Robert Kalfin who staged the original Broadway production in 1975. The 11-week limited engagement runs from October 15 through December 29. The show will inaugurate a new 199-seat playhouse at 344 West 36th Street that Folksbiene hopes will be its permanent home.

Yentl premiered on Broadway in 1975 and starred Tovah Feldshuh. The stage play by the Nobel laureate Singer and co-author Leah Napolin was an adaptation of Singer's 1950's story, "Yentl the Yeshiva Boy," originally penned in Yiddish, but this is the first time the play has been performed in Yiddish. While simultaneous English translation via headsets will be provided, Folksbiene will draw on *Yentl*'s wide popularity to bridge its Yiddish-speaking core audience with a younger, more mainstream crowd.

SHORT TAKES: No wonder Dana Ivey is one of the busiest character actresses in show business. Co-starring with Twiggy in the Bay Street Theatre's production of *Blythe Spirit*, Ms. Ivey was featured in *Home Alone II*. "I love everything I do," she said. "Television, film, theater. But theater is my first love because it's what I grew up in and spent a greater part of my life doing."

UP CLOSE: "Sex in the City's" "Mr. Big" (actor Chris Noth), with a couple of buddies, ordering a big steak at Strip House...Rock star Graham Nash releasing "Songs For Survivors," his first solo CD in 16 years this week at a party with DJs Scott Muni and Zach Martin from radio station Q104 at the Shoreham Hotel on West 55th Street...Coati Mundi, former Kid Creole & The Coconuts mainstay, now in a new movie *Servicing Sara* with Mathew Perry and Elizabeth Hurley, at Atlas restaurant...Miramax's Tina Brown, in white slacks and black tank top, getting into a black Mercedes on East 57th Street...Blythe Danner, a perennial Broadway star who's in the new CBS fall series, "Presidio Med," staying well into the night at TV Critics Association bash this week at the Ritz Carlton Hotel in Pasadena. Actors Michael Nouri and Anthony LaPaglia as well as producers Jerry Bruckheimer and Bertram van Munster, ("The Amazing Race") at same party.

The New York Sun, July 24, 2002.

◻ Grammy-Winner Schifrin Gives Up Car Chase Music

GREAT ARGENTINEAN-AMERICAN composer/pianist Lalo Schifrin is calling it quits with (doing the music for) car chases.

The four-time Grammy Award-winning composer, who scored the music for *Bullitt*, *Rush Hour*, *Rush Hour II*, *Cool Hand Luke*, and *Dirty Harry*, can't wait to write the music for *Drinking Down the House*, an upcoming Touchstone comedy starring Steve Martin.

"It's refreshing because I don't have to write chase music, and don't have to feel guilty about the demolition of so many vehicles!" the wiry, white-haired six-time Oscar nominee said in his dressing room at the Blue Note jazz club Wednesday night. Mr. Schifrin, who also conducted the London Philharmonic Orchestra and the Vienna Symphony, is at the Blue Note through Sunday for what is being billed as his 70th birthday celebration.

"The work of a composer is very, very isolated and playing the Blue Note is a different kind of challenge," said Mr. Schifrin. "In a big theater, the audience is far away. But in a club the respect you have for an audience is even bigger. At times, I am like a bullfighter who likes to go close to the horns of a bull. A club like this is the danger."

IT'S REALLY MUSIC to her ears. Felicity LaFortune, who understudies Mercedes Ruehl in *The Goat*, Edward Albee's controversial and emotionally charged Broadway play, has approached the role of Stevie, the wife of Martin, played by Bill Pullman, almost as if it were in an opera. "I was already familiar with a lot of Albee plays, but I went and read the ones I didn't know and realized that Edward has a musician's ear," said Ms. LaFortune, who went on for Ms. Ruehl Tuesday night. "His writing is very musical to me and as a trained singer, I sometimes find a hint as to the approach I should take. One of the things that makes the part of Stevie so exciting is that it is so operatic in size, and you can't shy away from that. For instance, she has three speeches in Scene 2 that are really like big arias."

WRITER/ACTOR STEPHEN BELBER, co-starring in celebrated French playwright Jean Luc Lagarce's *Only the End of the World*, which begins performances on Thursday, August 1 at Theatre 3 (311 West 43rd Street), just got an Emmy nomination as one of the writers on "The Laramie Project," about the life and death of Matthew Shepard which aired on HBO.

"I am completely flattered and ecstatic at the notion of an Emmy for 'The Laramie Project.'" Mr. Belber told the *Sun*. "What we wanted in working on

Laramie was to further a dialogue that had begun with Matthew's murder, and if the notoriety of an Emmy enhances that still, then I'm more than delighted."

VETERAN CHARACTER ACTRESS Abetha Aayer, who died recently, appeared in over 100 roles on and off-Broadway, in regional theater and summer stock. But her husband, Aaron Frankel, a Broadway director and retired Columbia University theater professor, didn't realize the extent of Aayer's gift for knowing how an audience would react to a line until he ran the Margo Jones Theatre in Dallas.

"I was directing rehearsals of a new play, *Penelope's Web*, by Sheridan Gibney, an Oscar winner. Abetha was playing Penelope and she had a speech on the phone and immediately after had to be on the other side of the stage. I couldn't find a line for her to cross on, and Sheridan couldn't come up with one either. Abetha said, 'Don't' worry. I'll cross on the laugh.' I worried. But, sure enough, when the audience came there was a laugh. Over to the other side she sailed!"

SHORT TAKES: Wearing four different outfits, a radiant Diana Ross did three encores at her one and only concert at the Westbury Music Fair this week, including her signature song "I Will Survive." "I've never seen such a giving performance," one fan in the audience told the *Sun*. "It was like she was trying to please each and every person in the audience."

Harvey Fierstein, who is in the new musical *Hairspray*, now in previews at Broadway's Neil Simon Theater, told Barbara Corcoran, head of the prestigious the Corcoran Group, that while he plays a real estate agent in his next movie, *Duplex*, he could not help a friend of his looking for an apartment. Ms. Corcoran said she would.

UP CLOSE: Kathleen Turner and Alicia Silverstone, co-starring in *The Graduate* on Broadway signing dozens of autographs for a full 15 minutes Tuesday night outside the stage door...Jimmy Nederlander, the legendary Broadway theater owner and producer, dining at Elio's on Second Avenue at 84th Street with son Jimmy Nederlander Jr., and Margo McNabe...Broadway Tony Award winning actress Zoe Caldwell, whose husband producer Robert Whitehead, died recently, at a nearby table with a lady friend the same night... Blake Edwards and wife Julie Andrews tasting samples at the organic foods deli counter at Brentwood's Whole Foods Market.

The New York Sun, July 26, 2002.

◻ Elvis Lives, on Broadway

ELVIS MAY HAVE LEFT the building, but he may be coming to Broadway soon. David Michael Spear, whose voice has been likened to a cross between the late Elvis Presley and Roy Orbison, will be performing two songs from the new CD "Elvis Movie: The Song" at the Planet Hollywood Times Square on August 13 to mark the 25th anniversary of Elvis's passing August 16. Mr. Spear is also attracting backers who are working with him to develop a musical called *Elvis Movie: the Song* for Broadway in 2004. David Briggs, Elvis' keyboard player and arranger from 1970-75, and Reggie Young, Elvis' guitar player from 1969-73, are on the CD.

The title song was inspired by an incident at one of his favorite Nashville watering holes. "I was just like any other guy with a broken heart, looking for a new flame to help me get over the old one, when Jimmy, the bartender, handed me my usual—a Black Lemon Twister," the New Jersey singer-songwriter said. "Jimmy turned on the TV above the bar and there was an Elvis flick I must have seen 100 times. I couldn't help noticing how the chicks drooled over Elvis. All I could think was, 'Man, I want a girl who makes me feel like I feel when I'm watchin' an Elvis movie.'"

Mr. Spear went home and fell asleep and had a dream about *Viva Las Vegas*, an Elvis movie. He kept thinking of the scene where Elvis is kissing Ann-Margret. Suddenly, in the dream, they were Mr. Spear's lips and when he awoke, he wrote the words and music in one sitting.

TANYA CLARK never expected her Broadway debut to be so much fun. "I've never been so happy," she told the *Sun* at a party in the penthouse apartment of entrepreneur Joel Newman, hosted by Tony Awards nominator Aubrey Reuben. Referring to *I'm Not Rappaport* co-stars Judd Hirsch and Ben Vereen, she said, "Judd and Ben are children, really; they're adorable; they're crazy—and they are the real thing. There was a kid who came on the set before the curtain and someone introduced him to Judd. And Judd became a giraffe; he became a tiger. He's always like that—he's so cute. He's a 12-year old in a 66-year old body. And he's got more energy than I ever imagine having."

After the show's official opening night performance last week, the cast went to playwright Herb Gardner's apartment to celebrate with him. According to Ms. Clark, Mr. Gardner, the author of *A Thousand Clowns* and other successful plays, was too ill to go to the opening. "He's going to be laid up for a while but his spirit is so insanely alive!" said Ms. Clark.

IT MAY BE HOTTER than the weather. Everyone on Broadway thought that *Hairspray*, the new $10.5 million musical spoof of the 1960s costarring Marissa Jaret Winokur and Harvey Fierstein (and based on the 1988 John Waters movie of the same name), would do well. But in an unusual set of circumstances, ticket sales have soared to such levels that *Hairspray* may be the first blockbuster of the new Broadway season. *Hairspray* began performances at the Neil Simon Theater July 18 and opens officially August 15.

Advance ticket sales for the musical, with a score by Marc Shaiman and Scott Wittman, have reached $6 million and climbing, amazing even some of the show's veteran producers. Last Friday alone, box office receipts topped $300,000.

"In today's market $6 million is a very healthy advance," one major Broadway producer told the *Sun*.

SHORT TAKES: Katlean DeMonchy, who appears regularly on "The View" talking about the latest lifestyle trends, is known around the Hamptons for her social column, "Kat's Eye," in Dan's Papers. "This year was supposed to be the summer we suffered," Ms. DeMonchy told the *Sun*. "But the charity events at $1,000 and up sold out and were turning people away at the door."

UP CLOSE: Prolific novelist Rona Jaffe, who wrote her first poem at age 2-1/2, telling the *Sun* she just turned in the manuscript of her latest novel, *The Room-Mating Season*, to her editor at Dutton, which will publish it next April. The novel, set in New York City, is based on "Things I knew about people having roommates. I never had any roommates, but I knew friends who did!"

The New York Sun, July 31, 2002.

JANE CURTIN had two Broadway offers she couldn't refuse, but she had to refuse one. Ms. Curtin, perhaps best known for being an original cast member of the TV show "Saturday Night Live," co-starred with Paul Newman in the Westport Country Playhouse's production of *Our Town* in June before she joined the cast of Michael Frayn's *Noises Off* on Broadway.

"I'm sorry I'm not going to be a part of the [upcoming] Broadway production of *Our Town*—it's a magical production." She told the *Sun* at a party for the new cast of *Noises Off*. "But, you know, it happens in this business. The opportunity to do *Our Town* happened and I had a glorious experience doing that and *Noises Off* is something that I said yes, I would do it, and now I'm having a fantastic time doing it. I'm contracted for six months. I can't imagine doing it longer. I think my body would give out—it's very physical!"

Would she ever like to do "Saturday Night Live" again? "I don't think so," she told the *Sun*. "And, honestly, I don't stay up that late!"

Kaitlin Hopkins, who plays the cheerful busybody in the new cast of *Noises Off*, says her mom, TV and film star Shirley Knight, tried to dissuade her from a career in show business "for about five minutes. And then she gave up and I know she's really, really thrilled I'm in this show."

"You know, they've restaged a good portion of the first and second acts," Ms. Hopkins, who is making her Broadway debut in the revival, also told the *Sun*. "So it looks like a new production, in a way. The director really allowed us to create our own characters and encouraged us to make it our own."

SHE MAY BE PLAYING a witch on stage but Vanessa Williams seems to be more like an angel these days to adoring fans. Last Saturday night in front of the stage door of Broadway's Broadhurst Theatre, where she's starring in a hit revival of Stephen Sondheim's *Into the Woods*, the recording and film star signed autographs for 20 minutes until almost each and every fan had either an autograph, photo or warm greeting. "Hello!" "How are you?" "Sure, you can take my picture!" she told several of the more than 100 fans who gathered outside the Broadhurst.

CHALK UP ANOTHER credit for legendary singer, actor, and activist Harry Belafonte—Broadway producer. Mr. Belafonte, one of the producers of *Harlem Song*, told the *Sun* opening night of the new Broadway style musical, that producing "is something I would like to do more of."

He also said he's co-producing it because "the Apollo Theatre means an awful lot to a lot of people and so does George C. Wolfe."

SHARON MCKNIGHT brought the church down with "Songs to Offend Almost Everyone" in a cabaret performance to raise money for the York Theatre at St. Peter's Church/Citicorp Center. Ms. McKnight wittily ad-libbed with the lively crowd in between songs such as "Poisoning Pigeons in the Park" and "I Should Put a Bullet Through Your Head." Whether throatily impersonating the late Mae West in an inspired "I'm Everybody's Girl" and growling out "Let's Drop the Big One Now," the audience kept clamoring for more. She treated the crowd to two encores after receiving a standing ovation.

SHORT TAKES: John Travolta has a special place he goes to for cheeseburgers in L.A. It's the Los Angeles International Airport's Encounter theme restaurant, which looks like a huge spider. Just recently, the actor threw himself a birthday party at Encounter, where friends and family enjoyed cheeseburgers and a specially created birthday cake.

Almost everyone knows that Mayor Giuliani is a great fan of HBO's "The Sopranos." But he also loves watching the real-life trials on "Court TV." Court TV CEO Henry Schlieff said Mr. Giuliani, a former prosecutor, told him, "It's a favorite of mine."

Stephen Mo Hanan, who plays the title role in the upcoming musical *Jolson & Company*, about the late Al Jolson, can't wait for performances to start at off-Broadway's Century Center September 12. He sadly notes some the Jolson standards "haven't been heard by a live theater audience for an entire generation."

The Tooth Fairy Legend: A Touch of Kindness, a popular children's book, is being readied for the stage. John Arthur Long and Chet Meyer, the book's coauthors, are doing a workshop of the new show next month.

UP CLOSE: Actor Michael Emerson at Marseilles Restaurant telling the *Sun* he's been cast in the Roundabout Theatre's production of Moliere's *Tartuffe*, which starts rehearsals in November…Playwright and two-time Academy Award-winning screenwriter Horton Foote telling the *Sun* he's going back home to Texas "to get some rest and think about writing my next play."…March 1999 Playboy Playmate Cindy Guyer, who has adorned the cover of several romance novels, telling the *Sun* she's penned a Harlequin novel of her own due out in the fall…Vice President Gore and "Friends" cast member David Schwimmer dining on Brancini (whole striped sea bass laced with herbs) on separate evenings at Beverly Hills' classy Italian bistro Il Cielo.

The New York Sun, August 7, 2002.

◻ A 'Crazy' Cline Celebration; No 'Hairspray' for Lake

PATSY CLINE MANIA is about to sweep the Big Apple with a musical about the legendary pop and country singer in the wings. On September 8, which would have been Cline's 70th birthday, Greenwich Village's Cowgirl Hall of Fame will celebrate with a birthday party that will feature Cline's recipes on the menu and a live musical tribute by Renee Lawless Orsini, the winner of the 2002 "St. Patsy's Day" Look-a-Like Contest.

Ellis Nassour, who wrote a biography of Cline, has also developed his book into a stage musical, complete with the Cline classics and an original score. He's so impressed with Ms. Orsini's ability to portray Cline that he's in discussions with her to star in his musical. March 2003 will mark the 40th anniversary of Cline's death, and in addition to the premiere of the musical, an all-star tribute CD is planned featuring k.d. lang, Lee Ann Womack (a favorite of President Bush and Laura Bush), Natalie Cole and jazz great Diana Krall, who'll offer her rendition of "Crazy."

TALK SHOW DIVA Ricki Lake says she can't go home again—to *Hairspray*. Asked if she would ever consider subbing for the musical's star, Marisa Janet Winokur, Ms. Lake, who starred in John Waters' 1980s movie, told the *Sun*, "I think I've been there and done that. I've come a long way. I have a very different life than I did then. I think I could still pass for 18 on stage. But, you know, I'm not heavy enough!"

RUSSIAN-BORN ACTRESS Lana Novac is playing a leading role in a top secret HBO pilot being filmed in California. In fact, the HBO pilot is so hush-hush that the cable channel is calling it "the untitled pilot." Hollywood sources say it's the genesis of a new "edgy, urban comedy series a la 'Sex in the City.'"

Ms. Lana, whom TV viewers may remember from "Law and Order: Special Victim's Unit," got some advice from Russell Crowe one day while waiting in the teller line at the bank they both used in Melbourne, Australia. She was a fledgling teenage actress, and Mr. Crowe was an unknown actor on the TV series, "Neighbors."

"Russell and I exchanged our views on stardom," Ms. Lana told the *Sun*. "He said to me 'trust me, I have been trying for years.' Well of course since that time he's gone on to see super stardom. I am so very happy for Russell...He is such a brilliant performer."

WALTER BOBBIE, who won a Tony Award for directing the current Broadway revival of *Chicago*, may have a new Broadway show in *The Road to Hol-*

lywood at Goodspeed Opera House's Norma Terris Theatre in Chester, Conn. Besides being extended to September, several major producers who have come to the show seem keen on the Hollywood spoof.

SHORT TAKES: Lyricist Tom Jones (no relation to the famous singer), who wrote the book for *The Fantasticks*, told the *Sun* that he and collaborator Joseph Thalken have "nearly finished the score" for *Harold and Maude*, a new musical based on the movie of the same name starring the late Ruth Gordon. He expects it to open in a regional theater or in London next year before coming to Broadway. *Damn Yankees* composer Richard Adler told the *Sun* "there's possibly going to be a movie of *Damn Yankees*."

UP CLOSE: Kathie Lee Gifford at her Greenwich, Conn., estate trying out love songs that she's planning to include in a show called "Songs in the Key of True" at Feinstein's at the Regency this fall…Billy Crystal and Jerry Seinfeld jogging instead of joking to The Pump, the health food restaurant on West 55th Street for energy shakes during a mid-morning jog…Cady Huffman, the blond co-star of *The Producers*, calling her handsome husband, Bill Healy, a basketball coach at Hunter College, "Broadway Bill," "because he hangs around Broadway hotspots so much—"with me!" Ms. Huffman tells the *Sun* she's producing an independent film…New Jersey pop-punk band The Stems (formerly Random) lunching with Nickelodeon execs at Cinnabar on West 56th Street…*Into the Woods* star Vanessa Williams stopping by Angus MacIndoe, the West 44th Street restaurant, with a bodyguard…Yankee stars Jason Giambi, Robin Ventura, David Wells, and Mike Mussina relaxing at Mickey Mantle's Restaurant…Mets star Mike Piazza and his brother dining at Strip House steak house two weeks in a row.

The New York Sun, August 28, 2002.

Luhrmann Gets a Loft; Cattrall and Abraham Get New Roles

HAPPY BIRTHDAY Lester Lanin, the legendary bandleader who turned 95 this week!

"Sex in the City," siren Kim Cattrall may be headed to Broadway in yet another steamy role—but don't think she's anything like her TV alter ego.

Ms. Cattrall will co-star with Martha Plimpton in the New York premiere of David Mamet's *Boston Marriage* at the Joseph Papp Public Theater in November. She "may move with the play to Broadway depending on how well it does at the Public," a source close to the production told the *Sun*. Sharon Stone had been previously mentioned to star in a Broadway production of the play, about two lesbians, which was first staged at the Donmar Warehouse in London.

Ms. Cattrall told the *Sun* she is not anything like the sexually promiscuous Samantha Jones, her "Sex in the City" character, even though some women tell her that Ms. Jones has been something of a role model for them. "Samantha's such a life-affirming character for many women who have been afraid of their sexuality for so long, and here's a woman who says 'yes' to life," Ms. Cattrall said at a benefit in the Hamptons for the anti-hate crime group BiasHELP of Long Island and the Long Island Association for AIDS Care.

OSCAR WINNER F. Murray Abraham—who made his New York City "acting" debut as a Macy's Santa Claus—will play Scrooge in the annual Radio City Music Hall production of *A Christmas Carol* at Madison Square Garden. Mr. Abraham, a veteran of some 60 films, is best known for his playing Antonio Salieri in the 1984 movie *Amadeus*.

BAZ LUHRMANN, the director of *Moulin Rouge* is bringing *La Boheme* to Broadway in December and doing his part for downtown real estate in the process. Mr. Luhrmann and his wife, Catherine Martin, are renting a downtown loft for a year through the Corcoran Group, as are Mr. Luhrmann's sister, Mandy, who is also his lawyer, and Adam Siberman, his general manager.

ONE OF THE HIGHLIGHTS of the hugely successful 2002 New York International Fringe Festival was *The Way Out*, a dramatic play about boxer Rubin "Hurricane" Carter, brilliantly performed by Shiek Mahmud-Bey. Mr. Mahmud-Bey won an Excellence Award for performance. Present Tense Productions' producer Suzannah Nolan tells the *Sun* the company has received offers to produce the show off-Broadway and for cable TV.

When Bob Watman and Tim Ouellette had the idea to decorate their first bar in Manhattan with old posters and memorabilia from the 1970s and to dub the club Polly Esther's, they never dreamed that over a decade later they would be opening their 30th nightclub. Before the end of September, The Culture Club '80s theme disco and Club Expo will open their doors in Cleveland. The Danceplex empire also includes clubs in Austin, Boston, Washington, D.C., San Francisco, San Deigo, Phoenix.

When Scott Cargle, the adapter and creator of the Shakespeare Project's production of *Falstaff*, ran into huge budget problems post-September 11 and was forced to scale back his production, he could only cast four actors for the 20 roles in the show. But in the spirit of "the show must go on," and with the help of lots of puppets and masks, the antics of Shakespeare's outrageous anti-hero comes to life each night.

Falstaff wears a fantastic fat-suit, of which Mr. Cargle says, "His belly is a huge, well-engineered apparatus with a mind of its own. It is the 21st character of the play!"

The play is touring city parks through September 15.

Short Takes: Israela Margaliti, the wife of "Guiding Light" executive producer Paul Pauch, has written a play called *Three O'Clock in Brooklyn*, which begins performances October 4 at the Access Theatre. Set in a Brooklyn coffee shop, the romantic comedy is directed by Margaret Perry and the cast includes Kim Zimmer, Jordan Charney, Jeremy Webb, and Erica Piccininni. Theater-lovers who can't wait to see the Westport (Conn.) Country Playhouse's Broadway-bound production of *Our Town*, starring Paul Newman, can see one of the production's stars in an off-Broadway play next month. Maggie Lacey, is playing the lead role in the Keen Company's revival of the 1933 Broadway him *Three-Cornered Moon*, which is at the Blue Heron Arts Center beginning September 6.

The New York Sun, September 1, 2002.

◻ Broadway Turns From Big-Name Stars to Best-Selling Songs

THE MONEY is in the music. This season music is in the air on Broadway! Broadway producers know they can guarantee advance box office sales by bringing in big name Hollywood stars like Kathleen Turner, Alicia Silverstone, Jason Biggs, Joey Fatone, and Anne Heche. In this new season, best-selling name music will be the big draw.

Already in pre-production are musicals based on the multimillion selling recordings by some of pop and classical music's biggest names. Eagerly anticipated are *Movin' Out*, based on the music of five-time Grammy Award winner Billy Joel and opening October 24; *Rocky Mountain High*, starring the music of the late John Denver and produced by his longtime accountant and manager; and a new version of Puccini's *La Boheme*, directed by one of the most creative talents in show business, Baz Luhrmann of *Moulin Rouge*, fame.

Following announcements last month that there are at least three musicals based on Elvis Presley in development, comes the news that David Bowie is considering a Broadway presentation of his music.

Years ago, the best songwriters of our time wrote for Broadway. Even modern masterpieces, like the music for *Cats*, were first popularized by stars like Barbra Streisand, who made a hit single out of "Memories" prior to the show's opening. But in the last 30 years, that has changed. Even *Rent* really failed to produce a hit single.

Multi-platinum record producer Tony Bongiovi, of Bongiovi Entertainment, (singer Jon Bon Jovi's cousin) said he sees potential in the new trend of creating musicals from songs that are already hits.

"Building theatrical musicals based around great music is a terrific idea. Even before the introduction of music videos, pop and rock music by its very nature is a total performance art," he told the *Sun*. "It would be great to see popular music as a catalyst to inspire a whole new generation of theatergoers and recording artists who write for the stage."

INTERNATIONALLY CELEBRATED concert pianist and composer Byron Janis is hoping to beat Disney at its own game. He's composed a stage musical based on Victor Hugo's classic *The Hunchback of Notre Dame*, which he hopes will open on Broadway before Disney's own *The Hunchback of Notre Dame*, which closed in Berlin this past June, opens as a stage musical in this country.

"There are no plans to bring it [*Hunchback*] to New York, Chicago or L.A. at this time," Chris Boneau, a spokesman for Disney said yesterday of the production, which will be developed as a TV movie for the "Wonderful World of Disney." "It will be a TV movie first and then we'll see."

Mr. Janis' version, meanwhile, has been workshopped in Havana with an all-Cuban cast. Mr. Janis was a favorite with Cuban concertgoers before Castro came to power. (He wrote his *Hunchback* score after arthritis left him unable to keep up with his vigorous concert-playing schedule.)

"I haven't seen Disney's production. But I know the way in which they do things," Mr. Janis told the *Sun* in a reference to Disney's musical versions of stories such as *Beauty and the Beast*. "I don't think bigger is necessarily better."

But a Disney source, noting the millions of dollars the company spends on marketing its shows even after poor to lackluster reviews (as was the case with Disney-produced *Aida*) said, "I don't care if it's Byron Janis' best work, they're crazy to try and compete with Disney on any level. If they don't open before Disney's, they're dead."

"Byron can't compete with Disney on sets and special effects. He's going to have to do it the old-fashioned way—by being inventive and having wonderful music and wonderful singers," said independent producer Ivan Kronenfeld, who helped mount Mr. Janis' *Hunchback* in Havana. "We used artifice to accomplish things that Disney has spent a fortune on. For example, the church in our set is just a skeletal structure and as dancers mount the structure they became the saints and gargoyles."

THE CALVIN KLEIN Equitation Championship at the 2002 Hampton Classic Horse Show concentrates on style. But when Mr. Klein showed up with ex-wife Kelly and daughter Marci, he was nonplused about the style displayed in the tony VIP tent. "Everyone used to get dressed up for this event, but this year no one seems to care," he told the *Sun*. "At one time you'd think it was Saratoga, but today it seems a lot more Long Island." Meaning? "Read into that what you like," he said.

The New York Sun, September 4, 2002.

◻ Mackie's Coming Back to Town!

AFTER SOLD-OUT engagements across the country, *Mack the Knife*, a new musical based on the life and music of the late Bobby Darin—the first musical done about Darin to have the backing of the Darin estate—is coming to Broadway or off-Broadway this spring. The musical will include many of his greatest hits, including "Mack the Knife," "Splish Splash," "Beyond the Sea," and "Dream Lover."

"We are trying to test it in different markets in the next few months and that's why we're going to do it in Springfield [Mass.] in late October and in late December or early January in Chicago—especially Chicago because it's a big market and a precursor to New York," said Charles Esposito., who plays Darin.

"I've had a fascination with the guy since I was a kid," the singer/actor said. "I remember my parents listening to him and also catching his NBC special. I remember my mother really enjoyed watching that. And he was kind of stuck in the back of my head as a kid. He was a cool, hip guy, and I started performing in some nightclub work and I'd always try and pop in a song of his. I did that work for years until I collaborated with my partner, Jim Haddon, who's a musical director and did all the arrangements for *Mack the Knife*."

"Bobby Darin was the quintessential performer," Mr. Esposito continued. "He could write a song; he could produce a song; he was a music publisher; he was a heck of an actor; he was very good at all those things, but what he did the best was perform."

HARVARDWOOD, an organization for Harvard graduates in the entertainment industry, held an "End-of-Summer Mixer" at Absolutely 4th, a bar in Greenwich Village, recently. Among the creative people who attended were: Jean Tang who is writing a book on the history of food "from an American perspective"; Yoshi Amao, who appeared in a Budweiser "Whassup?" commercial; Daniel Libin and Alex Twersky who are at work on a film about a man, pretending to be Jewish, who stalks an Orthodox woman; Matthew Saha, who plays a corrupt blackmailer who works in a deaf phone center in *Two Shades of Blue*; Jon Rubin, a comedian who calls himself "the Jewish Victor Borge" (the joke, of course, is that Borge was Jewish); attorney Charles Danziger, who writes a column on art law with his brother called "Brothers-in-Law"; Alexander Olch, who designed a luxury tie with small pictures of female breasts on it, and made a documentary about the world's most famous tailor of custom-made bras; Rob Dimaio, who is making a film about photographer Jerry Dantzig; and HSBC senior vice-president Jonathan Schorr, who has taken up swing dancing.

CAROL HIGGINS CLARK, mystery writer Mary Higgins Clark's daughter and a former actress, is a bestselling mystery writer in her own right. Her fifth novel, *Jinxed*, (Scribner) came out August 27, but as one reviewer said in comparing their respective books, "Mary goes for the jugular and Carol for the funny bone." Carol Higgins Clark also tends to draw a lot on her theater background.

"We both do extensive research on the locals and themes of our novels," Carol Higgins Clark said. "Where we differ is style—my mother's thrillers are meant to scare people, while a comic thread runs through my books." In *Jinxed* a major character is a 93-year-old former silent movie star who takes on a sixth husband and a ride on a motorbike with the same relish.

SHORT TAKES: Get to Riverside Church on time tomorrow or you won't get a seat for the funeral of the late jazz great Lionel Hampton who died last week. "We're going to have the full Lionel Hampton Orchestra and give Lionel a send-off in the tradition of a Mike Todd extravaganza," said Phil Leshin, Hampton's longtime press agent. The service begins at 9 a.m., and it's suggested that anyone who wants a seat get there two hours before if not earlier.

Harlem's Apollo Theater will present Salman Rushdie's stage adaptation of his 1981 novel *Midnight's Children* for two weeks starting March 20, *Variety* reports. Columbia University and the Royal Shakespeare Co. are producing Mr. Rushdie's play about modern India.

Candace Bergen, who grew up in the public eye, tells this month's *Readers' Digest* that "It gives you that bogus sense of entitlement. It's similar to when kids are little and have a birthday party. They get all these presents and all this attention and they go nuts and crash and burn and behave like an alien has invaded them. It's hard enough to be my age and try and have some perspective on it."

The New York Sun, September 6, 2002.

◻ McCartney Won't Sign; 'Goat' Gets New Stars

PAUL MCCARTNEY gave one young New Yorker an earful she didn't bargain for on Saturday afternoon.

Sydney, who is nine, was with her dad and sister in an Upper East Side luncheonette when Sydney spotted Mr. McCartney and his wife, Heather Mills, having lunch. Sydney waited until they were finished eating, and when Ms. Mills went to the ladies room she approached Mr. McCartney with a napkin and a pencil and asked if he would please sign an autograph.

"He very nicely told her it was not polite to ask for an autograph in a restaurant and that 'If I give you one everyone else will come up to me, too,'" said Sydney's father. He said Mr. McCartney then asked if she lived in New York and if she came to that restaurant often. "She was absolutely thrilled to speak to him but a bit disappointed about his refusal to give her an autograph," the girls' father said.

TWO-TIME OSCAR WINNER Sally Field, who is making her Broadway debut on Friday, says working in New York on the anniversary of September 11 "is a great privilege. It makes this time in my life all the more important," she said.

Ms. Field, who is perhaps best remembered for her performance in *Places in the Heart*, steps into Edward Albee's play *The Goat*, opposite Bill Irwin, "For a very limited run 'til the middle of December," Ms. Field told the *Sun*.

"Edward has been very helpful," she continued. "He has been with us frequently. He knows when to come [to rehearsal] and when to stay away—and that's definitely great! He doesn't talk about our interpretations of the characters, really." As for the play, which is about a man who falls in love with a goat, Ms. Field said, "It's a very complicated piece. It's Greek, basically. Contemporary Greek comedy—if there is such a thing!"

Mr. Irwin, winner of a Special Tony Award for co-creating and starring in the mime show *Fool Moon*, said he's thrilled to be working with Sally Field in *The Goat*—even though "she swears like a truck driver!" he told the *Sun*. He said he was scheduled to go to Japan with another production of *Fool Moon* when that fell through. "This was offered to me out of the blue and I love it," he said.

OCTOGENARIAN MICKEY ROONEY wants one last hurrah on Broadway—and producer Terry Allen Kramer may just grant him his wish.

"He calls me about it all the time and after he hangs up I'll go get a cup of coffee and the phone rings and it's Mickey on the line again!" said Ms.

Kramer who is one of the producers of the upcoming *Movin' Out* as well as *The Goat*.

ONE STORY THAT didn't surface at Lionel Hampton's funeral Saturday at Riverside Church concerns a New York City firefighter who was at the Apollo Theatre in the 1940s at a time when Mr. Hampton played a record 10 shows a day, often ending with his own composition, "Flyin' Home."

SHORT TAKES: Paul Shaffer of the "Late Show With David Letterman" has Oxtail soup five days a week at Gallagher's Steakhouse on 52nd Street. "It's my favorite dish," he said. "I must have already eaten a team of oxen!"

Broadway ticket sales may be in the post-Labor Day doldrums but final figures for the city's recent International Fringe Festival are heartening for organizers. "Ticket sales were up about 10 percent over last year—or about $20,000," Ron Lasko of the Festival told the *Sun*.

Don't ask Pulitzer Prize-winning playwright Edward Albee what new work of his will be produced this year. "I don't know," he told the *Sun* Monday. "There's a lot of talk about a lot of stuff. But I'm not ready to commit to anything."

Mr. Albee will be teaching at the University of Houston this winter, as he usually does. "I have a small residency chair there," he said, "and I want to go where it's warm!"

The New York Sun, September 11, 2002.

▢ The Joy of a Jazz Great Who Left a Legacy Beyond Music

Lionel Hampton, an extraordinary musician who was "King of the Vibraphone" for 60 years and a star of the Swing era, earned all the praise given him at a service last Saturday at New York's Riverside Church.

And not just for his groundbreaking music, many awards, and role in black-white relations in the musical industry.

His longtime friend, former President George Bush, said that Mr. Hampton not only "helped shape and even define an era in jazz [but] to know Lionel was to know joy—pure, simple joy."

Indeed, in three interviews with him over the past several years, I was struck by his radiance and love of music, and especially his humor.

In one interview, he talked about playing at Harlem's renovated Apollo Theatre, where Hampton holds the record for playing 10 shows a day. "If you got a standing ovation from people sitting in the second balcony, you knew you had made it!" he said.

Another jazz great, Illinois Jaquet, who was an early member of the Lionel Hampton band, told the story at the funeral of how "Hamp" one time rehearsed all day and all night, and finally went to change his clothes before a performance. "All of a sudden he comes running up on the bandstand and he had forgotten to put on his pants!" That brought smiles to others at the service, which included jazz legends Hank Jones, Clark Terry, and Wynton Marsalis, as well as the full Lionel Hampton Orchestra.

On a much more serious note, bandleader Benny Goodman heard Hampton play in the 1930s and, suddenly, the Benny Goodman Trio became the Benny Goodman Quartet. That made history by being the first racially integrated group of jazz musicians in America. In the early 1940s, Hampton formed his own band after the release of his hit single "Sunny Side of the Street" on which he sang as well as played the "vibes."

"Benny and I were close friends," Hampton told me before his passing. "The first time blacks and whites played together was with Benny. I had such respect for his musicianship. I liked him. Too, as a person. Some people thought he was too hard, but he had a good heart."

Hampton wrote some 200 original compositions, and his original ballad, "Midnight Sun," written with Johnny Mercer and Sonny Burke, has become an American jazz and popular music classic. His two major symphonic works, *The King David Suite* and *Blues Suite* are performed by leading symphonic orchestras around the world.

Music wasn't his only love. In the early 1970s, he developed the Lionel Hampton Houses as well as the Gladys Hampton Houses, named for his late wife, and to this day they are considered among the best examples of public housing in the nation.

Despite that success, Hampton said the highlight of his career was having the music school at the University of Idaho named for him.

Bob Hoover, president of the University of Idaho, told those at the funeral that Hampton's work to establish the school and his yearly appearances at its Lionel Hampton Jazz Festival were but a small fraction of his long and productive and giving life. I and thousands of others are privileged to have shared a much smaller fraction of Hampton's time and joy and enthusiasm.

The Christian Science Monitor, September 12, 2002.

◻ Miller May Allow Production of Monroe Play

PLAYWRIGHT ARTHUR MILLER may let *After the Fall*—his 1964 play based in part on his stormy marriage to Marilyn Monroe—be produced on Broadway this season, sources close to Mr. Miller say. No word on who would play the plum Monroe role, but a reading was scheduled for last night to see what, if anything, needs updating.

The play, first produced at the Lincoln Center Repertory Theater's temporary home near Washington Square in Greenwich Village, received excellent reviews, but caused a firestorm of controversy about whether the renowned author of *Death of a Salesman* and *All My Sons* was exploiting his relationship with his late wife.

That production starred Jason Robards, and Barbara Lodin as Monroe. Dianne Wiest co-starred in a more recent 1984 off-Broadway production of *After the Fall*, with Frank Langella, at Playhouse 91 on East 91st Street.

OSCAR WINNING ACTRESS Jill Clayburgh, who starred on Broadway in the musical *The Rothchilds* three decades ago, is coming back to the New York theater to co-star with Richard Dreyfuss in the gritty reality-based play *The Exonerated*, joining the growing number of Hollywood stars doing Off-Broadway shows this season.

Ms. Clayburgh won an Academy Award for Best Actress in *An Unmarried Woman* and a Golden Globe nomination for best actress in *Starting Over*. *The Exonerated*, by Eric Jensen and Jessica Blank, is about wrongly accused death row inmates. The authors claim more than 80 such inmates have been exonerated and freed since 1976.

At the same time, Sigourney Weaver, Al Pacino, Chazz Palminteri, Billy Crudup, Ione Skye, and other stars are set to twinkle Off-Broadway in the next few months. Mr. Pacino, Mr. Palminteri, and Mr. Crudup will be in the cast of the National Actors Theater's revival of *The Resistible Rise of Arturo Ui* at Pace University's downtown campus in next month. Ms. Skye will be in the Empire Theatre's production of *Evolution* starting later this month, and Ms. Weaver will costar in Neil LaBute's *The Mercy Seat* at the Acorn Theatre on West 42nd Street. That play is about a woman who has an affair the day after the terrorist attacks on the World Trade Center.

Additionally, "Sex and the City" actress Kim Cattrall will costar with Martha Plimpton in the New York premiere of David Mamet's *Boston Marriage* at the Joseph Papp Public Theater in November, a play some producers hope to take to Broadway. Lisa Eichhorn is also starring in a revival of Harold Pinter's drama *Betrayal* at the Actors Studio on West 44th Street.

It seems lighting is striking twice for actor and playwright Jay DiPietro. His new show *Peter and Vandy*, co-starring stunning Monique Vukovic, opens on September 12th at Tom Noonan's Paradise Theatre on East 4th Street, and buzz surrounding the two-character show has been so strong that it's just been extended through October 12th.

Long shots are nothing new for Mr. DiPietro, who began working with Mr. Noonan after writing the veteran actor and playwright a fan letter.

"I went home after seeing one of Tom's plays and immediately wrote him a long embarrassing letter about how I needed to be a part of what he was doing," Mr. DiPietro said.

The genesis of *Peter and Vandy*—a series of 11 nonlinear scenes from a couple's relationship—began when Mr. Noonan told Mr. DiPietro in a writing seminar, "You should really be doing something with your stuff. It needs to be seen. I could watch these two characters for hours. Write a play about them."

Ms. Vukovic has been in a number of productions in New York, including the premiere of Beth Henley's *Impossible Marriage* at the Roundabout Theatre.

Short Takes: *Menopause: The Musical*, which has played to big houses at Off-Broadway's Theatre Four, is moving to Playhouse 91 on East 91st Street where it will begin performances on September 26. Directed by Kathleen Lindsay, the show has songs such as "I Heard Through the Grapevine You'll No Longer See 39" and "Stayin' Awake."

T.S. Eliot's classic play *The Cocktail Party*, the original Broadway production of which starred the late Alec Guinness, will have a limited run of two weeks beginning Sept. 25 through Oct. 6 at Theatre 22, 54 W. 22nd Street. Directed by Terese Hayden, the cast includes Charles D. Cissel, Jacqueline Brookes, Elizabeth Nafpaktitis, and Richard Lollo.

The New York Sun, September 15, 2002.

▢ 'George' to Host a Sondheim Reunion; Rossellini Tells All

JASON ALEXANDER, aka George on "Seinfeld," is coming back to Broadway in something he says "really touches my heart."

On Monday, Mr. Alexander will host a reunion of the original Broadway cast of *Merrily We Roll Along*. It was Stephen Sondheim's infamous flop of 1981, but it's a musical that has one of the composer's most highly regarded scores.

"This whole notion of putting us back together again in this concert form really touches my heart because I think the lives of everyone that passed, now, singing that material, being those people with dreams revealed or dreams dashed, or reinvented, will sit on us in a very interesting way," Mr. Alexander, who was last on Broadway in *Jerome Robbins' Broadway*, told *The New York Sun*.

"I'm so looking forward to having that group back together and seeing what comes of it. It was the best of times; it was the worst of times. I had never been part of anything where a show was being built from scratch, so to see something created from its bones—and even more importantly to see something that is not working, in the hands of guys who I thought were gods, was a great learning experience. I probably learned more about life by having it not be a successful show than had it been a perfect show."

The reunion is a benefit for Musical Theatre Works and will take place at LaGuardia High School for the Performing Arts. Ticket prices start at $50. Aside from Mr. Alexander the concert version of *Merrily We Roll Along* features other members of the original cast, including Jim Walton (Franklin Shepard), Ann Morrison (Mary Flynn), Lonny Price (Charley Kringas), Terry Finn (Gussie), David Cady (Jerome), Donna Marie Elio Asbury (Terry), Maryrose Wood (Ms. Gordon), and Marc Moritz (Alex).

ISABELLA ROSSELLINI, whose mother Ingrid Bergman broke up the love affair between Roberto Rossellini, her father, and the film star Anna Magnani, was eager to provide the author of *Roman Nights*, the hit Off-Broadway play about the turbulent friendship of Magnani and Tennessee Williams, with information about her mother's relationship with Magnani.

"You know Magnani hated my mother," Ms. Rossellini told playwright Franco D'Alessandro before the curtain rose on a recent performance of *Roman Nights* at the DR2 Theatre, 103 East 15th St. "I know, it's all in the play," Mr. D'Alessandro told Ms. Rossellini.

"But do you know about the bowl of spaghetti Magnani threw onto my father's head?" Ms. Rossellini asked. "Go watch the play," replied Mr. D'Alessandro.

"By late 1949, Roberto Rossellini had begun the affair with Bergman and was still living with Anna Magnani—together by then for six years," Mr. D'Alessandro told the *Sun*. "A telegram arrived at the table in a restaurant where Rossellini and Magnani were dining, the waiter handed Rossellini the telegram and he put it in his pocket and never said anything. Magnani's famous instincts kicked in, and when the pasta arrived she asked Roberto if he 'wanted a taste'…and then dumped the whole bowl on his head. The telegram was from Bergman."

At the intermission of *Roman Nights*, Mr. D'Alessandro brought Ms. Rossellini champagne and they chatted about the play and she asked what inspired him to write it and how he did the research. "I mentioned the 90-year-old church custodian who told me about the images of Tennessee and Anna laughing and talking seriously in the piazza del Pantheon, 20 years of late-night walks, and then by 1970 the laughter had stopped," Mr. D'Alessandro said.

At the end of the play, a teary eyed Ms. Rossellini hugged the playwright and whispered: "It is so beautiful Franco! This story has moved me so much!"

ANTONIO BANDERAS has Italian-born playwright Mario Fratti sitting on cloud nine these days. The film star is set to star in a Roundabout Theatre revival of Mr. Fratti's musical *Nine*, based on Fellini's classic film *8-1/2*, when it opens at Broadway's Eugene O'Neill Theatre in February.

"We see him [Mr. Banderas] as a film actor, but he was very successful in *Evita* and he had a good voice," Mr. Fratti, who was honored for his achievements by the Castillo Theatre Monday night, told the *Sun*. "The director is also terribly satisfied; he's 100 percent satisfied." Mr. Fratti added that he believed that Mr. Banderas has signed a six-month contract "with a possible renewal."

The New York Sun, September 25, 2002.

◻ Al Pacino to Star in Brecht Play

FOR THE FIRST TIME in 40 years, Bertolt Brecht's kaleidoscopic drama *The Resistible Rise of Arturo Ui*—the story of the rise of the Nazis in 1930s Germany as portrayed by gangsters in 1920s Chicago—is headed to Broadway *The New York Sun* has learned.

The play, which is Off-Broadway at the Michael Schimmel Center for the Performing Arts at Pace University, stars Al Pacino and was last done on Broadway in 1963, with Christopher Plummer in the title role.

"Mr. Pacino is one of the people who's talking about moving it to Broadway in January," Gary Springer, the press agent for the show, told the *Sun*. "As far as I know, he is doing something in late November and early December and will be available in January." It's scheduled to run through Nov. 3 at Pace but may be extended another two weeks, Mr. Springer said. At the same time, well-placed theater sources say the powerful Shubert Organization, which owns 17 Broadway playhouses, is expected to help mount *Resistible* on Broadway.

In addition to Mr. Pacino, the $1.2 million Off-Broadway production boasts a star-studded cast rarely seen on or Off-Broadway these days, including Dominic Chianese, who plays "Uncle Junior" on HBO's "The Sopranos," Chazz Palminteri, Charles Durning, and Billy Crudup. And even though everyone, including Mr. Pacino, is working for scale, the minimum pay required by the Actors Equity union, ticket prices for the show are $100, the highest price in Off-Broadway history.

DONNA LYNNE CHAMPLIN, who plays Carol Burnett as a young adult in *Hollywood Arms*, the Broadway play written by Ms. Burnett and her late daughter Carrie Hamilton and directed by Hal Prince, thinks highly of Ms. Burnett. "I'd take a bullet for Carol Burnett," she said, laughing. The play started preview performances on Monday at the Cort Theatre.

Ms. Champlin, who was featured in *By Jeeves* and *The Dead* on Broadway, was Ms. Burnett's favorite to play her as a young woman. "I read a scene for Carol," Ms. Champlin told the *Sun*. "It was a very simple scene. Carol laughed and said to me, 'That's really interesting. You found things in it that are not on the page. Dysfunctional family?' I said, 'Just a little!'" In the play, Ms. Burnett's alter ego has two alcoholic parents and is raised by her loony grandmother played by Linda Lavin.

On Mr. Prince: "With Hal, you put all your energy in just doing whatever the man tells you! I felt so safe as an actress," Ms. Champlin told the *Sun*.

WITH SIX DISNEY musicals in development, speculation is rife about which will be the Mouse Factory's fourth musical simultaneously on Broadway along with the hits *The Lion King*, *Beauty and the Beast*, and *Aida*. "The farthest along in development is *The Little Mermaid*, Chris Boneau, A Disney spokesman, said.

At the same time, *Hoops*, another of the six in development, may be the first to be staged in America, but at the Trinity Repertory Theatre, a regional theater in Providence. "That production is about a year-and-a-half away," Mr. Boneau said. "Then we will see what happens to it."

The four other musicals in development are *Tarzan*, *Pinocchio*, *Mary Poppins*, and *The Hunchback of Notre Dame*, which as been staged in Berlin and is being turned into a made for TV Disney movie.

Actress Karen Young, who plays a tough federal agent trying to bring down the family in "The Sopranos," finds herself leading a kind of dual acting existence. She's worked mostly with men filming the HBO series and is mainly working with women Off-Broadway in Julie Jensen's *Cheat*, being produced by the Women's Project and Productions. Opening October 10 at the Women's Project Theater, 424 55th Street, *Cheat* tells the story of what happens to two women after they lose their jobs in a munitions plant at the end of World War II.

"During the entire time I shot 'The Sopranos' I only worked with one actress but at the Women's Project—the producers, the director, and most of the designers are women—and there is only one man in the cast of *Cheat* and I'm never on stage with him," Ms. Young said.

STUNNING DOMENICA Cameron-Scorsese, the youngest daughter of director Martin Scorsese and writer Julia Cameron, is having no problem relating to the character she's playing in John Picardi's play *The Sweepers*, set to open at Off-Broadway's Urban Stages Theatre on Oct. 19. Ms. Scorsese, who was featured in the films *Cape Fear* and *Age of Innocence*, plays one of three Italian-American women who have been neighbors and friends since childhood.

"Ms. Scorsese is a charming, lovely young woman, and a wonderful actress with a rich Italian heritage that she brings to the role," said Urban Stages' Artistic Director Frances Hill, who is also the director of *The Sweepers*. Ms. Hill added that Ms. Scorsese even brought a visual aid—*The Scorsese Family Cookbook* (Random House)—to rehearsals. "The cast has really enjoyed seeing the pictures of her grandparents in Little Italy."

UP CLOSE: *Hairspray* star Harvey Fierstein sitting on the lip of the stage at the Neil Simon Theatre for 10 minutes telling stories while stagehands fixed technical difficulties...Michael Weller telling friends at a performance of the revival of his *Split* at Off-Broadway's Lion Theatre that his longevity as a playwright "is a combination of craftiness and resilience and lots of coffee and vodka"...Action film star Vin Diesel, whose latest movie is *Knock-Around Guys*, telling the *Sun* that "I want to do a production of *Guys and Dolls*"...Film producer Steven Soderbergh telling the *Sun* that while "doing theater is too difficult, I would like to do a movie musical."

The New York Sun, October 9, 2002.

'Stars Walk' to Honor Broadway's Leading Lights

Carol Channing, Great White Way's 'Dolly,' to Get First Star

IN WHAT IS BEING hailed as another big step in the revitalization of Times Square, some of Broadway's brightest stars—and biggest business and civic leaders—yesterday unveiled plans to honor the legends of the Great White Way.

Borrowing the idea from Hollywood's Walk of Fame, which dates back to the 1950s with some 1,500 individual stars, they will create a "Walk of Stars" as a "long-overdue tribute to the greatest artists of our time," said actress Arlene Dahl, president and founder of the Broadway Walk of Stars Foundation.

"It will celebrate the talent, vitality and rich cultural history of New York City and is wonderful testimony to the enduring spirit of New York," Ms. Dahl said.

The 30-inch by 30-inch bronze stars will be placed in the sidewalks of Times Square from Duffy Square at Broadway and 47th Street to 42nd Street starting next spring.

They will honor old-timers from the worlds of theater, movies, music, dance and TV, including Fred Astaire, Irving Berlin, George Burns and Gracie Allen, John Barrymore, Helen Hayes, James Cagney, Humphrey Bogart, Noël Coward, Richard Burton, and Elizabeth Taylor.

Stars will also likely be placed for more contemporary luminaries such as Neil Simon, Barbra Streisand, Liza Minnelli, and Candice Bergen, and more current stars like Nathan Lane, Matthew Broderick, and Bebe Neuwirth.

Ms. Dahl said the first star to be placed in the sidewalk either in Duffy Square or outside the Palace Theatre will honor Carol Channing, best known for starring in *Hello, Dolly!* on Broadway.

Composer Jerry Herman, who wrote the score for *Hello, Dolly!*, presented Ms. Channing with a replica of her bronze star yesterday at the River House duplex of Broadway producer Marty Richards.

"I'm the first to get a star because everyone else is dead—Ethel Merman, Mary Martin, and Gwen Verdon," Ms. Channing said with a laugh. "New York would not have been the center of the world unless there was Broadway. If live theater were in New Jersey like it is in New York, New Jersey would have been the center of the world."

Among the guests at the ceremony were Charles Gargano, chairman and CEO of the Empire State Development Corporation, and honorary chairman of the Broadway Walk of Stars, and Tim Tompkins, President of the Times Square Business Improvement District.

Those getting stars will be honored for one or more of five performing arts disciplines: theater, film, television, music and dance. In rare cases, some stars will be adorned with symbols for several different disciplines, like Fred Astaire, a dancer who appeared in theater, movies and TV.

Ms. Dahl told *The New York Sun*, she and her advisory board, which includes Mr. Richards and George Kaufman, owner of the Kaufman Studios in Astoria, Queens, had raised $100,000 for the Broadway Walk of Stars. No public money will be used.

"We expect the first stars to be set into the sidewalks before next year's Tony Awards in June," she said.

Ms. Dahl said she hoped that a circle of some 100 bronze and terrazzo stars would be placed in the sidewalks in Duffy Square at Broadway and 47th Street near the TKTS half-price Broadway ticket booth.

"If this isn't done by next spring then we will start putting down stars in front of the Palace Theatre across the street from Duffy Square and run a ribbon of stars down Broadway and down Seventh Avenue to 42nd Street and eventually on the side streets of the theater district," she said.

The New York Sun, October 11, 2002.

◻ Burnett Goes the Distance

AFTER A NUMBER of negative reviews, *Hollywood Arms*, Carol Burnett's autobiographical play, may be fighting for its theatrical life at the Cort Theatre, but its plucky co-author is just grateful the play opened on Broadway.

"You know what? Carrie [Hamilton, her daughter] and I went the distance to Broadway," Ms. Burnett told *The New York Sun*. "With her help and because of [director] Hal Prince, she must be feeling very proud and excited—just like I'm feeling." Ms. Hamilton, the co-author of *Hollywood Arms*, died recently of lung cancer.

"She's with me—I know that," Ms. Burnett continued. "I get little signs all the time. It rained this week. That's really important because that was our favorite weather. I said, 'Okay, we've got to have rain the week it opens'—and we did."

"I can only imagine what Carol must be going through right now," Lauren Bacall, Ms. Burnett's longtime friend told the *Sun* at the opening of *Hollywood Arms*. "She's a very tough lady. She'll be fine," said singer Reba McEntire, who also attended the opening.

Is Ms. Burnett working on another play? "Not right now," she told the *Sun*. "This has been such a journey." While some Broadway insiders predict *Hollywood Arms* may close by Thanksgiving a spokesman for the show told the *Sun* it will be around for the foreseeable future.

Ms. McEntire, who's doing a sitcom series called "Reba" on the WB Network, would "love to come back to Broadway."

Her flaming red hair cut short, Ms. McEntire made a huge splash several years ago in the revival of *Annie Get Your Gun* and came to the opening of *Hollywood Arms*, she told the *Sun*, because "Carol Burnett is a fantastic entertainer, a wonderful friend and has given so much to the business. But, also, she's done so much for women in the business. I'm glad to be here to support her!"

NICE WORK IF you can get it. Actor Jordan Bridges (son of Beau Bridges and grandson of the late Lloyd Bridges), who has just been cast in *Big Al*, an Off-Broadway play that opens at the Arclight Theatre November 8, plays Kirsten Dunst's husband in *Mona Lisa Smile*, a film being shot that will star Julia Roberts and Marcia Gay Harden.

"The movie takes place in the early 1950s and we had to go to a cotillion and learn to dance, so I was the lucky guy who got to dance with all these beautiful women like Kirsten and Julia," Mr. Bridges told the *Sun*. The film is being directed by Hollywood veteran Mike Newell.

Big Al is about two screenwriters who are obsessed with getting Al Pacino to star in their movie. Mr. Bridges, who said he's never met Mr. Pacino, appeared in his first movie—about a Thanksgiving goose—when he was 12 years old. It starred grandfather Lloyd, who was perhaps best known for playing adventurer/scuba diver Mike Nelson in the TV series "Sea Hunt." "Whenever we have the time we love to strap on the tanks and pretend to be Mike Nelson for a few minutes," Mr. Bridges told the *Sun*.

THE ROAD FROM the entertainment biz to the restaurant biz is well traveled. Fans in New York can stop by to sample the culinary offerings of associates of Britney Spears, Sean (P Diddy) Combs, and Robert De Niro. Now, one SoHo restaurateur is turning the tables and venturing into the entertainment jungle—sans spatula. Samuel Roberts, the former Quilty's owner, has become a stage director. *Last Day*, which premieres November 10 at Off-Broadway's Altered Stages, is his second directorial effort. The dark comedy covers some familiar ground for Mr. Roberts, as a fictional chef's undercooked Moonfish leads to some unforeseen twists and turns.

The New York Sun, November 6, 2002

▣ Hey, Lady! Jerry Lewis Plans to Hit Broadway

Hopes to Celebrate his 78th Birthday with a Show on the Great White Way

Legendary comedian Jerry Lewis—who made his show business debut as a 5-year-old in 1931 singing "Brother, Can You Spare a Dime"—will celebrate his 78th birthday with an opening night on Broadway in a new show on March 16, 2004.

In an interview with *The New York Sun* at the Waldorf-Astoria hotel, where he is preparing to give a Learning Annex seminar on comedy on Thursday, Mr. Lewis also said:

- Next Labor Day "I'll be back to doing the (Jerry Lewis Muscular Dystrophy) Telethon 24 hours 'til I die. There's no way I will ever stop." Last Labor Day, illness forced him to cut back to 13 hours.

- Pain in his spine triggered by comedy pratfalls "finally got to the point where it was so severe I was ready to kill myself" but "for the first time in 37 years I'm without pain" through the use of a "Medtronic" medical device implanted in his back.

- "I had four years of grieving for Dean [Martin, Lewis' longtime partner] I cannot even explain" but "when I sat down and started to write *The Martin and Lewis Story* the grieving stopped."

- "When I'm writing the book I feel like Dean is in the room with me, I'm getting this wonderful plethora of beats and rhythms. I'm not Shirley MacLaine and not talking about channeling. I deeply feel Dean's presence. The grieving has stopped."

He said he hopes to turn in the manuscript by Christmas of 2003.

Martin and Mr. Lewis began their legendary show business partnership in 1946 when Mr. Lewis was performing at the 500 Club in Atlantic City and one of the entertainers quit.

Despite having gained more than 50 pounds in the wake of contracting pulmonary fibrosis and taking a drug called Prednizone for it, Mr. Lewis said "I've been pain free since I got it" (the Medtronic implant last April 20) and "I'm thrilled to be alive—you can't beat it!"

Getting back to his upcoming Broadway show, his first since he played "the Devil" in a revival of the musical *Damn Yankees* in 1994-95 before reprising his role in London, Mr. Lewis said it would partly be a musical tribute to Dean Martin and, "As long as they want me I'll stay on Broadway. Where am I going? I'll have my wife and daughter with me. That's all I'll need!"

As for the courage some thought it took for Mr. Lewis to do his telethon this past September with his face looking temporarily bloated, he said, "I never thought of it in terms of courage…I thought of it in terms of some of my kids were dying. They had bigger problems than I did."

The New York Sun, November 12, 2002.

◘ The 'Vicar of Vintage' Makes It Big

DANNY STILES—affectionately known to thousands of New York-area radio listeners as the "Vicar of Vintage" for spinning rare Broadway soundtracks—will finally be on Broadway himself. He'll attend a party on December 2 at John's Pizzeria next to the St. James Theatre to celebrate his 55th year in radio. It will also be his 79th birthday.

"I'm finally making a hit on Broadway after 55 years on radio!" Mr. Stiles, whose tag line is "Stiles on your dials," told *The New York Sun*. "I am thrilled for such a long ride in radio…I look forward to another 55. I'll probably die in front of a microphone."

Mr. Stiles, host of "Big Band Sounds" each Saturday from 8 to 10 p.m. on WNYC/820AM, began his radio career in New York on December 2, 1947 on station WOV. "Back then, WOV played 12 hours of English programming and 12 hours of Italian," he said. Today, he features such stars as Sophie Tucker, Harry ("Mr. Broadway") Richman, Guy Lombardo, Louis Prima, Xavier Cugat, the Ray Noble Orchestra, Buddy Clark, Bing Crosby, the Boswell Sisters, and Charlie Barnett.

IN WHAT MAY BE an Off-Broadway first, the Castillo Theatre is presenting *Moviemachine*—part seminar, part "The Making of…" to shed light on the process of creating an independent film. The film, called *Nothing Really Happens*, written and directed by Castillo's artistic director, Fred Newman, has just completed principal photography.

Nothing Really Happens examines the worlds of three very different women: a working class stripper from the Bronx, an Auschwitz survivor, and a social studies professor. It stars Judith Malina, co-founder of Off-Broadway's Living Theatre. Ms. Malina has starred and been featured in countless feature films including *Household Saints* (1993) and *Dog Day Afternoon* (1975).

YOU CAN GO HOME again—or at least across the street, says Oscar winner F. Murray Abraham. Mr. Abraham is playing Ebeneezer Scrooge in *A Christmas Carol*, which begins at the Theatre at Madison Square Garden on Friday, across the street from his first acting job. "My first job in New York was as a Macy's Santa Claus. So I feel I'm going home in a show across from Macy's," Mr. Abraham told the *Sun* between rehearsals. "Ebeneezer Scrooge is one of the greatest characters ever written. His transformation, as well as Dickens' underlying theme of good will toward men, is a story that everyone can embrace and understand."

Mr. Abraham, a veteran of some 60 films, is best known for playing Antonio Salieri in the 1984 movie *Amadeus*, for which he won an Academy Award. He also was featured in *The Last Action Hero* and Woody Allen's *Mighty Aphrodite*. He recently completed shooting a film called *Argua 555* starring Charlton Heston and, in a sharp departure from most of his roles, played a nice guy. "For the first time in a long time I played a nice guy, which is ironic because I'm really a nice guy." Ten different actors have played Scrooge in the annual Garden show over the last nine years, including Roger Daltrey and the late Roddy McDowell.

As FIRST PREDICTED in *The New York Sun* on June 7, the Westport Country Playhouse production of Thornton Wilder's *Our Town*, directed by Jim Naughton, has come to Broadway. But unlike most shows that take months if not years to recoup their investors' money, *Our Town*, which began previews November 22 and stars Paul Newman, has sold enough tickets for its scheduled nine-and-a-half-week run at the Booth Theatre to recoup its $1 million investment.

Likewise, *Frankie and Johnny*, Terrence McNally's two-character blue-collar comedy, which opened in August at the Belasco Theatre with Edie Falco and Stanley Tucci, recouped its $1.5 million investment weeks ago. And in what some Broadway insiders are calling an even greater masterstroke of casting, producers just announced that on New Year's Day Rosie Perez and "Sopranos" star Joe Pantoliano will step into the roles of two lovers who are either totally or partially nude for nearly half the show.

"Let's fact it, sex sells!" one Broadway producer, who asked not to be identified, told the *Sun*. "Whether it's an aging Hollywood icon like Paul Newman or Rosie Perez in the raw. I'd like to see them do *Frankie and Johnny* without the nudity and see how long it lasts." But that's not likely to happen. A spokeswoman for the show said the extensive nudity "will stay the same" when Ms. Perez and Mr. Pantoliano take over.

The New York Sun, November 27, 2002.

◘ From Hogwarts to the Great White Way

HOLD ONTO YOUR Nimbus 2000 broom and your magical cloak! Young wizard Harry Potter—who returned to Hogwarts for his second year in the blockbuster film *Harry Potter and the Chamber of Secrets*—may be bound for Broadway.

"Harry Potter's a natural for a musical," said New York producer Robert Blume, who tried unsuccessfully to get the *Batman* rights for Broadway from Warner Brothers. "But I'm sure it won't be done until after a third Harry Potter movie comes out, if there is one. Warner Brothers told me that only after they did all the *Batman* movies would they consider doing a Broadway show." *Batman: The Musical* is slated to be done out-of-town in 2004, after Tim Burton, who directed the films *Batman* and *Batman Returns*, fulfills existing commitments.

The new Harry Potter movie grossed some $32 million last weekend and more than $200 million in America alone since it opened last month. While Mr. Blume and Warners insiders say the Harry Potter books and movies would make a great musical, a Warners publicist said there are no plans to make it into a musical "at this time."

"A WORLD WITHOUT Adolph Green is not quite a world," lamented Lauren Bacall, one of many celebrities who paid tribute to the late Broadway author and lyricist, at the Shubert Theatre yesterday. Green and Betty Comden wrote the book and lyrics for *Peter Pan, Wonderful Town, Bells Are Ringing*, and many other musicals.

But for the most part, the comments were as lighthearted and humorous as Green, who died last month at age 87. "He was everything," Ms. Bacall told an overflowing audience that included a who's who of Broadway, from Kevin Kline and Mr. Green's widow, actress Phyllis Newman, to director Sidney Lumet and playwright Arthur Laurents. "He was crazy; he was talented; he was smart. He knew every note of music that was ever written. He was an original. He was, above all things, eccentric—truly eccentric. And he was a great friend."

Director Hal Prince vouched for Mr. Green's eccentricity, as well as his genius and originality. "There was the time Adolph went off to the veterinarian but forgot to take the dog! And just last year on his way to Betty Comden's to work he made his daily stop at Tower Records to shake hands with everyone who worked there and to fill his arms with free catalogues. On his way out he was pursued by an assistant manager, who said, 'Mr. Green, that CD you're holding—are you certain you paid for it?' Adolph said, 'It was at the entrance, so I thought it was a sample.' And finally, very recently, Phyllis was with my wife and me in Europe and Adolph called and asked my assistant [in New York] if he could dictate a message to Phyllis. This is the message: 'Who do you love? I hope...Who do you miss? I hope...Who are you hoping to see? I hope, I hope, I hope, it's me.'"

"All that inspired madness is at rest," playwright Peter Stone said. "But thanks to such modern marvels as tapes, CDs, films and the like the rest is not silent. Adolph remains with us loud and clear."

ACTOR, DIRECTOR, writer, producer Tim Robbins, who was honored at the 21st annual benefit for Off-Broadway's Vineyard Theatre Monday night, wants to act on Broadway, but only three nights a week.

"I'd be very interested in doing that," he told *The New York Sun*. "The problem with Broadway is that with my kids, I don't want to be gone on weekends. When you're doing a movie, you're away from home for five or six weeks. So when we're at home, we try and stay at home."

While acting on Broadway may present some personal hurdles, Mr. Robbins is keeping busy doing theater in Los Angeles and New York. "I have two plays running in L.A.," he said. "One that I've written called *Alagazam*, a kind of raucous vaudeville show. And both I've produced...Susan and I are also doing a Christmas show." Susan, of course, is Mr. Robbins' longtime girlfriend Susan Sarandon. For her part, she's shooting down rumors that Burt Lancaster fell in love with her during the filming of *Atlantic City*. "I don't know that he was in love with me but we kept in touch after the film," Ms. Sarandon said. "He was a sweet, dear man."

The New York Sun, December 4, 2002.

IN THE HOUSE: Don't go to *Movin' Out*, the new Billy Joel-Twyla Tharp megahit Broadway musical, expecting to see Billy Joel, who wrote the music for the show. But there's at least a chance the pop icon will be in the audience and may sing one or two of the numbers after the final curtain as he has done twice in the last several weeks. "Billy Joel's seen the show more than a dozen times and he doesn't try to die," a show source told the *Sun*. "Last Friday, for the first time, he signed autographs and went up on stage after the show to sing the title number. The time before that he sand 'New York State of Mind' and "Movin' Out.'"

"He's so nice and loves being there," the source added. "Only thing is that on Friday one lady said to Mr. Joel's date, 'Are you Christie Brinkley?' And his date graciously said, 'No, I'm not.'"

WITH HIS BROADWAY production of Puccini's *La Boheme* having opened on Sunday to almost universal critical acclaim, director Baz Luhrmann will turn two of his films, *Moulin Rouge* and *Strictly Ballroom*, into stage shows, he said as he arrived at the opening amid a plethora of some of Hollywood's hottest stars.

"*Strictly Ballroom* and *Moulin Rouge* will come to Broadway—but I'm very slow so it will take some time before they get here," he told the *Sun* as he followed Sandra Bullock, Hugh Grant, Marcia Gay Harden, and other stars into Broadway's historic Broadway theater.

Mr. Luhrmann is planning to produce *Moulin Rouge* in a hotel in Las Vegas before it comes to Broadway. As for *La Boheme*, Mr. Luhrmann told the *Sun*: "It's Broadway and a great night! Who would have imagined? The bottom line is it's a beautiful story told through beautiful music…it's the right time for a bit of beauty."

UP CLOSE: Anne Heche, who recently starred in *Proof* on Broadway, jumped out of her Rolls-Royce limousine at Fifth Avenue and Rockefeller Center the other day so she could take a photo of her young son with a "Sidewalk Santa," one of the Santas employed by the Volunteers of America. The Santa said a hearty "thank you" when Ms. Heche's husband threw a $20 bill into his collection box.

The New York Sun, December 11, 2002.

◻ Crepuscule With Monk

MONK, A NEW DRAMA about the late jazz pianist Thelonious Monk, will be produced in a brand-new theater in The Armory at 543 West 42nd Street, *The New York Sun* has learned.

Written by Lawrence Holder, author of the acclaimed play *Zora*, *Monk* is being produced by Five Points Productions, a new consortium of community-based theaters including the New Federal Theatre and the Castillo Theatre.

The All Stars Project, Inc., which runs the All Stars Talent Show Network, a performance-based youth program, and the Castillo Theatre, just bought 31,000 square feet in The Armory for $7 million with the aid of tax-exempt bonds from the New York City Industrial Development Agency (IDA).

Dominic Chianese, who plays Uncle Junior on the HBO series "The Sopranos" and is a spokesman for the All Stars, told the *Sun*: "This [the All Stars Project's] new center has been a long time coming—and it's a cause for celebrating not only for the All Stars' programs but for every one in the creative arts."

Thelonious Monk was one of a small group of jazz musicians who started bebop. In the 1940s, Monk played in Harlem clubs like Minton's and Munroe's Uptown House with Dizzy Gillespie and Charlie Parker. It wasn't until the 1950s that he became recognized for his contribution to so-called new jazz. Mr. Holder, a faculty member of New York's John Jay College, received the National Black Theatre Conference's Garland Anderson Playwriting Award for his body of work in 1995.

To some fans, superstar Julia Roberts may appear serious and even a bit cold off screen. But to Marian Seldes, who is in *Dinner at Eight* at the Vivian Beaumont Theatre on Broadway and has been filming *Mona Lisa Smiles* with Ms. Roberts, "Julia screams with laughter," Ms. Seldes told the *Sun*.

"She's very receptive to jokes and is sort of a pixie!" Ms. Seldes said. "But the moment she finishes her scene they come and take her away. And when she's called for a scene people bring her in. If she walks down corridors by herself the little girls at Wellesley and the people who do the extra work will tear her clothes off." In *Mona Lisa Smiles* Ms. Seldes plays the president of Wellesley College and Ms. Roberts comes to her looking for a job. "I give her the job but I reprimand her later on!" Ms. Seldes said with a big smile.

Besides Ms. Roberts' keen sense of humor, Ms. Seldes says she is happy to see how "serious" Ms. Roberts is as an actress. "She's so beautiful you almost can't believe she could be anyone but Julia Roberts," Ms. Seldes said. "She is a terrific person and the crew loves her. If they don't love the star it's like walking on eggs. She's not like that at all."

The New York Sun, January 8, 2003.

🗆 A New 'Fiddler' Waits for Death of 'Vampires'; Simon's Latest

ALFRED MOLINA may star in anew revival of *Fiddler on the Roof*—one of the greatest musicals ever written and bound for Broadway this spring or summer, *The New York Sun* has learned.

With music and lyrics by Jerry Bock and Sheldon Harnick and dialogue by Joseph Stein, *Fiddler on the Roof*, originally opened on Broadway in September, 1965. Zero Mostel played Tevye, a simple dairyman who dreams of being a rich man, in the musical based on Sholom Aleichem's short story, "Tevye and His Daughters."

"The last word I had is that it will open in June or July," said a high-placed source close to the Nederlander Organization, which owns 11 Broadway playhouses and is producing the revival of *Fiddler*. Another source close to the production said "it might even open before the 2002-2003 Broadway season ends in early May. But the producers want the Minskoff Theatre and *Dance of the Vampires* would have to close very soon for that to happen."

Dance of the Vampires, starring Michael Crawford, opened to a number of negative reviews and has been struggling at the box office.

If *Fiddler* opens before May, it would join the revivals of *Man of La Mancha*, starring Brian Stokes Mitchell, *Nine*, with Antonio Bandaras, and *Gypsy*, with Bernadette Peters in a four-way battle for the Tony Award for Best Musical Revival of the 2002-2003 season. *Fiddler* includes the classic show tunes "If I Were a Rich Man," and "Tradition." The original production ran for 3,242 performances.

NEIL SIMON'S latest play, *Rose and Walsh*, now in rehearsals for a five-week run at the Geffen Playhouse in Los Angeles starting January 28, may open on Broadway this year.

If it does open on Broadway in the next several months, it would join several other new plays already scheduled, including Richard Greenberg's baseball drama *Take Me Out*, which begins preview performances February 4 at the Walter Kerr Theatre, and the Lincoln Center Theater's production of *Vincent in Brixton*, about the young Vincent van Gogh, which starts performances at the Golden Theatre February 13. "If it gets great reviews at the Geffen then it may immediately move to Broadway," said one knowledgeable Broadway insider.

PAUL NEWMAN may be playing the role of the mild-mannered stage manager in the Broadway revival of *Our Town* but shades of his erstwhile tough-guy persona in *Cool Hand Luke* and other films surfaced last Saturday night on Broadway outside the stage door of the Booth Theatre. Some 25 die-hard fans braved the below-freezing temperature to catch sight of the superstar as he left the theater.

"He didn't come out until 11:30 last night and by then a lot of people had left," one fan waiting in the cold Saturday night told the *Sun*. Than an employee of the Booth Theatre told those still waiting at 10:50 p.m. on Saturday that, "It'll be another 15 minutes to a half hour before Mr. Newman comes out."

Some 15 minutes later—to a chorus of "You were great, Mr. Newman!" and "Can I shake your hand, Mr. Newman?"—the casually dressed star emerged from the stage door and began signing autographs, mostly on *Playbills* of *Our Town*. "Sure," Mr. Newman politely said to one man, "How's that?" But Mr. Newman's fatherly tone changed abruptly when one young man placed a *Playbill* under his nose. "You've got one already!" Mr. Newman said, looking right at the man, who backed away.

SINGER/PIANIST STEVE ROSS, who has been playing and singing the songs of Cole Porter and Noël Coward to overflow audiences at the Park Hyatt Stanhope Hotel on Fifth Avenue, may sing an entirely different tune at the hotel when he introduces a song he has written.

"I've never liked the songs I've written from scratch because the world doesn't need another 'B' song," Mr. Ross, who is one of New York's foremost cabaret draws, modestly told the *Sun*. "But this one kind of came to me—and I'm quite proud of it. It's a song about Paris called 'Whenever I Think of Paris.' But I don't wake up in the morning burning to write another song. I feel I can contribute a lot by arranging some of the great songs that have already been written."

The New York Sun, January 15, 2003.

Seinfeld Eyes Return; a Savior for 'Chicago'; the Importance of Plays

JERRY SEINFELD may return to Broadway later this year for the first time since making his Broadway debut five years ago, *The New York Sun* has learned.

"I want to do Broadway again [this year]," Mr. Seinfeld said. "I've been working on another stand-up show, going all around and doing new material." He's appearing at the Providence, R.I., Civic Center January 25 and the Des Moines, Iowa, Civic Center February 21, among other engagements.

He also told the *Sun* he was "very pleased" with the way audiences received *Comedian*, his recent Miramax film that is a behind-the-scenes look at his comedy act and the challenge of making people laugh. His limited engagement at Broadway's Broadhurst Theatre in the summer of 1998 sold out and was also presented on HBO.

SURROUNDED BY MORE than 100 screaming teens who had braved the bitter cold to see him and get his autograph, Kevin Richardson, a member of the Backstreet Boys pop group and new co-star of the Broadway musical *Chicago*, told the *Sun* that "I only hope the new movie [*Chicago*] helps the show. I liked the movie!"

But whether it is the movie—which won three Golden Globe Awards Sunday night—or Mr. Richardson, this much is certain: the weekly box office receipts for the musical have just chalked up their biggest weekly numbers for January since 1999, at more than $600,000.

After getting a standing ovation for his first night in the show Monday, Mr. Richardson emerged from the stage door at the Shubert Theatre, where he was greeted with the same kind of enthusiasm he got at the curtain call. Fans, mostly teenage girls, cried out: "Kevin I love you!" "Kevin, you were great." Most graciously, he told them right when he came out of the theater, "Don't worry. I'm going to sign for all of you." And he did.

Chicago moves from the Shubert to the Ambassador Theatre on January 29 to make room for the upcoming revival of *Gypsy*. Producers Barry and Fran Weissler worried the current revival of *Chicago*, which opened in November 1996, might lose steam when it reopens at the smaller Ambassador. But the blockbuster movie, together with Mr. Richardson—who's in the musical until March—appear to be giving the show new life.

THE PLAY'S THE THING on Broadway again. Suddenly the 2002-2003 season is coming alive with new plays.

After a modest beginning, with only two new plays—Nora Ephron's *Imaginary Friends* and *Say Goodnight, Gracie*, starring Frank Gorshin—still running, at least three new plays are set to open by May 1. Even some of the most conservative theater veterans are forecasting that the season will end on an upbeat note for plays as well as musicals.

"The Broadway theater can't exist without new plays," producer Aaron Frankel told the *Sun*. "Musicals may make more money—if they last—but plays are the origin of the Broadway theater, the source. So many musicals wouldn't exist if plays didn't exist first."

Producer Jeffrey Richards said Matthew Barber's *Enchanted April*, a stage version of Elizabeth von Arnim's novel, will open on Broadway in April with a cast headed by Molly Ringwald, Elizabeth Ashley, and Jayne Atkinson. Like the movie, the play is about women who decide to rent a villa in Italy for the month of April. The show was first done at Hartford Stage in March 2000.

NOVELIST JOYCE CAROL OATES has just completed a full-length play, she told the *Sun* at a reading of another of her plays at the National Arts Club.

"It's called *The Shadows*," the diminutive Ms. Oates told the *Sun*. "It has to do with issues of anti-Semitism and Holocaust denial, but it's also a love story…It's also exposing anti-Semitism in some ways. But I don't want to make it sound as if the play is propaganda. Basically, it's a love story. A lot of old emotions go back for centuries."

SHORT TAKES: As part of the curtain call of the Broadway hit comedy *Say Goodnight, Gracie*, Frank Gorshin will blow out 107 candles on a huge cake in celebration of what would have been George Burns' 107th birthday today. Mr. Gorshin has gotten rave reviews in the play, which brings the late Burns back to life. Didi Conn—the voice of Gracie—will also join the festivities at the Helen Hayes Theatre after the matinee performance.

The New York Sun, January 22, 2003.

◻ 'Chicago' Producer Turns to 'Bullets Over Broadway'

FRESH FROM THE overwhelming success of his movie *Chicago*, film and theater producer Martin Richards may next produce a stage musical version of *Bullets Over Broadway*, Woody Allen's popular 1994 movie, *The New York Sun* has learned.

"All of a sudden I've become the flavor of the week, so I'm just going to enjoy it for a while," Mr. Richards told the *Sun*. "Then I want to do a musical version of *Bullets Over Broadway* for the theater. We're working with Woody on it, trying to get a contract through with him. I was just waiting for his legal case with Jean Doumanian [Mr. Allen's former longtime partner] to clear. I love them both, so I've stayed away from the whole thing. Right now, I love everyone!" Ms. Doumanian produced the film.

Dianne Wiest won an Oscar as best supporting actress in *Bullets Over Broadway*, which is set in the 1920s and is about a promising young playwright whose play is brilliantly rewritten by a gangster, played by Chazz Palminteri. As for the possibility of Oscars for *Chicago*, Mr. Richards told the *Sun*, "I'm afraid to say it. But we look good for the Oscars, I hope."

Meanwhile, Mr. Allen is slated to direct two of his one-act plays, *Riverside Drive* and *New Milford*, at Off-Broadway's Atlantic Theatre Company in April.

Woody Guthrie: The Musical is bound for Broadway, the *Sun* has learned.

"It may open this year," said producer Pierre Cossette, who has produced the Grammy Awards for the last 33 years. I'm going for Broadway. Nothing's working [financially] Off-Broadway these days." Mr. Cossette said the ensemble cast would not have a star because "Woody Guthrie is the star."

Guthrie, an American icon, was best known as a singer-songwriter but was also an acclaimed novelist and a rousing public speaker. He was born in Okemah, Okla., in 1912, and he crisscrossed the country in his younger years, sometimes in railroad boxcars, singing about the plight of migrant workers and the beauty of the rural landscape. He died in 1967 at Creedmoor State Hospital in Queens after a series of mental and physical breakdowns.

CALL IT "STAR TREK" meets Katharine Hepburn. Katherine Mulgrew, best known as Captain Kathryn Janeway in the syndicated TV series "Star Trek: Voyager," will play four-time Oscar winner Hepburn in Matthew Lombardo's play *Tea at Five* at Off-Broadway's Promenade Theatre beginning February 25.

"Kate Mulgrew grew up watching and loving old Hepburn movies, and the whole play is a love letter to Miss Hepburn," David Gersten, the press representative for the one-person show, told the *Sun*. The play was first done at the Hartford Stage Company a few miles from where the real life Miss Hepburn grew up as the daughter of a physician in West Hartford. Since then it's gotten rave review in theaters in Cleveland and Boston.

The first act of *Tea at Five* takes place in 1938 on the eve of Miss Hepburn's stage and film comeback, after she had been labeled "box office poison." Act II takes place almost a half-century later in Miss Hepburn's Old Saybrook, Conn., country house. Now 95, she moved there permanently from her Manhattan townhouse several years ago. This reporter had the opportunity to interview Miss Hepburn twice, in 1993 and 1995, in her townhouse on East 49th Street and once at her Connecticut home overlooking Long Island Sound in March 2000. During the brief later interview, she sat in front of a roaring fire and, as she had done previously in New York, asked more questions than she answered.

IN A VARIATION of Stephen Sondheim's famous lyric, "Everything's Coming Up Roses," two classic Sondheim shows are coming up. The first is the New York City Opera's all-star revival *A Little Night Music*, Mr. Sondheim's 1973 musical. It stars Jeremy Irons, Claire Bloom, and Kate Burton.

Rehearsals for Sam Mendes' revival of *Gypsy*, with music by Jule Styne and lyrics by Mr. Sondheim, started Monday. It stars Bernadette Peters as "Mama Rose," the mother of famed stripper Gypsy Rose Lee, to be played by Tammy Blanchard.

The New York Sun, January 29, 2003.

MICKEY ROONEY and the late Judy Garland will be singing and dancing again in *Mickey and Judy*, a new two-person musical which is heading Off-Broadway.

With Jeff Harnar as Mickey and Shauna Hicks, who was in the cast of the Broadway musical *Blood Brothers*, as Judy, the two-person show has gotten the support of a number of high profile celebrities including Liza Minelli, Judy Garland's daughter.

"We went over to Liza Minnelli's [apartment] to do it for her," Mr. Harnar told the *Sun*. "She was going to have Michael Feinstein over for dinner so it was the two of us in front of the two of them!"

"We're not impersonating Mickey and Judy per se," Mr. Harnar continued. "There is a script [book] for the musical on what their relationship was on- and off-camera but it's mostly all the great Gershwin and Rodgers and Hart and other composers' songs they sang in their movies together." Mr. Harnar and Ms. Hicks have been doing the show around the country and it may open Off-Broadway in the next several months.

UP CLOSE: When Debbie Reynolds, who won an Oscar nomination for *The Unsinkable Molly Brown*, did her one-woman show with the Savannah Pops Symphony Orchestra at the Johnny Mercer Theatre in Savannah, Ga., last week, she told friends backstage she wants to take her show to Broadway... With Broadway shows setting an all-time ticket sales record Christmas week of more than $21 million, Roy Somlyo, president of the American Theatre, which co-produces the Tony Awards, says that despite "world tensions, despite all odds, theater is well on its feet!"

The New York Sun, January, 2003.

☐ Zellweger Has Eyes on Stage — and Oscar Night

RENEE ZELLWEGER SAYS she plans to do a play here—whether or not she wins an Oscar for her performance in *Chicago*.

"I'd love to do Broadway or Off-Broadway," Ms. Zellweger told *The New York Sun* after being in one of James Lipton's Actors Studio seminars at the New School last week.

"There hasn't been any opportunity before. I was asked to be in a play, but I couldn't because I was doing something. I couldn't have but I would have."

Asked about her doing the role of Roxy Hart in *Chicago*, the Texas native said, "It's been a good year for movies. We're all beneficiaries of that. And great women's roles. I can't wait for the Oscars, and [those nominated for Best Actress] are all my friends, so it's going to be a fun night out!"

Earlier at the New School, Mr. Lipton asked her how it was doing a love scene with Tom Cruise in *Jerry McGuire*. "He's fantastic. He puts you at ease right away," she said.

It was a lightning-swift transition. Suddenly, in an interview with the *Sun* in her spacious West End Avenue apartment, actress Kate Mulgrew, who on Monday began playing four-time Oscar winner Katharine Hepburn in *Tea at Five* at Off-Broadway's Promenade Theatre, started sounding exactly like Ms. Hepburn.

"This is the song of life. Get out there and give it hell! That was Miss Hepburn," said Ms. Mulgrew, best known for her role as Captain Kathryn Janeway on the hit TV series "Star Trek: Voyager."

"Miss Hepburn said over and over again that the big thing that separated her from others in Hollywood was her Connecticut Yankee roots." And though Ms. Mulgrew is from Iowa, she said that she shared a common bond with Ms. Hepburn by being from a family with "a lot of love of language and love of life."

Denying that she was in any way exploiting the famed actress, who will be 97 in May and has been well known for trying to preserve her privacy, Ms. Mulgrew said Matthew Lombardo's play "is a tribute to Ms. Hepburn. I would not have done it for one minute if I thought it was less than that."

CHITA RIVERA, who was one of the star attractions in Tuesday night's Drama League gala at the Pierre Hotel honoring Jerry Orbach, told the crowd in the hotel's grand ballroom, "It came as no surprise to me that Jerry would become one of TV's most extraordinary detectives [in the series "Law & Order"]. And if he told you that you played your scene well, you could be sure that it was the truth."

Ms. Rivera, who is to co-star with Antonio Banderas in the upcoming Broadway revival of *Nine*, got a big laugh when she joked she was reading from notes "because I've been having a painful life doing the tango with Anthony Banderas. Somebody's got to do it."

THEATERGOERS HUNGRY for Kathleen Turner's quick return to the stage will have the chance to see the sexy leading lady lend her famously throaty voice to two thrillers—"The Rats" by Agatha Christie and "The Tell-Tale Heart" by Edgar Allen Poe—at "Food for Thought" today. Ms. Turner, who recently left the cast of the Broadway production of *The Graduate*, is kicking off the spring 2003 season of the popular lunch-hour play-reading series staged at the National Arts Club at 15 Gramercy Park South. The series runs through May 29.

ON MARCH 5, playwright Arthur Miller makes a rare jaunt into New York City to direct a staged reading of his play *Elegy for a Lady*, also at the National Arts Club.

SHORT TAKES: Actor/director Phillip Seymour Hoffman, set to co-star next month in the Broadway revival of Eugene O'Neill's *Long Day's Journey Into Night*, with Brian Dennehy, Vanessa Redgrave, and Robert Sean Leonard, said staging the recent LAByrinth Theatre Company production of Stephen Adly Guirgis' *Our Lady of 121st Street*, set in a funeral home in Harlem, has helped him prepare for his role in the O'Neill classic.

The New York Sun, February 26, 2003.

◻ Swank's Bitten Nails, Turner's New Horizon

HILARY SWANK, who won an Oscar by playing a boy so convincingly in *Boys Don't Cry*, is more than a bit nervous about making her Broadway debut in *The Miracle Worker* on April 8.

"See, I have no nails because I've bitten them off," Ms. Swank, wearing a chic black dress and holding up her hands, told *The New York Sun*. "Anytime I embark on a new project I'm nervous and this is a whole new venue for me."

Ms. Swank will play the role of Annie Sullivan, who taught the late Helen Keller sign language. "[But] I'm really looking forward to the role. I like to challenge myself, and hopefully, I can live up to my own expectations." Ms. Swank, who was born in Lincoln, Neb., is no stranger to the stage. She played many roles in school and in regional theater before her Hollywood career took off.

KATHLEEN TURNER'S next major role may not be acting on or Off-Broadway.

"I'm working on a new angle right now—producing something," said Ms. Turner, who recently created a sensation playing a scene in *The Graduate* in the nude. She wouldn't say what she would produce.

As for acting, "I'll be back on Broadway in about a year. I'd like to take a year off from acting," she said. Having said that, she's been doing a number of play readings, including reading from *The Exonerated*, about death row inmates, at 45 Bleecker Street in Greenwich Village next week.

JESSE MARTIN, who plays Jerry Orbach's sidekick in the TV series "Law & Order," may be on the other side of the law this summer.

"I'm hoping to do the role of Mack the Knife in *Threepenny Opera* at the Williamstown [Mass.] Theatre Festival. I have been offered the role. Hopefully, I will get to do it when 'Law & Order' takes a break." Written by Bertolt Brecht and Kurt Weill, *Threepenny Opera* is considered to be a masterpiece of musical theater and Mack the Knife is the charismatic thief in the show.

BEBE NEUWIRTH got a standing ovation after doing the "All that Jazz" number from *Chicago* at the "Nothing Like a Dame" gala Monday night at the St. James Theatre. "I have no plans to go back in the cast," she told the *Sun* after the show, which benefited the Phyllis Newman Women's Health Initiative of the Actors Fund of America. "There's something happening for me probably Off-Broadway."

On stage at the benefit, syndicated columnist Liz Smith and Ann Richards, the former Texas governor, sang a duet of the song "I'm an Old Cowhand," after which Ms. Smith asked Ms. Richards, "Why didn't you ever run for president?" Ms. Richards replied: "Run for president? And give up show business!?" Ms. Richards replied.

The New York Sun, March 5, 2003.

◻ Ovations for 'Movin' Out'

WITH THE WAR in Iraq on everyone's minds, audience members and show insiders say it's extremely moving to see the reaction to a scene in *Movin' Out*, the Billy Joel-Twyla Tharp musical in which an American flag is waving during a funeral procession for a fallen Vietnam-era soldier. Every night, there are audience ovations and many are moved to tears.

"It's always been an emotional scene but even more so now with the war in Iraq," Robert Rea, who works at the Richard Rodgers Theatre where *Movin' Out* is playing, told the *Sun*. "*Movin' Out* has always been considered a contender for a Pulitzer Prize and this could put it over the top."

SET TO SHUTTER last Sunday after 26 previews and four regular performances, the $10 million musical *Urban Cowboy*, which received a number of negative reviews, has gotten a new lease on life from producers Chase Mishkin and Leonard Soloway.

Ms. Mishkin, who has produced 18 shows on and Off-Broadway in the past 10 years, said she got so many calls from friends and audience members saying how much they enjoyed *Urban Cowboy*, she reversed her earlier decision to close it.

"The cast is having a blast," Jenn Colella, who plays Sissy, the lead female role, told the *Sun*. "I can't ask for anything more than that. We're looking forward to a long run. We have all the faith in the world it will be."

The producers also told the *Sun* they are considering doing a movie version of the musical like *Chicago*. "We could do it," Mr. Soloway told the *Sun*. "There's never been a musical before," Ms. Mishkin eagerly chimed in. "But right now, producing this show is a 24-hour-a-day job!"

BROADWAY IS STAGING its annual spring revival. Eleven shows—six plays and five musicals—are slated to open between last Sunday, when *The Play What I Wrote*, directed by Kenneth Branagh, bowed, and May 6, with a revival of Eugene O'Neill's classic play *Long Day's Journey Into Night*, starring Brian Dennehy.

With the influx of tourists, a number of long-running Broadway hits like *Phantom of the Opera* and *Chicago*, have chalked up in ticket sales increases. Some upcoming shows like *Salome* with Al Pacino and *Gypsy*, starring Bernadette Peters, are already sold out for May performances.

Perhaps the hottest ticket in town is *Long Day's Journey Into Night*, O'Neill's autobiographical drama which originally premiered in Stockholm in 1956, well after the Nobel Prize winner's death. It co-stars Vanessa Redgrave, Philip Seymour Hoffman, and Robert Sean Leonard.

HARVEY FIERSTEIN, co-starring in *Hairspray*, will be honored May 7 at the 50th anniversary gala for the Christopher D. Smithers Foundation, Adele Smithers-Fornaci, the foundation's president, told the *Sun*. The Foundation is dedicated to helping alcoholics and Mr. Fierstein is a recovering alcoholic.

The New York Sun, April 21, 2003.

▣ 'Hairspray' Rocks Them at the Tony Awards

MOST EVERYTHING came up Tonys last night for *Hairspray*—the spectacular mega-hit spoof of the 1960s—which won eight awards—including best musical, leading actress and best actor.

Richard Greenberg's gay-themed ode to baseball won Tonys for best play, best direction of a play (Joe Mantello) and featured actor in a play (Denis O'Hare).

The other big Tony night news was that the costly but lackluster revival of *Gypsy*, starring Bernadette Peters, who missed a number of performances because of illness, failed to win a single award.

Other big winners included Eugene O'Neill's masterwork, *Long Day's Journey Into Night*, taking the Tony for best revival of a play, leading actor in a play (Brian Dennehy) and best actress in a play (Vanessa Redgrave).

Long Day's Journey Into Night won against three well-reviewed plays, *A Day in the Death of Joe Egg*, *Frankie and Johnny in the Clair de Lune*, and *Dinner at Eight*.

Hairspray, the Marc Shaiman-Scott Wittman-Thomas Meehan spoof, was nominated for 13 Tonys.

"I'm blessed every day of my life to act with each and every one of you," Mr. Fierstein said about his fellow *Hairspray* cast members in accepting his Tony Award. But he later told reporters that he was "uncomfortable" about being singled out in the Tony race with Antonio Banderas from the musical *Nine*, as the leading contenders when all the nominees were so talented.

In accepting her Tony Award on the cavernous stage of Radio City, Marissa Jaret Winokur, who won for best actress in a musical for *Hairspray*, said, "I want to thank my *Hairspray* family...and my sister, who made me a painting years ago saying, 'Fairy tales do come true.' If a 4-foot, 9-inch girl...can win a Tony, anything can happen!"

Lead *Hairspray* producer Margo Lion told the Tony audience that if "producing musicals is your dream, go for it."

The star-studded revival of the musical *Nine*, starring Mr. Banderas, and brilliantly directed by David Leveaux, won the Tony for leading featured actress (Jane Krakowski) and the hotly contested Tony for best revival of a musical. Mr. Banderas lost the Tony for leading actor in a musical to Mr. Fierstein.

Barbara Walters quipped that she was "asked to present the award for best revival of a musical because I was around when they were first presented."

Ms. Krakowski won against some of the toughest competition of any category against Chita Rivera and Mary Stuart Masterson—both also from *Nine*.

Ms. Krakowski said at first the cast of *Nine* was "very intimidated by Mr. Banderas because he's a movie star—and so gorgeous."

Mr. Banderas, making his Broadway debut in *Nine*, and Mr. Fierstein, a perennial Broadway star who won a Tony in *La Cage Aux Folles*, waged a tight race for best actor in a musical.

In fact, the two tied for best actor in the recent Drama Desk Awards that some consider a precursor to the Tonys. But Mr. Fierstein won the Tony.

Mr. Mantello, who won the Tony for best direction of *Take Me Out*, said the nudity in the other Broadway play he directed this season, *Frankie and Johnny in the Clair de Lune*, was necessary to provide the necessary raw element in the work.

Host Hugh Jackman from *X-Men* got the three-hour telecast off to a humorous start.

"I've really got to save my voice because I'm going to sing 'Rose's Turn,'" Mr. Jackman joked in a reference to the number from *Gypsy* that Bernadette Peters, nominated for a Tony for best actress in a musical, would sing later in the show.

In the press room after his Tony win for orchestration—and his appearance at the start of the show singing "New York State of Mind" in Times Square—Mr. Joel said he was "flabbergasted" by the success of *Movin' Out*.

When his collaborator, Twyla Tharp, won the Tony for best choreography, Mr. Joel clapped vigorously.

Tony producers Gary Smith and Elizabeth McCann sought to pump new life in what traditionally has been America's least-watched major awards show.

Despite being top-heavy with revivals of musicals and plays, no season in recent memory has featured such diversity, including an opera (Mr. Lurhmann's production of *La Boheme*), an evening of poetry (*Russell Simmons Def Jam Poetry on Broadway*), a rock musical with modern dance (*Movin' Out*), and British high farce (*The Play What I Wrote*, with celebrity guest stars like Kevin Kline and Roger Moore).

The New York Sun, June 9, 2003.

◻ Step Up For 'Edge"; Izzard's Roots; Hurt's Giggles; Springsteen's 'Run'

EDGE, A BLISTERING one-woman play starring Angelica Torn as the late poet Sylvia Plath, may move to Broadway in January. *The New York Sun* has learned.

Written and directed by Paul Alexander, *Edge* has been running Off-Broadway on Sunday and Monday evenings at the Culture Project at 45 Bleecker Theatre since June 8. Ms. Torn is the daughter of actor Rip Torn and the late Geraldine Page. She first appeared on stage years ago with her mother.

"We're moving to another Off-Broadway theater within the next three weeks and have set the opening date there," a well-placed source with the show told the *Sun*. "The money is there to go to Broadway, and we're planning to go there in January."

Plath committed suicide at age 30. She was the author of poems and short stories as well as *The Bell Jar*, her only published novel.

FILM AND STAGE ACTOR Eddie Izzard, who was nominated for a Tony Award for his performance in *A Day in the Death of Joe Egg*, is returning to his stand-up comedy roots.

Call it a comedy of (involuntary) giggles; Actress Mary Beth Hurt got so worked up during a recent performance of *Humble Boy* at the Manhattan Theatre Club that she began to laugh uncontrollably. Other cast members were tickled, with some ducking behind dinner napkins to regain their composure.

Later in the same play, co-star Blair Brown accidentally dropped a small honey pot containing her character's dead husband's ashes. The pot broke and the ashes flew all over the stage. Ms. Hurt and Ms. Brown later apologized to their colleagues in the Charlotte Jones comedy, which closes July 6.

NEW JERSEY NATIVE Bruce Springsteen, who says when he was younger he "ran to New York," now likes to relax with his kids in his home state. In an article headlined "Our America" in the July issue of *Reader's Digest*, an early copy of which was released exclusively to the *Sun*, the singer says, "It's funny. 'Born to Run' is a little anthem here in New Jersey. They talked about making it the state song, and yet it's about leaving New Jersey! It was often an oppressive place to be. When I was younger, I ran to New York. Now I like to take my kids to my hometown. They've got hotrod rallies and a nice main street, and my buddy's the mayor.

"I find enormous satisfaction from standing with my children on the same street where I stood with my father and mother. I like that a lot. I couldn't tell you exactly why."

In the same article, Don Hewitt, the "60 Minutes" producer, said he came to New York "believing that the Londoner who lived through the blitz was a breed of human the world would never see again. But I did see him again—on September 11, 2001, in the New York City police officers, firefighters, medical personnel, and volunteers."

In another interview in the July *Reader's Digest*, Harrison Ford discusses his life after the breakup of his 18-year marriage. He also covers Josh Hartnett, his co-star in the action comedy, *Hollywood Homicide*. Mr. Ford said his 12-year-old daughter Georgia calls him "Josh 'Hotnett.' I call him Josh 'Hairnet.' He's funny, charming, very serious about his work, which makes me laugh, he wants so bad to be good that sometimes he over-thinks it."

SHORT TAKES: Two-time Tony Award-winning actor Nathan Lane will co-star in a revival of Simon Gray's acclaimed play *Butley* at Boston's Huntington Theatre Company next January, the theater has announced…Yankees All-Star Bernie Williams may have a life as a musician after his professional baseball career is over. Mr. Williams, a guitarist and composer, has been signed by Sir Paul McCartney's MPL Communications Inc. "When I heard his CD I was blown away by his talent," Mr. McCartney reportedly said.

The New York Sun, June 18, 2003.

▢ Bob Hope 'Memories' at Walter Reade

ON WITH THE SHOW! Despite the death of Bob Hope on Sunday, the Film Society of Lincoln Center's Walter Reade Theater will celebrate the centenary of the comic genius with "Tanks for the Memories: Bob Hope's 100th Birthday," a 13-film selection representing the best of Hope's work in movies. It includes three of the popular "Road" pictures he made with Bing Crosby; his first screen test, and the hilarious shower sequence from *Star-Spangled Rhythm*.

On August 8, the series will kick off with an invitation-only reception hosted by Linda Hope, Hope's daughter who recently was nominated for an Emmy Award as a producer. Invited guests include Sarah Jessica Parker, who appeared with Hope on a U.S. Navy ship when she was playing the title role in *Annie* on Broadway, Woody Allen, Mel Brooks, Dick Cavett, Candace Bergen, and Lucy Arnaz, whose mother starred with Hope in the 1960 film *Facts of Life*.

MELANIE GRIFFITH, who joined the cast of *Chicago* as gold-digger Roxy on July 11, has helped the long-running hit show strike even more gold.

In fact, she has sparked attendance so much that last week *Chicago* even set a house record for ticket sales ($671,200) at Broadway's Ambassador Theatre. And on at least two occasions, the rousing standing ovations she's gotten were led by none other than husband Antonio Banderas, who is starring in the Tony Award-winning revival of *Nine*.

A NUMBER OF PAST and present TV and film stars—including Farrah Fawcett, Ashley Judd, and Alec Baldwin—may appear on Broadway this fall and winter. Ms. Fawcett, who became a household name in the original "Charlie's Angels" TV series, is reportedly in talks to co-star as a dutiful wife whose marriage is threatened by a 20-year-old new girl in town, in Nancy Hasty's play *Bobbi Boland*.

Scheduled to be directed by David Esbjornson, the play was done Off-Broadway at New York's Arclight Theatre two years ago. Alec Baldwin, meanwhile, has been in talks to do a Broadway revival of *Twentieth Century*, which originally opened in 1932, before becoming a 1934 movie of the same name with John Barrymore and Carol Lombard, at the Roundabout Theatre. Mr. Baldwin last was on Broadway in 1992 in a revival of *A Streetcar Named Desire*.

STEP ASIDE, HAIRSPRAY. *Cry Baby*, a musical version of John Waters' 1990 movie about a juvenile delinquent, who falls for a girl from the right side of the tracks, is Broadway-bound.

"It's very different from *Hairspray*," Adam Epstein, one of the producers of *Cry-Baby*, said. "For one thing, it's set in pre-Elvis 1954, while *Hairspray* is set in the pre-Beatles 1960s. I came to John with the idea last Christmas and he liked it. As he is with *Hairspray*, he will be the show's creative consultant." Mr. Epstein is also a producer of *Hairspray*.

"We don't have a creative team yet, so it's at least two to four years off from being done," Mr. Epstein said. "It took three years to do *Hairspray*, from the idea to the stage…It's a great story: bad boy gets the debutante."

Meanwhile, Mr. Waters expects to start shooting his next movie called *A Dirty Shame*, about sexual addiction, this fall.

The New York Sun, July 30, 2003.

◻ More Minnelli May Be in the Offing

BROADWAY PRODUCER Marty Richards, who won an Oscar for his film *Chicago*, has put production of the stage musical version of *Bullets Over Broadway*, Woody Allen's popular 1994 movie, on a "fast track." He said it might even be ready for Broadway next year.

"I am co-producing it with Harvey Weinstein of Miramax," Mr. Richards said. "I've signed Marvin Hamlisch (*A Chorus Line, Sweet Smell of Success*) to do the music. Harvey called me in my car coming over here and said, 'I miss working with you, honey!'" The Friars Club saluted Mr. Richards Monday night at the Ames Auditorium at The Lighthouse.

"*Bullets Over Broadway* is the thing I've wanted to do," Mr. Hamlisch said before the tribute. The Friars tribute featured Brent Barrett, Mario Cantone, Dee Hoty, Karen Ziemba, Judy Kaye, and others.

Bullets Over Broadway is set in the 1920s and is about a promising young playwright whose play is rewritten by a gangster. Dianne Wiest won an Academy Award as best supporting actress for the film.

Asked if he could get Catherine Zeta-Jones or another of his *Chicago* stars to be in the stage musical *Bullets Over Broadway*, Mr. Richards said, "I would be thrilled if she would just show up for the opening!"

FILM STAR Hugh Jackman, who plays the late singer-songwriter Peter Allen in the Broadway mega-musical "*The Boy From Oz*," which started previews last night, joked and adlibbed for several minutes when there was a glitch in a scene change in Monday night's dress rehearsal. "Hugh! Hugh!" shouted some in the audience, and Mr. Jackson shouted back, "My name's Peter!"

Some production insiders and audience members at the dress rehearsal say the work that needs to be done between now and the show's official opening in October is no joking matter. "They should cut some more songs!" one theater professional said.

WHEN *THE LONG CHRISTMAS RIDE HOME*, Pulitzer Prize-winning playwright Paula Vogel's new drama about the fallout from an automobile accident, starts previews at off-Broadway's Vineyard Theater October 14, it will bring to four the number of shows on and off-Broadway featuring puppets.

"I've never seen anything like it—puppets are taking over!" joked veteran Broadway producer and theater owner Stewart F. Lane, who is a co-producer of *Gypsy* and *Thoroughly Modern Millie*. "There are three musicals and a fourth show, the Vogel play, with puppets. They ought to have their own union!"

Besides *Avenue Q*, the first musical of the 2003-04 Broadway season at the Golden Theatre, Disney's long-running *The Lion King*, and *Little Shop of Horrors* feature non-human animated creatures. Incidentally, the name of the first play to open at the John Golden Theatre was *Puppets of Passion* in 1927, but its puppets were in the title only.

Up Close: Because "the very young, hip crowd" is clamoring for autographs from the cast, barriers have gone up outside the stage door of the Henry Miller Theatre where the long-running musical *Urinetown* is playing, *Urinetown* company manager Julie Crosby says.

The New York Sun, September 17, 2003.

◩ Rerun Eyed for 'What Makes Sammy Run?'

WHAT MAKES SAMMY RUN?, a 1964 musical that originally starred singer Steve Lawrence, may have its very first Broadway revival.

"We have been doing some revisions for a production either in London or here on Broadway," said Irwin Drake, the show's composer, who has written dozens of hit songs including "It Was a Very Good Year," sung by the late Frank Sinatra.

"The show has been done around the country but not revived on Broadway—and, ironically, its story of Hollywood greed and power is more relevant today than it was years ago," Mr. Drake said.

The musical is based on the 1941 novel by Budd Schulberg about an unscrupulous movie executive who began his career as a copyboy on a newspaper and gets his big break in the film business by "borrowing" a script from another writer. The 1964 production ran more than 500 performances.

FAMED FASHION DESIGNER Isaac Mizrahi, who did a one-man show several years ago, says he may soon be back on the off-Broadway boards.

"I'm in discussions about being in a revival of that one-man show of songs and stories," Mr. Mizrahi said when he was a guest at the recent National Design Awards at the Cooper-Hewitt National Design Museum.

"I'd also love to branch out and do a play sometime with other people's lines," he added. Meanwhile, Architect I.M. Pei and Massimo and Letta Vignelli were jointly honored with the museum's 2004 Lifetime Achievement Award. Architect Michael Graves, who has gone from designing hotels and kitchenware to residential buildings here in the city, attended the gala in a wheelchair, but said, "I'm busier than ever."

With almost perfect timing, Idina Menzell and Kristin Chenoweth, who play the Wicked Witch of the West, and Glenda the Good Witch, respectively, open officially tomorrow—the night before Halloween—in Stephen Schwartz's new musical *Wicked*.

Ms. Menzell took Broadway by storm when she was nominated for a Tony Award for her performance as Maureen in *Rent* and Ms. Chenoweth won a Tony in the musical *You're a Good Man, Charlie Brown*.

Based on a novel by Gregory McGuire, *Wicked* is one of the most eagerly anticipated shows this season because it comes on the heels of Mr. Schwartz's success in Hollywood as a composer of the animated films *The Hunchback of Notre Dame* and *Pocahontas*.

Ms. Menzell and Ms. Chenoweth are teamed with veteran Broadway star Joel Grey in *Wicked*.

It may be down, but don't count it out. Chicago City Limits, New York's longest-running comedy improvisational theater company, is actively looking for a new home downtown or in the Times Square area. It will take its final bow at its current location on First Avenue and 61st Street on Saturday, when it will have played 8,500 performances at this and two other locations. "I foresee us and other groups joining forces to establish a new space," founder Paul Zuckerman said.

The New York Sun, October 29, 2003.

▣ Rob Marshall: Heading Back to Broadway?

AFTER WINNING the best-picture Oscar for *Chicago*, Rob Marshall may be one of the hottest directors in Hollywood, but his heart belongs to Broadway. "I can never leave Broadway—it's still too much who I am," Mr. Marshall told *The New York Sun* Monday night, before he received a 2003 Genie Award presented by the Genesius Theatre Guild in TriBeCa.

He added, "The Weisslers [Barry and Fran] and I are working on something for Broadway. It's a new musical based on a play and a film. I'm going to do another film next year and following that will be the theater project. So 2004 for the film, and 2005 for the new Broadway musical."

Mr. Marshall has directed a number of Broadway shows, including *A Funny Thing Happened on the Way to the Forum*. He also co-directed the award-winning current production of *Cabaret*. The Weisslers are producers of the current stage version of *Chicago* and the revival of *Wonderful Town*, now in previews.

As for the success of the film version of *Chicago*, Mr. Marshall said, "I had great material and just kept my nose to the grindstone and did the work, but I could never have contemplated what happened with the picture could have happened."

GRAND DAMES: The new drama *Duet*, about the rivalry between stage legends Sarah Bernhardt and Eleonora Duse, will receive its New York premiere in a production starring veteran actresses Pamela Payton-Wright and Laura Esterman. The limited Off-Broadway engagement begins on November 18, opens officially on December 4, and runs through January 4 at the Greenwich Street Theatre in SoHo.

The play's author, Otho Eskin, is a Washington-based former diplomat turned playwright. *Duet* will be his New York playwriting debut.

Ms. Payton-Wright said that many of her insights into the character of Duse come from memories of working with the great Eva Le Gallienne, who cast her in her first play in New York, a production of *The Cherry Orchard* on Broadway in 1968. "Le Gallienne of course revered Duse," Ms. Payton-Wright said. "She studied her work on stage carefully. One of her most treasured possessions was a copy of the prayers of St. Thomas of Aquinas which Duse gave her and which she carried around with her everywhere."

Le Gallienne's biography of Duse, *The Mystic in the Theatre*, which she published in 1965, is still considered one of the most spellbinding and enlightening actor biographies of all time.

The New York Sun, November 12, 2003.

◻ Spring Again for Kirk Douglas

FILM LEGEND KIRK DOUGLAS, who turns 87 on December 9, is considering a return to the stage.

"I'm thinking about doing a one-man show about my life," he said in an interview with *The New York Sun*. Mr. Douglas, who suffered a stroke in 1995 which left his speech partially impaired, was in New York this past weekend and saw the revival of *Wonderful Town*.

"It's a very good show," he said of *Wonderful Town*, which was first produced a half-century ago. "It reminds me of the shows that were on Broadway when I was a young actor."

Mr. Douglas attended the American Academy of Dramatic Art here before parlaying his good looks and explosive energy into his Broadway debut as a singing Western Union boy in *Spring Again*.

Nominated for three Academy Awards, he received an honorary Oscar in 1995. In 1991, Mr. Douglas narrowly escaped death in a helicopter that collided with a small plane, and after his subsequent stroke many people thought his acting days were over. But since then he has starred in several films including one produced by his son, Michael Douglas.

Born Issur Danielovitch on December 9, 1916, in Amsterdam, N.Y., the son of illiterate and abjectly poor Jewish-Russian immigrants, Mr. Douglas went from being "an unhappy child who never got a pat on the back from his father," as he wrote in his 1997 book, *Climbing the Mountain: My Search for Meaning*, up to the very pinnacle of film stardom.

HERE IN SPIRIT: Michael Feinstein returned to Feinstein's at the Regency last night for his new holiday show, "The Great American Holiday Songbook," which runs through December 27. But his heart is heavy this season, because longtime friend Rosemary Clooney died earlier in the year.

"We always spent Christmas together, and this time of year is when I miss her the most," he told *The New York Sun*. To celebrate their friendship and the some 200 shows they performed together over the years, Mr. Feinstein sang a duet with Clooney's voice on tape. "We sang many duets together," he said.

Having recorded more than 20 albums and sung in some of the world's most famous nightclubs, Clooney is perhaps best known for co-starring in the film classic *White Christmas*, with Bing Crosby, Danny Kaye, and Vera Allen. Clooney told *The New York Sun* several years ago that she spent one of her happiest holidays in a suite at the Plaza Hotel. "We had seven rooms and a Christmas tree from FAO Schwartz, a live tree that they had decorated," she said. "It was one of the nicest Christmases I ever had."

CY HIGH: Cy Coleman will go from a stylized look at the Jazz Age to a whimsical adaptation of Wendy Wasserstein's book, *Pamela's First Musical*, he told the *Sun* last week.

The Friars Foundation International Gala and Ball hosted a ball at the Plaza last week honoring Mr. Coleman and Muriel Siebert. Mr. Coleman's New York-bound *Like Jazz* will open December 4 at the Mark Taper Forum in Los Angeles for an eight-week run. Marilyn and Alan Bergman wrote the lyrics.

"This musical is like nothing else," Mr. Coleman said. "There is no usual plotline. But it's not a revue. It glides from episode to episode, and the 18-piece orchestra is an integral part of it. It's stylized but very accessible. And it all started when Polly Austen commissioned me to write a couple of jazz songs."

Pamela's First Musical is "based on my children's book, about a little girl who goes to her first musical and then comes home to write her own," said Ms. Wasserstein, who also attended the gala. "Cy and I both have young daughters, and although I never dreamed I'd be working with Cy when I wrote the story, I created a character called 'Cy Songheim,' so I guess it was meant to be."

Meanwhile, a revival of Mr. Coleman's *Sweet Charity* is also headed to New York.

BRAVO: Musical Theatre Works, a not-for-profit organization dedicated to helping develop new songwriters and new musicals, grossed some $300,000 at its "Bravo Bernstein!" benefit at the Hudson Theatre Monday night. "We offer a composer, lyricist, or a creative team the opportunity of taking the first step and seeing their show on its feet in a reading," said executive director Randy Ellen Lutterman during the intermission of musical numbers, performed by Audra McDonald, Marin Mazzie, Michael Cerveris, and others.

Even actor David Hyde Piece, the evening's Emcee, got into the act, performing an ensemble number from the late Leonard Bernstein's rarely performed musical *1600 Pennsylvania Avenue*.

SECOND TO NUN: Georgia Engel, who has an ongoing feature role in the hit TV sitcom "The Ray Romano Show," will play a nun in a new revival of *Nunsense*. Ms. Engel made her first major splash in New York playing a nun in the original off-Broadway production of John Guare's *House of Blue Leaves*. She may be best known to fans of *The Mary Tyler Moore Show*, in which she had a supporting role. Ms. Moore is currently performing in Neil Simon's new play, *Rose's Dilemma*, at the Manhattan Theatre Club.

The New York Sun, November 26, 2003.

▣ Two New Musicals From Kathie Lee?

KATHIE LEE GIFFORD may be coming to Broadway—as a writer. "I've written two musicals that are both going to be produced this coming year," Ms. Gifford told *The New York Sun* in an interview. "One on the life of Aimee Semple McPherson that's called *Hurricane Aimee* and the other called *The Family Under the Bridge*, taken from a book that won a prize for best children's book in 1958. I read it with my daughter a few years ago and it absolutely charmed me."

"The Nederlander Organization is developing *Hurricane Aimee*," she continued. Nederlander, which owns 11 Broadway playhouses, is a major producer of Broadway musicals. "I wrote the book and all the lyrics and co-wrote some of the music. I was offered a TV sitcom but I said I can't do a sitcom and birth my 'babies' [musicals] at the same time." She says to expect both productions in September 2004.

Ms. Gifford said that even though *Hurricane Aimee* is about one of America's early religious temperance leaders, "It's funny and not religious at all." As for romance, "She was married three times and there's the question of who she was with six weeks she was missing!"

"I'm just loving what I'm doing. Now instead of sitting on a stool on 'Live' ["Live With Regis and Kathie Lee," now "Live with Regis and Kelly"], talking about my life, I'm actually living it." Any chance Ms. Gifford will act in one of the shows? "No, no, no. no!" she said.

GOTTA DANCE: The new musical *Never Gonna Dance*, based on a 1936 Fred Astaire-Ginger Rogers movie, has been rumored to be having problems with its book. Ted Hartley, a co-producer of *Never Gonna Dance*, told *The New York Sun* the show would be fine. "We're addressing them everyday," he said. "We don't freeze the show for another week." But he frankly admitted he at first had some serious doubts about the show.

"I'm basically a movie producer by trade and I wasn't sure how the Jerome Kern score and particularly the 1936 script would work on Broadway," he said. "Fortunately, we got some very talented people. It has the feeling of 1936 with the spirit of 2003." *Never Gonna Dance*, which costars Nancy Lemenager, is scheduled to open officially at the Broadhurst Theatre December 4.

GELB SERIES FOR PBS?: Arthur Gelb may be the former managing editor of *The New York Times* but he's also known for the scholarly biography of playwright Eugene O'Neill he co-wrote with his wife, Barbara Gelb. At a book party on Monday for his new book, *City Room* (Putnam Publishing Group) about his career at the *Times*, Mr. Gelb told *The New York Sun* that "My wife, Barbara, and I are doing a documentary on O'Neill with Rick Burns. WGBH is the sponsor. And it will be on PBS in the late spring [2004]. It's got an all-star cast. Al Pacino is brilliant in it. Zoe Caldwell and others."

HARRIS'S HOPES: Five-time Tony winner Julie Harris, who had a stroke three years ago that impaired her speaking ability, said she hopes to return to acting in the not-too-distant future. Ms. Harris attended a special benefit reading of Carson McCullers's *The Member of the Wedding* at the National Arts Club last Friday, more than 50 years after she appeared in the play on Broadway. "The Food for Thought-Julie Harris Playwriting Fellowship" was awarded to Renee E. D'Aoust. When someone suggested that Ms. Harris might want to do a one-woman show about her own life in the theater, her longtime friend, actress Patricia Neal, said "That's a good idea. That's a gorgeous idea!"

QUICK CHANGE: One day this week, instead of her usual vocal warm-ups before going onstage in *Our Sinatra*, Hilary Kole, who stars in the off-Broadway hit along with Tony DeSare and Adam James, was simply trying to keep her cool. Her costumes, all provided by Laurence Kazar Inc., still hadn't arrived. The beaded, hand-painted frocks finally made an appearance five minutes before curtain. "The dresses were all wrapped," Ms. Kole says. "During changes I just ripped off the wraps and jumped into whatever came out. Thank goodness they all fit perfectly." *Our Sinatra* officially opens at Birdland on Thursday, November 20. This tribute to the music of Frank Sinatra, which ran for almost 1,100 performances is back in New York after a 60-city tour.

UP CLOSE: "I am planning many more concerts after my run in *Thoroughly Modern Millie* ends and I will be sure to include the Bergman songs in my act," said Leslie Uggams as she signed her new CD, "On My Way to You: The Songs of Alan & Marilyn Bergman," (Fynsworth Alley) at Tower Records Lincoln Center…"It's not a busy year for me theater-wise because I plan to do a film," said prolific theater producer Chase Miskin, a co-producer of last year's *Urban Cowboy*, at a recent party that Louise Kerz Hirschfeld, the widow of artist Al Hirschfeld, threw for the publication of *The Speakeasies of 1932* (Glenn Young Books)…Composer Mary Rodgers, the daughter of late composer Richard Rodgers, said at a recent party at the Four Seasons restaurant that she's "given up writing for the theater. My son, Adam Guettel, does all the writing now." Mr. Guettel wrote the music for a show called *Light in the Piazza*, which Ms. Rodgers said may eventually be done on Broadway… Speaking of offspring of theater luminaries, David Lahm, who is the son of the late Broadway lyricist Dorothy Fields and is appearing with his wife Judy Kreston at Danny's Skylight Room through November 29, said "I've been singing Dorothy Fields's lyrics for a lot of years without giving much thought to how they work in a book show." But after seeing *Never Gonna Dance* on Broadway "I got a whole new exciting angle on what a superb writer she was."

The New York Sun, November 19, 2003.

◻ At Taping for Bravo, Jackman Talks About 'Oz' & 007

THE BOY FROM OZ has his eye on Bond, James Bond.

"What boy doesn't want to be James Bond?" actor Hugh Jackman, who currently is playing legendary singer/son writer Peter Allen in *The Boy From Oz* on Broadway, said in an interview with *The New York Sun*.

James Lipton had just interviewed Mr. Jackman for a taping on Monday night of his Bravo talk show, "Inside the Actors Studio." He asked him whether the rumors were true that he might play the lead in a new James Bond movie. "I've heard more rumors than I've heard official contact through my agent," Mr. Jackman replied. "So there's nothing official to tell you." Mr. Lipton is also dean of the drama department of New School University.

In his dressing room after the taping, Mr. Jackman told the *Sun* that aside from wanting to play Bond (he didn't get the role), "I'd love to do Shakespeare on stage." He also indicated that although he's signed to be in *The Boy From Oz* until next September, he might consider extending his engagement. "A year, that's a long time. We'll see how we go," he said.

He also told the *Sun* that every performance in *The Boy From Oz* "feels like the first time, since I love it. I only sign on to a show I really love and want to do. And doing it for a year you have to love it."

Earlier in the evening, he told the audience that, "You have to love the character you play. And the gift for me [playing the role of Peter Allen] is the [direct] contact I have talking to the audience. I feel it's easier to communicate with members of the audience in America than in Australia, because I feel their very open spirit."

DISCOUNT INFERNO: In the next few weeks, a number of shows On- and Off-Broadway are expected to announce deep ticket discounts for the next two months. Beginning January 1, producers traditionally make extra efforts to sell seats that may go unfilled because of bad winter weather.

"I know there have been production meetings to discuss specials but I have no official word," said Sam Rudy, the press representative for the hit musical *Avenue Q*.

REVEL YELL: Veteran Broadway actor Michael Burke, who played Leonardo da Vinci in the 24th annual amateur production of "New York Revels" this past weekend at the Peter Norton Symphony Space, says that there's something special about doing amateur theatricals in New York, the professional theater capital of the country.

"It's very comfortable—like doing summer stock in the middle of Manhattan," he told the *Sun* backstage Sunday night. "There's a great rapport between the actors and audience you often don't get on Broadway."

The New York Sun, December 17, 2003.

◻ Renée Decked Out As Holly?

RENÉE ZELLWEGER in *Breakfast at Tiffany's*? Martin Jurow, the Brooklyn-born producer of the classic film *Breakfast at Tiffany's*, starring Audrey Hepburn, is urging Ms. Zellweger and Paramount, which has the rights to the movie based on the Truman Capote book, to remake it.

"Renée would make a fabulous Holly Golightly in *Breakfast at Tiffany's*, and be truer than Audrey because Renée comes from a small town in Texas," Mr. Jurow told *The New York Sun* from Dallas, where he now lives.

"She would really understand the role. I think she's just brilliant in everything she does. If she wanted it she could get it. If she wanted to do it again, Paramount would probably let her do it." Producer Robert Evans, Mr. Jurow said, is interested in doing a remake of the movie.

In his long career, which began in the New York theater, Mr. Jurow also produced the first *Pink Panther* film and co-produced *Terms of Endearment* with Jack Nicholson and Shirley MacLaine.

REPRISE FOR DUET: The new drama *Duet*, by Otho Eskin, about a backstage encounter between the super-divas Sarah Bernhardt and Eleonora Duse, may reopen Off-Broadway in the Spring after it closes this Sunday. A number of prominent industry producers are fans of the production, and actor Brian Murray who actually incorporated a plug for the show in his performance of *Beckett/Albee* one evening recently.

Producer Ludovica Villar-Hauser says what she's seeing reminds her of the grassroots enthusiasm that propelled her dark horse hit *The Countess*, which went on to be the longest-running drama of the 1999-2000 season. While she admitted that the play needs some revisions, she's particularly bullish about her actresses—Laura Esterman, who portrays Bernhardt, and Pamela Payton-Wright, who plays Duse.

"I absolutely want to stay with our stars," she told the *Sun*. "Pamela and Laura are gems in these roles. Casting them has been a blessing. Keeping them is a priority."

DON'T TAKE IT OUT: The deep-fried turkey and potato soufflé are some of the dishes being prepared on stage by playwright/food writer/performer Jonathan Reynolds in *Dinner With Demons* at off-Broadway's Second Stage Theatre. They certainly appear delectable enough to eat, and many people in the audience leave the show wondering who gets to take the food home. Behind-the-scenes sources say that while cast members may sometimes nibble or pick at it, the theater doesn't have a food license—so it throws most of it out.

UTE'S DEBUT: Ute Lemper, the international chanteuse who made her professional debut as Grizabella in the original Vienna production of *Cats* and starred in the revival of *Chicago* on Broadway a few years ago, is currently making her Café Carlyle debut.

"My musical program at the Carlyle will be a journey through the sleepless cities and places of the world, between yesterday and tomorrow, either right here or somewhere at the end of the world," Ms. Lemper told me.

"The journey includes musical reflections in Yiddish, Hebrew and Arabic, the dances of Piazzolla, sleepless nights of Brel and Piaf and always a walk on the 'Weill' side. I'll also include such offbeat contemporary writers as Tom Waits, Nick Cave, and Elvis Costello." Ms. Lemper will perform Tuesday Through Saturdays from January 9 to 31.

A MODERN MAJOR ANNUAL: One might think it's hard to gather a cast, crew and orchestra members to perform on New Year's Eve but "this New Year's Eve concert marks a 20-year tradition for the New York Gilbert & Sullivan Players and Symphony Space," Albert Bergeret, artistic director of the Gilbert & Sullivan Players said in an interview with *The New York Sun*. "It's the only musical event quite like it in the city."

"Unfortunately, we did not present the concert the last two years—so this is a very special event," he said. "The highlight of the evening is when the audience shouts out their favorite numbers and cast and orchestra instantly perform! Talking about keeping them on their toes…

UP CLOSE: After attending a performance of *Avenue Q* last weekend, former President Bill Clinton, his wife Senator Clinton, and their daughter Chelsea went on stage to greet the cast and were mobbed by the show's puppet stars Kate Monster, Princeton, Rod, and Trekkie Monster.

The New York Sun, December 31, 2003.

▣ Can You See a 'Broadway' Show in Chicago?

THE WAY PLAYS and musicals continue to be advertised and promoted in Chicago, Los Angeles, and Miami could have a big impact on whether or not union actors on Broadway, who are members of the Actors Equity Association, continue to work past their current production contract, which ends June 27, 2004.

At issue are the so-called "non-Equity road shows," which are sometimes advertised as part of a "Broadway" series but employ non-Equity actors who haven't been on Broadway or have dropped their unions affiliation.

"The unions are prepared to strike over this issue unless a lot of progress is made between now and June," a well-placed union source told *The New York Sun*. "There has to be honest promotion and advertising so at the very least audiences across the country know when they are seeing shows which have non-Equity casts."

"We've reached a crisis stage," says Equity Executive Director Alan Eisenberg about the issue on the Actors Equity Web site. "According to our latest statistics, 40 percent of all road tours are non-Equity." The union has earmarked $1.6 million in a campaign against non-Equity shows.

One Broadway producer, who requested that he not be named, said producers would fight to preserve their rights to produce non-Equity shows because many can't afford to pay higher Equity salaries and the pension and welfare benefits Equity requires.

Another producer, however, said that he was not opposed to "more honest promotion of shows to say their employees are nonunion actors."

MONROEMANIA?: The Roundabout Theatre Company is preparing to present the first ever revival of Arthur Miller's *After the Fall* with performances scheduled to begin June 11.

The play hasn't been done in New York since 1964 when it received generally good reviews but Mr. Miller was criticized by some in the media for permitting the play—based on his relationship with Ms. Monroe, his second wife—to be produced little more than a year after her death.

Hilary Swank is reportedly in talks to play "Maggie," the Monroe character in *After the Fall*, and one knowledgeable source told the *Sun* that Mr. Miller has made a number of revisions in the play to focus more attention on the play and less on its widely assumed connection with the late screen idol.

HAPPILY HAUNTED: Christine Andreas, one of the many big Broadway stars who performed in Scott Siegel's 2004 Nightlife Awards at Town Hall on

Monday night, will return to the Café Carlyle for the month of February, to one of the "few stages in New York I feel is happily haunted."

"The Palace Theatre is one, where I did *Oklahoma*, Carnegie Hall is one, and the Carlyle is the other," she told the *Sun*. "You sort of sense all the spirits of past performers that you have admired through the years."

UP CLOSE: "Life is beautiful, the steaks are beautiful, and even the orchestra is beautiful!" Ute Lemper told her opening night audience, which included Joan Rivers, Barbara Cook, and John Simon, at the Café Carlyle Friday…"I can't wait to call daddy and tell him we ended up the night singing with Kitty Carlisle Hart," said one socialite leaving the Café Pierre after Ms. Hart joined singer Kathleen Landis and the audience in singing "I'll Be Loving You, Always."

The New York Sun, January 14, 2004.

🔲 Scoundrels Onstage

DIRTY ROTTEN SCOUNDRELS, a new musical based on the popular 1998 film of the same name starring Steve Martin and Michael Caine, "will open on Broadway next Spring," producer Martin Bell confirmed in an interview with *The New York Sun*. Published reports in *Playbill* and elsewhere have reported that the show will open at the Old Globe Theatre in San Diego in September 2004 and then on Broadway in February 2005. Mr. Bell confirmed the former but not the latter.

With music and lyrics by David Yazbek (*The Full Monty*), the musical will be directed by Jack O'Brien, artistic director of the Old Globe, and choreographed by Jerry Mitchell, with a book or dialogue by Jeffrey Lane. Don't expect Mr. Caine to repeat his performance on Broadway, Mr. Bell said. "I'm not sure he's right for it," he laughed.

STAYING ALIVE: Julian Lennon, the talented actor and singer who is one of two sons of late Beatle John Lennon, may be bound for off-Broadway as a producer of a new play about his late father. "Julian has read the play (*Ears on a Beatle*) and would love for it to move—he's really 100 percent behind it," said Dan Lauria, who in the new two-character production plays the older of two FBI agents assigned to track the pop star. "He wants it to stay alive."

Mr. Lauria, perhaps best known as the Dad in the ABC series "The Wonder Years," said that the drama "is not a 'whitewash' of John Lennon. No one plays John Lennon in the play. But he's there—he's felt. In the very first scene we're in the park watching him."

Ears on a Beatle by Mark St. Germain started previews at the DR2 Theatre last night and opens officially March 28. The show is currently being presented by veteran Broadway and off-Broadway producer Daryl Roth.

REMEMBERING BETTE DAVIS: *Me and Jezebel*, a stage production based on the real life experience of writer Liz Fuller when the famous Hollywood star Bette Davis in 1985 asked if she had a room to spare for one night in her Connecticut house and then decided to stay for one-month—turning Fuller into a guest in her own home—was presented by producer Robert Blume for one special performance at the National Arts Club last Thursday evening.

With Ms. Fuller playing herself and actor Kelly Moore portraying Bette Davis, a role he performed to rave reviews in stage productions of *Me and Jezebel* in London and Australia, the special performance was attended by a number of New York City theatrical producers that Mr. Blume is trying to interest in becoming co-producers of a new off-Broadway revival of the stage comedy.

Over the past 10 years, productions of *Me and Jezebel* have had successful runs across the United States with Karen Valentine playing Ms. Fuller as well as in the U.K. and Australia where Katy Manning is currently portraying Ms. Fuller. It was originally mounted at the Actors Playhouse in New York City in 1994.

The New York Sun, March 17, 2004.

◻ Will Wasserman Bring Duke to Broadway?

CHOOSERS, NOT BEGGARS: *Beggar's Holiday*, the late Duke Ellington's only Broadway musical, is being revamped and may return to Broadway, *The New York Sun* has learned. Its new book is by two-time Tony Award-winning author Dale Wasserman.

"I have now written a completely new book for it, and I've also done some new lyrics," Mr. Wasserman, who wrote the play *One Flew Over the Cuckoo's Nest* and the book for the musical *Man of La Mancha*, told the *Sun* in a phone interview from his home near Phoenix.

But *Beggar's Holiday* will have the original Ellington score when it opens at the Marin Theatre in Mill Valley, Calif., just across the Golden Gate Bridge from San Francisco. After that, "It's our intention to move it to San Francisco" before it comes to Broadway, Mr. Wasserman said. *Beggar's Holiday*, which originally opened at Broadway's Broadway Theater in 1946, is based on John Gay's *The Beggar's Opera* of 1728.

Donald York, a veteran Broadway musical director and arranger, is writing new orchestrations for the Ellington score. "The score had to sound like 'today,'" Mr. Wasserman told the *Sun*. The acclaimed author was actually a co-producer of the original Broadway musical and said he may play a producing role until it opens in San Francisco. "I'm not in love with being a producer but that kind of stubbornness is sometimes the only way you can get something to move!" he said. "At this point the show will speak for itself."

The New York Sun, Wednesday, March 24, 2004.

◻ Judith Ivey's Stage Designs

TWO-TIME TONY AWARD-winning actress Judith Ivey will be returning to her acting roots when she plays the late Martha Mitchell, the flamboyant wife of late U.S. Attorney General John Mitchell, in a new play at the Public Theater next fall, *The New York Sun* has learned.

Perhaps best known for a recurring role in the hit TV series "Designing Women," Ms. Ivey won her Tony Awards in the plays *Steaming* and *Hurlyburly*. Recently, she directed *More*, a one-woman show written by and starring Yeardley Smith, which opened officially last week at the Union Square Theatre and is closing April 18 after receiving mixed reviews.

Following *More*, Ms. Ivey said, she is "going back to being a mother and then I do a film in May. The film is a PBS docudrama and I'm playing Margo Jones, who was the woman who actually crated regional theater." Jones was for years the driving artistic force behind the Dallas Theater Center. For her part, Ms. Smith said that she expects to take *More* on tour. "I hope to take it to Los Angeles, and maybe Chicago," she told the *Sun*.

HUGH'S SIDESHOW: Call it the Hugh Jackman sideshow. What began as an occasional lark now has become an integral part of *The Boy from Oz*. One of Mr. Jackman's latest give-and-takes with an audience member was with an 8-year-old girl. He tried to get the girl and her mother to move closer to the stage, but her mother appeared too shy to change seats. Mr. Jackman talked to the girl throughout the show and even asked her to cover her ears at one point because he said the material was not for her young ears. Another time, he offered the young lady some "sweets"; she promptly shared her bag of Hershey's Kisses with those around her. Finally, he asked the girl to come up on stage and dance with him. She was too shy—but her mother was not.

LOOKING BACK ON BROADWAY: Fifty years ago on March 31, 1941, a play with the intriguing title of *Mrs. January 7 and Mr. Ex* by Zoe Akins and starring Billie Burke opened at the Belasco Theatre. "The amazingly youthful Billie Burke and the droll and ever-recurrent Frank Craven are pleasantly teamed in the new comedy," the critic for *The New York Sun* wrote in his review in the April 1, 1944 edition of the paper.

UP CLOSE: Liza Minnelli stepped up on the stage of the Gershwin Theatre where *Wicked* is playing on Saturday night and sang part of "Wilkommen" from *Cabaret* with Joel Grey, a costar of *Wicked* who costarred with Ms. Minnelli in the film version of *Cabaret*.

The New York Sun, March 31, 2004.

▣ 'La Cage' Back to Roost

JERRY HERMAN'S musical comedy *La Cage aux Folles* is going home. This first ever Broadway musical to deal with a gay love affair—it was originally produced in 1983 at Broadway's historic Palace Theatre, under the direction of the great Arthur Laurents—is scheduled to be revived at the Palace this fall, knowledgeable production sources have told *The New York Sun*.

Jerry Zaks will stage the revival, which has music and lyrics by Jerry Herman and a book by Harvey Fierstein (based on the play *La Cage aux Folles* by Jean Poiret), sources also said. Sources said casting for the lead roles, first played by Gene Barry and George Hearn, is not set.

La Cage aux Folles is being produced by the Nederlander Organization, Clear Channel, and others. "I feel it's great material," said one source close to the production. "I'm very excited."

AFFAIRS OF THE HART: Kitty Carlisle Hart, the actress, singer, and former chairman of the New York State Council on the Arts, which supports a wide spectrum of arts endeavors, retired from her state post some years ago. But she says "the theater, the off-Broadway theater," remains "nearest and dearest to my heart."

In an interview with the *Sun* in her Madison Avenue Apartment, the 93-year-old Ms. Hart, the widow of the late playwright and director Moss Hart, who collaborated on *The Man Who Came to Dinner* and other classic comedies with George S. Kaufman and directed *My Fair Lady* and many other hit shows, said that not a day goes by when she doesn't think about and miss the late Moss Hart.

TRUE WIT: Singer Steve Ross, who is doing a show called *Rhythm and Romance* at the Stanhope Hotel, is putting special emphasis on the romantic ballads of the late Noël Coward. "Coward is known for his more catchy songs like 'Mad Dogs and Englishmen' but he had not only rhythm but romance," Mr. Ross told the *Sun* after a show this past Saturday night. "I wanted to present a broad picture of his work." One of the most romantic songs Mr. Ross sings is "Someday I'll Find You," which was not in a Coward musical at all but served as background music for his play *Private Lives*.

Mr. Ross also told the *Sun* he is planning a two-character review about the life of the late Dorothy Parker. But he said choosing an actress/singer to palsy the late poet, pundit, and short-story writer won't be easy.

UP CLOSE: *7 Habits of Highly Effective Mistresses*, a one-woman show by Lisa Faith Phillips about helping to pay her way through the London School of

Economics by working as a stripper, opens at Dillon's on May 7. She told the *Sun*, jokingly, that President George Bush's strong support for the traditional institution of marriage "means there will be more demand than ever for mistresses."...Alec Baldwin and Frank Langella, stars of the Broadway plays *Twentieth Century* and *Match*, respectively, attended a Sunday evening performance of Stephen Sondheim's musical *Assassins* at Studio 54.

The New York Sun, April 28, 2004.

🔲 Drama Desk Awards

IN WHAT MANY BELIEVE to be a precursor of the Tony Awards on June 6, Hugh Jackman, *Wicked*, and *Assassins* were big winners at the 49th annual Drama Desk Awards yesterday at Fiorello H. LaGuardia High School. The organization of drama critics, columnists, and reporters, handed out awards in 25 categories.

The Drama Desk Awards, bestowed for excellence in both Broadway and Off-Broadway theater, were hosted by Harvey Fierstein, who received the 2003 Tony Award for Best Actor in a Musical.

"Last year the Tony's reflected what happened here at the Drama Desk almost exactly, except for two awards," executive consultant for the Drama Desk, Roy Somlyo, told *The New York Sun*.

Wicked headed the list of Drama Desk winners with 6 awards, trailed by *Assassins* with 4 awards and *Henry IV* with 3 awards. The play *I Am MY Own Wife* was voted outstanding new play.

The New York Sun, May 17, 2004.

◘ Well, Hello Carol!

BROADWAY LEGEND Carol Channing—who has long been identified with the role of Dolly Gallagher Levi in Jerry Herman's blockbuster 1964 musical *Hello Dolly!*—may be coming back to Broadway in a one-woman show.

"It's the show I always wanted to do," Ms. Channing, now 83, told *The New York Sun*. "I am just in heaven, because I am playing myself." The Nederlander Organization, which owns 11 Broadway playhouses, "is in talks to put the show in one of their theaters," Harlan Boll, Ms. Channing's publicist, told the *Sun*.

On June 7 the York Theater Company will honor Ms. Channing with the Oscar Hammerstein Award and a reception at the University Club, followed by a 7 p.m. concert and award ceremony at the Citigroup Executive Auditorium, 399 Park Avenue.

"I am a bit surprised, but then I find myself almost in shock every time I am told that someone wants to give me an award," Ms. Channing told the *Sun*. "They keep using words like 'legend' and 'icon.' I just don't think of myself that way, and I think the moment anyone does they should give it up."

The gala, which is the main fund-raising event for the York Theatre Company, will feature performances by Kristin Chenoweth, Christine Ebersole, and Debra Monk. The honorary chair is Mr. Herman. Barbara Walters, Arlene Dahl, Marge Champion, and Liz Smith will also be there.

MUSICAL DICKENS: A musical version of Charles Dickens's *A Tale of Two Cities* may be Off-Broadway bound.

With a book by veteran playwright Joe McDonald and a score by Robert Hoover, *A Tale of Two Cities: The Musical*, was originally produced at the Helen Hayes Performing Arts Center in Nyack, N.Y. in 2000. A reading of the show was done recently at the Lambs Club, and producer Heather Duke and others are now hoping to mount it Off-Broadway early next year.

"We had 18 actors in the Nyack production," Mr. McDonald said in an interview with the *Sun*. "I've gotten it down to 9 [actors] to make it more economical to produce these days. But there are still going to be more rewrites. It's a constant thing, which is fine."

IN THE WINGS: Shannen Doherty, once the costar of the hit 1990s TV series "Beverly Hills 90210," may make her New York Theatrical debut in a new Off-Broadway-bound play called *In the Wings* by Stewart F. Lane.

"I think I was 12 when I did my last play," Ms. Doherty told the *Sun* after a reading of the play last week at the Revelation Theatre. "You couldn't tell I was nervous? I think I had hives." In *In the Wings*, Ms. Doherty would play a character called Melinda Donahugh, an actress who gets her first big break with a role in a Broadway play and leaves her longtime boyfriend for the play's director.

Playwright Lane, who is also a Tony Award-winning producer, said, "I'm still working on it" but added he hopes it will be ready for production later this year or early next year.

The New York Sun, June 2, 2004.

◻ On the Town, 2004 Tony Winners Shine

ASSASSINS, WICKED, and *Avenue Q* dominated the Tony Awards last night at Broadway's annual celebration of itself.

The revival of *A Raisin in the Sun* helped make Tony history when Phylicia Rashad won for Best Leading Actress in a Play, the first time a black actress has won in this category. Audra McDonald won her fourth Tony for Best Featured Actress in the play.

Assassins, the offbeat musical about people who have shot American presidents, won five awards—more than any other show—including Best Revival of a Musical, Best Featured Actor in a Musical (Michael Cerveris), and Best Direction of a Musical.

Avenue Q, the cheeky musical that uses puppets, four-letter words, and catchy tunes, took home Tonys for Best Musical, Best Original Score, and Best Book of a Musical.

Idina Menzel, who made her Broadway debut in *Rent*, won for Best Leading Actress in *Wicked*, which also received awards for Best Costume Design and Best Scenic Design.

Jefferson Mays won for Best Leading Actor in a Musical for his performance in the Pulitzer Price-winning *I Am MY Own Wife* (in which he plays over 40 characters), which also won for Best Play.

Hugh Jackman, who hosted the show, won Best Actor in a Musical in *The Boy from Oz*.

Anika Noni Rose won for Best Featured Actress in a Musical in *Caroline, or Change*. Brian F. O'Byrne won for Best Featured Actor in a Play in *Frozen*.

Jack O'Brien won Best Direction of a Play for staging *Henry IV* starring Kevin Kline.

The New York Sun, June 7, 2004.

WHO WOULD HAVE THOUGHT? Hip Hop record mogul Sean (P. Diddy) Combs, who is in the Broadway revival of "*A Raisin in the Sun*," says he's "addicted" to Broadway players.

"It's just curious how you get addicted to the people involved with Broadway," he told reporters backstage at Sunday's Tony Awards. "Everyone from the doormen to the stagehands have a certain love for the art [of Broadway] and anything I can do for the art I will. It helped me so much. It's changed by life."

Phylicia Rashad, who won the Tony for Best Leading Actress in *A Raisin in the Sun*, called Mr. Combs "an incredible cheerleader."

Joanne Woodward and Paul Newman, one of the greatest husband-and-wife acting teams in Hollywood history, may act together in a new stage revival of Joseph Kesselring's classic 1940s farce *Arsenic and Old Lace*. It would be done in Westport, Ct. first and, if successful, possibly move to Broadway.

Twenty-nine year old Broadway producer Adam Epstein's hair is turning gray but it's not for lack of success. A co-producer of the blockbuster musical *Hairspray*, Mr. Epstein tells *amNewYork* that he's well into development of a stage musical version of John Waters' movie *Cry Baby*, which he hopes will see the light of Broadway in 2006. "It's about a Marlon Brando/James Dean type of guy who's trying to get a girl from the upper crust," he told *amNewYork* between segments of "The Joey Reynolds Show" on WOR radio Tuesday morning.

amNewYork, June 11, 2004.

RICHARD DREYFUSS, who is preparing to play the role of Max Bialystock in the upcoming London production of *The Producers*, may also appear on Broadway in the role, Dreyfuss told *amNewYork*. "If they put enough laurels in my path—make it worthwhile, I would do it on Broadway," the *Jaws* and *Close Encounters of the Third Kind* star said in an interview with *amNewYork* Monday. "But right now I'm getting ready for the London production." The London production of *The Producers* starts rehearsals next month.

GEORGE C. WOLFE, one of theater's most esteemed directors and writers, will be honored by the Princess Grace Awards and Gala this fall and a special award named in honor of him and underwritten by the gala's co-chair HBO will be given to a young theater artist. The Princess Grace Awards are named after the late Grace Kelly, Princess of Monaco. Wolfe's Tony Award winning work includes *Angels in America* and *Caroline, or Change*.

A NEW REVIVAL of *Let My People Come*, Earl Wilson Jr.s' musical spoof of the sexual revolution of the 1970s, is coming back to New York, *amNewYork* has learned. Robert Blume, executive producer of the Drama Desk Awards, is one of several producers planning to mount the show off-Broadway later this year. The show, which was nominated for a Grammy as Best Original Score played The Village Gate for three years.

"AS A CHILD Jackie Kennedy Onassis wanted to run away and join the circus because of the problems within her family, which is why I titled the play *Cirque Jacqueline*, Andrea Reese told *amNewYork* as she rehearsed her one-woman show which opens at the Triad Theater (158 West 72nd Street) June 24.

amNewYork, Weekend, June 18-20, 2004.

KATHLEEN TURNER—who bared all in the movie *Body Heat* and the stage version of *The Graduate*—will get the chance to tear passions to taters when she co-stars with Bill Irwin in the revival of Edward Albee's *Who's Afraid of Virginia Woolf?* on Broadway. Performances begin at a yet unnamed theater on February 12, 2005.

First produced on Broadway in 1963, the film version co-starred Richard Burton and Elizabeth Taylor. It was later revived on Broadway in 1976 with the late Colleen Dewhurst and Ben Gazarra. The current Broadway-bound revival is being co-produced by Elizabeth Ireland McCann and Daryl Roth, who co-produced Mr. Albee's Pulitzer Prize winning *Three Tall Women* off-Broadway. Mr. Irwin appeared on Broadway with Sally Field in Mr. Albee's play *The Goat*.

JEALOUSY, A HIGHLY sensational two-character play about newlyweds who will do anything for each other, including murder, may open later this year or early next off-Broadway. Written by Eugene Walter, the often-revived *Jealousy* was one of the hits of the 1927-28 Broadway season when 267 other plays and musicals opened.

It's currently at the East Lynne Theater Company in Cape May, N.J., whose artistic director Gayle Stahlhuth told *amNewYork* that she's talking to Studio Dante and others about moving it off-Broadway. "It has some incredibly written scenes," she said. Walter also wrote *The Easiest Way*, which was banned in Boston.

Chip Deffaa, who conceived and directed the "George M. Cohan Revue" now at Danny's on West 46th Street, is writing a one-man show about Cohan for Broadway. The review of Cohan songs, including "Give My Regards to Broadway," stars Jon Peterson who played the Emcee in *Cabaret* and last year starred in Mr. Deffaa's off-Broadway musical *George M. Cohan: In His Own Words*.

THANK YOU *AVENUE Q*. No, that's not another Tony Awards show speech but the role puppeteer Basil Twist feels the Broadway musical has played in putting "puppetry on the radar," and may have even helped lead to a midtown home for his own show, Mr. Twist told *amNewYork*. "Q's success definitely piques theatergoers' interest in the art form," he said.

Mr. Twist's *Symphonie Fantastique* opens next month at the Dodgers Stages on W. 50th St. after first being done at HERE in 1998. The fact that Dodger Stages is "underground means that we will be able to maintain the intimacy of the original production at HERE," he said.

Jay Johnson's *The Two and Only*—which celebrates its 100th performance tomorrow—will move to Broadway after its Atlantic Theatre run ends Aug. 15, *amNewYork* has learned.

"We're ready to move to Broadway—we're just looking for the right venue," producer Stewart F. Lane told *amNewYork*. "We need an intimate theater but definitely a Broadway house. I wouldn't move it to another theater off-Broadway." The show is about Johnson's lifelong love affair with ventriloquism. Johnson told *amNewYork* that being in the play has already "exceeded my dreams."

amNewYork, Weekend, July 9-11, 2004.

SEVERAL BROADWAY PRODUCERS are considering reviving Tony Kushner's 1991 Pulitzer Prize-winning play *Angels in America* following news yesterday that Mike Nichols' HBO version netted a record 21 Emmy Award nominations in the miniseries category.

"It would do very well—AIDS and gay rights are hot topics of our time," one Broadway producer told *amNewYork*. Another Broadway producer, Fred Zollo, who was one of the original producers of *Angels in America*, told *amNewYork* in an interview yesterday that, "If Tony called me tomorrow and wanted to revive it, I'd say OK....What would be fantastic would be to do it like Eugene O'Neill's *The Iceman Cometh* was done in the '50s off-Broadway—a down and dirty production. But it would be hard to get the kind of cast you'd want."

Al Pacino, Meryl Streep and Emma Thompson were nominated in the leading actor category with Mary-Louise Parker, Patrick Wilson, Justin Kirk and others nominated for supporting roles. Nichols got a nomination for direction and Kushner for the adaptation of his play, Kushner, who wrote the book for this year's Tony-nominated musical, *Caroline, or Change*, will discuss it and *Angels in America* next Wednesday at SOHO House as part of a new series of roundtable discussions.

BERTOLT BRECHT and his close circle of artistic collaborators believed they could change the world through the theater—and change the theater through politics. Now, a decade-and-a-half after the fall of the Berlin Wall, the highly respected Castillo Theatre will produce *Revising Germany*, a new play by Castillo's artistic director Fred Newman early next year at the All Stars Project's new performing arts center (at 543 W. 42nd Street). *Revising Germany* is a montage of performed conversations between Bertolt Brecht, Helene Weigel, Elisabeth Hauptmann, Ruth Berlau and Margarete Steffin, four women some scholars believe collaborated with Brecht on some of his most enduring stage work, including *Threepenny Opera* and *The Resistible Rise of Arturo Ui*. The Castillo Theatre's 2004-05 season opens October 8, 2004 with *Stealin' Home*, about Jackie Robinson, the great black ballplayer who broke the color barrier in major league baseball in 1947.

PRODUCER AL TAPPER's documentary, "Broadway: The Golden Age," has been so well received that several Hollywood directors are interested in doing a movie based on a play he wrote called *Bettinger's Luggage*. "That's my next focus," he told *amNewYork*.

"When I was a kid I had two dreams," he continued. "One was to play center field for the Boston Red Sox and the other was to write the music and lyrics to a Broadway musical. As hard as I tried, I didn't make the major leagues, but I did write three off-Broadway musicals and my love for theater grew as a result."

ROGER BART, who starred in *The Producers*, has joined Nathan Lane, in the cast of Lincoln Center Theater's *The Frogs...Cirque Jacqueline*, a one-woman show about Jackie Onassis, is extending at the Triad Theatre to August 7.

amNewYork, Weekend, July 16-18, 2004.

SUPERSTAR RUSSELL CROWE will sing on Broadway for a fraction of what he makes in the movies if the producers of *Princesses* are successful in casting him in the upcoming musical based loosely on a classic children's story.

"Crowe would play the role of the father of the teenage girl in the show," one of the producers of *Princesses* told *amNewYork*. But Crowe and other marquee-name stars will not be in the workshop production of the show at the Goodspeed Theatre in Connecticut in November. "That's not necessarily the cast that will go to Broadway next year," this same producer said.

Anna Deveare Smith, whose one-woman shows uniquely recreate the disparate voices of neighbors affected by such community crisis as the Crown Heights and Los Angeles riots, is turning her attention to last year's four student suicides at NYU, where she is a professor. She will debut that material in "An Evening with Anna Deveare Smith: Connecting the Dots," at the NYU Skirball Center, Sept. 10. "I gathered interviews from students, faculty and trustees," she told *amNewYork* at the Watermill Center Summer Benefit. "We have a new president now who has an idea about creating a new kind of intellectual community. I really want to be a part of shaping the future of the university, and performance is one way to do that."

amNewYork, Weekend, August 6-8, 2004.

JACKIE HOFFMAN, the Broadway actress and downtown comedienne—whose Joe's Pub comedy show is being extended to Oct. 11—may radically shift gears as an actress this fall.

amNewYork has learned that she is negotiating with the Folksbiene Yiddish Theatre to star in *The Novel Romance*, a Yiddish musical by Abraham Goldfaden, in November.

Originally produced in New York in the late 1800s, the show's about a woman with incredibly modern ideas (for the 1800s) about love and how to land the perfect man. Hoffman will have to learn more Yiddish "but you really do have to have the culture in your blood and with Jackie that's not a problem!" director Allen Lewis Rickman told *amNewYork*.

MICKEY ROONEY, now 83, may come to Broadway one more time next spring, says his wife and costar, Jan Rooney.

Mr. Rooney has been appearing with Jan Rooney in *Let's Put on a Show!* at Off-Broadway's Irish Repertory Theatre and "we would love to do the show on Broadway," Ms. Rooney told *amNewYork*. "We're booked for six weeks in Branson, Missouri, and then do our Christmas show but after we might come to Broadway." Mr. Rooney, who is celebrating 80 years in show business, was once the number one film box office star in the country. He won a Tony nomination in the musical *Sugar Babies* in 1980.

ZANY ERIC IDLE, who wrote the book for *Spamalot*, a Broadway-bound musical based on the film *Monty Python and the Holy Grail*, and laconic mega film director Mike Nichols may shape up to be one of the theater's most unusual partnerships. The musical is slated to begin performances at Broadway's Shubert Theatre on February 7, 2005.

"I like the title *Spamalot* a lot," said Idle in an announcement of the show. "We tested it with audiences on my recent U.S. tour and they liked it as much as I did, which is gratifying. After all, they are the ones, who will be paying Broadway prices to see the show." Mr. Nichols, whose film critics include *The Graduate* and *Carnal Knowledge*, directed *Barefoot in the Park* on Broadway and HBO's *Angels in America*. Mr. Nichols is also directing Whoopi Goldberg in a revival this fall at the Lyceum Theatre of her 1984 one-woman show.

THE FIRST (AND LAST) MUSICAL ON MARS, a new musical with previews beginning Sept. 10 at the Mint Space on W. 43rd St., may be the first musical to make the transition from the Internet to the stage. "It began life as the first original musical on the Net on the Sci Fi Seeing Ear Theatre website," George Zarr, who wrote the book and music and is directing the musical, told *amNewYork*. "And it's certainly unique in portraying the romance between a backpack-toting Earthling from Chagrin Falls, Ohio, and a cybernetic crown-wearing princess from the planet Jupiter as created by a writer/composer from Manhattan."

amNewYork, Weekend, August 20-22, 2004.

PAUL ALEXANDER'S one-woman drama *Edge*, starring Angelica Torn as the late poet Sylvia Plath, is slowly making its way to Broadway.

"Producers are coming to us about the play on Broadway," a well-placed source close to two off-Broadway productions of *Edge* as well as its more recent ones in London and Texas, told *amNewYork*. But *Edge* may not be done on Broadway until later next year.

Film and TV star Ann Wedgeworth, who was last on Broadway in Neil Simon's *Chapter II*, is making her directing debut, co-staging with her husband, Ernie Martin, in *Before the Next Blue Norther*, opening Sept. 23 at the Abington Theatre Complex. "The play takes place in west Texas where I was raised and I'm helping the actors with their dialect," Mr. Wedgeworth told *amNewYork*. "Ann's done other things besides helping on the dialect—she's co-directing with me!" Martin, who once ran the California branch of the Actors Studio, chimed in. *Blue Norther* is produced by the Actors Creative Theatre and runs through Oct. 10.

amNewYork, Weekend, September 10-12, 2004.

ANNIE, THE 1977 MUSICAL with book by Thomas Meehan (*The Producers*) music by Charles Strouse and lyrics by Martin Charnin, is coming back to Broadway. "There's going to be the 30th anniversary production of *Annie*, which goes into rehearsal in July," Charnin told *amNewYork* about the bighearted show based on "Little Orphan Annie." "It will play 80 weeks before coming to Broadway."

KITTY CARLISLE HART, the Broadway and Hollywood star, is celebrating her 94th birthday with a three-night engagement at Feinstein's at the Regency starting next Tuesday. Hart has sung in New York nightclubs like the legendary Persian Room that was in the Plaza Hotel, where Hart told *amNewYork*, laughing. "The Persian Room was so chic. Everybody came. I got a brand new dress and I had everything so beautifully organized. And I was singing my first number and forgot the words. So I thought the orchestra would give me a chance to sing it again. But they went right on with the second number. "I'm singing one song and they're playing another. It was pandemonium!"

amNewYork, Weekend, September 17-19, 2004.

"WE JUST STARTED rehearsals for *On the Record*, the show that's going to be done all over the country, starting in November," says Ken Cerniglia of Disney Theatrical. "It celebrates the 80 years of Disney musicals. It's really been fun working on it."

The new Disney stage musical *Mary Poppins*, based on the film of the same name starring Julie Andrews, is in Bristol, England, prior to opening at the Prince Edward Theatre in London Dec. 15. It's not expected to come here and join Disney's productions of *The Lion King* and *Beauty and the Beast* before late next year.

BROOKE SHIELDS is pumping new life into the Broadway revival of *Wonderful Town*, which opened last November, "Beauty sells as well as talent!" said one source connected to the show at the Al Hirschfeld Theatre. Shields, who was also in *Cabaret* and *Grease* on Broadway, stepped into the role of Ruth Sherwood Tuesday night to an enthusiastic standing ovation. She's currently scheduled to be in *Wonderful Town* until the first week in January.

amNewYork, Weekend, October 1-3, 2004.

WENDY WASSERSTEIN, the great American playwright whose work includes *The Heidi Chronicles* and *Isn't It Romantic?*, will have her new play, *Third*, produced by the Lincoln Center Theatre next season.
"I did it as a one-act play last year in Washington and turned it into a full-length play," Wasserstein told *amNewYork*.
Wasserstein is also working on a musical with composer Cy Coleman called *Pamela's First Musical*. [Ms. Wasserstein has, sadly, since died.]
"It's going to be done first at the Norma Terris Theatre in Connecticut," she said.

MOVE OVER, DRACULA. *Frankenstein, The Musical*, the latest collaboration of Mel Brooks and Thomas Meehan (*The Producers*) is now on a fast track to Broadway.
"Mel has already written eight songs for the show and he's going to write another eight to bring it to 16," a close friend and associate of Brooks' told *amNewYork*. "Mel is so busy working on the show I hardly ever see him at the St. James Theatre," where *The Producers* is playing. Brooks' screen version of *Frankenstein* starred Gene Wilder. No casting has been announced for the musical.

GRACE, A NEW MUSICAL about Grace Kelly, the late actress and Princess of Monaco, is being written by playwright A. H. Gurney and composer Cy Coleman.

"It was done in Holland and it's coming here with Pete Gurney writing the book and Michael Blakemore directing," Coleman, who is currently doing a cabaret show at Feinstein's at the Regency, told *amNewYork*.

Wildcat, starring the late Lucille Ball, was Coleman's first Broadway show and a revival of *Sweet Charity* will be done later this season.

amNewYork, Weekend, October 15-17, 2004.

◻ Best of Theater Spots

BROADWAY AFTER DARK THEATER DISTRICT FAVORITES

WHEN SHE ISN'T before the cameras or on runways, Roshumba Williams, the supermodel and television host, soon-to-be-seen on NBC TV's "Sports Illustrated Swimsuit" series, likes to dine at Cite. "They have a beautiful wine dinner that pairs wonderful champagne and wines with each course," she told *amNewYork*.

"Our regular waiter, Charlie, is an aspiring screenwriter, and I hope he'll write a part for me. I've been shooting back-to-back television shows in Los Angeles most of the year and I can't wait to get back home to NYC. I'm most looking forward to seeing *Avenue Q* which all my friends say is terrific." Cite is at 120 W. 51st St. 212-956-7100.

Broadway actor Jack Noseworthy's favorite restaurant is "Angus McIndoe. I love it. It's the [theater] community that goes there and I love the cheeseburgers. I love the chicken. I love the salmon and I take everyone who comes to town there." His choice of theater is easy, he told *amNewYork*. "The Imperial. My memories of it go back to when I was in high school. I saw *Dream Girls* there, which is one of the first musicals I ever saw and I had my Broadway debut there five years later in the original production of *Jerome Robbins' Broadway*."

Actress/dancer Zina Goldrich's favorite theater is also tied to her own performance there—the Vivian Beaumont Theatre in Lincoln Center where she danced in *Contact*. Her favorite dining spot: Café Luxembourg, 200 W. 70th St., between Broadway and West End Ave., 212-873-7411. "One reason I like it is it's across the street from me and, two, I like the bar! It's very comfortable, convenient and always open after the show."

Cabaret star Craig Rubano says "you can't do better that Joe Allen's," 326 W. 46th St. "or Esca," 402 W. 43rd St. "And an Argentine restaurant on Ninth Avenue called Chimichurri Grill." 606 Ninth Ave., near 44th St. 212-586-8655. "I grew up in Argentina and I love it." As for Mr. Rubano's favorite theater, he told *amNewYork* "I'm partial to the Imperial. I did *Les Miserables* there. There are so many ghosts there on that stage. It was just magical to be on that stage."

When asked his favorite restaurant, Tim Tomkins, president of the Times Square Alliance, which represents a cross section of businesses in the Crossroads of the World, said diplomatically, "I like them all!"

Julio Peterson, director, real estate and special projects, for the Shubert Organization, which owns 16 Broadway playhouses, says he goes to HARU (205 W. 43rd St. 212-398-9810) "when I want great sushi. The best steak in

Times Square is Frankie & Johnnie's Steakhouse [269 W. 45th St. 212-997-9494] which used to be a speakeasy in the late 1920's." As for theaters, "I actually like the façade of the Lyceum," he told *amNewYork*, "where *I Am MY Own Wife* is playing. The Little Shubert Theatre on West 42nd Street is my favorite off-Broadway theater. Great leg room. I'm 6'5'."

LeRoy Neiman's favorite restaurant is Tavern on the Green, off the beaten track from the Broadway theater district but close to Lincoln Center and his studio in Hotel Des Artistes. "I could never pick just one show or theater out of so many," the world famous artist told *amNewYork*. "That's why my original serigraph edition of 450, 'The Lights of Broadway' depicts 46 plays and musicals." The glitzy, glass-enclosed dining palace is at Central Park West between 66th and 67th St. 212-873-3200.

JAMIE MASADA, owner of the Laugh Factory Comedy Club in Times Square, told *amNewYork* she's looking forward to seeing yet another comedy act—this one on Broadway. "I can't wait to see and cheer on Billy Crystal on Broadway—he's enormously talented!" she said. "He used to perform his comedy at our Los Angeles club and we've been friends for 25 years." *Billy Crystal—700 Sundays*, opens Nov. 12 at the Broadhurst Theatre. For tickets, call Telecharge at 212-239-6200.

amNewYork, Weekend, October 22-24, 2004.

A NEW MUSICAL about American folk music legend Woody Guthrie is heading for Broadway.

"We're in the middle of working on it and, actually, I'm working with producer Pierre Cossette," Nora Guthrie, the late Woody Guthrie's daughter, told *amNewYork* at the Huntington's Society of America's annual Guthrie Awards gala sponsored in part by the Amarin Corporation. Guthrie died of Huntington's Disease, a nerve disorder. "There was one Woody Guthrie show before, which was just his songs," a close associate of Guthrie told *amNewYork*, "but we want to tell a bigger story, the story of his life."

JACKIE MASON, who is trying out his new comedy act at the Café Carlyle, will play the fight manager, a role originally played by the late Rod Steiger, in a new version of Budd Schulberg's *The Harder They Fall*, for BBC Radio.

STAGE.SPACE.COM will soon be offering deep discounts to Broadway and Off-Broadway shows. "We will launch a major new Broadway and Off-

Broadway ticket discount service in the next several months," Ryan Davis, a co-founder with Joe Drymala of Stage.Space.com says. The Web site has received over a million "hits" since it was officially launched last month.

THE PRODUCERS of *Toulouse*, a Broadway-bound musical about the life and times of Toulouse Lautrec, say they have raised nearly half the $9.5 million capital investment needed to mount the show on Broadway "We have raised $4 million," composer Ronnie Britton, who did the music and lyrics for the show, told *amNewYork*. "But we can't touch that money until three-fourths of the show's budget is raised."

amNewYork, Weekend, October 29-31, 2004.

SUPER FUNNYMAN Mario Cantone wants to do drama in the worst way.
"I wish someone would write me a drama," he told *amNewYork* after a recent performance of his one-man show *Laugh Whore* at Broadway's Cort Theatre.
"Then I wouldn't have to worry about being funny all the time and carrying the whole show!" Playwright Terrence McNally attended the same performance and Cantone told *amNewYork* that he had said, "I want to do a play with you again." McNally wrote *Love, Valour, Compassion!* which co-starred Cantone, Nathan Lane and others.

ACTRESS JULIA MURNEY, the stunning co-star of the hit TV series "Law & Order," will try out a new one-woman show, tentatively called "Julia Murney Sings Tunes," at Birdland on Feb. 7 that she hopes may evolve into an off-Broadway show and an album. "Aside from 'Law & Order,' I do a lot of singing at benefits—it's flattering to be asked," Murney told *amNewYork* at the Fourth Annual Only Make Believe children's charity benefit on Monday night at SHOW. Murney has costarred in *The Wild Party* and *Queenie 2000*. Harvey Fierstein, Dick Latessa, Christiane Noll and others also performed at the benefit.

FILM STAR HAYLEY MILLS, who hosted the benefit with Brad Oscar, told *amNewYork* she has no plans to do theater but that "every now and again I do something in the theater in London and this country. I have a little house in London and I also live here so I'm able to act in both places." Mills added that John Mills, her father and legendary British actor, is 97 and "doing nicely" for his age.

BRITISH PLAYWRIGHT and actor Kerry Shale is on a role—in fact, many of them. Shale, who has penned a radio play for Jackie Mason that will air on the BBC's radio drama series, has written and is performing in the one-person show, *The Prince of West End Avenue*, at 59E59 Theatres, playing all 15 roles, male and female. In January, he and Henry Goodman will do a one-night-only staged reading of Wallace Shawn's *My Dinner with Andre* on a West End theater stage as a benefit for Great Britain's The Actors Centre.

"THERE WILL BE LOTS, lots, lots of changes," composer Cy Coleman told *amNewYork* at Feinstein's at the Regency about the upcoming Broadway revival of his classic 1966 musical *Sweet Charity*, set to star Christina Applegate as Charity Hope Valentine. "We have a new opening and a new director, Walter Bobbie," Coleman said, "and I've put in some new songs that Dorothy Fields, the lyricist, and I wrote and will be heard for the first time in this show." It opens on April 21. Meanwhile, Broadway diva Patti Lupone opens at the Regency Nov. 8.

BROADWAY ACTRESS Jessica Molaskey will make her debut singing at the legendary Oak Room of the Algonquin Hotel in January but her husband, guitarist and actor John Pizzarelli, who has starred on Broadway and at Radio City, will just be a back-up musician, *amNewYork* has learned. Molaskey is also returning to her Broadway roots with her new PS Classics CD called "Make Believe" which just hit stores.

"It was so fabulous I got to sing songs that I would never be hired to sing in the shows, Like 'Make Believe'!" Molaskey told *amNewYork*.

amNewYork, Weekend, November 5-7, 2004.

LIAM NEESON is set to star in a Roundabout Theatre production of Eugene O'Neill's complex lyrical drama *A Touch of the Poet* next September, well-placed sources told *amNewYork*.

Ed Hall, the son of renowned English director Sir Peter Hall, has been tapped to direct the play at Broadway's American Airlines Theatre, insiders said. Roundabout is looking to cast two other stars to play the female leads.

Neeson will play Cornelius Melody, the eloquent owner of a shabby New England tavern who claims he's from an aristocratic family. *A Touch of the Poet*, first produced in 1958, five years after the great dramatist's death, was the first part of a cycle of plays O'Neill envisioned but never completed. The 1958 production starred Eric Portman, Helen Hayes and Kim Stanley.

PATTI LUPONE, who once bowled Broadway over in Andrew Lloyd Webber's *Evita*, will be doing a show at Carnegie Hall early next year which may act as a springboard to her starring in a Broadway or off-Broadway show about the late, great French chanteuse Edith Piaf.

"Patti will be doing a Carnegie Hall show in March and there will be a lot of Piaf stuff in it," Scott Whitman, who along with Marc Shaman wrote the lyrics and music to the hit musical *Hairspray*, told *amNewYork*.

NOSTALGIA MAVEN and radio/TV legend Joe Franklin, who has been packing in the small theater at The Laugh Factory on Times Square with his one man show, *I Came to Reminisce*, has been approached by some producers, who asked him to consider letting them move the show to Broadway for a limited run.

"No way, right now," Franklin told *amNewYork*, "I don't want to compete with the youngsters Billy Crystal, Whoopi and Dame Edna!" Already, Tony Curtis, Sylvia Miles, Captain Lou Albano, Jackie "The Joke Man" Martling and Sally Kirkland have all caught his show in which he talks about his exclusive TV interviews with Charlie Chaplin, John Wayne, Cary Grant, and Elvis Presley.

amNewYork, Weekend, November 19-21, 2004.

DIRECTOR/PRODUCER Peter Bogdanovich, whose movie *The Cat's Meow* about Charlie Chaplin and William Randolph Hearst has become a cult favorite, wants to direct or possibly act in a New York play. "I'd love to do a play," he told *amNewYork*. "I started in the theater. I haven't done a play in 40 years…but recently someone has talked to me about a play."

A new one-character play about the life and times of the late Bobby Kennedy is headed for Broadway or Off-Broadway. "There's so much on Broadway this season I think we're going to wait until next to bring it in," said a well-placed source close to the production. In one scene, the character of Bobby Kennedy talks about looking at a little girl who has been severely bitten by rats and saying, "How can this happen in New York? How can this happen in my city?"

WILL FILM STAR Leonardo DiCaprio do a play? Larry Moss, director, acting coach and author of *Intent to Live: Achieving Your True Potential as an Actor*, who coached Leo for *The Aviator* and Oscar-winning Hilary Swank for *Million Dollar Baby*, told *amNewYork* that he urges all fine actors, including Di-

Caprio and Swank, "to do both plays and films." Swank was scheduled to be in a revival of *The Miracle Worker* on Broadway but bowed out for a film. About Moss, she has said, "I wouldn't take on another role without working with him."

amNewYork, Weekend, March 4-6, 2005.

CHLOE SEVIGNY, who co-stars in Woody Allen's new movie, *Melinda and Melinda*, says *Hurlyburly* director Scott Elliott has asked her to do a play, "but the timing was wrong."

She told *amNewYork* at the premiere of Woody's new movie at Chelsea West Cinemas Wednesday night, "I'm going to Los Angeles to do a series for HBO, so theatre will have to wait but I'd love to go back to the stage. I'm going to see *Doubt* on Friday and I'm very excited. I'd love to do Broadway and have my own dressing room!"

Amanda Peet, her co-star in *Melinda and Melinda*, is co-starring with Ben Stiller in Neil LaBute's new play *This Is How It Goes* at the Public Theatre.

SPAMALOT, WHICH HAD a star-studded opening last night, already has a huge $20 million ticket sale advance. At a recent performance, ushers walked Nicolette Sheridan ("Desperate Housewives") down the aisle as she told everyone, "They're kicking me out, they're kicking me out." But her fears were unjustified. She had merely sat in the wrong seat.

amNewYork, Weekend, March 18-20, 2005.

A MUSICAL BASED on the life and music of the country music legend Johnny Cash is being developed for Broadway, *amNewYork* has learned.

The "Man in Black," as he was sometimes called, left a rich legacy of 1500 recorded songs and 45 albums. The book for the musical is expected to be as gritty and serious as was Cash, who was born a sharecropper's son, served time in prison but became one of the biggest stars in American music history.

ED ASNER AND CLORIS LEACHMAN are being wooed to do an off-Broadway production of a new comedy by L.A.-based playwright Jennifer Maisel called

The Last Seder. A backers' audition for the play is scheduled to take place at the Manhattan Theatre Club in early May.

amNewYork, Weekend, April 1-3, 2005.

THE STARS CONTINUE to come out for *Red Light Winter*, the new play written and directed by Adam Rapp. Recently spotted at performances were stars such as Steve Martin, Harvey Keitel, Marian Seldes, and Ed Norton. *Red Light Winter* is currently playing at the Barrow Street Theatre (27 Barrow Street at 7th Avenue).

A STREET WAS JUST named after Barbara Walters' late father, Lou Walters, who ran the famous Lou Walters' Latin Quarter on 48th St. and Broadway in the '40s and '50s. Her friend, Barbara Corcoran, the real estate queen, who is now preparing TV packages, unearthed a 1947 program of that nightclub. She sent it to Barbara, who was most appreciative as she had never seen it before.

DR. OLIVER SACKS, who inspired the film *Awakenings* starring Robin Williams and Robert De Niro, will present the Isobel Robins Konecky Creative Award to Lukas Foss, the noted composer, pianist and symphony conductor at Page Morton Black's Parkinson's Disease Foundation gala May 17 at the Pierre Hotel.

The Epoch Times, May 1-3, 2006.

THE 51ST ANNUAL Village Voice Obie Awards, Off-Broadway's highest awards, are honoring Eric Bentley with the Lifetime Achievement Award, *The Epoch Times* has learned exclusively. The complete names of the winners won't be announced until the night of the awards, which will be handed out tonight, Monday, May 15th. The citation that will appear on his OBIE award will read:

"For the past 60 years, if you love the theater, you have found yourself consulting certain books. If you wanted to know the entire range of the world's drama, modern and classic, there were anthologies of plays you could reach for. If you wanted to confront the great playwrights of the modern age, there were volumes of essays by a man who had not only studied them deeply but had met or worked with many of them. If you wanted to know the day-to-day experience of theatergoing, there were volumes of reviews by this same man. If you wanted to understand the whole life of drama, from the lowest farce up to the highest tragedy, a book by this man would be your guide. He has not shied away from any confrontation or from any experience: In addition to writer, editor, social commentator and thinker, he has been teacher, performer, director, playwright and translator. For his untiring service to the theater, his omnivorous curiosity, his panoramic attentiveness, his bracing prose—and for his 90th birthday—the judges are honored to present this year's Sustained Achievement Award to ERIC BENTLEY."

LILI TAYLOR AND ERIC BOGOSIAN were announced as hosts of the 51st annual Village Voice Obie Awards. Christine Lahti, scheduled to be a presenter, has dropped out of the Obies as well as her play at Playwright's Horizons. She was replaced by S. Epatha Merkerson, a wonderful actor who moves seamlessly from the stage to television to film.

REBECCA LUKER, the lauded Broadway star of *The Music Man*, *Show Boat* and *The Phantom of the Opera*, is saluting female songwriters at her new show at the Park Avenue nightclub Feinstein's at the Regency through May 20. Most people think of classic American song as the work of George Gershwin, Irving Berlin and Harold Arlen, but many of the standards in the great American songbook have been written by women. Rebecca is highlighting the work of Betty Comden (who wrote the lyrics with Adolph Green for Bernstein's *On The Town*), Dorothy Fields (who wrote lyrics to many songs by Jerome Kern, including "The Way You Look Tonight") and Carolyn Leigh (who wrote lyrics to many Cy Coleman melodies, including "The Best Is Yet to Come"). She also includes songs from many of the current generation of female songwriters, including Marcy Heisler & Zina Goldrich (who are writing new musicals for Disney based on *101 Dalmatians*, *Cinderella* and *The Jungle Book*), Debra Barsha (who co-wrote the Public Theatre's musical *Radiant Baby* about Keith Haring) and Jessica Molaskey (best known for being John Pizzarelli's writing and singing partner).

FRANC D'AMBROSIO, who I believe has played the title role in Andrew Lloyd Webber's *Phantom of the Opera* longer than any other actor, played to standing ovations and a packed house at Manhattan's Joe's Pub last week. The show consisted of popular and classic show favorites. Celebrities and press who flew in from all over to attend the one-night-only engagement included Olympic gold medalist Brian Boitano, NBC Skating producer Steve Disson of Disson Skating in Washington, D.C., choreographer Lea Ann Miller, ABC award-winning television director Jeff Kay and a young actress ballyhooed as "one to watch," Nicole Disson.

THEATER HISTORY is sometimes found in the most interesting and least expected places. Take the Viennese psychoanalyst Sigmund Freud. This being the 150-year anniversary of his birth, many public programs have revolved around his life. On May 5, the Austrian Cultural Center hosted a lecture by the noted writer Dr. Edith Kurzweil on Sigmund Freud. An audience member during the Q&A portion remarked that plays by the playwright Arthur Schnitzler (1862-1931) in reality were dramatizations of Freud's thoughts. That he dramatized Freud's ideas on stage. Dr. Kurzweil concurred with this opinion. She also pointed out that Freud was considered an excellent writer, thereby being able to concisely express his thoughts. Among other evening highlights was an audience member recalling her first-hand accounts of having observed Freud walking his dog around her and Freud's neighborhood in pre-war Vienna.

The Epoch Times, May 15-17, 2006.

OPERA LOVERS RUDY and Judy Giuliani say they haven't seen much on Broadway this year, but they have seen one show three times: *Mama Mia*. "Our girls loved it," they said of their daughters, 16 and 21, from previous marriages, "so we kept going back to take their friends."

The Giuliani's were honored at the American Heart Association's 10th Annual Heart of the Hamptons Gala on June 10. The Master of Ceremonies for the evening, Ed Bradley of "60 Minutes," on the other hand, went for a completely different night at the theater. He recently saw the Broadway production of *Faith Healer*.

"I thought those were masterful performances," he told *The Epoch Times*. "Ian McDiarmid [who won a Tony the following evening] stole the show. But I kept wondering what happened. There were three of us who saw it and we had three different opinions. I thought it left a lot hanging. I'm a reporter and I want to know the beginning, middle and end. My wife tells me I'm like Jack Webb in 'Dragnet,' always looking for 'just the facts ma'am.' The guy who played the manager was astounding. I expected greatness from Ralph Fiennes and Cherry Jones, but I didn't expect anything from McDiarmid and I thought he was amazing."

As if three-time Academy Award nominee, film and stage actor, television star, producer, director and grandmother are not enough titles, there is one more credit in the works for the beautiful and talented Diane Ladd—author. Her new book is *Spiraling Through the School of Life—A Mental, Physical and Spiritual Discovery; Finding Your Own Miracles*. (Hay House Books) Simply put, it's part autobiography, part self-help and a lot of Southern charm and horse sense.

I asked Ms. Ladd what the impetus was for this book and she explained, "I began handing out a page or two of 'Pragmatic Suggestions.' Those suggestions grew and grew until they became this book." It took her a year to complete, fitting it in between a busy acting schedule.

"I wrote it because I felt I had to," she continued. "I wanted to give payback to my fellow human beings. I always thought there are other people who need someone to inspire them, to fight for their dreams.

"You can't always change someone's karma, but you can have a miracle. You can magnetize better things into your life, but in order to do that you have to kick dirt and you have to remove anger. People have said that I wrote this book because I want to save lives. No, I let God save the lives. I wrote a book because I wanted to inspire and help my fellow human beings while also, hopefully, fulfilling my destiny."

Diane will make a rare personal appearance in Manhattan to sign copies of her book at Borders, Columbus Circle, on Wednesday, June 28 at 7:00 p.m.

Rob Bartlett, who just completed an engagement in Broadway's *The Odd Couple*, was a big hit at the Police Athletic League's gala at the Pierre Hotel when he did an impression of Luciano Pavarotti. Among those attending was superstar nutritionist Olinka Podany, who gave tips on dieting to people at her table.

The Epoch Times, June 22-25, 2006.

◩ Robert Downey Jr. Gets Iron Man Buff; OBIE Awards Gets New Chairman

NEW YORK—Jake Gyllenhaal, Aretha Franklin, Kitty Carlisle Hart, and Jeff Koons were honored at this year's Americans for the Arts National Arts Awards chaired by Maria Bell at Cipriani 42 Street. The elegant event, which raised more than a million dollars, brought out the likes of actor Ronald Perlman and former New York Governor Mario Cuomo.

Presenter Robert Downey Jr.—toned and taut in preparation for his upcoming superhero role as Iron Man, in Marvel Entertainment's first independent film, directed by Jon Favreau—told me, "I've been working on something for Broadway for 10 years, but I'll be engaged for awhile in this film, which I hope will be successful."

Downey, a well-respected talent, presented Gyllenhaal with the Young Artist Award.

Downey reflected on his contemporaries: "Mark Ruffalo, is between Jake's generation and mine. We just did this *Zodiac* film, and it turned out great." (The three actors star in *Zodiac*, a film slated for 2007 based on the serial killer who terrorized San Francisco in the 60s and 70s). "I have to say after watching *The Departed* last week, that Leonardo DiCaprio is a very established actor. He's always pushing new ground. Even the established actors of my generation like Mark Wahlberg and the like are continuing to grow and try different stuff. And it's inspiring."

VETERAN BROADWAY ACTOR Jason Alexander, the famed George Costanza on TV's "Seinfeld," has directed his first TV commercial. It's a public service announcement concerning the ills of second-hand smoke.

JACK NICHOLSON'S date at the New York premiere of his movie, *The Departed, Paz de la Huerta*, wore red hair recently. Previously a honey blond, she acquired the new do on the advice of her long-time hairdresser, Maureen McLeod, of Benistry Beauty Salon at 152 West 26th Street.

It has just been announced that Michael Feingold, chief theater critic of the *Village Voice*, where he has been a contributor since 1981 and a staff writer since 1980, will be the new OBIE Chairman.

The Village Voice OBIE Awards, off-Broadway's highest honor, has often been a forecaster of shows and artists who often receive their first acknowledgements from the OBIES and then go on to make their mark in the mainstream.

Mr. Feingold is a graduate of Columbia University and the Yale School of Drama. He sustains an ongoing second career in theater as a playwright, translator, director and dramaturge. His translations of plays and operas, which now number over 50, have been heard on and off Broadway, in resident theaters across the country, and in major opera houses. A Pulitzer Prize finalist in Criticism, a Guggenheim Fellow, and a Senior Fellow of the National Arts Journalism Program, Feingold has received the coveted George Jean Nathan Award for his *Voice* reviews.

WHAT DO TONY BENNETT, Luciano Pavoratti, Steve Martin, and Marty Short have in common? A love for fabulous Italian food, such as served at San Domenico restaurant. On any given night you can see one or all of them at this close-to-Broadway gastronomic palace. The other day, Tony May, owner of San Domenico, hosted the historic signing of the collaborative agreement between Hartford's Connecticut Culinary Institute and the Italian Culinary Institute for Foreign Professionals of Costigliole d'Asti, Italy.

The Italian Culinary Institute has relationships with many foreign countries throughout the world, sending professional chefs to teach local culinary students recipes and procedures for making fine Italian food. This is their first relationship with a cooking school in the United States. A fully accredited course, the 27-week curriculum includes 12 weeks at the Connecticut Culinary Institute hotel in Hartford, followed by 15 weeks at Costigliole d'Asti in Piemonte. The hands-on course in Italy includes internship at well-known Italian restaurants. "We wish to make Americans understand Italian cuisine has evolved so much," said Tony May. He should know. His award-winning kitchen is vigorously watched over by acclaimed executive chef Odette Fada.

DONNY OSMOND, currently starring in *Beauty and the Beast* on Broadway, Euan Morton (Tony nominee, *Taboo*), Felicia P. Fields (Tony nominee, *The Color Purple*), Liz McCartney (*Mama Mia*, *Taboo*), Merle Dandridge (*Tarzan*), Christine Pedi ("Forbidden Broadway"), and KENiMATTix (world renowned acrobats Ken Berkeley and Matthew Cusick) will be part of the sixth annual gala benefit for "Only Make Believe," hosted by Kathie Lee Gifford, on Monday, Nov. 6 at 7:30 p.m. at the Hudson Theatre at the Millennium Hotel (145 West 44th Street).

The charity brings theater to chronically ill children. Jeremy Gilley, founder of the international non-profit peace organization Peace One Day, will receive the 2006 James Hammerstein Award for his outstanding dedication to children in need.

SOURCE: *Broadway After Dark* column by Ward Morehouse III, Special to *The Epoch Times*, October 23-29, 2006, page B8.

🇨🇿 former Czech Prez Playwright; Honoring Broadway Star Julie Harris

NEW YORK—In honor of Vaclav Havel's 70th birthday and two-month residency at Columbia University's Untitled Theater Company #61, the same company that brought us the Ionesco Festival and recently the NEU-ROfest presents The Havel Festival, a collection of all of the plays by the internationally acclaimed playwright and former President of the Czech Republic.

Events began October 5 and end on December 4. Performances run from October 26 through December 2. And for the first time ever, the complete works of Vaclav Havel will be presented in a festival that includes one world premiere, four English language premieres, and five additional new translations. All told, there will be 18 productions to complete the collection.

"It seems as if this festival is happening at the perfect time. Havel's 70th birthday, his residency at Columbia, our political situation in the United States, and this festival all fit together," said Edward Einhorn, Artist Director for the Havel Festival and Untitled Theater Company. "This may be the most deeply rewarding project I've worked on…Havel is a very quiet man, and when [you] work on his plays you realize that silence, in his writing, means power. It is always those who say less who have the power on stage, whether they are the interrogators or the interrogated."

Performances will take place at The Brick in Williamsburg, Brooklyn, and The Ohio Theater in SOHO, with a special engagement of *The Beggar's Opera* at Columbia's Miller Theatre.

THE LOVELY AND TALENTED Alexa Ray Joel will perform for a very special audience on Nov. 2 at the Princess Grace Awards Gala at Cipriani in Manhattan. The Princess Grace Foundation-USA was founded to continue the work that Princess Grace began during her lifetime to help financially young emerging talent in theater, dance, and film.

The beautiful and talented singer/songwriter Ms. Joel, is currently on tour in support of her independently recorded and distributed debut EP, "Sketches."

She was raised in a musical home on Long Island, where Ms. Joel's gift for singing and songwriting was strongly encouraged by her parents. Among her earliest memories is her father singing and playing nursery rhymes for her on the piano. Ms. Joel underwent classical piano training for many years before developing a love of songwriting, discovering her piano training to be a solid foundation for her songwriting.

Ms. Joel recognizes the importance of supporting young artists in their studies and in addition to the young recipients who include 17-year-old John

Mark Giragosian who will receive a scholarship to the Maryland Youth Ballet and top Statue honorees Adam Rapp and Maria Kowroski.

The ceremony will be emceed again by CNN's Larry King who is a long-time supporter and friend of the Princess Grace Foundation-USA. Awards will be presented by Chita Rivera, Jesse L. Martin, and Ethan Stiefel. The second annual Prince Ranier III award, created by Madison Avenue Jewelers Di Modolo, will be presented by Norma Kamali to dance veteran Twyla Tharp.

CHRIS SEEGER, the lawyer who is well known in show business circles for winning over a billion dollars in class action lawsuits, is giving a fundraiser for his friend Andrew Cuomo, who's running for attorney general, on Monday, Oct. 30, at Sparks Restaurant. They are long-time friends.

Literally off the bus and onto the New York stage comes emerging young playwright Keith Boynton. Boynton, a former pupil of Constance Congdon while at Amherst College, will premiere two of his one-acts at NYC's Altered Stages in an evening entitled "Love, Death, and Interior Decorating." His mother Sandra Boynton, the Grammy nominated songwriter and noted cartoonist, will direct one of the evening's plays. Although new to the New York stage, Boynton's work has been performed by such luminaries as Sam Waterston, Liam Neeson, and Meryl Streep.

Julie Harris, one of Broadway's greatest actresses, will be honored at Primary Stages 22nd Anniversary Gala Benefit in The Crystal Room at Tavern on the Green on Monday evening, November 6. "Each year, we honor an artist who has made significant contributions to the American theater and the development of new plays in particular," said Primary Stages Artistic Director Andrew Leynse. "The legendary Julie Harris is most deserving of such an honor." Harris won the Tony Award for Best Actress for *I Am a Camera* (1952), *The Lark* (1956), *Forty Carats* (1969), *The Last of Mrs. Lincoln* (1973), and *The Belle of Amherst* (1977), as well as five nominations for Best Actress.

SOURCE: *Broadway After Dark* column by Ward Morehouse III, Special to *The Epoch Times*, October 30–November 5, 2006, page B8.

◻ Neil Simon (1926 –)

DURING MY FATHER'S Broadway reporting heyday, being a successful, productive playwright of witty comedies was something to be proud of. When the majority of the Broadway audience was locals who showed up in suits, such writers were prized. A new George S. Kaufman play? The box office was besieged. Neil Simon was the last of these great comedy dramatists. He, in many ways, was the transition from the "old" Broadway, where entertainment was the goal, to the "new" Broadway, where playwrighting had turned into an "art." Well, Doc Simon went blithely along with his bulletproof fan base of locals for decades, but even he had to change eventually. He started writing "great drama." And, you know what? He's pretty good at that, too. This interview dates from 1993, when Simon was mounting *Laughter on the 23rd Floor*, his tribute to his Sid Caesar "Your Show of Shows" writing-pool days.

PLAYWRIGHTS ARE OFTEN acknowledged as great long before becoming popular, condemned to be admired by critics but ignored by the general public. Neil Simon may be the only example of the reverse—a man who after 25 years as the world's most popular playwright had won only a single Tony Award for Best Play (for 1965's *The Odd Couple*.)

For years, Simon's comedies had been sure-fire Broadway hits, but the critics weren't impressed. Whenever the playwright dared venture into serious matters, the response was similar to that of *The New York Times'* Frank Rich, who wrote: "I'm sorry but Neil Simon sentimental isn't as good as Neil Simon funny."

Simon seemed destined to join the ranks of the rich-and-famous-but-critically-despised. But then Simon threw a curve ball. In his 1983 *Brighton Beach Memoirs*, the playwright began to explore new ground, funny and sentimental, and it worked. After 25 years of all-but-total frustration in the major awards department, he's garnered two Tonys and a Pulitzer Prize in the last seven years. He's even seen a theater named after him.

It would be understandable if Simon sported an air of self-satisfied vindication. He's actually refreshingly down-to-earth, a quality that reflects the unpretentious tone of his works—as wittily self-depreciating in person as his works are funny on stage. Recounting a time early in his career when he and his first wife Joan spent some time in Italy while he was working on a movie, he says with a laugh, "It was a mess. The director couldn't speak English, the assistant directors couldn't speak English—and I can't speak English."

I interviewed Simon in his midtown New York apartment. Broadway rehearsals had just started for *Laughter on the 23rd Floor*, and it was noticeable that, at this point in his life, the notoriously dissatisfied Simon was relaxed, a happy many at last. At peace with his past, he looks forward as much as backward.

In Simon's life as in his plays, however, the past and the present are inextricably linked. He and his current wife Diane share a midtown apartment in the same building where he lived with his second wife, actress Marsha Mason, but they occupy a lower floor. He and Mason lived on the 35th floor, the playwright explains, and enjoyed a magnificent view. But the building boom in the late 1970s and 1980s largely blocked the once-great views, and anyway he wouldn't want to live there now, with a new wife.

Diane Simon herself links both Simon's past and present. She's his fourth wife, she was also his third: the two had an unhappy divorce in 1988, only to reconcile subsequently. Their marriage reportedly features an unusual clause in the prenuptial agreement, forbidding Simon to write about either his wife or her young daughter.

"The divorce was really—I don't know how to put it because it sounds frivolous—it never should have taken place, and we both knew it," says Simon ruefully. "She was going through a tough time and, as a result, I was, too; and I thought maybe it was not going to work out. So we just disappeared from each other for a while, and then we got divorced.

"But I don't think we ever stopped caring about each other. She had a little girl before I met her. When we got together again, I adopted the little girl and she's my daughter. Everything's terrific with us now."

The playwright also has two daughters by his first marriage: Ellen, a 35-year old writer, and Nancy, a 33-year old filmmaker, who is the mother of Simon's two grandchildren, Andrew and Sofia.

Looking back over his career, Simon doesn't see his early years on Broadway as a struggle for critical respect. If the critics weren't exactly rip-roaring fans, he says, they certainly weren't the diehard detractors some have become in recent years.

"Those were the good days," Simon says. "I used to know critics and go have dinner with critics, Walter Kerr and Richard Watts on *The Post* and Clive Barnes [then on *The New York Times*]. I mean, you could talk to them and they would say, 'Well, I don't think this play was so and so, or something else.'

"I like the idea of having some communications with critics," Simon continues.

☐ Index

A
Aayer, Abetha 257
Abady, Josephine 233
Abbott, George 54, 55
Abraham, F. Murray 264, 287, 288
Abraham, Saul 56
Actors' Theater, The 53
Adams, Annie 10
Adams, Maude 10, 11, 12, 13, 14, 15, 16, 26, 79
Adams, Tony 202, 203
Adler, Richard 263
Ahrens, Lynn 221
Albee, Edward 133, 176, 195, 233, 256, 270, 271, 339
Alexander, Jason 276, 357
Alexander, Paul 308, 343
Algonquin, The 54, 171
Alien Corn 21, 65
Allen, Lewis 170
Allen, Woody 171, 190, 245, 246, 288, 297, 310, 312, 352
Altman, Robert 162
amNewYork 92, 93, 338-353
Anders, Glenn 66
Anderson, Judith 26, 66
Anderson, Laurie 247
Anderson, Maxwell 7, 32, 53, 83
Andreas, Christine 229, 326
Andrews, Julie 87, 184, 201, 203, 230, 254, 257
Andrews, Neal 55
Anglin, Margaret 29
Anna Christie 57
Annie Get Your Gun 43
Annie Warbucks 153, 154
Anthony, Marc 212
Anthony, Mark 13
Applegate, Christina 350
Arlen, Michael 20
Arliss, George 29
Asbury, Donna Marie Elio 276

Asbury, Herbert 244
Ash, Jeffrey 195
Ashley, Elizabeth 296
Asner, Ed 352
Associated Press 77, 80
Astaire, Fred 282
Astor Hotel 34
Atkins, Eileen 170, 249
Atkinson, Jayne 296
Atlee, Clement 52
Auburn, David 237
Austen, Polly 318
Axelrod, George 70
Azenberg, Emanuel 143, 198

B
Bacall, Lauren 203, 289
Bacon, Kevin 224
Bailey, Pearl 128
Baker, Anne 189
Baker, Jordan 176
Baldwin, Alec 135, 310, 333
Ballard, Lucinda 52
Bancroft Award 31
Banderas, Antonio 277, 293, 301, 306, 307, 310
Bankhead, Tallulah 7, 66, 88, 117
Barber, Matthew 296
Barrett, Elizabeth 20
Barretts of Wimpole Street, The 20, 21, 64, 65
Barrie, James M. 10-12, 14, 15, 18, 50
Barron, Mark 53, 79
Barrymore, Ethel 18, 79, 136
Barrymore, John 7, 18, 47, 85, 96, 120, 123, 310
Barrymore, Lionel 18, 85
Barrymore, Maurice 18
Bart, Roger 341
Bartlett, Rob 356
Baryshnikov, Mikhail 245
Beatty, Warren 96, 190
Beggar's Holiday 330

Behrman, S.N. 28, 70
Belafonte, Harry 260
Belasco Theater 65
Belber, Stephen 256
Bell, Martin 328
Benchley, Robert 171
Bening, Annette 96, 190
Bennet, Richard 66
Benson, Raymond 249
Bentley, Eric 354
Bergen, Candice 269, 281, 310
Bergeret, Albert 325
Bergman, Ingrid 276
Berhman, Sam 32
Berlin, Irving 34
Bernhardt, Sarah 30
Bernstein, Leonard 318
Biggs, Jason 245
Bill of Divorcement, A 20, 21, 64
Billings, Donald 125
Bitter Sweet 38
Black, Jeremy 247
Blades, Ruben 207
Blake, Betty 131
Blake, Robert 249
Blakemore, Michael 346
Blanchard, Tammy 298
Blank, Jessica 274
Blinkoff, Susannah 168, 169
Blinn, Holbrook 48
Bloom, Claire 230, 298
Bloomgarden, Kermit 74
Blume, Robert 289, 328, 339
Bobbie, Walter 224, 262
Bock, Jerry 293
Bodne, Ben 121
Boesky, Billy 177
Boesky, Ivan 177
Bogdanovich, Peter 254, 351
Bogosian, Eric 354
Boll, Harlan 335
Boneau, Chris 266, 279
Bongiovi, Tony 266
Bonstelle, Jessie 21

365

Booth Theater 75, 176, 204, 294
Boston, Mass. 51
Bowie, David 266
Boyd, William 84
Boyer, Charles 69
Boynton, Keith 360
Brackett, Charles 24
Bradley, Ed 355
Brady, Alice 84
Brady, William A. 21
Branagh, Kenneth 176, 304
Braun, Jennifer 109, 110
Bridges, Jordan 283, 284
Briers, Richard 222
Briggs, David 258
Britton, Ronnie 349
Brixton Burglary, The 75
Broderick, Matthew 188, 281
Broken Glass 164, 166, 176
Brookes, Jacqueline 275
Brooks, Mel 237, 310, 345
Broun, Heywood 21, 47, 55, 56
Brown, Blair 308
Brown, Tina 255
Bruckheimer, Jerry 248, 255
Bryan-Brown, Adrian 193
Bryant, Mary 204
Buckley, Betty 199, 200
Burke, Michael 322
Burnett, Carol 134, 278, 283
Burton, Bruce 244
Burton, Kate 298
Bush, George 156, 272, 333
Busker Alley 183
Busley, Jessie 17
Button, Dick 169

C
Cacciotti, Tony 234
Caddick, David 199
Cady, David 276
Caldwell, Zoe 257, 320
Calhoun, Jeff 162, 183
Cameron, Julie 279
Cameron-Scorsese, Domenica 279
Campion, Sean 238

Canadian Black Watch 31
Candida 20, 21, 65
Cantone, Mario 349
Cantor, Arthur 213, 236
Cantor, David 236
Capote, Truman 239, 324
Cargle, Scott 265
Cariou, Len 105–107
Carroll, Barbara 246
Carter, Myra 176
Caruso, David 195
Cates, Phoebe 249
Cats 149, 150, 189, 192, 199
Cattrall, Kim 264, 274
Cerniglia, Ken 344
Cesa, Jamie 210
Chaiken, Howard 189
Chamberlain, Richard 161, 168
Champlin, Donna Lynne 278
Channing, Carol 128, 151, 230, 281, 335
Channing, Stockard 219
Chaplin, Charlie 24
Charles, Walter 151
Charney, Jordan 265
Charnin, Martin 153, 344
Chase, Mary 5, 7
Chekhov, Anton 21
Chenoweth, Kristin 314
Chianese, Dominic 278, 292
Childs, Timothy 200
Chip Chop 22
Chopin 16
Christian Science Monitor, The 92, 93, 102, 104, 109, 112, 114, 161, 238, 241, 273
Christie, Audrey 67
Christopher Blake 35
Christopher, Sybil 254
Churchill, Winston 29
Cissel, Charles D. 275
Clapool, Veronica 232
Clark, Bobby 45
Clark, Carol Higgins 269
Clark, Tanya 258
Clayburgh, Jill 181, 274
Cline, Patsy 262

Clinton, Bill 153, 325
Clooney, Rosemary 317
Close, Glenn 173, 180, 181, 195, 199, 200
Cobb, Lee J. 88
Coe, Fred 70
Coffey, Tom 116
Cohan, George M. 77, 81, 82, 88, 101, 102, 112, 115, 116, 120, 340
Cohen, Alexander H. 196
Cohen, Daniel Linden 247
Cohen, John S. Jr. 53, 54, 79
Colbert, Claudette 76
Cole, David 151
Cole, Gloria 118
Colella, Jenn 304
Coleman, Cy 318, 345, 346, 350, 354
Collier, Constance 90
Colony Club, The 11, 13
Colton, John 87
Combs, Sean (P. Diddy) 338
Comden, Betty 70, 289, 354
Connelly, Marc 28, 86
Connery, Sean 220, 222
Cooper, Gary 117
Cooper, Max 196
Coote, Robert 87
Copeland, Carolyn Rossi 243
Corcoran, Barbara 257, 353
Corcoran, Joe 163
Cornell, Katharine 7, 20–23, 26, 64, 65, 86
Cornell, Peter 20, 64
Corvette, David 232
Cossette, Pierre 297, 348
Cottrill, Olan 180
Coustas, Mary 164
Coward, Noлl 28, 29, 37–40, 252, 332
Cowl, Jane 7, 88
Crawford, Michael 293
Cromarty, Peter 184
Cromwell, John 54
Crookston, Jim 181
Crosby, Julie 313
Cross, Ben 164
Crouse, Russel 56

Crowe, Russell 262, 342
Crudup, Billy 274, 278
Crystal, Billy 263
Cugat, Xavier 112
Cukor, George 26
Cumming, Alan 220, 222
Curtin, Jane 260
Curtis, Simon 164

D
D'Alessandro, Franco 276, 277
D'Amboise, Charlotte 194
D'Ambrosio, Franc 354
Dahl, Arlene 281, 282
Dali, Salvador 243
Dalrymple, Jean 117, 124, 146, 170
Daltrey, Roger 229
Daly, Augustin 41
Damn Yankees 194, 197
Danielle, Marlene 192
Danner, Blythe 255
Darin, Bobby 268
Davies, Howard 161
Davis, Ryan 349
Daykin, Judith E. 146
Dear Brutus 18, 50, 52
Death of a Salesman 74, 88
Deffaa, Chip 340
Dekle, Bernard 73
DeMille, Cecil B. 24
DeMonchy, Katlean 259
Dennehy, Brian 181, 301, 304, 306
Dennis, Sandy 129
Denver, John 266
DeSare, Tony 320
Diaz, Cameron 243
DiCaprio, Leonardo 243, 351, 352, 357
Diehel, Matt 92
Diesel, Vin 280
Digges, Dudley 88
DiPietro, Jay 275
Dirty Rotten Scoundrels 328
Doganieri, Elise 248
Doherty, Shannen 335
Donen, Stanley 248, 249
Doro, Marie 16

Douglas, Kirk 317
Doumanian, Jean 245, 297
Downey, Robert Jr. 357
Doyle, Arthur Conan 16, 18, 122
Drabinsky, Garth 180, 186, 188, 191, 193, 204, 210
Drake, Irwin 314
Dramatic Mirror, The 34
Drew, John 11
Drewes, Caroline 111, 113
Dreyfuss, Richard 274, 338
Duke, Heather 335
Dukes, David 176
Dunaway, Faye 173, 183, 200
Dunnock, Mildred 74
Dunst, Kirsten 254, 283
Durning, Charles 278
Durst, Douglas 228

E
Eagels, Jeanne 7, 46–48, 53, 83
Easiest Way, The 46, 87
Eason, Myles 76
Ebersol, Christine 141
Ecklund, Helen 76
Edge 308
Edson, Margaret 237
Edwards, Blake 203, 240, 257
Egan, Susan 165
Eichhorn, Lisa 274
Einhorn, Edward 359
Eisenberg, Alan 326
Elephant House, The 60, 62
Elizabeth the Queen 7, 28
Elliot, T.S. 149, 275
Elliott, Scott 352
Ellis, Edward 53
Elmore, John 97
Emerson, Michael 261
Empire Theater 11, 12, 17, 64
Engel, Georgia 318
Ephron, Nora 296
Epoch Times, The 92, 93, 142, 353, 355, 356, 358, 360

Epstein, Adam 310, 311, 338
Errico, Melissa 183
Esbjornson, David 310
Eskin, Otho 316, 324
Esposito, Charles 268
Esterman, Laura 316, 324
Evans, Robert 324
Evening Post, The 56

F
Fairbanks, Douglas 15
Falco, Edie 288
Farr, Jamie 174
Farrow, Mia 171, 190
Fawcett, Farrah 310
Fay, Frank 7
Feingold, Michael 357, 358
Feinstein, Michael 249, 299, 317
Feldshuh, Tovah 255
Ferrer, Jose 25, 67
Feuer, Cy 188
Field, Sally 270, 339
Fields, Dorothy 321, 350, 354
Fields, William 32, 56
Fierstein, Harvey 257, 259, 279, 305–307, 332, 334, 349
Finn, Terry 276
Fisher, David 148
Fitch, Clyde 29
Flaherty, Stephen 221
Fontaine, Joan 70
Fontanne, Lynn 7, 15, 28–30, 32, 39, 58, 64, 66, 84
Foote, Horton 261
Footloose 224
Ford, Harrison 309
Forever Plaid 155, 156, 163
Forty-Five Minutes Past Eight 46, 48, 53, 79
Foss, Lukas 353
Fox, Robert 170
Frankel, Aaron 257
Franklin, Joe 351
Franklin, Rebecca 115, 116, 136
Fratti, Mario 277
Frayn, Michael 260

Frazier, Michael 224
Freedley, Vinton 177
Freeman, Lea 5
Fresco, Robert 214
Frings, Kitti 74
Frohman, Charles 10, 11, 12, 14–17, 19
Fry, Christopher 20
Fuller, Liz 328

G
Gabriel, Gilbert 55, 56
Gallagher, Leonard 53, 54
Galpotthawela, Asoka 181
Garber, Victor 194, 197
Gardner, Ava 218
Gardner, Herb 258
Gargano, Charles 281
Garland, Judy 87, 223, 299
Garrett, Betty 216
Garrick Theater 18
Garrison, Dyke 234
Gatien, Peter 228
Geisler, Robert 165
Gelb, Arthur 319, 320
Gelb, Barbara 319
Gentlemen of the Press 53–56, 79, 116, 117
George, Grace 21
Georgia 11
Gere, Richard 126
Gershwin, George 34, 137
Gersten, David 297
Gibney, Sheridan 257
Gielgud, John 233, 249
Gifford, Kathie Lee 263, 319, 358
Gilbert, John 46
Gillette, William 5, 16–19, 52, 122
Gilley, Jeremy 358
Gish, Lillian 127
Giuliani, Rudolph 162, 261, 355
Glass Menagerie, The 7–9, 52
Glover, Corey 176
Goggin, Dan 182
Goldberg, Whoopi 205, 206, 230, 343
Goldin, Ricky Paul 162

Goldrich, Zina 347
Goodman, Benny 272
Goodman, Dody 182
Goodman, Henry 350
Goodrich, Frances 79
Gordon, Leslie 115
Gordon, Max 27
Gordon, Ruth 26, 27, 89, 263
Gore, Al 261
Gorshin, Frank 296
Gottlieb, Morton 70
Grant, Ellsworth 97, 99
Gray, Simon 309
Green Hat, The 20, 64, 65
Green, Adolph 70, 289, 290, 354
Green, Jackie 206
Greenberg, Richard 293, 306
Grey, Joel 139, 314, 331
Grier, David Alan 205
Griffith, Melanie 310
Grimaldi, Dennis 153, 154, 211
Gruzinski, Frank 210
Guettel, Adam 320
Guinness, Alec 88, 275
Gurney, A.H. 345
Gurney, Pete 346
Guthrie, Nora 348
Guthrie, Woody 297, 348
Guyer, Cindy 261
Gyllenhaal, Jake 357

H
Haggai, Tom 251
Haimes, Todd 205
Hairy Ape, The 57, 58
Hall, Carol 168
Hall, Dorothy 55
Hall, Ed 350
Halliday, Richard 68, 69
Hamilton, Carrie 278, 283
Hamlisch, Marvin 312
Hammerstein, Oscar II 41–43, 51, 52
Hampton, Lionel 250, 269, 271–273
Hanan, Stephen Mo 261
Hannele 38

Haran, Mary Cleere 171
Harden, Marcia Gay 283
Harnar, Jeff 299
Harnick, Sheldon 134, 293
Harper, Valerie 234, 235
Harris, Jed 35, 36, 52, 55
Harris, Joseph 181
Harris, Julie 320, 359, 360
Harris, Radie 177
Harris, Rosemary 174
Harris, Sam 34, 35, 120
Harris, William 65
Harrison, Rex 87, 168
Harrison, Richard B. 7, 86
Hart, Kitty Carlisle 137, 327, 332, 344
Hart, Lorenz 34, 41–43
Hart, Moss 34–36, 66, 137, 332
Hartley, Ted 319
Harvey 5, 7
Havel, Vaclav 228, 359
Hawkins, Tim 229
Hayden, Terese 275
Hayes, Helen 21, 30, 50–52, 88
Hayward, Leland 70
Healy, Bill 263
Heche, Anne 266, 291
Hecht, Ben 55
Helburn, Theresa 42
Held, Scottie 189
Hellman, Lillian 7
Henry, William A. 3d 175
Hepburn, Katharine 5, 6, 26, 89–92, 95–100, 161, 162, 171, 240, 297, 298, 300
Herman, Jerry 128, 151, 152, 281, 332, 335
Herrmann, Edward 254
Hewitt, Don 309
Hicks, Shauna 299
Hill, Conleth 238
Hill, Frances 279
Hilliard, Robert 81
Hines, Gregory 215
Hines, Maurice 215
Hirsch, Judd 258
Hirschfeld, Al 243, 320
Hoffman, Bill 100
Hoffman, Jackie 342

Hoffman, Phillip Seymour 301, 304
Holder, Lawrence 292
Hollywood Reporter, The 177
Hoover, Bob 273
Hoover, Robert 335
Hope, Bob 310
Hope, Linda 310
Hopkins, Harry 31
Hopkins, Kaitlin 260
Hopkins, Miriam 54
Hopkins, Ryan 214
Hopper, Dennis 164
Howard, Leslie 46, 65
Howard, Sidney 21, 32, 65
Hudson, Kate 249
Huffman, Cady 263
Hull, Josephine 7, 88
Hunt, Helen 222
Hunter, Alberta 103, 104
Hunter, Jeffrey 206
Hurt, Mary Beth 308
Huston, Walter 58
Hynes, Garry 219, 221

I
Ibsen, Henrik 7, 27
Idiot's Delight 7, 28, 31, 33
Idle, Eric 343
Inaba, Noriko 72
Irby-Ranniar, Scott 214
Irons, Jeremy 298
Irving, Amy 164, 176
Irwin, Bill 270, 339
It Happened in New York 79
Ivey, Dana 255
Ivey, Judith 331
Izzard, Eddie 308

J
Jackman, Hugh 307, 312, 322, 331, 334, 337
Jackson, Anne 126, 138
Jackson, Tommy 54
Jaffe, Rona 259
James, Adam 320
Janis, Byron 266, 267
Jaquet, Illinois 272
Jay-Alexander, Richard 148
Jensen, Eric 274

Jensen, Julie 279
Joel, Alexa Ray 359
Joel, Billy 266, 291, 304, 307
Johnson, Jay 340
Jones, A.L. 55
Jones, Al 56
Jones, Clayton 93
Jones, Marie 238
Jones, Tom 263
Jordan, Leslie 165
Josephson, Barney 103, 104
Josten, Henry 97, 99, 100
Jurow, Martin 239, 240, 241, 324

K
Kahn, Otto 75
Kalfin, Robert 255
Kanin, Garson 26, 27
Kaufman, George 282
Kaufman, George S. 27, 28, 34, 35, 77, 137, 332
Kaye, Judy 187, 188
Keefe, Willard 53, 79
Kennedy, Kathryn 47
Khrushchev, Nikita 112
King, Larry 360
Kipling, Rudyard 15
Kiskadden, James 10
Kitchen, Guy 151
Klein, Calvin 267
Klein, William 76
Kline, Kevin 249, 289, 307, 337
Klores, Dan 209
Knight, Gladys 232, 233
Knight, Shirley 260
Kociolek, Ted 233
Kole, Hilary 320
Kornberg, Richard 161, 168, 215
Kraft, Hy 54
Krakowski, Jane 306, 307
Kramer, Terry Allen 270, 271
Krasna, Norman 69
Kreston, Judy 321
Krieger, Barbara 253
Kronenfeld, Ivan 267
Kuhnert, George 48
Kurzweil, Edith Dr. 355

Kushner, Tony 182, 227, 237, 340, 341
Kushnier, Jerry 224

L
Lacey, Maggie 265
Ladd, Diane 356
LaFortune, Felicity 256
Lagarce, Jean Luc 256
Lahm, David 320
Lahr, Bert 124
Lahti, Christine 354
Lait, Jack 55
Lake, Ricki 262
Lambs Club, The 5, 53, 76
Lamos, Mark 233
Landis, Kathleen 327
Lane, Clifford 210
Lane, Jeffrey 328
Lane, Nathan 143, 174, 205, 281, 309, 341, 349
Lane, Stewart F. 210, 312, 335, 336, 340
Langella, Frank 274, 333
Langner, Lawrence 42
Lanin, Lester 244, 264
Lansbury, Angela 152
LaPaglia, Anthony 222
Lapine, James 166, 167
Larson, Jonathan 226
Lasko, Ron 271
Laurents, Arthur 289, 332
Lauria, Dan 328
Lavin, Linda 278
Lawrence, Carol 158
Lawrence, Gertrude 35, 38, 66, 88
Leachman, Cloris 352
Leahy, Thomas F. 147
LeDonne, Peter 152
Leguizamo, John 204, 222
Leigh, Carolyn 354
Lemenager, Nancy 319
Lemper, Ute 325, 327
Lennon, Julian 328
Leonard, Robert Sean 301, 304
Leshin, Phil 269
Letter, The 21, 46, 65
Letterman, David 187, 271
Leveaux, David 306

Levene, Sam 67
Levine, Carol 224
Lewis, Jerry 194, 197, 285, 286
Lewis, Shari 192
Leynse, Andrew 360
Lieberman, Joseph 97
Life With Father 29, 74
Light Up the Sky 35, 36, 66, 67
Linden, Hal 237, 238
Lindsay, John 127
Lindsay, Kathleen 275
Lindsay, Leon 93
Lion King, The 178, 179, 192, 210, 214, 219, 220, 221, 279, 313
Lion, Margo 306
Lipsky, Seth 242
Lipton, James 300, 322
Little Women 21, 64
Logan, Joshua 51, 68–70
Lollo, Richard 275
Lombardo, Matthew 300
Long Island Daily Press, The 74
Long, John Arthur 261
Longworth, Mrs. Nicholas 15
Loos, Anita 51, 52
Lord, Pauline 66, 88
Lucas, Craig 227
Luhrmann, Baz 264, 266, 291, 307
Lukas, Paul 88
Luker, Rebecca 354
Lunt, Alfred 7, 28–30, 32, 39, 52, 84
LuPone, Patti 200, 351
Lutterman, Randy Ellen 318

M
MacArthur, Charles 55
MacArthur, Mary Hayes 50, 51
Macbeth 12, 66
Mackintosh, Cameron 148
Magnani, Anna 276, 277
Mahmud-Bey, Sheik 264
Maisel, Jennifer 352
Malick, Terrence 165

Malina, Judith 287
Mamet, David 190, 264, 274
Manahan, Anna 221
Mancini, Henry 184
Manitoba Theatre Center 107
Mann, Abby 238
Mann, Ted 190
Mann, Terrence 229
Manners, Hartley 8, 9
Manning, Katy 329
Mantello, Joe 306, 307
Margaliti, Israela 265
Marguer, Stuart 92, 93
Margulies, Donald 237
Marlowe, Julia 66
Marshall, Rob 316
Martha's Vineyard 22
Martin, Catherine 264
Martin, Dean 285, 286
Martin, Ernie 188, 344
Martin, Jesse 302
Martin, Mary 68–70, 88
Martin, Steve 162, 172, 256
Masada, Jamie 348
Mason, Jackie 166, 170, 171, 173, 174, 348, 350
Massey, Raymond 7, 32
Masterson, Mary Stuart 307
Matchmaker, The 26
Maugham, Somerset 20, 21, 46
Maxwell, Elsa 111, 112
Maxwell, Mitchell 194, 197
May, Elaine 190, 248, 249
May, Tony 358
Mayer, Michael 219
Mays, Jefferson 337
Mazzle, Marin 167
McArdle, Andrea 148, 214, 215
McBroom, Amanda 196
McCann, Elizabeth 195, 233, 307
McCann, Elizabeth Ireland 339
McCartney, Paul 252, 270, 309
McClintic, Guthrie 8, 20, 53, 55
McCollum, Kevin 223

McConaughey, Matthew 249
McDiarmid, Ian 355
McDonald, Audra 221, 337
McDonald, Joe 335
McEntire, Reba 283
McGovern, Elizabeth 164
McGuire, Toby 254
McKechnie, Donna 140
McKnight, Sharon 260, 261
McMahon, Judi 203
McNally, Terrence 221, 288, 349
McNamara, Brooks 253
McTyre, Robert 178
Medea 66, 177
Meegan, Jean 70
Meehan, Thomas 344, 345
Meehan, Tom 153, 154
Mendes, Sam 298
Menzel, Idina 337
Menzell, Idina 314
Merchant of Venice, The 10, 11, 13, 15
Merkerson, S. Epatha 354
Merman, Ethel 70
Merrick, David 201, 202
Mexican Hayride 44, 45
Meyer, Chet 261
Mielziner, Jo 52
Miles, Sylvia 247
Miller, Arthur 164, 166, 176, 206, 274, 301, 326
Miller, Gilbert 52
Mills, Hayley 349
Mills, Heather 252, 270
Mills, John 349
Minkus, Jacques 71
Minnelli, Liza 125, 223, 281, 299, 331
Mirren, Helen 187
Mishkin, Chase 304
Miskin, Chase 320
Mitchell, Brian Stokes 293
Mitchell, Jerry 328
Mizrahi, Isaac 314
Molaskey, Jessica 350
Molina, Alfred 222, 293
Monk, Thelonious 292
Monterey, Carlotta 57, 58
Moore, Kelly 328

Moore, Roger 307
Morehouse, Ward 5, 78–82, 101, 109, 111, 113, 115–117, 121, 130, 142, 161
Morehouse, Ward III 109–115, 117, 161
Moriarty, Michael 161
Moritz, Marc 276
Morley, Robert 121
Morley, Sheridan 121
Morris, Mark 209, 213, 245
Morris, Richard 230
Morrison, Ann 276
Moss, Larry 351, 352
Mostel, Zero 131
Mr. Doom Gets a Letter 109, 113, 115
Mulgrew, Katherine 297, 300
Mullen, Marie 221
Murney, Julia 349
Murphy, Donna 170
Murphy, Mary 249
Murphy, Tom 220, 221
Murray, Brian 324
Myers, Alan 198

N
Nackman, David 247
Nafpaktitis, Elizabeth 275
Napolin, Leah 255
Nassour, Ellis 262
Naughton, James 244, 252
Naughton, Jim 288
Neal, Patricia 320
Nederlander, Jimmy Jr. 192
Neeson, Liam 222, 350
Neiman, LeRoy 243, 348
Nesbitt, Cathleen 88
Nethersole, Olga 29
Neuwirth, Bebe 194, 281, 302
New York Daily News, The 143, 146
New York magazine 105
New York Morning World, The 56
New York Post, The 92, 93, 96–100, 109, 142, 145, 147, 148, 150, 157, 163, 165, 169, 172, 175, 177, 179, 182, 184, 186, 188, 191, 192, 195, 196, 198, 200, 202–206, 208–211, 213–215, 218–220, 222, 223, 225–233, 235, 236
New York Sun, The 5, 48, 50, 54, 55, 59, 67, 76, 78, 79, 92, 93, 142, 161, 242, 244, 245, 247–249, 251–259, 261–267, 269–271, 275–278, 280, 282–288, 290–301, 303–305, 307–309, 311, 313, 315–337
New York Telegram, The 55
New York Times, The 27, 77, 82, 88, 105, 113, 114, 236
New York Tribune, The 53
New York World Telegram, The 71, 73
Newark Star-Ledger, The 110
Newell, Mike 283
Newman, Fred 246, 287, 341
Newman, Joel 258
Newman, Paul 250–252, 260, 265, 293, 294, 338
Newman, Phyllis 289, 290
Nichols, Mike 208, 209, 248, 340, 341, 343
Nicholson, Jack 357
Niki, Mariko 72
Nolan, Suzannah 264
Noonan, Tom 275
Noseworthy, Jack 347
Noto, Tony 247
Novac, Lana 262

O
O'Brien, Jack 328, 337
O'Byrne, Brian F. 337
O'Daly, Larry 169
O'Donnell, Rosie 168, 219, 220, 222
O'Hare, Denis 306
O'Neill, Eugene 32, 56–58, 84, 304, 306, 350
O. Henry 16
Oates, Joyce Carol 296
Olivier, Laurence 88
Orbach, Jerry 300

Orsini, Renee Lawless 262
Osmond, Donny 358
Ouchi, Kiyoshi 72
Ouchi, Sachiko 73
Ouchi, Umeyo 72, 73
Ouchi, Yoko 73
Ouellette, Tim 265
Our Town 252, 260, 265, 288, 293
Owens, Frank 183

P
Pacino, Al 190, 274, 278, 284, 304, 320
Pacitti, Joanna 215
Page, Geraldine 308
Paige, Elaine 199
Palmer, Bob 173
Palminteri, Chazz 274, 278, 297
Pantoliano, Joe 288
Papert, Fred 163
Paris 57, 58
Parker, Dorothy 85
Parker, Sarah Jessica 215, 310
Parker, Woody 70
Parsons, Estelle 247
Passion 167, 188, 191
Patterson, Patsy 195
Pauch, Paul 265
Payton-Wright, Pamela 316, 324
Peck, Gail 207, 208
Peet, Amanda 352
Pegler, Arthur James 53
Pegler, Westbrook 53
Perez, Rosie 288
Perry, Ryan 168
Peter Pan 10–14, 26, 27, 38, 70
Peters, Bernadette 200, 293, 298, 304, 306, 307
Peterson, Jon 340
Peterson, Julio 347
Phillips, Lisa Faith 332
Picardi, John 279
Piccininni, Erica 265
Pickford, Mary 46
Pierce, David Hyde 318
Pitman, Richard 13

Pizzarelli, John 350
Playbill 328
Plimpton, Martha 264
Plummer, Christopher 132
Pollock, Alan 21
Porter, Cole 34
Povah, Phyllis 67
Powers, Susan 192
Presnell, Harve 153
Price, Lonny 276
Prince, Hal 278, 289
Prince, Harold 158, 159, 185, 186
Priory, Willy 130
Pulitzer Prize 34, 66, 176, 358, 361
Pullman, Bill 256
Purcell, Charles 62

Q
Quinn, Anthony 162

R
Rabe, David 181
Racheff, James 233
Rahe, Joan Marlowe 130, 131
Rain 7, 46, 48, 74
Randall, Tony 187
Rapp, Adam 353, 360
Rapp, Anthony 247
Rashad, Phylicia 337, 338
Rea, Robert 304
Redford, Robert 184
Redgrave, Vanessa 170, 249, 301, 304, 306
Reed, Florence 87
Reed, Ishmael 247
Reese, Andrea 339
Reeve, Christopher 181
Reissa, Eleanor 255
Reney, Laurence 97
Reuben, Aubrey 258
Reunion in Vienna 15, 28, 31, 32
Reuters 92, 152–154, 156, 158–160, 166
Reynolds, Debbie 299
Reynolds, Jonathan 324
Reynolds, Susan 216

Rheims, LeRoy 151
Rice, Elmer 32
Rich, Frank 105, 361
Richards, Ann 302, 303
Richards, Jeffrey 296
Richards, Martin 297
Richards, Marty 167, 281, 282, 312
Richardson, Kevin 295
Richardson, Natasha 205, 221, 222
Richardson, Ralph 88
Rickman, Allen Lewis 342
Rifkin, Ron 176, 222
Rigg, Diana 166, 177
Ringwald, Molly 296
Rise and Fall of Little Voice, The 164, 169
Rivera, Chita 158, 188, 300, 301, 307, 360
Rivers, Joan 167, 196
Robbins, Tim 181, 290
Roberdeau, John 165
Roberts, Jennifer 252
Roberts, Julia 283, 292
Roberts, Samuel 284
Robeson, Paul 58
Rodgers, Gaby 70
Rodgers, Mary 320
Rodgers, Richard 34, 41–43, 51, 52
Rogers, Ginger 70
Rooney, Jan 342, 343
Rooney, Mickey 270, 299, 342, 343
Roosevelt, Alice 15
Roosevelt, Franklin 31
Rose, Anika Noni 337
Rosenberg, Edgar 167
Rosenberg, Jill 173, 174
Rosenkrantz, Peggy Hill 169
Rosenthal, Craig 244
Ross, Annie 162
Ross, Diana 257
Ross, Steve 294, 332
Ross, Stuart 155
Rossellini, Isabella 276, 277
Rossellini, Roberto 276, 277
Roth, Daryl 176, 195, 233, 328, 339

Rubano, Craig 347
Rudy, Sam 322
Rushdie, Salman 269

S
Sabinson, Harvey 144, 145, 174, 197
Sachs, Mel 173
Sacks, Oliver Dr. 353
Samrock, Vic 32
San Francisco Examiner, The 113
Sandum, Howard 223
Sarandon, Susan 181, 290
Sardi's 53, 76, 131
Saturday's Children 26, 53
Savannah Morning News, The 116
Scanlan, Dick 230
Schifrin, Lalo 256
Schlieff, Henry 261
Schlossberg, Julian 190, 248, 249
Schmidt, Harvey 223
Schoenfeld, Gerald 149, 150, 166, 188
Schoenholtz, Julius 102
Schulman, Susan 201, 219
Schuster, Alan 245
Schwimmer, David 261
Scorsese, Martin 243, 279
Scott, Martha 88
Seeger, Chris 360
Seinfeld, Jerry 263, 295
Selden, Albert 70
Seldes, Marian 133, 176, 292
Sennett, Mack 24
Severance, Elbert 54
Sevigny, Chloe 352
Shaffer, Paul 271
Shaiman, Marc 259
Shale, Kerry 350
Shaman, Marc 351
Sharp, Peter 246
Shaw, Arje 237
Shaw, George Bernard 86, 117
Shea, Jere 167
Sheldon, Ned 27
Shepard, Richard F. 114

Sherlock Holmes 16, 18, 122
Sherman, Keith 201
Sherwood, Madeline 27
Sherwood, Robert E. 7, 28, 31–33
Shields, Brooke 345
Show Boat 42, 185, 186, 189, 191–193, 195
Showalter, Max 99, 100
Shubert Theater, The 75
Shubert, J.J. 75, 76
Shubert, John 75, 76
Shubert, Lee 75, 76
Shubert, Sam S. 75, 76
Sills, Douglas 229
Silverstone, Alicia 257, 266
Simmons, Russell 307
Simon, Diane 362
Simon, John 105
Simon, Neil 143, 198, 237, 281, 293, 361, 362
Simon, Paul 207–209, 212, 213
Simonson, Eric 209
Sinatra, Frank 112, 216–218, 240, 243, 314
Sinatra, Frank Jr. 216
Sinatra, Tina 216
Singer, Isaac Bashevis 255
Sinise, Gary 237, 238
Skye, Ione 274
Slaughter, Harriet 189
Smith, Alison 56
Smith, Anna Devere 166, 342
Smith, Donald 140
Smith, Gary 307
Smith, Liz 302, 303
Smith, Rex 229
Smith, Russell 226, 227
Soderbergh, Steven 280
Soloway, Leonard 304
Somlyo, Roy 299, 334
Sondheim, Stephen 95, 166, 167, 188, 260, 276, 298, 333
Sound of Music, The 41, 214
South Pacific 41, 42, 68, 69, 88

Spamalot 343
Spear, David Michael 258
Spielberg, Steven 164
Springer, Gary 278
Springsteen, Bruce 308
St. Germain, Mark 328
Stahlhuth, Gayle 339
Stallings, Laurence 83
Starr, Frances 87
Statesboro, Ga. 73
Stein, Joseph 293
Stein, Laura 156
Stern, Henry 97
Stevens, Emily 7, 48, 88
Stevenson, Isabelle 171, 173
Stiles, Danny 287
Stiller, Ben 352
Sting 160
Stone, Peter 290
Stone, Sharon 264
Strange Interlude 58, 66
Streetcar Named Desire, A 74, 88
Streisand, Barbra 255, 266, 281
Strouse, Charles 153, 154, 344
Styne, Jule 70, 298
Summerhays, Heather 107
Sunset Boulevard 24, 25, 173, 185, 187–189, 192, 193, 195, 199
Sutlive, William G. 115
Swank, Hillary 302, 326, 351, 352
Swanson, Gloria 24, 25, 123, 173, 195
Swit, Loretta 174
Symington, Sidney 171

T
Tandy, Jessica 88
Tapper, Al 341
Tarkington, Booth 7, 26, 50, 52
Taylor, Charles A. 8
Taylor, Elaine 132
Taylor, Elizabeth 44, 119
Taylor, Eloise 54
Taylor, James 160

Taylor, Laurette 5, 7–9, 85
Taylor, Lili 354
Taymor, Julie 219, 221
Tea and Sympathy 32, 70
Teichmann, Howard M. 75, 76
Tesori, Jeanine 230
Thalken, Joseph 263
Tharp, Twyla 291, 304, 307, 360
Theater Guild 21, 42, 58
Theater Magazine 34
Theater Week 107
Thomas, Danny 101
Thompson, Kay 223
Thomson, Lynn 226, 227
Thoroughly Modern Millie 230
Thousand Islands Sun 193
Three Sisters, The 21, 26
Tiger Cats 21, 64, 65
Time magazine 175
Tiny Alice 233
Todd, Mike 44, 45, 119
Tomkins, Tim 347
Tompkins, Tim 282
Toots Shor's 76
Torme, Mel 216
Torn, Angelica 308, 343
Torn, Rip 308
Tracy, Spencer 26, 90, 96, 97, 162
Travolta, John 261
Tubert, Susana 209
Tucci, Stanley 288
Tune, Tommy 162, 168, 183, 252
Turner, Kathleen 257, 266, 301, 302, 339
Twain, Mark 16, 243
Twiggy 252, 255
Twist, Basil 340

U
Uggams, Leslie 320
Up in Central Park 44, 45

V
Vacco, Dennis 232
Valentine, Karen 329

Valentino, Rudolph 24
Van Druten, John 244
van Munster, Bertram 248, 255
Variety 34, 55, 148, 158, 176, 188, 269
Vereen, Ben 258
Victoria Regina 50
Villar-Hauser, Ludovica 324
Vinton, Doris 70
Vogel, Paul 312
Vukovic, Monique 275

W

Wachtel, George 162, 178, 211
Wagenhals, Lincoln A. 74
Wagner, Robert 124
Waldorf Astoria: America's Gilded Dream, The 109–111, 114, 115, 161
Walker, Fred 187
Wallach, Eli 126, 138, 164
Walsh, Tracy 214
Walt Disney Co., The 157, 163, 166, 178, 179, 192, 210, 211, 214, 220, 266, 267, 278, 313, 344, 345
Walter, Eugene 46, 339, 340
Walters, Barbara 306, 353
Walton, Emma 254
Walton, Jim 276
Wanamaker, Zoe 230
Wasserman, Dale 238, 330
Wasserstein, Wendy 174, 318, 345
Waters, John 259, 262, 310, 311, 338
Watman, Bob 265
Watson, Lucille 88
Watts, Richard Jr. 53, 54, 79
Weaver, Sigourney 274
Webb, Arthur 247
Webb, Jeremy 265
Webber, Andrew Lloyd 149, 159, 173, 180, 183–185, 187, 193, 195, 196, 199, 351, 354
Wedgeworth, Ann 344
Weinstein, Harvey 312
Weintraub, Jerry 216

Weissler, Barry 220, 295, 316
Weissler, Fran 168, 183, 220, 295, 316
Welch, Raquel 203
Weller, Michael 279
West, Mae 45, 261
Whitehead, Robert 176, 257
Whitman, Scott 351
Wiest, Dianne 274, 297, 312
Wilbourn, Phyllis 95
Wilder, Billy 24, 196
Wilder, Thornton 50, 288
Wildhorn, Frank 229
Will Shakespeare 21, 65
Williams, Bernie 309
Williams, Roshumba 347
Williams, Tennessee 5, 7, 8, 85, 126, 276, 277
Williams, Vanessa 260, 263
Wilner, Jon 152
Wilson, August 237
Wilson, Claggett 30
Wilson, John C. 39
Winokur, Marissa Jaret 259, 306
Wittman, Scott 259
Wolcott, Derek 213
Wolfe, George C. 260, 338, 339
Wolheim, Louis 7, 84
Wolsk, Eugene 155, 156
Wood, Audrey 5
Wood, Maryrose 276
Woods, A.H. 64
Woodward, Joanne 244, 251, 338
Woollcott, Alexander 21, 27, 35, 39, 47, 84, 117
Wuntch, Philip 239
Wynters, Gail 183

Y

Yazbek, David 328
York, Donald 330
York, Rachel 229
You Can't Take It With You 34, 36
Young, Glenn 320
Young, Karen 279
Young, Reggie 258

Z

Zaks, Jerry 212, 332
Zaremba, Kathryn 153
Zarr, George 343
Zellweger, Renee 300, 324
Zimmer, Kim 265
Zollo, Fred 340
Zuckerman, Paul 315

www.ingramcontent.com/pod-product-compliance
Lightning Source LLC
Chambersburg PA
CBHW021759220426
43662CB00006B/123